Conservation Biology

This beautifully illustrated textbook introduces students to conservation biology, the science of preserving biodiversity. Conservation biology is fast emerging as a major new discipline, which incorporates biological principles in the design of effective strategies for the sustainable management of populations, species and entire ecosystems. This book begins by taking the reader on a tour of the many and varied ecosystems of our planet, providing a setting in which to explore the factors that have led to the alarming loss of biodiversity that we now see. In particular the fundamental problems of habitat loss and fragmentation, habitat disturbance and the non-sustainable exploitation of species in both aquatic and terrestrial ecosystems are explored. The methods that have been developed to address these problems, from the most traditional forms of conservation, creation of protected areas and single-species programmes, to new approaches at genetic to landscape scales are then discussed, showing how the science can be put into practice.

ANDREW S. PULLIN is a Senior Lecturer in the School of Biosciences at the University of Birmingham, where he has been teaching Environmental Biology, Ecology and Conservation Biology for a number of years. His research interests include the ecology and conservation of invertebrates, the assessment of biodiversity at species and genetic levels, and the relationship between conservation science and practice. His work has taken him to many exotic locations, including the tropics and the Arctic, where he has obtained first-hand experience of a wide range of conservation problems. In addition to his academic work, he is also involved in the practical aspects of conservation, and serves on the council of several non-governmental conservation organisations. He is involved in the implementation of several species and habitat action plans, placing him in an excellent position to consider the relationship between conservation problems, conservation science and conservation action. Andrew is the Editor of *Ecology and Conservation of Butterflies* (1995) and the *Journal of Insect Conservation*.

Conservation Biology

Andrew S. Pullin

PUBLISHED BY THE PRESS SYNDICATE OF THE UNIVERSITY OF CAMBRIDGE
The Pitt Building, Trumpington Street, Cambridge, United Kingdom

CAMBRIDGE UNIVERSITY PRESS
The Edinburgh Building, Cambridge CB2 2RU, UK
40 West 20th Street, New York, NY 10011-4211, USA
477 Williamstown Road, Port Melbourne, VIC 3207, Australia
Ruiz de Alarcón 13, 28014 Madrid, Spain
Dock House, The Waterfront, Cape Town 8001, South Africa

http://www.cambridge.org

First published 2002

Printed in the United Kingdom at the University Press, Cambridge

Typeface Swift 9.5/12.25pt. *System* QuarkXPress™ [SE]

A catalogue record for this book is available from the British Library

Library of Congress Cataloguing in Publication data

Pullin, Andrew S.
Conservation biology / Andrew S. Pullin.
    p.   cm.
Includes bibliographical references (p.   ).
ISBN 0 521 64284 1 (hardback) – ISBN 0 521 64482 8 (pbk.)
1. Conservation biology.   I. Title.
QH75.P85   2002   333.95′16–dc21   2001037844

ISBN 0 521 64284 1 hardback
ISBN 0 521 64482 8 paperback

To George and his generation

Contents

Preface

At the time of writing I have just spent the last 24 hours or so celebrating the coming of the year 2001, the real new Millennium. Having to stay at home looking after my young son and therefore being unable to go out to any parties this year, I watched the New Year celebrations take place around the globe beamed by satellite to my TV set. One overpowering message that came to me, and I know to many others, is how closely connected we have now become and how much smaller the Earth feels as a result. Now more than ever before, it should be obvious to all just how limited the earth's resources are and how crowded the planet is becoming. We need to manage these resources very skilfully if we are to prosper as a species.

This book is intended as an introduction to the science of conservation biology: a science that I believe will become one of the most important to us in the twenty-first century. It seeks to provide the information about our natural world that will enable the sustainable management of genes, species and communities and to maintain the biodiversity that characterises the richness of our planet. We have a significant challenge on our hands, but we must face it head-on and develop our knowledge rapidly to give us the tools to do the job.

The text is written primarily as an aid to undergraduate-level teaching, supporting either short courses or modules in conservation biology within broader degree programmes. It is written with the presumption that readers have a fundamental knowledge of basic biology and some ecology. The book is based on the course in conservation biology that I taught first at Keele University and lately at The University of Birmingham, UK. One of the key motives for writing this text was that in teaching conservation biology I was frustrated by the lack of a text that reflected European as well as North American conservation issues. Europe is more crowded and has a longer history of human occupation than most of the rest of the world and most of its ecosystems have been fundamentally altered and degraded for millennia. Other continents may be able to learn by our mistakes. This book has a global perspective but includes many examples from Europe that may be indicators of problems to come elsewhere.

The content of the book is deliberately confined to the science of conservation biology and the mechanisms by which the science can influence practical actions. There is no attempt to cover wider conservation issues involving politics, economics and social sciences. In my view these subjects are often covered inadequately in conservation biology texts and I did not want to repeat the mistakes. There are a number of textbooks dedicated to these aspects of conservation and some are listed as further reading.

I have separated the text into three basic sections. The first two chapters introduce biodiversity and the characteristic ecosystems of the planet. These chapters may be too basic for some who will want to skip over them, but I find that many students need this basic information to fully appreciate more complex conservation issues. The second section (Chapters 3–6) explores the factors that have led to problems in conservation and threats to biodiversity: loss and fragmentation of habitats, habitat disturbance and non-sustainable exploitation of species. The final section (Chapters 7–15) explores the development of conservation biology, the conservation actions that have been taken and those that might be considered in the future. Early chapters in this section cover the most traditional forms of conservation, formation of protected areas and single species programmes and later chapters move on to developing aspects of the science, exploring both strengths and weaknesses in our knowledge that underpins conservation strategies.

I am very grateful to my undergraduates for giving me feedback on earlier drafts of the manuscript and for spotting minor mistakes. My thanks go to Ward Cooper, Barnaby Willetts, Jayne Aldhouse and Shana Coates at Cambridge University Press for encouragement and advice and to many others who have provided me with information and allowed me to present their data. My greatest debt goes to my partner Teri Knight for her unceasing support and expert comments on the manuscript.

Andrew S. Pullin
Birmingham
1st January 2001

Chapter 1

The natural world

In order to understand and evaluate the threat that human activity poses to the natural world we must first consider what the natural world consists of and how to describe it. This chapter sets the scene by introducing the term biodiversity and considering how our living heritage is quantified and distributed, both geographically and among taxonomic groups. The different ways in which we value natural resources are also considered to help us understand the need for their conservation.

By reading this chapter students will gain knowledge of how biodiversity has developed historically and how it is now distributed taxonomically and globally. They will also gain an understanding of some of the possible natural causes of these patterns and of the value of natural resources to human civilisation.

What have we got to lose?

Life has existed on Earth for around four billion years, constantly evolving to form the spectacular richness of our current living world. In fact the fossil record indicates that, on average, life has steadily increased in diversity and complexity over time to produce the richness we see today (Box 1.1). We have benefited from this natural richness in so many ways, we ourselves are products of it and we continue to benefit from it. How strange it would look, then, to any historian looking back in several thousand years time, that the most intelligent species on earth should, in such a short period, destroy and degrade the environment on which it depends to the degree we have, and continue to do.

Box 1.1	Historical changes in biodiversity – lessons from the past

The increasingly well-catalogued fossil record provides us with a window on levels of biodiversity throughout geological time and a fascinating measure of change. The first and most obvious pattern is that biodiversity has increased over time. We started with nothing and now we have a lot. A closer look suggests that biodiversity has not

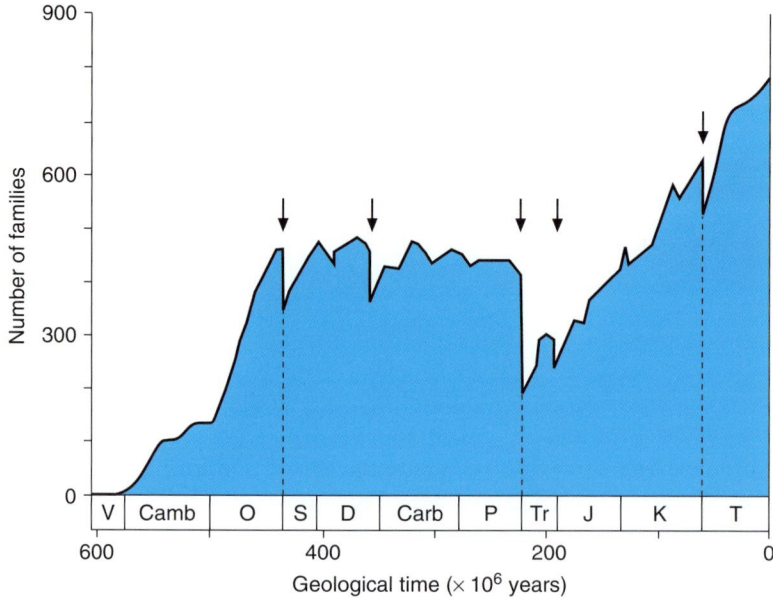

Fig. 1.1 Change in biodiversity over time represented by the taxonomic richness of marine skeletonised animals. The arrows mark mass extinction events. The current mass extinction is not shown. Reproduced from Erwin *et al.* (1987) with kind permission of the Society for the Study of Evolution.

increased at a steady rate, but is punctuated by sharp drops in biodiversity when many taxa disappear (so-called megaextinction events), usually followed by rapid recovery as many new taxa appear in their place (Fig. 1.1).

The megaextinction events are thought to have been caused by major climatic changes at these times. Many species were not able to cope with the rapid changes in their environments and so perished. Subsequent rapid radiation of life forms could have been because of the empty niches left behind. However, whilst there is some evidence to support the climatic reasons for megaextinction (see below), we do not as yet understand what conditions favour rapid increases in biodiversity. Such a major increase occurred during the Cambrian era, 550 My before present (BP), before any recorded megaextinction. This period has been richly described by Gould (1989) in his account of the Burgess Shale fossils which record a rapid diversification of multi-cellular hard-bodied animals (metazoans). This may have been due to an evolutionary advance in body form that enabled the exploitation of new niches.

A useful lesson for our future comes from the evidence that megaextinctions may be caused by rapid environmental change. The last and most famous mega-extinction event of all, which led to the demise of the dinosaurs, was almost certainly the result of rapid environmental change, caused either by intrinsic climatic factors or by extraterrestrial impact. The evidence we shall consider in the next few chapters of this book suggests that we are currently experiencing the sixth megaextinction event. This is the result of rapid environmental change as before, but this time the change is faster than ever before and we are the driving force of that change. Whether or not we suffer the same fate as the dinosaurs is a matter for debate; what is not in doubt is that, if we continue with our increasing impact on the natural environment, many other species will suffer that fate.

As we begin a new Millennium, it is interesting to consider what we, the few generations of *Homo sapiens* to traverse this point in time, might be remembered for. I wager it will not be for the Cold War between East and West, the rise and fall of communism, not for various wars in the

Middle East or for terrorist acts; not for rises in living standards or wide-spread famine. All of these will be continuations of normal historical events. We will probably be celebrated for putting the first person on the Moon, and the computer/information revolution, but we will certainly be condemned for presiding over large-scale habitat destruction and the mass extinction of species on earth. The latter is the crime of our generations for which future generations will never forgive us. It is happening now, concentrated over just a few decades, destroying what four billion years of evolution has created. We must find ways of limiting the severity of this crime, for although history will find us guilty of it, it is not we who will be sentenced, but our children.

Our actions look increasingly short-sighted when we consider how much we depend on our environment for goods and services. It would be a supremely arrogant person who claimed that humans were in control of their environment, yet this is what our political actions appear to presume or at least seek. We are still almost totally dependent on natural resources for the production of our food, the air that we breathe and the water that we drink. The natural environment frequently reminds us of our vulnerability in the form of natural disasters that appear on our television sets almost daily. Our lack of control is blatantly obvious, even more so if you consider that some of the disasters are not entirely natural but result in part from our attempts at control. But there are some reasons for optimism. There are signs that human society has begun to realise that it is part of the natural environment and that our future depends not on control but on coexistence. The science of conservation biology has a crucial part to play in providing the tools for this environmental revolution.

We will look in more detail at our impact on the natural environment in later chapters but in order to understand the problems that we face in conserving our natural heritage we must first know something of what we have got to lose. We therefore start with an appraisal of our assets.

Diversity among living organisms

One of the major reasons why I became a biologist was my early impression of the bewildering diversity of species that were apparently out there in the wild, living lives that I did not (and in most cases still do not) understand. My direct experience as a child living in the British countryside is partly responsible for this. I was able to walk out of my parents' front door in a Wiltshire village and stroll down to the local river, wander through rich chalk grassland and play in woodland dominated by oak and beech. Diversity was all around me. But, just as influential, was the increasing number of high-quality nature programmes on television. These showed me the contrasting diversity of other places and the bewildering facts of their existence. Along with these experiences came the desire to see and understand more. I was hooked.

Many other people are also hooked on nature, but don't necessarily recognise it. You just have to look at the traffic pouring out of our cities

Table 1.1 | General explanations of the term 'biodiversity'

1. Term commonly used to describe the number, variety and variability of living organisms (Groombridge 1992)
2. The variety among living organisms from all sources including, *inter alia*, terrestrial, marine and other aquatic ecosystems and the ecological complexes of which they are part; this includes diversity within species, between species and of ecosystems (Article 2, Biodiversity Convention)
3. The total variability of life on earth (Heywood 1995)

to try and find the open countryside during fine summer weekends. They are looking for many things, but one is that feeling of wildness and richness that, in contrast to concrete, even a small patch of woodland or grassland can offer. Nature seems to be a reference that we seek, a comfort to help us cope with our increasingly stressful lives, estranged from the natural world. The aesthetic or spiritual value of nature may be argument enough for its conservation but, in comparison with the value of economic development, estimating the hard value of nature can be difficult and illusive.

As a science, conservation biology must formalise the value of the natural world by quantifying its richness and diversity. The current popular term for the richness and diversity of life is **biodiversity**. This is simply short for **biological diversity** and it has no strict scientific definition (Table 1.1). However, it has become widely used in both the scientific and political fields as a measure of the value of the living world and we need to try and understand what it means. It is used in the literature to cover both the number of different populations and species that exist and the complex interactions that occur among them. Biodiversity is therefore commonly considered at three different levels:

1. within-species (intraspecific) diversity; usually measured in terms of genetic differences between individuals or populations;
2. species (interspecific) diversity; measured as a combination of the number and evenness of abundance of species;
3. community or ecosystem diversity; measured as the number of different species assemblages.

Biodiversity is therefore an expression of both numbers and difference and can be seen as a measure of complexity (Gaston & Spicer 1998). Its measurement at all levels presents significant challenges to the conservation biologist and we still largely rely on descriptive rather than quantitative measure of biodiversity to assess value, as illustrated in later chapters.

Biodiversity varies at all spatial scales from the 1 cm^3 sample of water or soil through the 1 m^2 quadrat vegetation sample to the continental scale. No one book can hope to describe these changes in full detail, but a general overview at the ecosystem scale is illustrative of the biodiversity and living resources we are fortunate enough to be borrowing from future generations. This is provided in the following chapter, where we also explore how major environmental factors influence diversity among ecosystems. Below, we try to draw some conclusions about general patterns of biodiversity.

Patterns of biodiversity

A fundamental starting point for conservation is to have a record of the living world in terms of the number of species that currently exist and how they are distributed. A pressing and difficult task for taxonomists, mostly working out of museums, is to painstakingly catalogue and report the discovery of new species. Unfortunately there are far too few taxonomists for this task. We are still very uncertain of how many species we have and there is a very long way to go. In fact it is certain that we will never be able to describe and name all species (to date approximately 1.5 million species have been described). It has therefore become necessary to try and estimate the total number of species currently present on earth. Box 1.2 summarises a method used for this daunting task.

Box 1.2 | **Estimates of the current number of species on Earth**

In order to arrive at an estimate of total number of species, the most common method employed is to sample and then scale up to the whole. An early estimate that initiated considerable debate on this problem was made by Erwin (1982), who was interested in the beetle fauna of tropical forest canopies. He collected beetles from a single species of tree by canopy fogging (an insecticide is released into the canopy of the tree and the insects collected as they fall to the ground). By estimating the number of species confined to that species of tree (162) and scaling this up by multiplying by the number of tree species in tropical forests (50,000) he estimated that tropical forests might contain as many as 8 million beetle species. He then further scaled up by assuming beetles were only 40% of total canopy arthropods and that canopy arthropods were only two thirds of the total arthropod fauna. This gave a total of 30 million tropical forest arthropods! Obviously there are many assumptions in this estimate and it was subsequently criticised, particularly for the assumption that all tropical tree species support such a large number of specialist insects. Subsequent estimates have been significantly lower, some based on more conservative scaling-up procedures and others based on the rate at which new species are being discovered in a range of taxonomic groups. There is now less variability in overall estimates and a general consensus is being reached that there are between 10 and 15 million species currently on Earth.

All of these estimates assume that there are no more surprises in terms of hidden diversity. This assessment may have to be revised if, for example, we find higher than expected numbers of species in the deep oceans. There is also a problem with the species concept in taxonomic groups such as the viruses and bacteria. Since there is no agreement on whether the species concept is applicable to these groups it is difficult to compare their diversity or richness with other groups. Genetic diversity may be a more appropriate measure in this case. I wonder how many genes there are on Earth?

If we cannot accurately count how many species occur in a given area then, clearly, measuring its biodiversity is also going to be an estimate. Different methods of estimating biodiversity will be considered in Chapter 8, but it is important to note here that the majority of the information gathered to date on the geographical distribution of biodiversity is based solely on the number of species (usually within one of the better recorded taxonomic groups) recorded in a given area. Thus the unit of measurement is the species and relative biodiversity is expressed in terms of **species richness** of selected taxonomic groups. Even though these measures are crude, they do suggest some inequalities in distribution that are of significance for conservation.

How is biodiversity distributed among taxonomic groups?

Species are not distributed evenly among higher taxonomic groups and most belong to those taxa that are least appreciated and understood. To anyone cataloguing species on earth it quickly becomes apparent that in terms of species number, the world is dominated by the Class Insecta and its close relatives (other Arthropods such as spiders) (Fig. 1.2). Of the species currently described, more than half are insects. Some of the best known taxonomic groups such as the mammals and birds, in which most species are already described, actually make up a small proportion of the total species. But what would the proportions look like if all species, known and unknown, were included? Based on the current estimates described in Box 1.2, species richness is likely to be dominated by the insects to an even greater extent than estimates currently based on named species. Other poorly recorded taxa, such as the algae, fungi and perhaps deep-ocean invertebrates, will probably rise as a proportion of the total as our knowledge of them advances.

Fig. 1.2 Proportion of all species currently recorded belonging to each major taxonomic group. Note the vertebrates (on which most conservation effort is expended) constitute an almost vanishingly small slice of the pie. Data from Groombridge (1992).

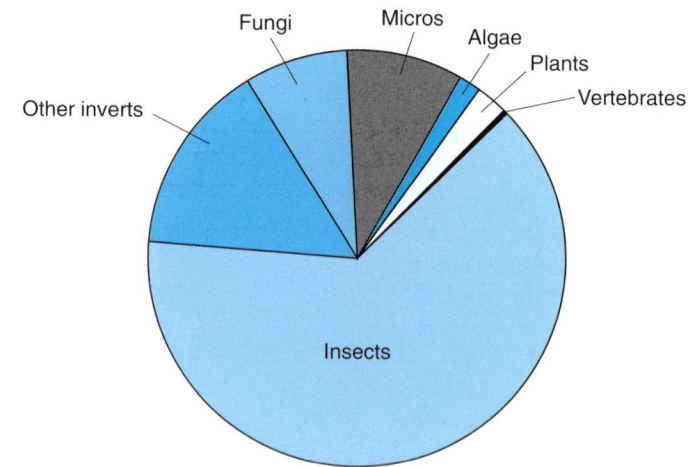

What do we know about global patterns of diversity?

Across a whole range of taxonomic groups there is a tendency for species richness to decrease from the tropics to the poles (Fig. 1.3). A decrease in species richness of American land birds from the tropics of Central America to the Arctic tundra of northern Canada is shown in Fig. 1.4.

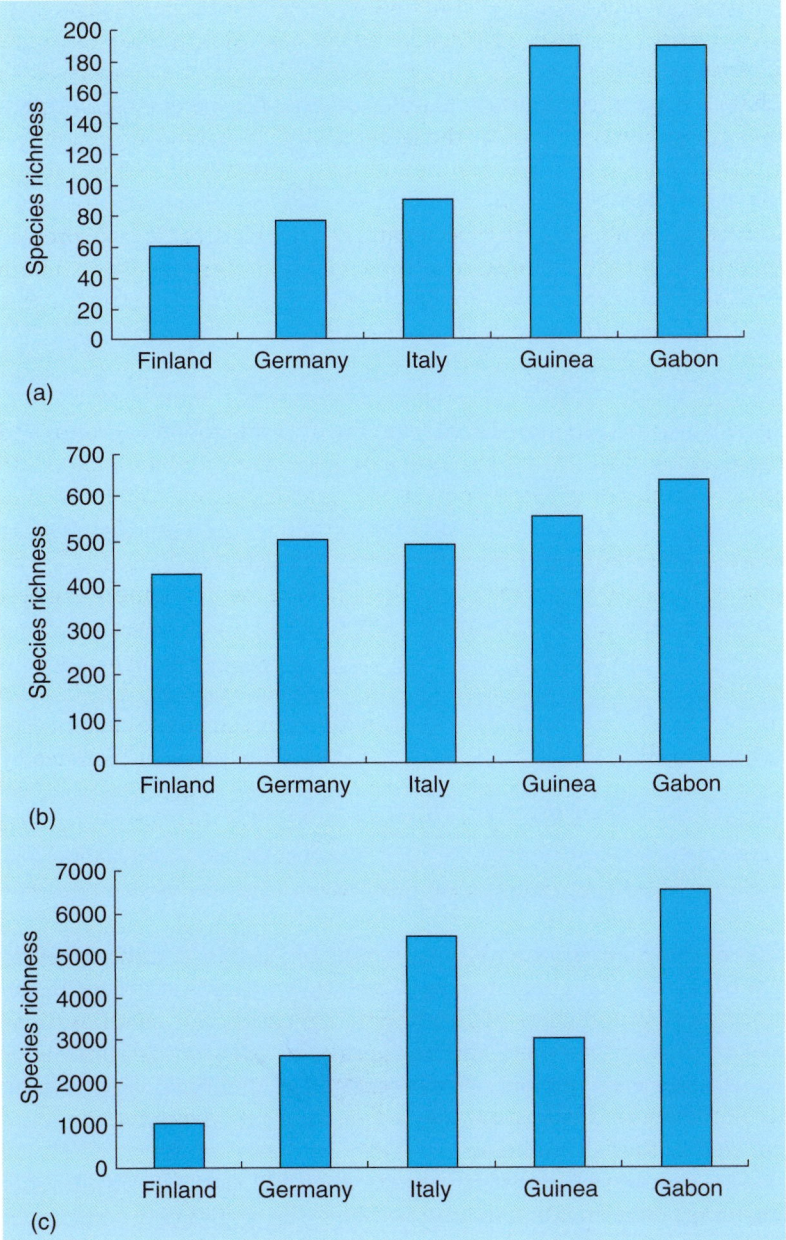

Fig. 1.3 Variation in species richness in (a) mammals, (b) birds and (c) flowering plants, among countries of similar size, but from different latitudes. All show a progressive increase from high to low latitudes.

This pattern is mirrored for many taxonomic groups, but is often complicated by physiographic and climatic factors such as mountain ranges and rainfall patterns. This is shown in the pattern for American land mammals and for tree species (Fig. 1.5). In both, the general trend is for a decrease from the tropics to the poles, but in mammals, species richness increases in the Rocky Mountain ranges, whilst trees reach a high species richness in the moister climate of the southeastern USA. Across all species, there is also a trend for decreasing species richness from low to high altitudes. The reason for these global trends has been the subject of much debate. The reason may at first seem obvious in that polar and

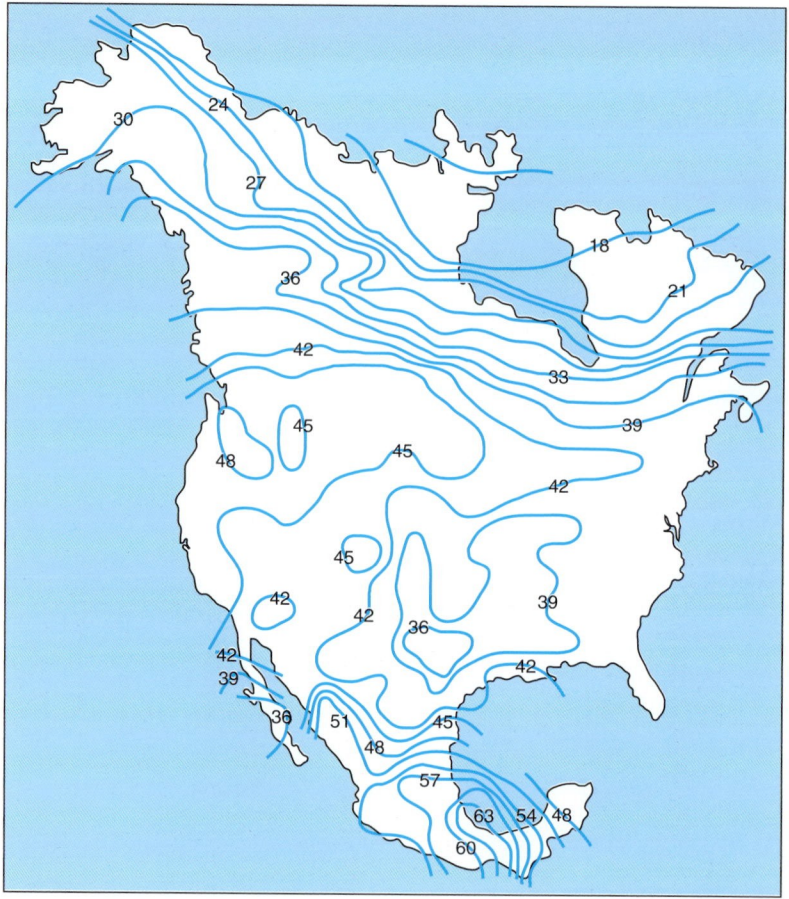

Fig. 1.4 Density of families of breeding birds in North America showing general decrease from the tropics to North Pole. Redrawn from Cook (1969) with kind permission of the Society for Systematic Zoology.

high-altitude environments are 'harsh' or 'extreme' and therefore present significant challenges for survival, but this a rather anthropomorphic view and these environments are clearly not harsh to those species that survive there and nowhere else. Many explanations have been put forward to explain the latitudinal gradient in diversity; none is completely satisfactory but they are not mutually exclusive and some can be effectively combined.

The *catastrophe hypothesis* argues that all stable environments encourage diversification in time and since the tropics have been stable for longer than temperate regions, which have suffered catastrophic changes in climate in the form of ice ages (Box 1.3), one would expect greater diversity in lower latitudes. Regions that have suffered other sorts of catastrophes such as volcanic activity have lower diversity and therefore provide good supporting evidence. However, coral reefs are prone to catastrophic changes in sea level but have very high diversity, thus undermining this hypothesis. The related *evolutionary speed hypothesis* similarly argues that because conditions are more favourable in the tropics, organisms develop faster and go through more generations per unit time. Biotas in warmer climates will evolve at more rapid rates than those in cold climates because of the more constant favourable

Fig. 1.5 (a) Species richness of terrestrial mammals in North America showing general decrease from tropics to pole, but also variance due to habitat heterogeneity. Redrawn from Simpson (1964) with kind permission of the Society for Systematic Zoology.

Fig. 1.5 (cont.) (b) Species richness of trees in North America showing general decrease from tropics to pole but also increase from west to east suggesting an influence of rainfall. Reprinted by permission from *Nature* 329: 326–327 copyright (1987) Macmillan Magazines Ltd.

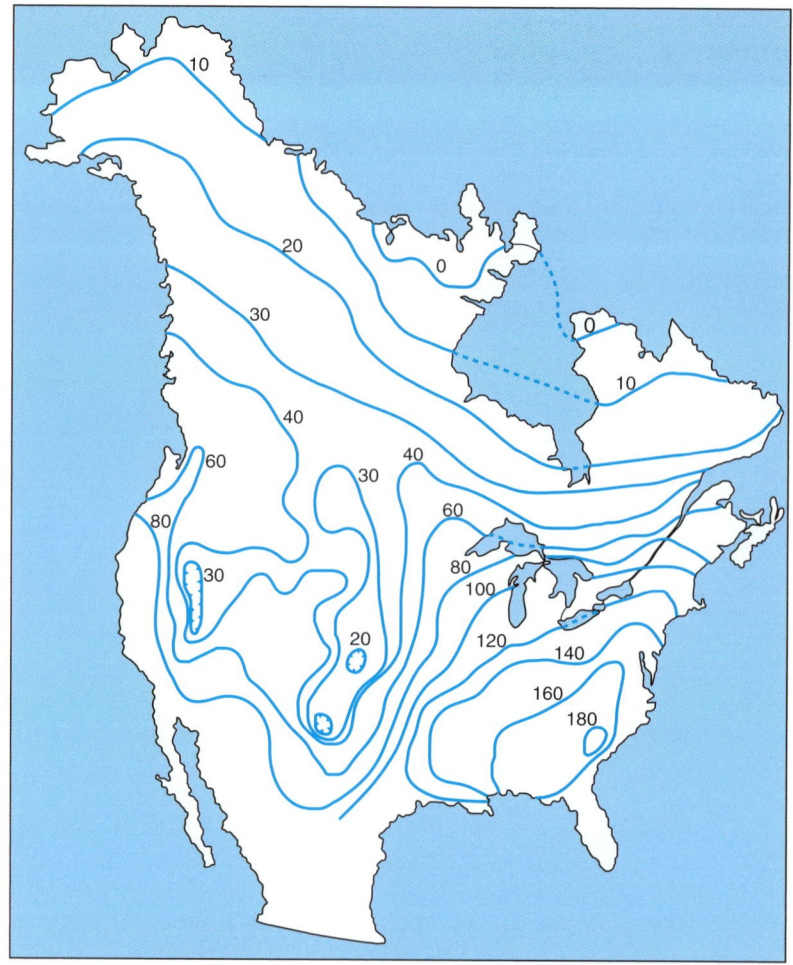

conditions throughout the year, and therefore faster generation times. Since temperate and polar regions are also younger, because of recent glaciations, the result is greater diversity in the tropics, whilst temperate regions are presumably still filling up with species.

The *energy input hypothesis* argues that diversity is related to the available solar energy at a given location. Since the tropics receive more solar energy than the poles, one would predict a diversity gradient (Brown 1981). Although there is a lot of supporting evidence for this general view (e.g. Turner *et al.* 1988), it is only a correlation and the causative factors involved are uncertain. Critics point to hot deserts that are often stable high energy input areas, but with low diversity. It is probable therefore that water balance should also be included in this model. This is the case in the *productivity hypothesis*, which predicts that diversity is dependent upon the realised annual evapotranspiration (RAE; which is dependent on both energy input and water availability). The RAE in a tropical rainforest is very high, but is very low in a hot desert, explaining the difference in the level of primary productivity in these two environments. This does not of course apply to aquatic environments and there are many examples in both terrestrial and aquatic envi-

Box 1.3 | Natural climate change and the impact of glacial cycles

The environment is not constant and major changes in our atmosphere have occurred ever since the appearance of the Earth some 5000 million years BP. More recently, it has become evident that our climate has followed a cyclic pattern of warming and cooling referred to as glacial cycles or ice ages. These fluctuations can clearly be seen in ocean-core and ice-core stratigraphy, enabling an accurate record of time scale to be constructed. The onset of the most recent period of glacial cycling (referred to as the beginning of the Quaternary period) is thought to be from 2 to 3 My BP. Since that time there have probably been nine glacial cycles (nine glaciations and nine interglacial periods), with the distinct possibility that we are currently in a tenth interglacial. The cause of glacial cycles is not fully resolved but an early theory of James Croll, that the eccentricity of the earth's orbit around the sun may lead to such cycles, was revived by Milutin Milankovitch in the first half of the twentieth century, and seems to have gained acceptance as new geological and astronomical evidence has come to light.

Whatever the cause, the impact of glaciations on terrestrial and aquatic ecosystems is profound, particularly in the temperate zones. Rapid changes in temperature as the climate cools and then warms lead to rapid changes in the distribution and abundance of species as they attempt to track their environment. The landscape of northern Europe today would be unrecognisable to someone living 15000 years ago, not only because of the human impact but also because of the considerable change in climate. Those species that have survived such events have done so through a cycle of contraction into climatic refugia during cool periods and a subsequent expansion in range during the interglacial periods. The impact that humans are currently having on our biodiversity must be understood against a background of already dynamic change: a crucial issue for conservation which will be expanded on in later chapters.

ronments of low productivity ecosystems that are diverse, such as some tropical seas and calcareous grasslands, suggesting that this hypothesis is not entirely satisfactory.

Perhaps the simplest explanation is the *area hypothesis*, which predicts that larger areas of uniform climate will support more species than similar but smaller areas. The basis of this idea is that larger areas provide more opportunity for isolation of populations and therefore speciation. Rosenweig (1995) compared the Pacific with the Atlantic Ocean as a test of this hypothesis. These oceans provide similar environmental conditions but the former covers a greater area and one might therefore predict greater diversity in the Pacific. This is supported by findings that the number of species of bivalve molluscs is greater in the Pacific than in the Atlantic, and the same pattern is found in butterfly fishes on coral reefs. Since the tropics cover a larger area than the temperate and polar zones, the area hypothesis would seem to be well supported, but it does not explain the relatively low diversity in large land masses such as central Asia, nor why Central America should have a greater species richness than the much larger North American continent. Again the explanation appears to be only partial.

There is also evidence that a number of local factors important in the study of conservation biology may influence diversity both positively and negatively. One of these is disturbance. The effect this has on bio-diversity is very much dependent on how much occurs. Very low levels of disturbance over long periods of time will tend to allow later succes-sional species to become dominant by exclusion of others. High levels of disturbance will eliminate many species that are relatively specialised and cannot cope with rapid changes in their environment (a subject returned to in Chapter 5). A modest level of disturbance confined to small patches of the total area, such as those caused by natural fires or treefalls (Fig. 1.6), can allow early successional species to persist, without eliminating more specialised species, resulting in higher diversity. This is the basis of the *intermediate disturbance hypothesis* (Connell 1978).

Whatever the reason for the observed geographical trends in bio-diversity it will probably remain a subject of lively debate for some time and the answer may well lie in a combination of the above.

Fig. 1.6 Natural treefalls in forest areas provide a low but frequent level of disturbance that increases diversity by creating gaps in the canopy that can be exploited by opportunist species.

The utility of the natural world

However difficult it may be to measure comparatively, there are many reasons for humankind to value its environment and biological richness. Many arguments for conservation are based on the direct value of natural systems to humans. They provide us with many of the goods and services we depend on and therefore act as good leverage in political debate. Humans have always relied on the natural world and, despite our technological development, this remains just as true today. A wide range of natural products are harvested for food and materials for clothing and construction, and we rely on the health of ecosystems to provide us with a reliable source of freshwater and clean air as well as maintaining the population of those species we directly exploit. It is not the purpose of this book to make these arguments in detail; we will concentrate on biology and only stray into politics and economics when absolutely necessary. This is not because these subjects are unimportant, but to cover them adequately would require whole textbooks to themselves. A brief overview of economic values placed on the natural world is provided below, with some suggestions for further reading at the end of the chapter.

Conservationists are often asked to defend the existence of habitats or species in economic terms, particularly when there is an alternative use, such as agricultural or industrial development, for the area they occupy. Some different economic values of biodiversity have therefore been defined as follows;

Direct Use Value: The economic (current market) value of natural goods such as timber or fish stocks. This makes some living resources directly comparable with other commodities on the market.

Indirect Use Value: The economic value of natural services such as provision of water, clean air, recreational space. Environmental economists have valued such global services at between 16 and 54 trillion US dollars per year, but add that the average of 33 trillion dollars is probably a minimum estimate (Costanza *et al.* 1997). The value here can be calculated as the amount that it would cost to provide these services by other means, if that is possible at all.

Option Value: The economic value of future benefits (as yet unseen) that a natural area could provide, e.g. new food sources, new medicines etc. The number of wild species that we utilise is currently increasing rapidly, not least because of the potential for new drugs from the chemicals naturally occurring in plants. A race is on among pharmaceutical companies to survey plant species for their medicinal properties and exploit the traditional use of plant chemicals by native peoples.

Existence Value: The economic value of a habitat or species based on the amount people would be willing to pay to avoid its destruction. How much would you pay to save the tiger?

Despite these useful terms, even the most enthusiastic conservationist can have problems when faced with the question "why bother to save this ugly little insect" or "that small piece of unproductive land" for conservation? The economic value may be small or non-existent, but this does not mean that the argument is lost. The reasons run deeper and are more complex, some might argue that they are more spiritually or ethically based, but they involve our fundamental relationship with nature which is the subject of the next section.

The wild experience

Earlier in this chapter the value of natural systems to human welfare was cited as an effective argument for conservation policies in a political arena. It would be wrong, though, to claim that this is the primary reason why so many people feel that conservation is an important activity. Most individuals contribute to conservation charities in response to the plight of charismatic species such as pandas and tigers, yet the vast majority of these contributors will never get to see those species in their natural environments. Why do they care? The answer was most eloquently explained by Ed Wilson (1994) in describing his experience of watching a thunderstorm over the Amazonian rainforest.

> The storm grew until sheet lightning spread across the western sky. The thundercloud reared up like a top heavy monster in slow motion, tilted forward, blotting out the stars. The forest erupted in a simulation of violent life. Lightning bolts broke to the front and then closer, to the right and left, 10,000 volts dropping along an ionizing path at 800 kilometers an hour, kicking a countersurge skyward ten times faster, the whole perceived as a single flash and crack of sound. The wind freshened, and rain came stalking through the forest.
>
> In the midst of chaos something to the side caught my attention. The lightning bolts were acting like strobe flashes to illuminate the wall of the rain forest. The forest was framed for a few moments in this theatrical setting.
>
> About the orchids of that place we knew very little. About flies and beetles, almost nothing, fungi nothing. Most kinds of organisms nothing. Five thousand kinds of bacteria might be found in a pinch of soil, and about them we knew absolutely nothing. This was wilderness in the sixteenth-century sense, as it must have formed in the minds of the Portuguese explorers, its interior still largely unexplored and filled with strange, myth-engendering plants and animals. And I thought: there is still time to see this land in such a manner.
>
> The unsolved mysteries of the rain forest are formless and seductive. They are like unnamed islands hidden in the blank spaces of old maps, like dark shapes glimpsed descending the far wall of the reef into the abyss. They draw us forward and stir strange apprehensions. The unknown and prodigious are drugs to the scientific imagination, stirring insatiable hunger with a single taste. In our hearts we hope we will never discover everything. We pray that there will always be a world like this one at whose edge I sat in darkness. The rain forest in its richness is one of the last repositories of that timeless dream.

I can directly relate to this experience as I have been privileged enough to be in a similar position. But perhaps it isn't necessary to actually experience wilderness at first hand to recognise its importance: it may be enough simply to be able to imagine it or see it second-hand. Few of us will ever visit the deep oceans but we are fascinated by what we might find there. The information revolution has undoubtedly helped in bringing the wonder and also the plight of species and natural ecosystems to the living rooms of affluent people with money to give.

Just as with economic reasons for conservation these spiritual reasons are not strictly the subject of this book, but it is worth reflecting on what sort of world it might be if there were nowhere left that we could call wild.

Summary

1. Life on Earth has existed for 4 billion years during which it has increased in diversity to the richness we see today. Human activity is threatening to wipe out a large proportion of this diversity within a tiny fraction of that time.

2. To date, some 1.5 million species have been described, but the vast majority are still unknown.

3. Biodiversity is unevenly distributed among taxonomic groups with a disproportionately large number of species in the Class Insecta.

4. Biodiversity increases from the poles to the tropics but there is no consensus as to why this is so. It has been suggested that this is because the tropics are more climatically stable or because the tropics receive more energy input from the sun.

5. Economic values have been placed on biodiversity to enable us to compare benefits of conservation versus development, but the spiritual value of biodiversity remains fundamentally important to many peoples.

Discussion points

- For what or for whom are we wishing to conserve biodiversity?
- What are the causes of global species richness gradients?
- Why are insects so successful and what are the implications for conserving biodiversity?
- How do we weight economic versus ethical reasons for conservation?
- Should we argue for the spiritual need for wildness as a reason for conservation?

Further reading

Costanza, R., dArge, R., deGroot, R., Farber, S., Grasso, M., Hannon, B., Limburg, K., Naeem, S., Oneill, R.V., Paruelo, J., Raskin, R.G., Sutton, P. & vandenBelt, M. (1997). The value of the world's ecosystem services and natural capital. *Nature* **387**, 253–260.

Daily, G.C. (ed.) (1997). *Nature's services: societal dependence on ecosystem services.* Washington, DC: Island Press.

Gaston, K.J. & Spicer, J.I. (1998). *Biodiversity: an introduction.* Oxford: Blackwell Science.

Groombridge, B. (ed.) (2000). *Global biodiversity: earth's living resources in the 21st century.* Cambridge: World Conservation Monitoring Centre.

Wilson, E. O. (1994). *The diversity of life.* Harmondsworth: Penguin Books.

Web sites

World Conservation Monitoring Centre – www.wcmc.org.uk/

Convention on Biological Diversity – www.biodiv.org/

The Natural History Museum, London – www.nhm.ac.uk/

The Smithsonian Institution, National Museum of Natural History: www.mnh.si.edu/

UK National Biodiversity Network: www.nbn.org.uk/

Chapter 2

Major world ecosystems

This chapter builds on the previous one by cataloguing the world's ecosystems, describing major types of terrestrial and aquatic environments and how these are shaped by prevailing environmental conditions. For reasons of space, the coverage of some subjects in this chapter is rather superficial and you may already be familiar with parts and wish to skip over them. Guidance is given to further reading for those who wish to study particular aspects in more detail.

By reading this chapter, students will gain an understanding of some major terms used in describing the natural world; of the major types of ecosystems that presently exist and how major environmental factors dictate the distribution of ecosystem types.

The ecosystem concept

An ecosystem is a community of living organisms together with the physical processes that occur within an environment. All organisms are faced with environmental variables to cope with. These are usually divided into abiotic factors, including the broad climate and geology as well as specific factors such as temperature, water (rainfall and humidity), light, salinity, pressure and soil and water chemistry (pH and mineral content), and biotic factors, which are interactions with other organisms, including competition, predation, parasitism and symbiosis. Thus there are abiotic (non-living) and biotic (living) components of an ecosystem, all potentially interacting to form a functioning unit, distinguishable, although not isolated, from other ecosystems. The concept of the ecosystem is central to our understanding of the natural world. Ecological studies have shown how energy flows through ecosystems, from the capture of light energy by plants and conversion to the chemical energy in sugars, to its passage through successive trophic levels and constant escape back into the environment (Fig. 2.1). Equally, we have learnt how nutrients and water are cycled from the atmosphere to the soil, through plants, animals, decomposers and back again; the intricacies of food webs and the interdependence of species in coevolved mutualisms (the evolution of relationships between species because of the

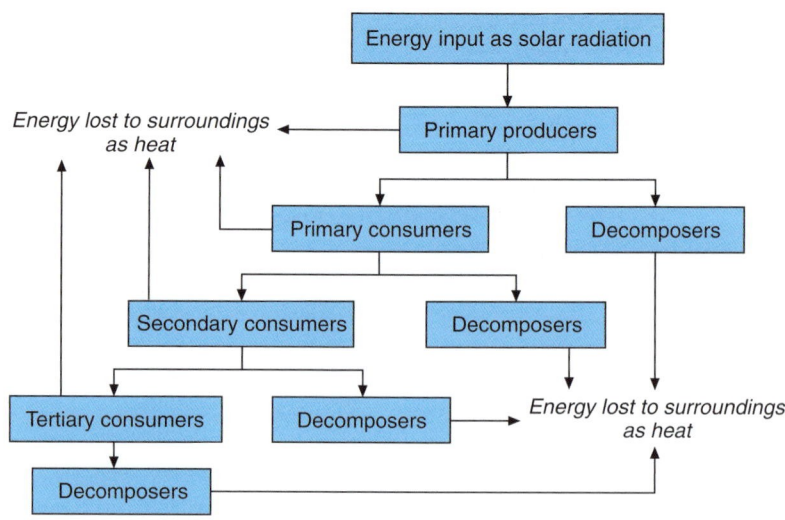

Fig. 2.1 Schematic diagram of energy flow through an ecosystem. Flow of energy from one trophic level to the next is only about 10% efficient and most energy is lost as heat back to the abiotic environment.

benefit to both, e.g. pollinators and flowering plants); and how our ecosystems are shaped by the challenges of the abiotic environment.

The study of the spatial distribution of species and habitats has led to the classification of the environments or ecosystem types we have on our planet in terms of the flora and fauna that prevail in them. This is most developed for terrestrial environments, but applies to aquatic ones as well. In this chapter we briefly review major world ecosystems. Brief descriptions are given of the prevailing environmental factors, the way these shape the communities, and how the organisms that live there have evolved to cope with the prevailing conditions. The descriptions given are, as far as is possible, of the natural systems before human influence, although in some cases it is not entirely clear what these would have been (see Chapter 3).

Terrestrial environments

Terrestrial environments are often divided into biomes, distinguishable on the basis of their prevailing climate and dominant vegetation (Fig. 2.2). Differences in climate are predominantly related to the uneven heating of the earth's surface by the sun. These differences in turn influence the type of vegetation that develops. The following descriptions are based on the biome concept but no attempt is made to subdivide these zones to the extent that Holdridge (1967) has done (see Box 2.1). We are going to take a imaginary journey from the polar regions to the tropics, considering each major ecosystem in turn and how it contrasts with its neighbours.

The polar environment

This environment is included for completeness although, in reality, the climate is so extreme that very few terrestrial organisms can persist and no true terrestrial ecosystem exists. The North Pole is not a truly terrestrial environment since it is not a land mass, but frozen seawater. The

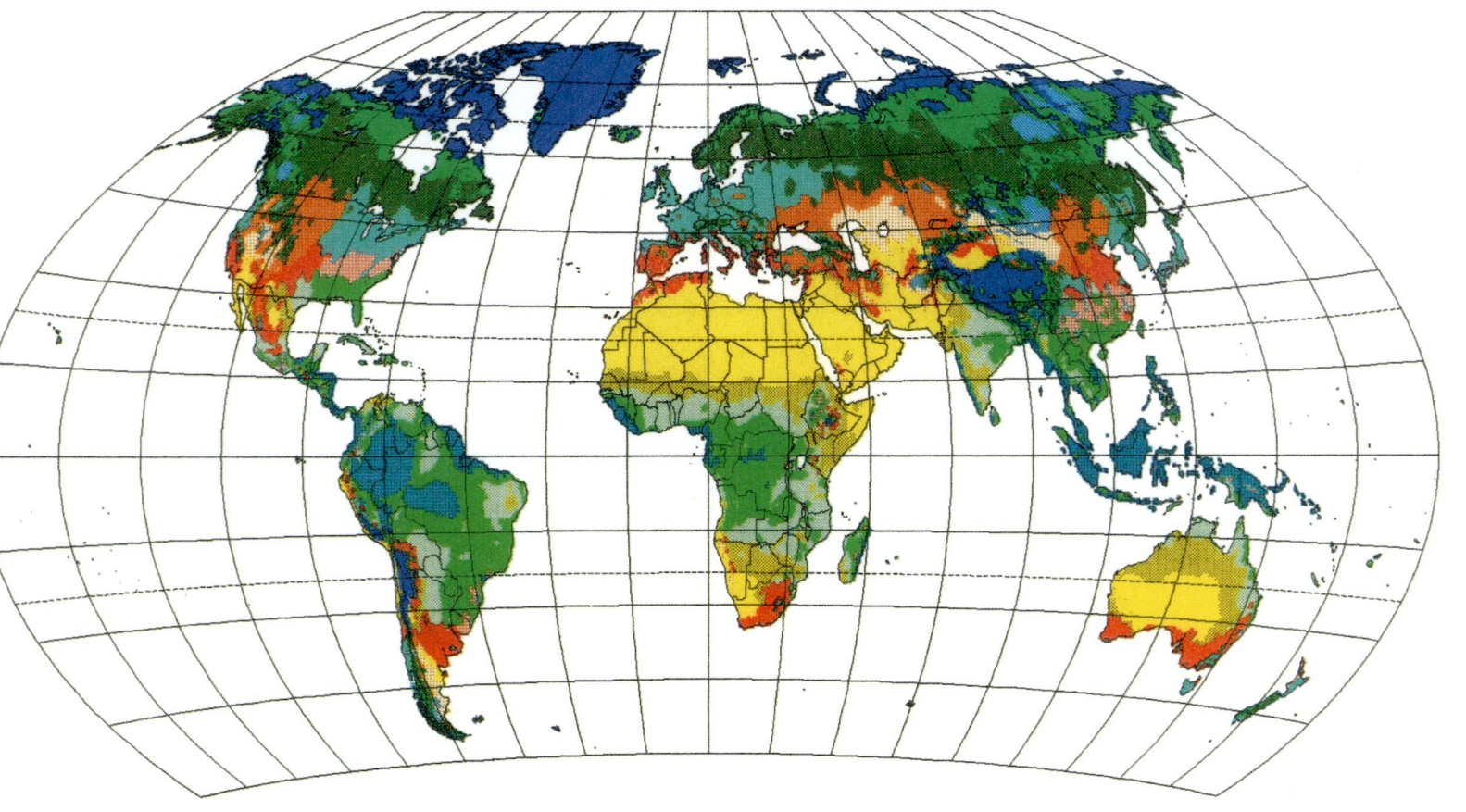

Fig. 2.2 World map of terrestrial biomes based on the Holdridge Life Zone classification. Colour coding is matched with Fig 2.4. Reproduced from Groombridge (1992) with kind permission of Kluwer Academic Publishers.

Box 2.1 | Dominant features of the abiotic environment

The world's terrestrial biomes are largely defined by climatic factors and the way they change with latitude and to some extent altitude, and we will concentrate on the two dominant climatic factors, temperature and water availability, together with their seasonal variation.

Temperature

This planet gets its heat from the sun, but unevenly, so that surface temperatures are relatively low at the poles and high at the equator (Fig. 2.3). This is complicated by the atmosphere around the earth, in that cloudy areas have more stable temperatures and clear areas more extreme. The equator is cloudy so has stable temperatures which do not reach as high (or low) as the clear areas at latitudes 30° north and south, where desert dominates. Also, land close to oceans is influenced by sea temperatures so that seasonal changes are less extreme.

Fig. 2.3 The sun's rays heat the earth's surface unevenly due to the angle at which they hit the surface at different locations. Each unit of energy hits the equator at an angle close to 90° and is therefore concentrated over a smaller area and achieves more warming compared with a unit of energy striking the poles at an oblique angle.

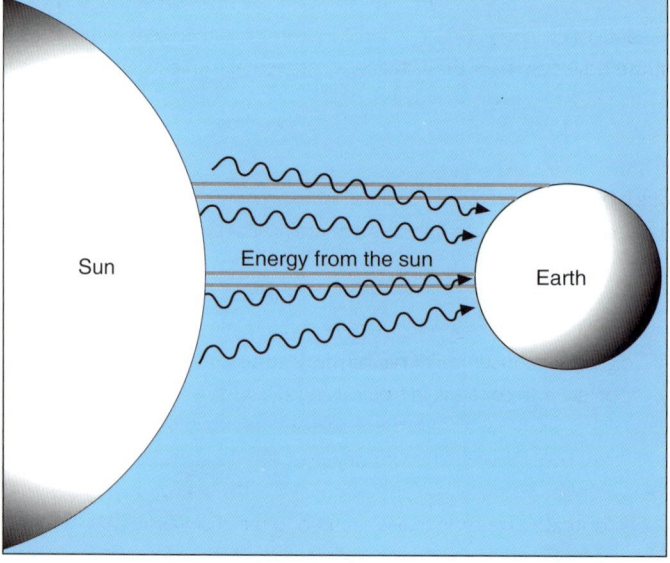

The range of temperatures on the earth's surface is quite large. A typical surface minimum for Siberia is −40 °C with an absolute minimum sometimes below −60 °C. In contrast, temperatures in some desert areas such as north Africa may reach 50 °C. Such extremes of temperature pose very great problems for living organisms.

Subzero temperatures will, of course, cause water to freeze. Since most of our bodies consist of water and we depend on its fluidity and solvent properties within our cells for vital biochemical processes, freezing of that intracellular water is almost invariably lethal. However, many organisms have evolved specific adaptations to survive subzero temperatures.

At the other extreme, high temperature threatens desiccation. The amount of water in our bodies needs to be maintained for the integrity of biochemical processes and all terrestrial organisms retain a greater concentration of water than their surroundings. Therefore water tends to be lost by evaporation from the body surface, through respiration, excretion and through methods of cooling such as sweating and panting. This water has to be replaced quickly. High temperature itself can be lethal if a way of cooling is not found. Many enzymes that are vital to our bodily functions become denatured at temperatures above 40 °C.

Water availability

The second dominant feature of the abiotic environment is water. Water is cycled within the environment but, as with temperature, precipitation (rainfall, snowfall, etc.) is distributed very unevenly over terrestrial environments. Some monsoon areas of India, Bangladesh and Burma receive over 1000 cm of rain per year, in contrast to some desert and tundra (sometimes called cold desert) areas which receive less than 20 cm a year, and in many years may have no rain at all. As a general pattern, rainfall is high over the equator where low pressure systems dominate and low over areas 30° north and south where high pressure dominates and where, as noted above, most deserts are located. Rainfall then increases moving towards temperate areas at 50° latitude and decreases again around the poles themselves where high pressure again dominates.

Using these two factors of temperature and water availability, Holdridge (1967) constructed a table of life zones (Fig. 2.4) which, although rather generalised, does serve to illustrate how dominant these two environmental variables are in shaping our terrestrial communities and ecosystems.

Seasonality

The way in which both temperature and rainfall influence environments depends, to an extent, on seasonality. Neither temperature nor rainfall is constant throughout the year, but some environments are far more seasonal than others. In terms of temperature it is clear that polar and high-latitude environments are far more seasonal than equatorial environments. The dominant seasons in temperate and polar regions are cold and warm (e.g. winter and summer); rainfall may also be seasonal but this is usually of secondary importance. In contrast, in tropical and subtropical areas the dominant seasons are wet and dry. Rainfall is often highly seasonal, as in monsoon areas, which means that organisms have to withstand long dry seasons. Only in relatively few areas on earth are both temperature and rainfall at all constant. This seasonality means that organisms have to operate a life cycle that is adapted to the changes in their environment. Reproduction and growth must occur at favourable times of the year and survival strategies (e.g. dormancy) must be used at unfavourable times.

Antarctic is a real continent and has a significant flora and fauna, but this is concentrated around the coastal margins and offshore islands where conditions are ameliorated by the sea and not truly polar. The polar environment is characterised by permanent snow cover and subzero temperatures, with six months of continual darkness during the winter. As a result, it has no significant primary production (no plants) and the only animals found there are endotherms ('warm blooded' or, more accurately, able to regulate their body temperature internally and maintain it despite their surroundings), which are transient visitors largely getting their food from the surrounding sea, penguins and seals being prominent examples. The polar bear (*Ursus maritimus*), an Arctic species, is not truly polar although it can exist on

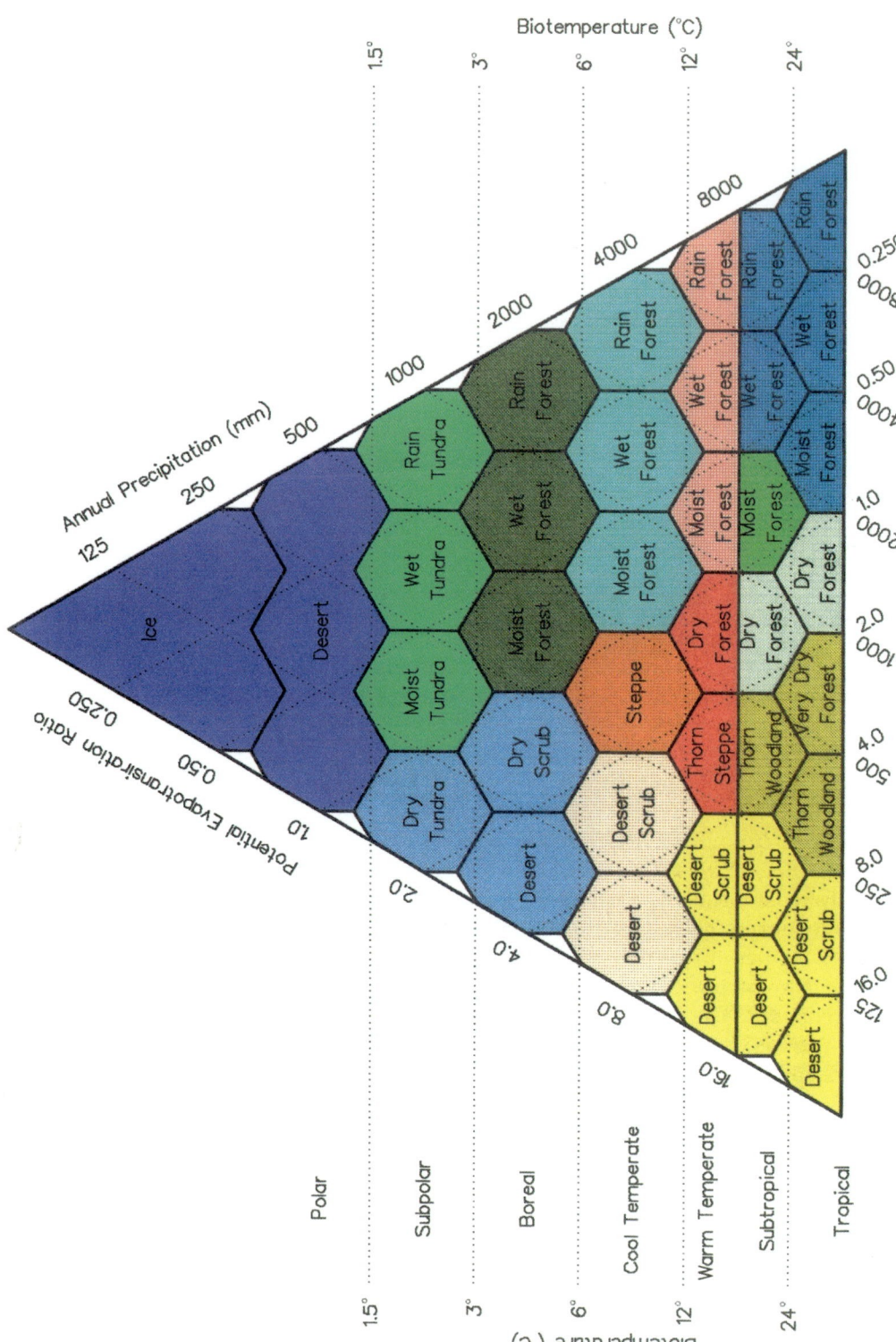

Fig. 2.4 The Holdridge Life Zone classification system based on the combination of average temperature and annual precipitation. Note that because of the combinations of temperature and precipitation that commonly occur on earth, some of the life zones are much commoner than others. See Fig. 2.2. for global distribution of life zones. Reproduced from Groombridge (1992) with kind permission of Kluwer Academic Publishers.

icefields up to 300 km from land, drifting as the ice breaks up during the short summer and surviving by catching seals, its main prey.

The tundra ecosystem

Tundra fringes the North Pole in areas of northern Canada, Alaska, Russia and Siberia, Greenland and other Arctic islands. In contrast, only a small area of the Antarctic extends far enough away from the South Pole to support this type of ecosystem. Tundra may be characterised by a combination of criteria:

1. a short vegetative growing period of generally less than 50 days (between spring and autumn frosts);
2. permanently frozen subsoil (permafrost);
3. a very low precipitation of less than 40 cm a year;
4. a very low productivity, usually less than 1 g of dry matter produced per square metre per day (however, areas where plentiful water is available can be far more productive).

The severity of this environment excludes tree growth and gives it the windswept, barren appearance from which it gets its name (Fig. 2.5): tundra is a Finnish word meaning barren land.

Average annual temperatures are not far in excess of 1°C, with 6–10 months having averages below freezing. This, though, does not tell the full story because the tundra is a highly seasonal environment, with continuous darkness during midwinter, but continuous light during the short summer, promoting rapid plant growth. The major inhibitor of plant growth is permafrost: permanently frozen subsoil that underlies the active soil layer that freezes and thaws with the seasons. Permafrost prevents root penetration below a few centimetres in places and is one reason for the lack of trees. Soil organisms such as bacteria and fungi are numerous near the soil surface but decrease rapidly in abundance with depth.

Despite the harsh conditions, there is primary productivity in the form of plants on which an ecosystem can be based. The vegetation is characteristically dwarf in form and may be widely dispersed so that plants have little influence on their microclimate or that of their neighbours. Some species such as dwarf willows (*Salix* sp.) grow outwards, creeping close to the ground rather than upwards, making use of the higher temperatures close to the ground in the summer. Others grow like a cushion, maintaining a microclimate of high humidity and high nutrient status as dead material accumulates around them. Such perennial herbs must be both cold- and drought-hardy. One of the most common groups of organisms is the lichens which are well adapted through their crustose growth habit and their tolerance of drought and low nutrient conditions.

Invertebrates can appear in summer in large numbers. Among these are soil nematodes, earthworms, springtails and insects whose larvae live in pools or streams, e.g. chironomid flies, mosquitoes and blackflies. Some of these are tolerant of the freezing of their extracellular tissues during the winter. Most feed either on decaying plant material or the blood of vertebrates.

Fig. 2.5 Two typical tundra landscapes. (a) Dry tundra and (b) wet tundra in northern Canada. The vegetation cover is much greater in wet tundra but the absence of trees is still evident.

There are no ectothermic ('cold-blooded') vertebrates such as reptiles or amphibians in the tundra: conditions are simply too cold. Of the endothermic animals, relatively few are resident over the winter. Some small rodents, such as lemmings (e.g. *Lemmus lemmus* and *Dicrostonyx groenlandicus*), survive the winter by remaining active under the snow and so cannot survive in dry windswept areas, which are snowless. Small carnivores in turn stay active and hunt small rodents; the Arctic fox (*Alopex lagopus*), and the stoat (*Mustela erminea*) are two examples, both of which grow a white winter coat for camouflage. Of the large herbivores, the musk ox (*Ovibos moschatus*) is a true resident of the tundra regions of North America and Greenland. Its large body size and therefore large surface-to-volume ratio, together with its thick coat, enable it to retain heat and resist the cold. Some species, such as the caribou (*Rangifer tarandus*), are migrants and move down into the boreal forests (see below), normally followed by their predators, packs of wolves (*Canis lupus*). The specialist polar bear is one of the few hibernators, making a den in the snow to pass the long winter. Bears build up fat reserves prior to hibernation and once in the den their metabolic rate slows as their body temperature cools (but always staying above freezing). The winter is too long for many smaller mammals to hibernate. Most birds are migrants and breed in large numbers during the short summer, typically geese, ducks and wading birds. Their mobility enables them to exploit the high seasonal plant and insect abundance and escape more numerous predators in temperate areas.

The boreal ecosystem

This ecosystem occupies a circumpolar subarctic region, ranging across Canada and Eurasia approximately between the July 13 °C and 18 °C isotherms. There is no equivalent region in the southern hemisphere, since the Southern Ocean dominates these latitudes. Boreal ecosystems experience snow cover for over half of the year, accompanied by very low temperatures, but with a longer summer season and higher summer temperatures than the tundra. They are characterised by:

1. greater precipitation than the tundra, although most still falls as snow. Mean annual precipitation is typically between 25 and 100 cm;
2. mean monthly temperatures that may fall as low as −35 °C, but during summer may be as high as +23 °C;
3. a very seasonal environment with a very long winter and short frost-free summer lasting about 2 months.

The boreal zone is dominated by stands of coniferous trees (plants that bear their seeds in cones, in contrast to flowering plants). The boreal forest forms one of the most prominent plant formations on earth but contains relatively few species compared with forests in warmer regions. The dominant species are coniferous trees of the spruce, fir, pine and larch families interspersed with deciduous hardwoods of alder, birch and poplar in more sheltered areas. At the northerly end of the range the forest is open and these areas grade into tundra dominated by lichens and mosses (Fig. 2.6). The limit of tree growth is

Fig. 2.6 A typical boreal landscape in northern Canada, close to the transition to tundra with scattered coniferous trees interspersed with tundra-type vegetation.

ultimately set by temperature as this dictates the soil depth above the permafrost. At the northerly limit of tree growth the permafrost is only a few inches below the soil surface, preventing sufficient root penetration of the soil for stability and nutrient and water uptake, and exposing the roots to permanently low temperatures.

The needle-shaped leaves typical of coniferous trees are thick and waxy on the surface, reducing transpiration (water loss) from the leaf. This is important during the long winter season when water cannot easily be replaced from the frozen soil. Water is also withdrawn from the leaf, concentrating the remaining solution and thus reducing the risk of freezing. This ability to retain leaves throughout the winter means that conifers are able to resume photosynthesis (and therefore growth and reproduction) as soon as conditions become suitable, thus making best use of the short summer. Deciduous trees have to spend some of this time growing new leaves and are at a competitive disadvantage. Coniferous forests let little light through the canopy, so when the forest is closed there is virtually no understorey but, importantly, the presence of trees creates a milder microclimate within the forest.

Animals are more diverse in the boreal than the tundra, but they are still limited by the length and severity of the winter. The trees add an extra layer or dimension of complexity, providing new niches for colonisation, especially by insects, birds and arboreal mammals such as squirrels. Many of the tundra vertebrates (such as the caribou mentioned above) migrate into the boreal forests during the winter, but resident species include several bears, otters, badger, lynx, moose, and even the

Siberian tiger (*Panthera tigris altaica*) is a boreal subspecies. Most birds are migratory as in the tundra and exploit the summer harvest of fruits, seeds and insects. Amphibians occur here, especially frogs, but reptiles are still poorly represented. Insects are particularly abundant if not diverse; many are phytophagous and attack the trees. Caterpillars of moths and sawflies can cause considerable damage, as can larvae of bark beetles. Many of these animals, from the insects to the bears, survive the winter by going through a period of dormancy.

Cool temperate ecosystems

This group of ecosystems is spread across the northern hemisphere, south of the boreal zone approximately delimited by the July 15 °C and 25 °C isotherms and the January −10 °C and +5 °C isotherms. There are also scattered examples in the southern hemisphere, including the southern tip of South America, Tasmania and the South Island of New Zealand. The climate is more favourable to plant growth than the Boreal zone and the winters are milder and shorter with a growing season of 4–6 months.

There is still a clear and dominant winter–summer cycle and no clear wet–dry cycle, although the pattern of rainfall can dictate the development of forest or grassland.

Cool temperate forest is found in the north-eastern USA, north-west, central and eastern Europe, northern China, Korea, Japan and far eastern Russia. In the southern hemisphere a few forests of a similar nature occur, acting as strong evidence that similar environments independently develop similar plant formations. In contrast to the evergreen conifers of the Boreal, this ecosystem is dominated by deciduous hardwood trees (Fig. 2.7). The growing season is long enough to favour the habit of shedding leaves and becoming dormant during the winter and growing new, highly efficient but not cold-tolerant leaves in the spring. In Europe dominant trees are beech (*Fagus*), hornbeam (*Carpinus*), lime (*Tilia*), oaks (*Quercus*), elm (*Ulmus*), birch (*Betula*) and sweet chestnut (*Castanea*). Related species are also dominant in North America but hickories (*Carya*) and maples (*Acer*) are particularly prominent. Because these forests are deciduous they are more open than boreal coniferous forests, particularly in the spring. This enables a clear understorey of shrubs and herbs to grow and benefit from leaf fall, providing nutrients. The large quantity of leaf litter is broken down, mainly by a diverse community of fungi, and the soil is rich in humus from leaf mould supporting a diverse soil fauna. The greater structural diversity again seems to enable greater species diversity to be sustained, though one should be careful about such interpretations (see Chapter 1).

The forest provides a rich but seasonal food source for herbivores and there are more animal taxa than found in the boreal. Many species are resident all year round, but many of the birds are summer migrants that take advantage of this seasonal flush of food. Reptiles and amphibians are notably more common as the summers get warmer and longer.

Temperate grasslands occur in regions of low rainfall where tree growth is inhibited. This is common in the interior of large continents such as North America (the prairies) and Eurasia (the steppes), although

(a)

Fig. 2.7 Examples of cool temperate vegetation. (a) A European beech (*Fagus sylvatica*)-dominated woodland in winter showing deciduous habit; (b) same site in late spring showing closed canopy with vernal ground flora; (c) cool temperate grassland created by herbivore pressure in mid-western USA.

the extent to which human activity has excluded trees from such areas is not clear. Grasslands also form the pampas region in South America. These areas are subjected to highly seasonal conditions with hot, dry summers and cold winters.

The dominant plants are perennial grasses (together with some herbs) which are tolerant of grazing by large mammals and the occasional fires that scorch the ground during the summer; but the grassland is far from uniform over such vast areas. For example, in the prairie region of the USA there is a recognisable transition from tall grass prairie in the east to short grass in the west, following a pattern of decreasing rainfall.

The most conspicuous animals are large herbivores. In the steppes of Russia there are saiga antelope (*Saiga tatarica*) and Mongolian gazelle (*Procapra gutturosa*). In the USA their equivalents are pronghorn antelope (*Antilocapra americana*) and the once widespread bison (*Bison bison*). Since there is little cover in grassland compared with forest many smaller mammals are burrowers, such as prairie dogs, gophers, mole rats and marmots. These hibernate in their burrows during the winter and may also aestivate (summer/dry season form of hibernation) during the hot dry summer. The herbivores have predators such as the wolf, coyotes and foxes as well as eagles and other large birds of prey that find the open grassland much more suited to hunting than forest. Invertebrates are also important grazers of grassland, particularly the grasshoppers and crickets (Orthoptera) and the ants (Formicidae).

(b)

(c)

Reptiles are more numerous here than in the cool temperate forest because the warm dry summers allow sufficient time to feed and reproduce.

In South America the temperate grasslands have a less seasonal climate, which is milder and wetter. Tussocky grasses dominate, including the familiar garden favourite, pampas grass (*Cortaderia* sp.). The reason for the lack of trees is uncertain but may be due to a combination of high winds and heavy grazing. Pampas deer (*Ozotoceros bezoarcticus*) take the place of the northern hemisphere antelope, and rodents like the rabbit-like viscacha (*Lagostomus maximus*) and mara (*Dolichotis patogona*) are the main burrowers. One notable addition is the large flightless bird, the rhea (*Rhea* sp.), a relative of the ostrich (*Struthio camelus*).

Warm temperate ecosystems

These ecosystems represent zones of transition in our journey from the poles to the tropics, from the dominance of temperature to precipitation as the primary seasonal variable (see Box 2.1). Warm temperate regions are just as heterogeneous as cool temperate ones but are influenced equally by seasonal temperatures and seasonal rains, partly explaining their complexity. Warm temperate ecosystems occur in southern North America, southern Europe and in Asia across to Japan. In the southern hemisphere this zone covers much of southern Australia as well as significant areas of South America and southern Africa. A 6–12 month growing season, with infrequent frosts, reduces the influence of temperature, although most plants have evolved some cold tolerance.

The pattern of rainfall dictates the development of the vegetation and two major zones are recognised within this region: warm temperate deciduous forest and the summer-drought – sclerophyllous community. Winters are mild in both of these zones with only infrequent frosts, but growth may still be arrested for a few months of the year because of low temperatures. Year-round rain allows the eastern continental regions to be more productive than the summer-drought region in the west of continents where the seasonality of rain necessitates adaptations of plants and many animals to drought conditions.

Warm temperate forest occurs on the eastern side of continents where rainfall is distributed evenly throughout the year. Examples are the south-eastern USA, south-east Australia and southern China. These forests are dominated by broadleaved trees, but in contrast to cool temperate forest, many trees are evergreen (Fig. 2.8). The infrequency of frosts means that leaves can be retained all year round. Typical species in the USA are oaks, hickories and magnolias (*Magnolia* spp.), whereas in Australia the evergreen *Eucalyptus* are dominant, but *Acacia* are also common. Conditions are very moist under the canopy and there is a well-developed understorey in places where sufficient light penetrates.

In the USA typical herbivores are deer and tree squirrels, along with turkeys (*Meleagris gallopavo*) which forage on the forest floor. Omnivores are well represented and include bears, racoons, skunks and opossums. Resident carnivores include wolves, fox and bobcats (*Felis rufus*). The diversity of insects and birds increases along with tree diversity as cool temperate forest grades into warm temperate down the east coast of the USA. In Australia this zone has many characteristic marsupials including the koala (*Phascolarctos cinereus*), wallabies and possums; it was the habitat of a recently extinct carnivore, the thylacine or marsupial wolf (*Thylacinus cynocephalus*).

The **summer-drought – sclerophyllous community**, often called the Mediterranean zone, occurs on the western side of continents where rainfall is highly seasonal, with wet winters and dry summers. Examples are the Mediterranean region of Europe, southern California, western Australia and the Cape Region of South Africa. Vegetation is dominated by drought-tolerant plants with thick, hard, waxy leaves that reduce transpiration (sclerophyllous means hard-leaved). Trees are few and scattered into small woodland fragments (although they may have been more widespread before human colonisation); in the Mediterranean, cork and evergreen oak are most characteristic and similar oak species are found in California. In Australia, however, it is the eucalyptus family that dominates as in the warm temperate forest, though with largely different species. Shrubby plants, up to 2 m tall, are more common than trees in the sclerophyllous community and form dense thickets referred to as Maquis in some parts of Europe and Chapparal in California. These plants are not only drought-tolerant but fire-tolerant as well. Fires are frequent in these areas towards the end of the summer when the vegetation is very dry. Annual grasses that pass the dry season as seeds and other plants relying on underground bulbs and corms to survive the drought, are common and highly diverse in some regions (Fig. 2.9).

In the northern hemisphere the fauna is not very distinct from that of the cool temperate zone; however, reptiles are more common and diverse. There are not many large herbivores because the vegetation is unpalatable during the summer, but wild ancestors of goats and donkeys probably once lived in the Mediterranean region. Deer are the common large herbivores in California, with rabbits and ground squirrels. Their predators include puma (*Felis concolor*), bobcat, coyote and golden eagle (*Aquila chrysaetos*). The winter is mild enough for most animals to remain active throughout, but some may become dormant (aestivate) during the long dry summer. Many insects also use this strategy here. In western Australia the fauna is very different: the major herbivores are kangaroos, wallabies and emus, and no large predators now exist although large marsupial carnivores equivalent to the large cats on other continents have existed in the past.

Hot desert and arid ecosystems

In deserts, lack of water is the dominant factor driving specialised adaptations in resident organisms. Desert conditions prevail in approximately 30% of the earth's land surface, but much of this area is cold desert in the tundra biome. Most hot deserts lie in the regions of dry

Fig. 2.8 Two examples of warm temperate forest (a) The interior of a humid forest in North Carolina, USA and (b) a dry forest of eucalypts in southern Australia.

(a)

trade winds in high pressure areas on either side of the equator (Fig. 2.2). Organisms must cope with three major problems: low rainfall, low humidity and intense insolation. Annual precipitation is far less than potential evaporation and there is often a high diurnal range in temperature (over 30 °C). Temperatures may go below freezing on some nights, but during the day shade temperatures over 50 °C have been recorded. Average rainfall is below 25 cm a year, but periodicity is just as important and many areas may go for years without rain. Extensive evaporation in valley bottoms may lead to salt pan formation as in Death Valley, California; this area receives less than 9 cm of rain annually. Typical characteristics of hot deserts therefore include:

(b)

1. average rainfall below 25 cm a year;
2. high daytime temperatures in excess of 40 °C;
3. large diurnal range in temperature;
4. high insolation.

Trees are generally excluded because of aridity, except around oases or where groundwater is reachable by roots. Drought-tolerant scrubby bushes are common; in Africa, Asia and Australia (Fig 2.10) these are usually members of the acacia family and are thorny in character. In America a locally dominant species is the creosote bush (*Larrea divaricata*), which covers large areas sometimes in association with the yucca plant. However, it is the cacti and the succulents that are the desert specialists; in America these are represented by the saguaro (*Carnegiea gigantica*), *Opuntia* and *Agave*; in Africa most succulents are members of the Crassulaceae or Euphorbiaceae. Australia has few succulents.

The gradual increase in diversity and structural complexity of ecosystems noted so far as one travels from the poles towards the equator is interrupted here and both decrease because of the dry conditions. In very dry areas many plants are opportunists, surviving long dry periods as dormant seeds, germinating only after rain, and completing their life cycles in a few weeks before drought returns. The adaptations of longer-lived species are varied but many have evolved mechanisms of photosynthesis which make more efficient use of water. The Crassulaceae and some other plants possess what is called crassulacean acid metabolism, where carbon dioxide taken into the leaf through the stomata during the night is stored in organic molecules and used in

Fig. 2.9 Dry sclerophyllous vegetation dominated by *Stipa tenacissima*, southern Spain.

photosynthesis during the day. This avoids water loss through open stomata during the heat of the day. A further adaptation is the ability to concentrate salts in the roots and therefore attract more water from the surrounding soil into the roots by osmosis. Whilst both of these adaptations are water-efficient they are also energy-intensive, so growth is slow and many plants are very long-lived. In this situation, attack by herbivores would be difficult to withstand and recover from. This may be why some desert plants have evolved antiherbivore defences such as spines and thorns, whilst others like the creosote bush exude toxic resins when damaged.

Despite the harsh conditions, deserts harbour a wide range of animals, principally because there are areas of lesser severity scattered throughout the desert, such as oases providing food and water. Large herbivores are rare, but of course in Africa and Asia include the camel (*Camelus* sp.), which is able to use up 30% of its body water before needing to drink. Some antelope, including the oryx (*Oryx leucoryx*), and wild ass (*Equus onager*) are able to get most of the water they require from the plant material they eat. In America, white-tailed deer (*Odocoileus virginianus*) and peccary (*Tayassu* sp.) are most abundant. Carnivores are even rarer and these are often largely reliant on scavenging. In Africa these include vultures and the fennec fox (*Fennecus zerda*) of the Sahara. In America the desert coyote (*Canis latrans*) and the kit fox (*Vulpes velox*) are common. Many smaller vertebrates and invertebrates are burrowers. They escape the heat of the day by staying in their burrows, which

Fig. 2.10 (a) Desert region in the mid-western USA and (b) desert scrub in western Australia.

provide a humid refuge, and forage during the cool night. Small herbivores such as the kangaroo rat of America and the jerboa (*Jaculus* sp.) of Africa and Asia never drink but gain all their water from the food they eat and as a by-product of their metabolism. Reptiles become one of the commoner vertebrate groups, using the sun's heat to become active hunters of insects and small mammals, whilst all but a few amphibians are excluded by the dry conditions.

Savannas

This is a specialised environment of the tropical zone that experiences a short rainy season and long dry season. Typical characteristics include warm temperatures all year round, rarely dropping below 20 °C, and rainfall that may be plentiful but is highly seasonal with 50–200 cm per annum falling during 3–4 months of the year and an 8–9 month dry season.

Savanna is found in eastern Brazil, eastern India, part of Australia and West Africa, but is most highly developed in East Africa where it forms one of the most spectacular communities on earth (Fig. 2.11). The dominant plants are tall perennial grasses, usually up to 80 cm in height but sometimes, in the case of elephant grass, up to 5 m. The leaves of these grasses dry out and die during drought but the plant regenerates rapidly from the base after rain. The dry season is too harsh for extensive tree growth, but small trees such as acacias grow where their deep roots reach groundwater. Some trees shed their leaves during the dry season to reduce water loss. Most plants are resistant to fires, which are common during the dry season. They must also be grazing-tolerant because of high numbers of herbivores present. Acacias are thorny and resistant to vertebrate grazing but grasses seem to tolerate high levels of grazing damage.

In the East African savanna, grass is highly productive during the wet season and supports a high density of large herbivores including antelope, zebra, warthogs, impala, buffalo, hippos and elephant. Most of these have their attendant carnivores. The lion (*Panthera leo*) is a savanna specialist as are the cheetah (*Acinonyx jubatus*), spotted hyaena (*Crocuta crocuta*) and the African wild dog (*Lycaon pictus*). The leopard (*Panthera pardus*) is also common in more wooded areas. There are many smaller mammals including several burrowers. Droughts are common as rain belts move north and south on the savanna, so many herbivores are migratory, following the rains, the most famous being the wildebeest (*Connochaetes* sp.). The threat of predation has led to the evolution of either swift and agile runners in the form of the antelopes or large body size and group defence such as elephant and buffalo.

Invertebrates are also common here and the most important are probably the termites (Isoptera) and ants. The termites attack plant material including wood and are a major factor in limiting tree growth.

Tropical seasonal forest/dry forest

In tropical areas where the rainy season is longer than that in the Savanna, but where there is still a significant dry season of up to six

Fig. 2.11 (a) Savanna region in northern Australia. (b) Giraffe feeding on acacia in a typical savanna region in southern Africa.

Fig. 2.12 Seasonal dry monsoon forest in southern India. This picture was taken during the middle of the dry season in February.

months' duration, the dominant community is seasonal or monsoon forest (Fig. 2.12). These forests are found primarily in India, Burma through to Indo-China, in northern Australia and on the margins of major rainforests in South and Central America and Central Africa. Rainfall is monsoonal, with high rainfall during wet season, usually over 150 cm a year and frequently more than 250 cm.

In most areas where it occurs, tropical seasonal forest is dominated by deciduous trees, as in the cool temperate forest, but these trees shed leaves in the dry season rather than in the winter. This strategy minimises water loss through transpiration from the leaves and enables a tree to survive the drought. However, some trees flower during the dry season, thus gaining the attention of the few pollinators that are active. Because of the open canopy during the dry season there is a distinct undergrowth that flowers after the first rains, taking advantage of light before trees leaf out. There are some evergreens in moister areas and these become progressively more common in regions where the wet season is longer. In Australia the eucalypt-dominated forest is predominantly evergreen. The diversity of trees in this ecosystem is generally higher than in temperate zones.

The animals as a community are intermediate between savanna and rainforest communities. There are still some large herbivores feeding predominantly on grass understorey, such as deer and elephant, and these still have their carnivores, most notably the tiger, but other cats and wild dogs are also present. Here, too, more arboreal (tree dwelling) species start to become abundant, including the primates. As in the savanna, insect abundance is very seasonal with many species becoming active after rains and feeding on the newly green grass and leaves and becoming dormant again during the dry season. Ants and termites are also dominant here and in terms of biomass per unit area are more dominant than the large herbivores. Reptiles are common in this tropical climate, as they are in savanna.

Tropical rainforest

This ecosystem occurs in areas where the climate is warm and stable with moderately high temperatures (21–30 °C) all year round, with more diurnal than annual fluctuation in mean monthly temperatures. Even more important is the distribution of rainfall: usually over 200 cm falls during a year with at least 10 cm in every month. Humidity within the forest is consistently high and therefore organisms have no problems with either low temperature or drought. Rainforest occurs in South and Central America, particularly in the Amazon basin; in West and Central Africa, centred around the Congo basin; and in the Far East Indo-Malay region, New Guinea and small areas of north-eastern Australia.

Characterised by the dominance of broadleaved evergreen trees with high species diversity (Fig. 2.13), the complex canopy structure traps most of the light so the forest floor is very dark and little grows. Competition for nutrients and light is fierce. Young trees can only grow in light gaps caused by falling mature trees (Fig 1.6). Consequently some species have found alternative ways to reach light or alternative energy sources. Epiphytes are able to grow in the canopy using forks in trees to establish roots, thus bypassing the problem of growing from far below on the ground. Saprophytes do not need to compete for light as they do not photosynthesize, but obtain energy from decomposing litter on the forest floor. Climbers such as vines and lianas use trees as a support to climb and reach light without having to grow trunks of large biomass. Parasitic plants have roots that penetrate the tissues of other plants and use them as a source of energy. All of these groups are far more abundant in the rainforest than in other environments.

The rainforest soil is often very poor and has a thin humus layer. All nutrients falling as litter are recycled very quickly by fungi and invertebrates on the forest floor and back into the trees. Most of the nutrient pool is therefore stored in the living trees rather than in the soil.

Since there is little vegetation on the ground, large herbivores are relatively rare and many people are surprised when they visit rainforest to find how deserted it seems for an environment famous for its abundance of life. In fact, all the action is up in the trees. On the ground in American rainforest there are a few species of deer, tapirs, peccaries and smaller mammals such as coatis and agoutis, which feed on fruits and nuts falling from the trees. There are also fewer large carnivores than in the savanna, mainly cats, some of which can hunt in trees, such as ocelot (*Felis pardalis*). The largest of all, the jaguar (*Felis onca*), is mainly ground dwelling. Most animals are arboreal, including some specialists such as the anteaters, and sloths in America and possums in Australasia.

(a)

Fig. 2.13 (a) Edge and (b) interior of rainforest at Barro Colorado Island, Panama.

A high diversity of primates lives in the canopy, feeding on fruits, leaves and some insects. Birds are also largely canopy feeders, as are fruit bats. The apes may be arboreal such as the orang-utan and gibbon of Indo-Malaysia, or semi-arboreal such as the chimpanzee (*Pan troglodytes*) and gorilla (*Gorilla gorilla*) of Africa. Reptiles and amphibians are numerous because of the warm humid conditions. Some frogs will complete their whole life cycle in the small pool of water collected inside an epiphytic plant in the canopy. Insects are highly abundant in the canopy as leaf eaters, pollinators and hunters. But pride of place among them must go to the ants for their abundance and the diverse roles they play.

Montane environments

A special group of terrestrial environments are primarily influenced, not by the latitude at which they occur, but the altitude. Changes with altitude to some extent mirror those with latitude, except that conditions change over much smaller distances (Fig. 2.14). Literally, one can walk from the equivalent of tropical rainforest to that of Arctic tundra in the space of one day. There are other important differences too, such as the diurnal temperature range at high altitude which can be as great as the annual range, so that temperature at high altitude can drop very quickly at night. The thin air also has an effect on respiration and photo-

(b)

synthesis as well as permitting high levels of potentially damaging ultraviolet radiation.

Montane areas are very varied and cannot be easily categorised, but much of their fauna is adapted to absorbing or conserving as much heat as possible. Insects often show greater concentrations of melanin, making them darker and more efficient heat sinks. Mammals often show increased coat length and density to help conserve heat during the cold nights. One special feature of montane communities is their isolation from others. They are effectively isolated in a sea of low altitude. Many populations have therefore evolved independently and are considered to be separate species or subspecies.

Fig. 2.14 The Nyiragongo volcano in Central Africa showing clear zonation of vegetation from tropical rainforest at the base from where the photo is taken through montane forest, a tree heath zone (dark green), and an Afro-alpine zone dominated by giant *Senecio* and *Lobelia* species.

Aquatic environments

Water has to be considered and characterised in a different way from land: as well as temperature, nutrient status and oxygen content are key factors dictating the biota. Over 70% of the Earth's surface is covered by water, so this is essentially an aquatic planet, but the difficulty in studying aquatic systems as 'alien' environments has meant that our understanding of them and an appreciation of their biodiversity has lagged far behind terrestrial systems. New technology is changing this and deep ocean systems are currently very active areas for research. In contrast to terrestrial systems, aquatic environments are usually classified according to their chemistry (e.g. fresh and salt water) and their basic morphology (e.g. rivers, lakes & oceans).

River systems

Rivers and streams are characterised by their linear dynamics, in other words water flows from the source downstream to the sink (e.g. ocean, lake or marsh). Much of the ecology downstream therefore depends on what is happening upstream. The water carries nutrients and other chemicals downstream with its flow making rivers very dynamic systems to study and a particular conservation challenge (Fig. 2.15).

The rate of flow and its fluctuation also have important impacts on

Fig. 2.15 The River Orinoco forming the Venezuela–Colombia border. The extreme linear dynamics of such rivers means that inputs upstream have a profound influence on the ecology downstream.

the types of flora and fauna that are found. High rates of flow will make it difficult for aquatic flora to establish and accumulate and for free swimming invertebrates to persist. However, bottom-dwelling (benthic) invertebrates and algae can survive such conditions more easily.

Nutrient levels in the river have an important influence on the community that develops. Low-nutrient (oligotrophic) rivers may have a low biomass, but high species richness, whereas high nutrient (eutrophic) rivers may have a high biomass, but be dominated by a few competitive species which thrive under these conditions.

Seasonal variation in rainfall causes fluctuation in water levels and rates of flow. The river may flood on a seasonal basis and thus influence the surrounding land within its floodplain. There is therefore a specialised community at the interface between the aquatic and terrestrial along the banks of rivers, referred to as the riparian community. Plants of this community are not aquatic but show adaptations to survive periods of submergence.

Many of the fish species inhabiting rivers move up and downstream with seasonal changes and throughout their life cycle. Other species move between rivers and the sea. Salmon species spawn in freshwater but migrate to the sea to mature, later returning to complete their life cycle. Such a strategy is termed anadromous. Other species, such as some eels, do essentially the opposite and spawn in the sea, whilst living the majority of their lives in freshwater, and are termed catadromous.

Lakes and wetlands

Lakes, as stationary water bodies, are extremely varied and a long list of factors dictates their flora and fauna. Among the most important is their size. Some lakes are extremely large water bodies approaching the size of smaller seas; at the other extreme are water bodies which we would commonly call small ponds which may be no larger than a few metres in diameter. Another important variable, as with rivers, is nutrient status: oligotrophic (nutrient-poor) lakes contain communities very different from eutrophic (nutrient-rich) ones. Although not as dynamic as rivers, lakes can have inflow and outflow producing turnover of the water body and can fluctuate in volume according to seasonal conditions.

Temperate lakes undergo seasonal cycles as the relative temperatures of surface and deep water change. In warm weather, the lake water tends to have a stable vertical structure. Since water is most dense at 4 °C, water warmed by the air above stays at the surface, whilst water at the bottom remains cold and close to 4 °C. Thus two zones are formed, the warm epilimnion and the cold hypolimnion separated by a zone of rapid temperature change termed the thermocline (Fig. 2.16). However, in colder weather when the air temperature is close to or below 4 °C, the surface water cools, the lake becomes unstable and mixing occurs. Winds blowing across the surface can increase the mixing of surface and deep water. This cycle has major implications for the nutrient and oxygen content of the water and therefore the distribution of biomass in the lake. The mixing usually occurs twice a year, in spring and autumn, and distributes nutrients from the bottom sediments throughout the water body. The primary source of oxygen is usually through diffusion from the surface and therefore the hypolimnion may become depleted of oxygen during the summer and all aerobic organisms may be confined to the epilimnion. Temperate eutrophic lakes can become largely deoxygenated during the summer because of high build-up of oxygen-demanding cyanobacteria (blue-green algae) in the

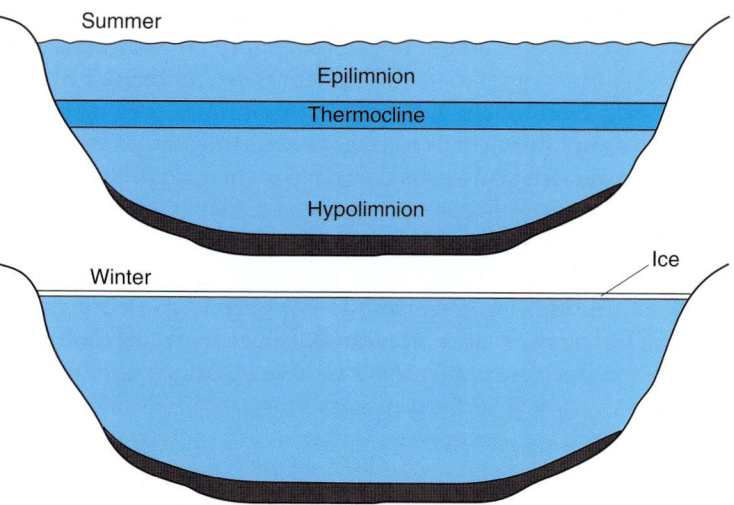

Fig. 2.16 Stratification of lakes in temperate zones during the summer, and mixing during the winter, has a fundamental influence on their ecology.

epilimnion. Conversely, in the winter, if such lakes freeze over, they can again deoxygenate because oxygen is no longer available through diffusion from the air–water interface. Smaller lakes and ponds are particularly vulnerable to deoxygenation.

Tropical lakes are more stable on account of the consistently warm surface temperature, but smaller lakes can fluctuate greatly in volume according to seasonal rainfall patterns and some may dry up completely. The more extreme this fluctuation is, the more ephemeral (transitory and opportunistic) or drought-tolerant the flora and fauna have to be.

Wetlands, like riparian ecosystems, are at the interface between terrestrial and aquatic. They are characterised by shallow water with emergent vegetation, which is terrestrial in origin but tolerant of waterlogged soils. Much of the fauna is semi-aquatic, spending portions of their life cycle above and below water. Largely as a result of this interface and therefore the variety of niches provided, wetlands are among our most biodiverse ecosystems. Wetlands are usually low lying and often coastal and their nature is dependent on the source of water. Some are fed purely from freshwater sources whilst others are fed by saltwater or a mixture of both. The salinity of the water largely dictates the type of plant communities as well as much of the aquatic fauna. Fenlands and acid mires develop where freshwater predominates whilst saltmarshes and mangrove swamps are found in saltwater areas. As in lakes, nutrient inputs have a profound influence on the type of community that develops.

Oceans

As mentioned above, marine ecosystems have not been classified in the same way as terrestrial. They are less influenced by climate and more by ocean currents and topography. These factors influence the flow of nutrients, the temperature and pressure of any given volume of water and the amount of sunlight received. Therefore, rather than a journey from the poles to the tropics it is more appropriate to travel from the deep ocean through shallower waters to coastal areas.

The deep oceans make up the largest ecosystem on the Earth by some margin – roughly as large as all the rest (aquatic and terrestrial) put together – yet it is one of the least studied and understood. The deep oceans are areas of low nutrient levels and therefore low productivity, comparable to a terrestrial desert, but this does not mean they have few species; on the contrary, as the ocean depths are increasingly studied using new diving technology, we are beginning to appreciate the high diversity of aquatic fauna that lives on or near the ocean floor, where nutrients accumulate. These creatures are highly adapted to the low light and high pressure of these environments and complex food webs may exist, awaiting to be discovered. The basis of the food chain in most cases seems to be particles of food falling from the upper waters but, in exceptional cases, energy is generated chemically by certain bacteria, enabling entire ecosystems to exist independent of sunlight. Near to the surface where sunlight penetrates, phytoplankton form the base of the food chain. They are mostly microscopic algae that photosynthesise in the same way as terrestrial plants and are consumed by zooplankton (small invertebrate animals). The zooplankton in turn are food for fish which are prey for still larger fish (e.g. tuna), marine mammals (e.g. dolphins) and seabirds (e.g. albatross) that patrol the open ocean.

Greater productivity is found in the shallower waters around the continents, termed **continental shelves**, where nutrients are supplied from the outflows of rivers. The biomass of fish is high in these waters as is that of marine mammals, and most of the world's fisheries are concentrated here. Species such as cod, herring, flounder and hake are to be found here, along with their invertebrate counterparts, shrimps, crabs and lobsters. In turn, a higher biomass of marine mammals and seabirds persists in these waters.

A special feature of some coastal areas is upwelling, where deep ocean waters are drawn upward as offshore winds push surface waters away. Rich in nutrients that have been accumulated from ocean sediments, these **marine upwellings** carry a high biomass of marine invertebrates such as krill (*Euphausia* sp.) a small planktonic shrimp that is a primary food source for many fish and marine mammals. These areas, chiefly found off the west coast of continental land masses, are particular 'hot-spots' for marine productivity and biodiversity.

In tropical areas, coastal waters which are shallow enough to allow light penetration to the bottom are colonised by corals, colonial animals containing symbiotic algae (zooxanthellae) which accumulate to form **coral reefs**, refuges for some of the most diverse communities on Earth. The corals act as both a food source for some and protection for many others. Beside the corals there is a high diversity of crustaceans, molluscs and other invertebrates, and particularly of fish. Many species of fish use reefs as spawning areas as they provide numerous hiding places for their fry to avoid the attention of predators.

Estuarine areas, transitional between freshwater and sea, are surprisingly high in diversity considering the dynamic nature of their environment, with constantly changing water and salinity levels. Their biomass of benthic invertebrates can be very high and when these mud and sandbanks are exposed at low tide they make very productive feeding grounds for wading birds. In tropical regions mangrove swamps develop around these areas and provide important spawning grounds for many species of fish. Shorelines where the tidal range is sufficient can also hold a specialised **littoral zone** (the zone between mean high and low tides) community. This zone can be very rich in seaweeds and harbour a very high diversity of invertebrates.

Summary

1. Terrestrial ecosystems can be categorised and described according to the prevailing plant species and physical structure.

2. In terrestrial ecosystems, increasing biodiversity is associated with increasing structure of vegetation.

3. Aquatic environments are more easily classified by their water chemistry and the dynamics of the water body.

4. In both cases abiotic factors have a primary role in shaping the community, producing predictable changes from the poles to the tropics and from low to high altitude.

Discussion points

- What are the similarities and differences between environments at high latitudes and altitudes?
- What factors dictate the presence or absence of trees in terrestrial environments?
- Why are rivers such a conservation problem?
- What impact is increased nutrient loading likely to have on lake ecosystems?
- What parallels can be drawn between highly biodiverse terrestrial and aquatic environments?

Further reading

Brown, J.H. & Lomolino, M.V. (1998). *Biogeography*. 2nd edn. Sunderland, Mass: Sinauer Associates.

Cole, M.M. (1986). *The savannas: biogeography and geobotany*. London: Academic Press.

Dobson, M. & Frid, C. (1998). *Ecology of aquatic systems*. Harlow: Longman.

Mann, K.H. (1996). *Dynamics of marine ecosystems: biological–physical interactions in the ocean*. 2nd edn. Oxford: Blackwell Science.

Whitmore, T.C. (1998). *An introduction to tropical rain forests*. Oxford: Oxford University Press.

Woodin, S.J. & Marquiss, M. (eds) (1997). *Ecology of Arctic environments*. Oxford: Blackwell Science.

Web sites
World Conservation Monitoring Centre: www.wcmc.org.uk/
UC Berkeley World Vegetation Maps:
www.lib.berkeley.edu/EART/vegmaps.html
Biomes of the world: www.snowcrest.net/geography/slides/biomes/

Part 2

Chapter 3

The human impact

The natural world is fast disappearing under the influence of human activity. In this chapter we cover the rise in human populations; cultural, agricultural and industrial development; the consequences of these advances on natural systems; and we identify the major threats to biodiversity. These major threats are then described in more detail in Chapters 4 to 6.

By reading this chapter students will gain an understanding of the impact of the growth of the human population on the natural world; the impact of agricultural and industrial activity; and a knowledge of the quantitative impact of humans on species and their habitats.

The rise of human populations

Conservation is often thought of as a twentieth century phenomenon. Something we have only needed within the recent past. But some lessons could have been learnt early in the rise of the human race, as in the example of Easter Island. A small isolated land mass of volcanic origin lying in the Pacific Ocean off the coast of Chile, Easter Island is best known for its stone statues that remain as a record of a culture which has long since passed. The presence of the statues has led to detailed study to try and learn more of the community that built them. Recent pollen analysis by Flenley *et al.* (1991) suggests that the island was once covered by forests of palm trees, but human colonisation led to deforestation between 1200 and 800 years ago. The disappearance of trees and the resources they provided for food and building materials, together with the disappearance of the animals of the forest, probably led to the collapse of the island system on which the human settlement depended and in turn caused the extinction of their own culture. All we see today is a treeless landscape whose relief is broken only by the eerie presence of the statues as a reminder that the island was once far richer. Unfortunately the story of colonisation and overexploitation, followed by the collapse of the ecosystem and the human population, was not generally known until late last century.

Homo sapiens seems to have evolved from its primate ancestors

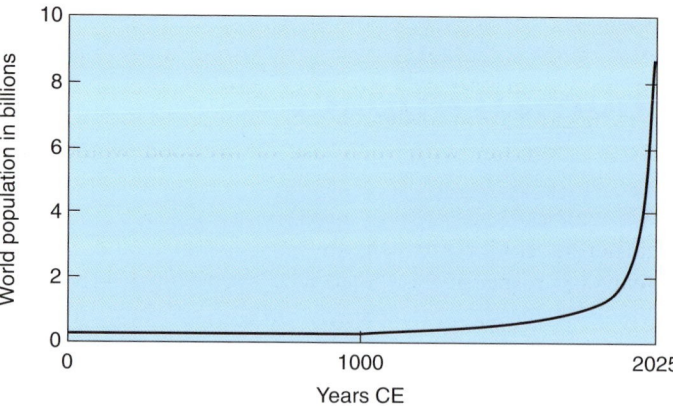

Fig. 3.1 Change in the size of the global human population over time. Note the exponential rise following the industrial revolution.

around 3 million years ago, first appearing in the rift valleys of East Africa. Populations survived as hunter-gatherers, gradually expanding in range through the Middle East, Europe and Asia, down to Australasia and across the Bering Strait into America, but remaining dependent on the natural resources available until the first agricultural revolution some 10–12000 years BP. The number of individuals on the planet at this time was probably no more than 5 million (Ehrlich *et al.* 1977). The agricultural revolution enabled the population to grow and colonise new areas so that by the beginning of the Bronze Age, some 5000 years BP, it reached 100 million. Even quite recently, around AD 1650 the world population was only 500 million. Today it has soared to 6000 million or 6 billion people (Fig. 3.1). The exponential rise occurring in the last 100 years has largely been brought about by the reduction in the death rate (particularly of children) through advances in public health (sanitation and nutrition), supported by developments in agriculture resulting from the industrial revolution. It is not the purpose of this Chapter to analyse these events in detail, but we are concerned with the impact this explosion of human presence has had on the global environment.

Early relationships with the environment

The first humans were hunter-gatherers. They used primitive tools to hunt for game and dig for root vegetables, both of which could be found living wild within their immediate environment. They were also probably opportunistic in gathering and consuming fruits whenever they became available. Tribes are likely to have had a home range, much as many primates do today, and would move through it, perhaps on a seasonal basis, exploiting sources of food as they became available. Their impact on the environment would have been little different from any other large animal of the time. Their populations would probably have fluctuated in response to availability of food and incidence of disease within their local environment. In short, the ecosystem had more impact on them than they had on the ecosystem.

The first major impact humans had on the environment was probably through use of fire. Evidence of this comes from archaeological sites in East Africa which date from some 60 000 years BP. Natural fires caused by lightning strikes would have occurred continuously in drier areas, but humans would have increased the frequency of fires, perhaps, at first, for driving game from cover and improving grassland to attract game. The latter, together with their use of firewood would have increased grassland at the expense of forest. This is a subject we will return to in Chapter 4.

Hunter-gatherers reached Australia and North America about 50 000 and 12 000 years ago respectively. Armed with fire and primitive tools they were able to have a significant impact on the environments they colonised. The fossil record shows a sudden extinction of many large mammals in both Australia and America, which appears to coincide with human colonisation, but the evidence for cause and effect is equivocal. There is some debate as to whether the extinctions were caused by human activity or by a period of rapid climate change to which many species were unable to adapt. During the late Pleistocene, humans arrived in Australia and more than 85% of large (body mass exceeding 44 kg) marsupials and birds went extinct. Was this just coincidence? Miller et al. (1999) examined evidence for the cause of extinction of the mihirung (*Genyornis newtoni*) a large flightless bird related to the emu (*Dromicieus* sp.). The time of extinction corresponds to a period of only moderate climate change and they conclude that human impact on this bird's habitat is the most likely cause. However, Choquenot & Bowman (1998) argue that there is no convincing evidence that human predation was the direct cause of the extinction of such a large amount of the Australian megafauna unless the aboriginal population was considerably denser than today. A more likely scenario is that the impact of the use of fire by early aboriginal populations changed the landscape so radically that many species were unable to survive. Aboriginal landscape burning played a central role in the formation of typical Australian grassland plant communities before the arrival of Europeans (Bowman 1998). This has created habitats suitable for some species that are adapted to grazing, but hostile to many browsing animals reliant on scrubby vegetation: browsing is a characteristic of many of the extinct species.

There has also been an ongoing debate on whether it was the spread of human activity or the climate changes (associated with the most recent ice ages; see Box 1.3) that caused the apparent extinction of many large mammals in America during the Pleistocene. Martin (1973) proposed that humans had colonised the American continent like a wave, with high population densities at the front of the wave as they exploited the naive prey that they found and decreasing densities behind as the prey was exhausted (Fig. 3.2). This has since been disputed many times by supporters of the climate-driven extinction model, who cite evidence that extinctions did not follow this wave pattern chronologically as you would expect from Martin's model, but followed deterioration in climate. Some resolution to this debate has been sought by suggesting it was the coincidence of climate changes and human colonisation that may have caused the synchronous extinction of a large proportion of

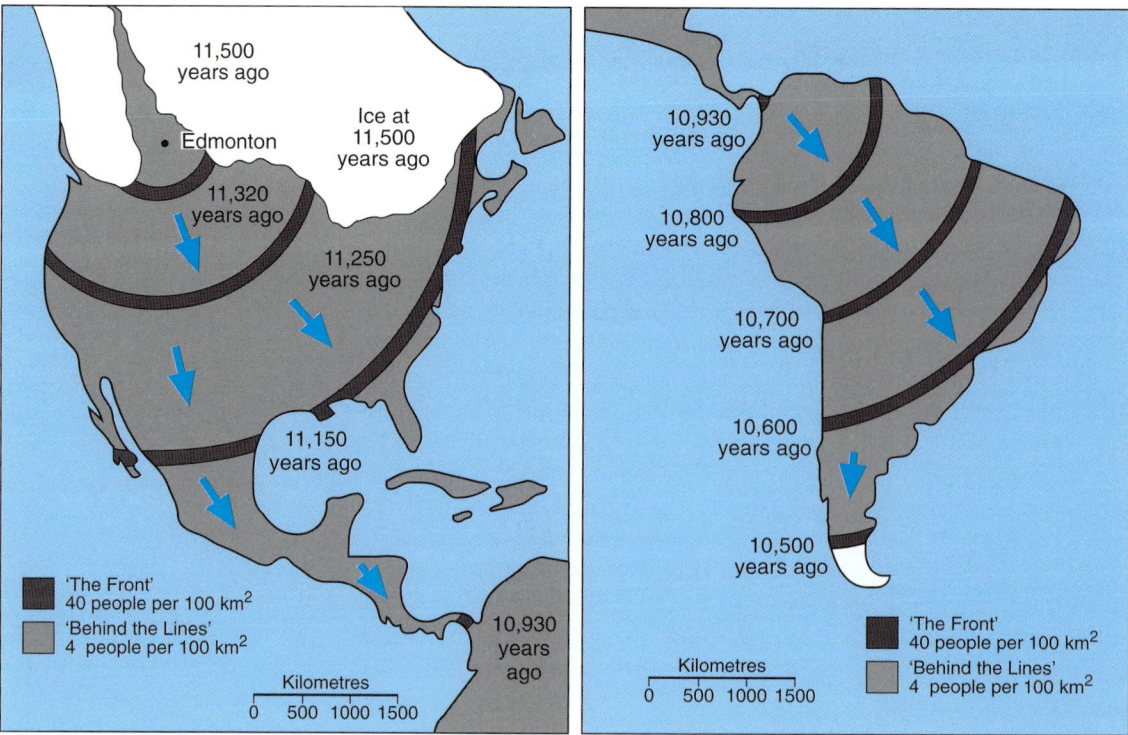

Fig. 3.2 Geographical spread of humans down through North and South America following the initial crossing of the Bering Strait from Asia. Reprinted with permission from Martin, P.S. (1973). The discovery of America. *Science*, **179**, 969–974. Copyright 1973 American Association for the Advancement of Science.

the American megafauna. Large mammal extinctions in Europe (which was colonised much earlier) were asynchronous (some mammals are known to have gone extinct, but not all at the same time) supporting the coincidence model (Stuart 1991).

Early Old World agriculture

The beginnings of agriculture are difficult to pinpoint, because of the lack of clear definition of what constitutes an agricultural system. Some kind of management of livestock or cultivation of crops is required, but the extent of its development before it is considered agriculture is debatable. Nevertheless, good evidence for the domestication of livestock has been found as early as 11 000 BP in the Middle East (Zohary & Hoff 1993). The first domesticated animals were probably the goat (*Capra haraus*) and the sheep (*Ovis aries*). The intensification of grazing that almost certainly resulted from this would have had a profound impact on the local vegetation.

The influence of this early agricultural revolution seems to have spread rapidly around the Mediterranean coast of North Africa and Europe. The dominant forest cover was both burnt and exploited for construction materials, tools and firewood, and the resulting cleared land was grazed by domestic animals such as goats, sheep and cattle and also cultivated for the first crops of wheat (*Triticum* sp.) and later barley (*Hordeum* sp.). This would have systematically eliminated many native plant species that were intolerant of grazing or disturbance of the soil

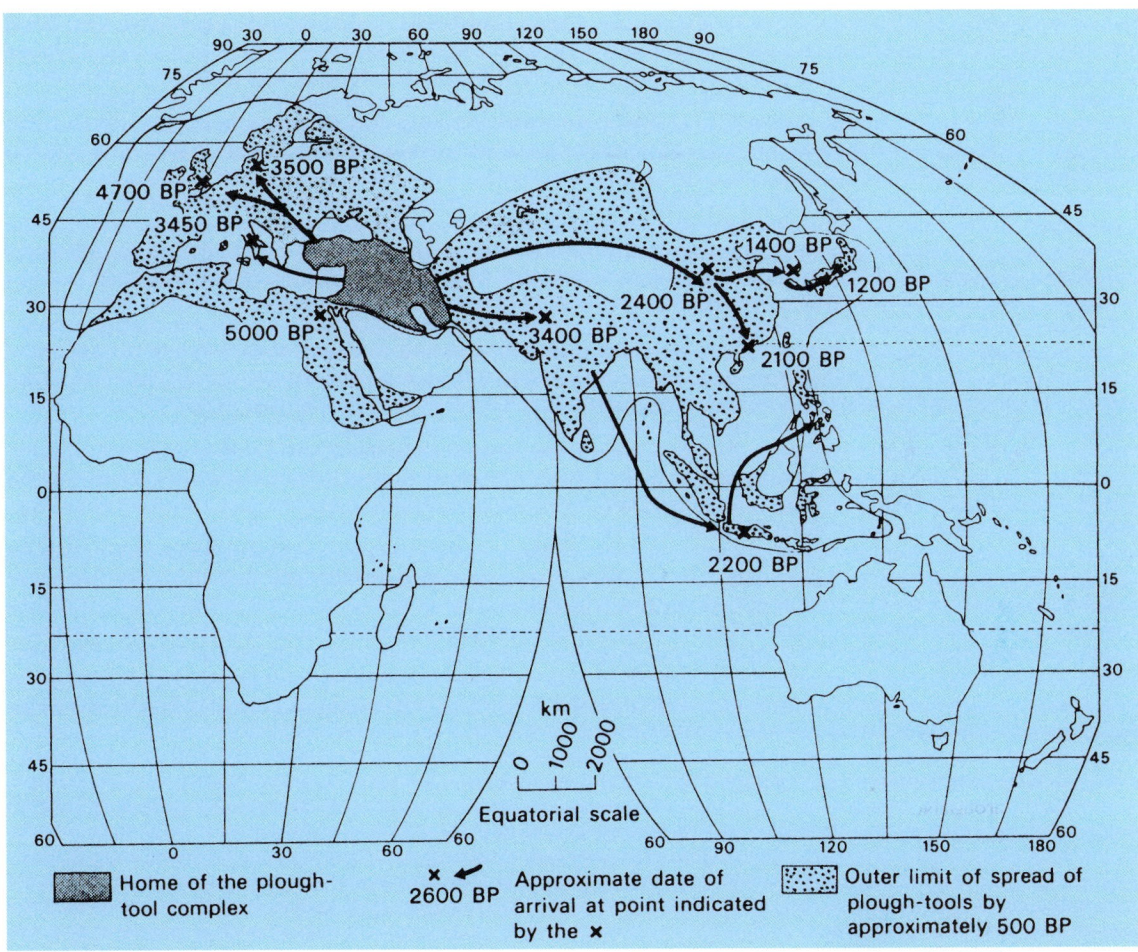

Fig. 3.3 The spread of the plough and associated agriculture through the Old World. Reproduced from Spencer & Thomas (1978) with kind permission from John Wiley & Sons.

surface. Technological development in agriculture, such as the use of the plough and the wheel, also spread rapidly through the Old World, further increasing the area under cultivation (Fig. 3.3).

There is evidence that agricultural practices quickly caused environmental problems. Human population density probably rose rapidly in areas where agriculture developed. The intensive use of land seems to have played a part in widespread climate change and desertification of the North African and Mediterranean region through deforestation and soil erosion. This in turn probably resulted in widespread famine and the disappearance of many early civilisations. Homer recorded cases of soil erosion in Greece around 2800 BP, when it was probably already a serious problem. Intensive grazing, particularly by goats, and increasing use of fire, prevented regeneration of forest and led to the development of a flora dominated by grazing-resistant and fire-tolerant scrub species, thus reducing its value as pasture land. Human communities probably practised shifting cultivation at this time, moving around the Mediterranean basin as they overexploited patch after patch of fertile land. Available land would have quickly been exhausted; few areas would have been left unused and no areas unaffected, at least indirectly. This region had already become a collection of **semi-natural communities** (communities in which the distribution and abundance of the native species have been fundamentally altered by human activity, but which still contain many characteristics of the natural communities).

The Tell region of North Africa was described by Roman authors as being abundantly wooded, today it is largely semi-desert, highly eroded by flash flooding. Plato wrote some 2400 years BP of the Grecian landscape: 'What now remains of the formerly rich land is like the skeleton of a sick man, with all the fat and soft earth having wasted away and only the bare framework remaining' (cited in Hillel 1991).

The large-scale exploitation of land in the Mediterranean region is intimately linked with the rise and fall of civilisations, such as the Egyptian, Greek and Roman. Yet early lessons were unfortunately not passed on and the story has been repeated many times elsewhere in Europe, North Africa, and also in America and Australia as European-style agriculture spread.

Agriculture spread north in Europe and was accompanied by large-scale clearance of forest, firstly with stone and later, with metal axes. Box 3.1 gives a detailed account of the changes in the UK landscape since

Box 3.1 | Climate and human impacts on the UK landscape

The northern European ice sheets of the last glacial period began receding around 14 000 years ago. As a result of climate warming, species rapidly reinvaded regions that had previously been covered in ice. Additionally ecosystems such as tundra that were present south of the ice underwent adjustment and moved northwards as the climate warmed. Mainland Britain was not completely free of permanent ice until 10 000 BP, but the subsequent period has been a time of rapid change in flora and fauna, as well as changes in soils.

Information on the nature of community change comes mainly from fossil and pollen records. The technique of pollen analysis depends on the fact that under certain natural conditions the walls of pollen grains do not decompose and may be preserved for thousands of years. Moreover, the pollen grains of many species can be recognised by their shape and pattern of pores, ridges and other surface markings. When airborne pollen settles on a lake or pond it may sink to the bottom or when it settles in an area where peat is forming it accumulates in the layers and forms a chronological sequence, provided waterlogged conditions remain. The frequency of pollen grains can then be analysed by taking core samples through the peat or sediment layers and major changes in vegetation over time can be detected and expressed in the form of a pollen diagram (Fig 3.4).

As the ice receded the bare ground was invaded by small arctic-alpine plants and relicts of these communities still remain in the coldest parts of upland Britain such as Teesdale and Ben Lawers. In wetter regions, tundra vegetation, dominated by mosses and lichens, developed. The cold winters still prevented large-scale tree invasion, but

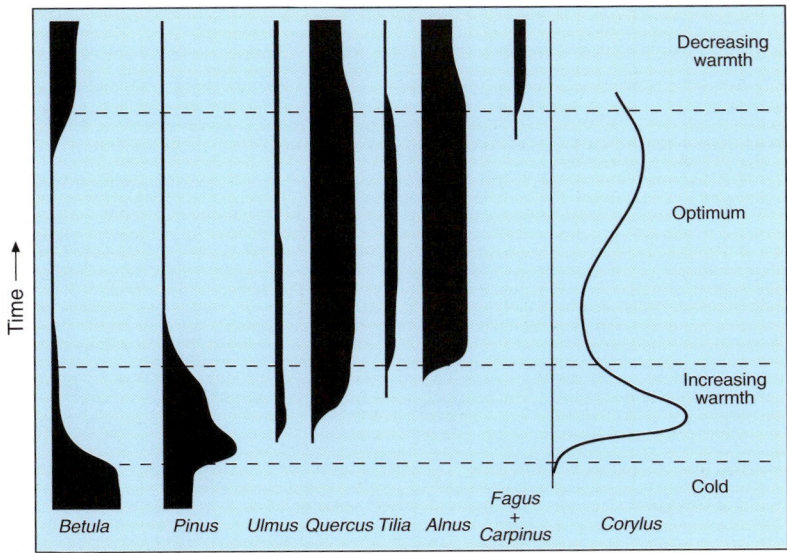

Fig. 3.4 A generalised pollen diagram recording changes in vegetation cover in East Anglia, UK since the last ice age (c. 10000 years). Note the early presence of birch (*Betula*) and pine (*Pinus*) at the bottom of the diagram followed by elm (*Ulmus*), oak (*Quercus*) and hazel (*Corylus*) and later arrival of lime (*Tilia*), alder (*Alnus*) and finally beech (*Fagus*) and hornbeam (*Carpinus*). Reproduced from Godwin (1981) with kind permission of Cambridge University Press.

the summers were warm and in southern Britain large areas of herb-rich grassland developed. The later invasion of tree species into what was basically open grassland vegetation is well documented in the pollen record. The formation of a rudimentary soil structure allowed the first invasion by birch, (*Betula pubescens* and *B. pendula*) and Scots pine (*Pinus sylvestris*) around 11000 BP. After several fluctuations in climate causing temporary retreat, these species were well established around 9500 BP, together with a ground flora dominated by heather (*Calluna vulgaris*) and *Vaccinium* spp.

At around 10000 BP the climate began to warm further and the UK had an essentially continental climate with more difference between warm dry summers and cold winters than at present. This is often referred to as the Boreal period. Once a sufficiently rich soil was established, species such as Hazel (*Corylus avellana*) appeared and by 8000 BP oak (*Quercus* spp.) and elm (*Ulmus* spp.) had invaded and subsequently replaced birch and pine in southern England; Alder (*Alnus glutinosa*), colonised wetter areas. The spread of this type of vegetation may have owed as much to the development of humus soils as the warming climate. Along with the woodland came the herbivores; aurochs (wild ox *Bos primigenius*), red deer (*Cervus elaphus*), and roe deer (*Capreolus capreolus*) probably invaded with the first trees. The woodmouse (*Apodemus sylvaticus*), bank vole (*Clethrionomys glareolus*), hedgehog (*Erinaceus europaeus*), badger (*Meles meles*), wild boar (*Sus scrofa*), beaver (*Castor fiber*), brown bear (*Ursus arctos*), wolf (*Canis lupus*), lynx (*Felis lynx*) and pine marten (*Martes martes*) also appeared during this time. The last major tree to appear was probably the small-leaved lime, (*Tilia cordata*), around 7500 BP, reaching its northerly limit around 5000 BP. Crucially, at about 8000 BP the land bridge between mainland Britain and the continent was cut by the formation of the English Channel. This meant that the rate of invasion slowed dramatically and many mainland species failed to reach these islands, even though the climate may have subsequently become suitable for them.

At the warmest time in recent history around 5000 years ago, the landscape of

Britain was dominated by cool-temperate forest (Fig. 3.5). Lowland Britain was dominated by deciduous woodland with oak, lime and field maple (*Acer campestris*), with understorey species such as hazel, yew and holly. On calcareous soils the dominant trees were ash (*Fraxinus excelsior*) and beech (*Fagus sylvatica*) whilst on more water-logged acid soils in the upland of northern England, Wales and Scotland, sessile oak (*Quercus petraea*) birch and pine were dominant. Only the highest peaks (over 800 m) and most exposed slopes would have been free of trees.

Fig. 3.5 The probable extent and composition of UK forests 5000 years before present. Reproduced from Ingrouille (1995) with kind permission of Kluwer Academic Publishers.

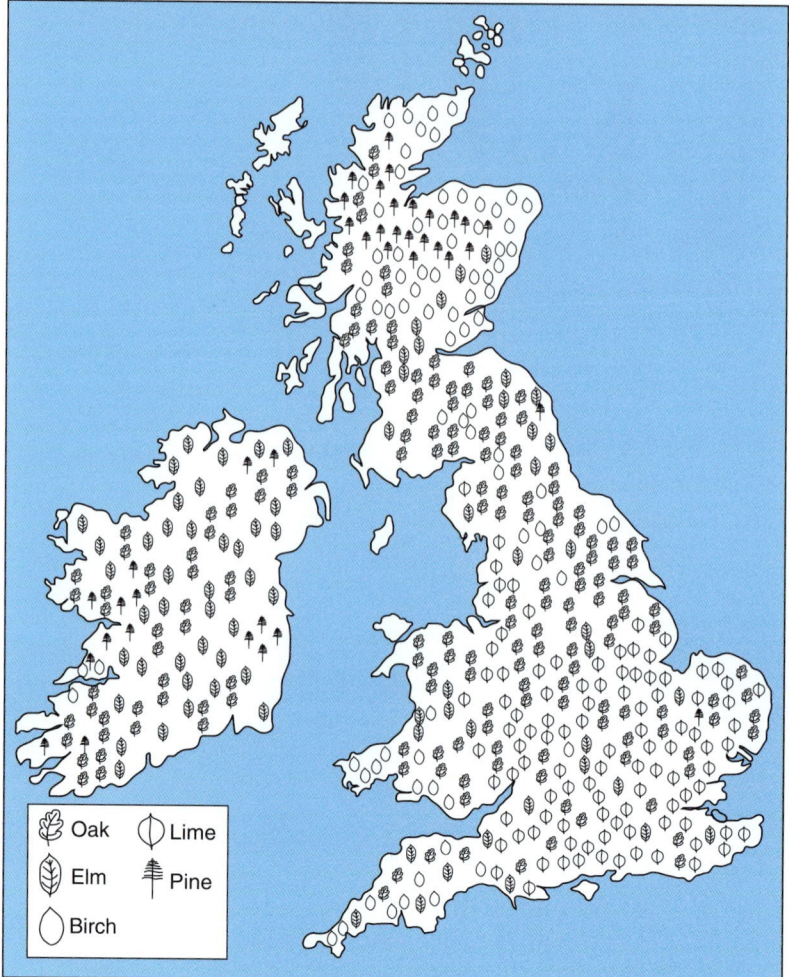

The presence of large herbivores and the occurrence of some natural fires would, by the creation of clearings and tracks, have ensured that the forest was not uniformly dense, thus creating microclimates for other species (Fig. 2.7c). Additionally, the deciduous nature of the trees would have allowed the development of a vernal (spring flowering) woodland flora.

There is good evidence that after 5000 BP the climate became more oceanic, with wetter cooler summers. This is the start of the so-called Atlantic period. This may have led to the extinction of some recent invaders in Britain. One of these was probably the European pond tortoise (*Emys orbicularis*). The northern limit of this species is set by temperature and cloudiness. A mean July temperature of 17–18 °C with abundant sunshine is necessary for reproductive success. Fossils are found in Britain dating from the period 10000–5000 BP but not afterwards, suggesting that the climate has cooled by 1–3 °C.

As we move closer to the present day the influence of humans becomes increasingly marked and during the period 6000–4000 BP it is not easy to distinguish natural and anthropogenic causes of change. The clearance of the forests began during this period and pollen records suggest that the abundance of elms declined by 50%. It is not known whether this represents climate change, selective cutting for fodder or an earlier disease event similar to the present Dutch elm disease epidemic (Ingrouille 1995). There is evidence for the first use of fire early in this period and the appearance of pollen from wild grasses, suggesting increase in cleared disturbed areas and perhaps pastoralism. Extensive moorland and heathland, dominated by heather and *Vaccinium* spp. were probably formed at this time, particularly in upland areas by clearance of waterlogged acid and dry sandy soils respectively. The wet oceanic climate would have also favoured the development of raised bogs and the accumulation of peat.

About 4000 BP, the Bronze Age reached Britain and trees could be felled using metal axes instead of stone. This resulted in a considerable acceleration of forest clearance. The great majority of the forests of southern Britain were cleared during the next 2000 years, particularly at the beginning of the Iron Age 2500 BP. The Romans invaded an island that may have already been largely deforested and heavily populated by humans and their domesticated animals. Extinctions of the large mammal fauna had already begun at this time and the elk and lynx had disappeared. The auroch died out around 2600 BP, the brown bear around 1100 BP and the beaver was last reported in AD 1188 in Wales. Perhaps surprisingly, the wolf survived until relatively recently. It was still present in Yorkshire during the reign of Henry VII and it did not disappear from Scotland until sometime between 1680 and 1743. The wild boar disappeared in 1676.

The Romans left during a period of climatic deterioration and agricultural abandonment and there may have been some recovery of woodland during the subsequent 'Dark Ages'. However, open field farming had re-established by the time of the appearance of the Domesday Book in 1086, a unique record of the agricultural landscape produced almost a millennium ago (Darby 1976). During the Middle Ages extensive tracts of woodland, such as the New Forest and Sherwood Forest were protected as royal hunting forests, but drainage of wetlands for agriculture became technically feasible and extensive destruction of lowland fenlands took place during sixteenth to nineteenth centuries.

The industrial revolution brought with it increasing demand for fuel wood and timber for construction, so that by the end of the First World War only 5% of Britain was under woodland of some kind. The formation of the Forestry Commission in 1919 saw the beginning of the practice of afforestation; the planting of trees in even-aged stands for timber production. The trees planted were exotic, quick growing conifers, such as pine, spruce, fir and larch, at first in place of clear-felled lowland deciduous forest, but later, many plantations were sited in upland areas of low agricultural productivity.

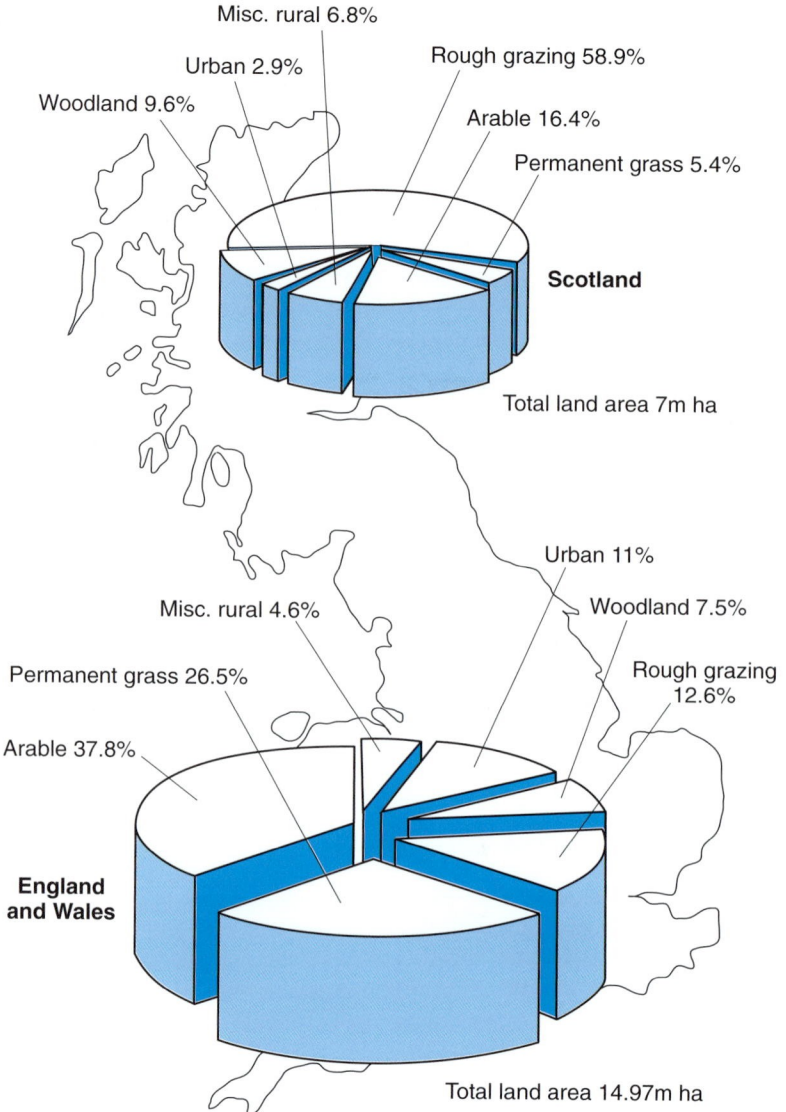

Fig. 3.6 Land use in the UK at the present time. Note the differences between the largely upland and sparsely populated Scotland and largely lowland and densely populated England and Wales. Reproduced with kind permission from the Joint Nature Conservation Committee, UK.

Misc. rural 6.8%

Urban 2.9%

Woodland 9.6%

Rough grazing 58.9%

Arable 16.4%

Permanent grass 5.4%

Scotland

Total land area 7m ha

Misc. rural 4.6%

Permanent grass 26.5%

Arable 37.8%

Urban 11%

Woodland 7.5%

Rough grazing 12.6%

England and Wales

Total land area 14.97m ha

After the Second World War the modern agricultural revolution took hold of the landscape, fuelled by advances in technology allowing use of increasingly sophisticated machinery along with chemical fertilisers and pesticides. Government policy (in the form of subsidies) encouraged farmers to intensify their use of the land, increase acreage of arable crops and increase productivity. This led to large-scale drainage of land to bring it into production and the large-scale destruction of hedgerows to increase field size. Consequently many areas of lowland England have been described as agricultural deserts of low diversity, dominated by the planted monocultures of industrial scale food production.

The picture we see today (Fig. 3.6) is a landscape mosaic of intensive land use, mostly for agriculture and urban development, with no natural habitat remaining and only small patches of semi-natural vegetation, in which much of our specialised native fauna and flora find their only refuge.

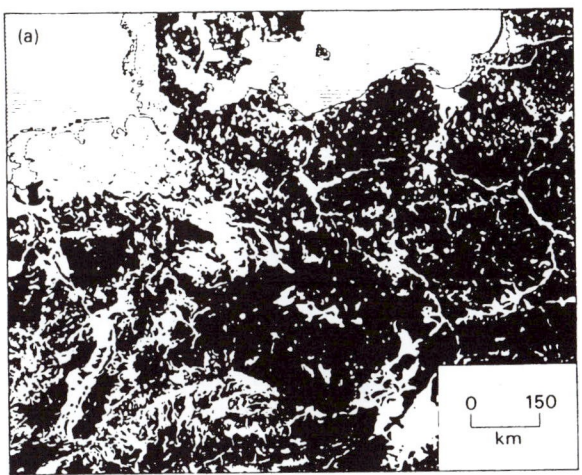

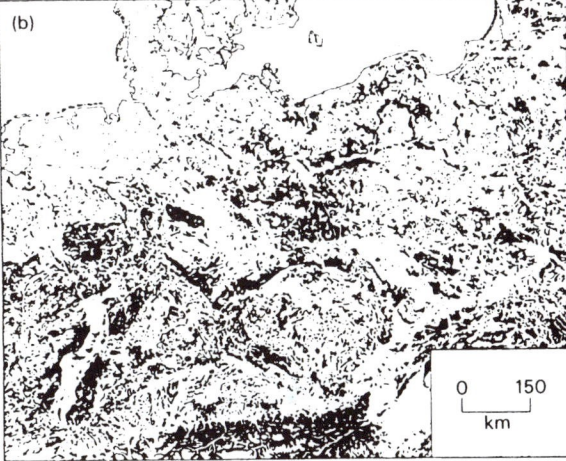

Fig. 3.7 The scale of central European deforestation in the thousand years between (a) c. 900 and (b) 1900. Reproduced from Thomas (1956) with kind permission of University of Chicago Press.

the end of the last ice age. The story is similar in many countries in north-west Europe, except that the clearance of forest was less rapid and less complete (Fig. 3.7)

As farming techniques and skills improved, individual plots of land were used on a more sustainable basis and a patchwork of land use, typical of modern European landscapes began to form. Agricultural communities were based around market towns that developed for sale and exchange of produce. This resulted in the type of European network of villages and towns that still exists in some areas today. This key transition by human populations, from existing by exploiting the natural products of their surroundings to exploiting the land itself to grow the products of their choice (and later consumer choice) was to have the most profound effect on the landscape.

Desertification

One issue concerning human impact on the environment that has been the subject of some debate is to what extent the recent spread of deserts has been due to human activity. Deserts changed in size many times before humans became an important environmental factor, and both local and global climate changes are constantly exerting their influence. The issue of greatest contention is whether human activity at the edges of deserts accelerates their spread. It is not disputed that increasing human population pressure in these areas leads to reduced tree cover and to overgrazing through increasing livestock densities. These factors both accelerate soil erosion and promote desert conditions, and evidence for this in the Mediterranean area has been presented above. What is disputed is whether changes in rainfall patterns are also a precondition for this process or whether they are a result of it. Examination of rainfall patterns at desert margins shows that they are characterised by variability, resulting in some drought years and some periods of heavy rain which cause severe soil erosion. The productivity of the natural vegetation seems to have been mistaken for a sign of agricultural potential by populations desperate for land and short-term gains have quickly been succeeded by long-term desertification as human activity combines with climatic extremes (in this case drought) to disrupt a fragile ecosystem. This was the harsh lesson learnt in the 1930s 'Dust Bowl' in the USA (Box 3.2) and appears to have been a periodic problem in the Sahel region of Africa. There is considerable dispute over the question of whether the Sahara desert is advancing relentlessly southward or whether fluctuations in rainfall patterns cause periodic drought situations in the Sahel leading to the human suffering that has been witnessed in recent decades. There is little doubt though that the human pressure on the area plays a fundamental role in the scale of the problem. Today, approximately 6 million hectares of land worldwide may be turning into desert each year.

Box 3.2 | America's Dust Bowl: a lesson learnt?

The increasing mechanisation of agriculture and improved transportation to distant markets during the early part of the last century, encouraged farmers to cultivate and overgraze every square metre of soil. Vast areas of the midwestern states of the USA were put under the plough during the 1920s and 1930s. Shortly afterward, a prolonged drought caused crop failure and the once-fertile topsoil dried up and turned to dust. Strong winds picked up the dust in storms carrying it far away and causing widespread erosion. In May 1934, a dust storm lasting four days transported 300 million tons of soil across the USA, darkening New York skies some 1500 miles away and depositing dust on the decks of ships 300 miles out in the Atlantic Ocean (Coffey 1978). Farmers had to abandon their land and seek a living elsewhere. When the extent of the damage had been recognised, expensive soil conservation measures were introduced in some areas, largely through the use of rows of trees as windbreaks.

However, it seems that this expensive lesson has not been fully learnt, even in the USA. Soil erosion through overexploitation is still a major problem in some states. Pimentel (1976) estimated that topsoil is lost from US agricultural land at a rate of around 30 tonnes per hectare annually, approximately eight times quicker than it is formed. It seems that to farmers, the incentive of short-term profits from high crop yields continues to outweigh the long-term consequences of soil erosion.

Post-industrial accelerated change

The start of the industrial revolution in Western Europe brought with it a whole new range of impacts and a new scale of human activity. Humans from then on would have a global rather than local impact on the environment. Unfortunately, society largely took the view that nature was for humans to control and the resources were there to be exploited. Chiras (1994) expresses this mind set as the 'frontier ethic' that many societies, religious groups and nations espoused. The frontier ethic has three tenets:

1. *There's always more and its all for us.* In which the earth is viewed as an unlimited supplier of resources for human use.
2. *Humans are apart from nature and immune to natural laws.* Originating from religious-based philosophy in which humans view themselves as so special that they are somehow unrelated to the rest of the living world.
3. *Human success derives from the control of nature.* Since humans are apart from nature they are in competition with it and must dominate and control it to be successful.

If confronted with these three tenets, I wager that most world leaders would distance themselves from them and claim that they are outdated, historical influences on human development. However, in reality the world economic strategy and the measurements of its success still embrace these ethics.

The result has been the rapid growth of industrial economies and (whilst resources remain) the rapid increase in the standard of living of people in the developed world. At the same time as the world population is increasing exponentially, resource use per capita has also increased, so we are all, as individuals, using an increasing amount of the earth's resources to the extent that there is now global competition for them (Table 3.1). In consequence, the standard of living in many less

Table 3.1 Energy consumption in developed countries (1995–1996) both as total and as an average per person

Country	Energy consumption: million tonnes of oil equivalent	% change 1986–1996	Energy use tonnes oil equivalent per capita
Australia	66.1	+31.1	3.6
Canada	181.9	+19.9	6.1
France	162.0	+19.1	2.8
Germany	249.0	−3.0	3.0
Japan	337.1	+34.6	2.7
Korea	119.8	+163.1	2.6
Mexico	101.6	+29.7	1.1
Sweden	36.1	+6.6	4.1
UK	162.4	+14.8	2.8
USA	1 443.5	+12.6	5.4

Source: OECD.

competitive developing countries has decreased and the integrity of the earth's ecosystems has been seriously challenged. The next section introduces the most serious impacts on our environment and biodiversity that are the subject of the following three chapters.

Current human impacts

Habitat destruction

The most direct threat to biodiversity comes from destruction of the habitat on which it depends. Levels of habitat destruction are probably at their greatest in Europe, where human population density is among the highest and industrial activity widespread and long established. In most European countries, as we saw in the UK landscape (Box 3.1), no natural habitats remain and therefore destruction can in this sense be considered complete. However, many semi-natural habitats that have been managed for their long-term sustainability have high biodiversity value. For example, many traditional agricultural practices developed in the Middle Ages, such as annual mowing of meadows for hay, coppicing of woodland for construction materials and cutting of wetland reed for thatching, have produced high-value wildlife habitats (see Chapter 9). These too are now under threat and have been disappearing rapidly, due to the industrialisation of farming methods and changes in the economy that have resulted in traditional practices becoming uneconomic. Changes since 1950 have been the most profound, caused by the mechanisation of farming practices and the increased productivity of crops through use of inorganic fertilisers. Intensification of agriculture in many regions has been driven by technology, enabling fertilisation of soils otherwise uneconomic to farm, ploughing of previously intractable soils and drainage of wetlands. All have contributed greatly to the disappearance of natural habitats, leaving many areas of intensively farmed arable land that have deservedly been described as 'agricultural deserts'. For example, the UK has lost 40% of lowland heathland and over 50% of lowland raised bogs and lowland wet grassland (Wynne *et al.* 1995).

In developing countries, the patterns and causes of habitat destruction can be very different. Instead of being linked to economic growth they can result from poverty and landlessness among the local human population. Clearing of tropical forest for subsistence agriculture has been practised for centuries by indigenous peoples, but the sustainability of the system is crucially dependent on the number of individuals reliant on it and so the frequency and extent of clearance. As populations have risen, forests have disappeared and fertility of the soil has declined rapidly. Populations have been forced to move ever further into the primary forest, until in many areas none remains. This link between human population, economics and habitat destruction is explored in Box 3.3.

Destruction can equally result from developing countries becoming heavily in debt and being forced to sell off their natural assets, particu-

Box 3.3 | Is there a link between human population growth and conservation problems?

Many conservationists would maintain that the problems they face are largely caused by the side effects of rapid human population growth, whilst some of their opponents deny any link between these factors. Which is right? Joel Cohen has written successive articles on this subject and concludes that whilst there is undoubtedly a link between rapid human population growth and environmental degradation (and hence conservation problems), the link depends crucially on economic and social factors prevailing in an area (Cohen 1995, 1997). The link may in fact be an indirect rather than direct one. In economically weak developing countries rapid population growth causes economic and political problems that require resources. These are provided at the expense of the environment, through forest clearance or mineral extraction, because there is no alternative source of income, and conservation problems arise. The economic liberation in developed countries has enabled greater freedom of choice and population growth has slowed and the same problem does not arise.

Ehrlich (1995) develops the argument that habitat destruction is linked to human enterprise (activity), which in turn is directly correlated with energy usage. Therefore if habitat destruction is a major cause of species extinction (see Chapter 4), both of these will increase as the human population grows, because the more of us there are the more energy we use. However, energy use is not simply linked to population growth, but also depends on resource use per capita. Unfortunately this makes the situation even worse because at the same time as the population is growing exponentially, each one of us is also using more energy. Ehrlich uses these links to suggest that future species extinction rates can be predicted by forecasts of future energy consumption.

larly tropical forest timber. Logging companies from rich developed nations have been able to do pretty much as they pleased in exploiting tropical forests because of the desperate need for cash in developing nations. Rates of logging have been limited in some areas only by the inaccessibility of the forests. The construction of roads for the removal of the timber has resulted in the immigration of peasant farmers in to the area and consequent further forest destruction. Brazil is currently losing 2 554 000 hectares of forest annually, equivalent to 0.5% of its forest area (Fig. 3.8). Costa Rica's 1 220 000 hectares of natural forest are currently decreasing by 41 000 hectares (3%) per year (Table 3.2).

Use of fire for forest clearance

The use of fire to clear forest is long established and traditional farming practices based on slash and burn systems have increased with the human population. The trees are cut down to form a clearing and the sun dries the leaf litter and allows the area to be set alight thus clearing it for cultivation. Standing forest is much more resistant to fire, the ground litter is heavily shaded and the humidity is high, so it doesn't normally spread beyond the boundaries of the clearing. However, when severe droughts occur, forests where the canopy has been reduced by

Fig. 3.8 The current extent of deforestation in the Amazon region. Reproduced with kind permission of Harper Collins.

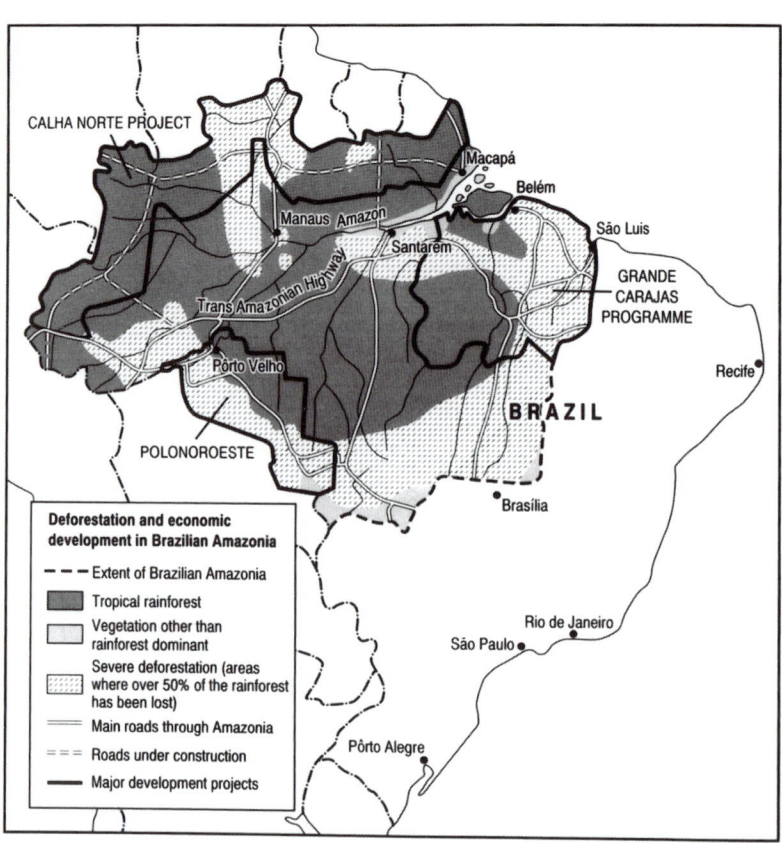

Table 3.2 | Annual loss of tropical forest cover in a sample of developing countries

Country	Current annual loss of forest cover in thousands of hectares (percentage of total)
Brazil	2554 (0.5)
Cameroon	129 (0.6)
Columbia	581 (1.2)
Costa Rica	41 (3.0)
Ghana	117 (1.3)
Indonesia	1084 (1.0)
Laos	148 (1.2)
Madagascar	130 (0.8)
Mexico	508 (0.9)
Nigeria	121 (0.9)
Peru	217 (0.3)
Tanzania	323 (1.0)
Thailand	329 (2.6)
Venezuela	503 (1.1)
Vietnam	135 (1.4)
Zaire	740 (0.7)

local felling or logging operations will become drier and be susceptible to fire. This has led to the destruction (accidental and deliberate) of large areas of tropical forest in recent years.

A catastrophic series of fires swept through the forests of Indonesia in 1997, after prolonged drought thought to have been caused by a periodic El Niño event (a change in Pacific Ocean current systems). An area of up to 5 million hectares may have been affected by the fires (Kinnaird & O'Brien 1998). Much of this seems to have been caused by local people seeing the drought as an opportunity to clear further areas of forest for cultivation. Many local fires spread out of control and devastated large areas. The smoke produced spread across South-East Asia affecting the health of 70 million people and costing an estimated US$4.4 billion.

Habitat disturbance

Whilst we are destroying habitat we are also are causing disturbance to all corners of the earth (see Chapter 5). The following are some examples.

Pollution

Pollutants emitted from early industrial processes are measurable as deposits around the globe and the simultaneous increases in industrialisation and pollution are all too evident. Since most industrial activity was based on burning of fossil fuels, the rise in activity can be measured by the increase in the atmosphere of the major product of combustion, carbon dioxide (Fig. 3.9). Evidence such as this, clearly

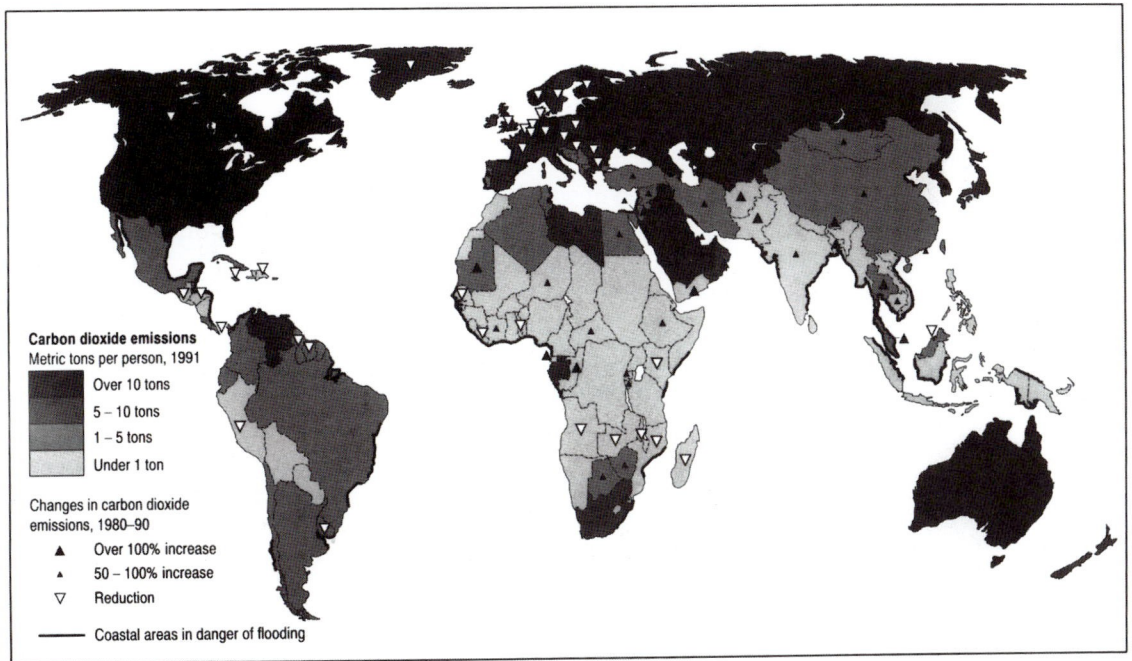

Fig. 3.9 Geographical distribution of carbon dioxide emissions. Note the higher levels in developed countries and oil-producing countries. Reproduced with kind permission of George Philip.

Table 3.3 Use of fertilisers and pesticides per unit area in a selection of developed countries

Country	Nitrogenous fertiliser use (tonnes per sq. km of arable land)	Pesticide use (tonnes per sq. km of arable land)
Canada	4	0.1
Denmark	12	0.2
Germany	15	0.3
Ireland	46	0.3
Japan	12	1.4
Mexico	4	0.1
Netherlands	37	1.1
New Zealand	34	0.9
UK	23	0.6
USA	6	0.2

showing a substantial rise, has profound implications for our environment as discussed below under climate change.

Large-scale industrial processes which burn coal, and involve smelting of metals, produce other pollutants such as sulphur dioxide and nitrogen oxides. These can cause pollution locally or be carried by prevailing winds to pollute areas some distance from source (see acid rain, Chapter 5). Other toxic waste products, such as heavy metals and synthetic organic compounds, were most conveniently and cheaply dumped into nearby rivers causing severe pollution in many industrialised nations.

The industrialisation of farming was made possible on the back of the easy availability of synthetic chemical fertilisers and pesticides (Table 3.3), both of which have caused pollution of natural ecosystems through eutrophication and toxicity to non-target organisms respectively.

The climate change scenario

Whilst the short-term effects of human activity are increasingly well documented, the longer-term influences on our global environment are rapidly becoming the focus of political debate. Foremost among these is the effect of some atmospheric pollutants on climate. Some chemicals present in the atmosphere block the reflective infrared heat from the earth's surface and therefore act like a blanket or greenhouse, keeping us warm. This process has been vital for the development of life on earth, but the production of excess concentrations of natural greenhouse gases (primarily carbon dioxide and methane) and the production of new ones (e.g. chloroflourocarbons) seems to be further warming the planet (Table 3.4). This in itself may not be a problem. The earth has been warmer than it is now at many times in the past. The problem lies in the rapidity with which the warming may be taking place. Projected global warming scenarios of an average of 1–4 °C over

Table 3.4 Carbon dioxide emissions expressed as millions of metric tonnes of carbon from selected countries in 1980 and 1994

Country	1980	1994	% change
USA	1259.3	1387.3	+10.2
Japan	254.9	303.3	+19.0
South Korea	34.3	91.9	+167.9
China	406.4	828.4	+103.8
India	95.6	236.5	+147.4
Germany	291.7	230.3	−21.0
UK	160.6	149.7	−6.8
Brazil	48.2	64.4	+33.6
Mexico	71.0	97.7	+37.6
Australia	55.4	75.9	+37.0
South Africa	58.2	85.5	+46.9

Source: OECD.

the next 50 years may not seem very dramatic, but they represent a more rapid change in our global climate than has ever been recorded before. So why is this a particular conservation problem? Most species are adapted to a relatively narrow range of environmental conditions. Their evolution is a result of the interaction between genes and environment. The species present today are here because they have been able to adapt to changing conditions in the past, but conditions in the future could change faster than ever before and many species will not be able to evolve sufficiently rapidly to persist. Their capacity to adapt will be insufficient to track the environmental changes. On top of this is the problem that in the past many species could cope by moving with their environment, for example, as the climate warms species move to higher latitudes and/or altitudes, as has been the case at the end of each ice age. But the rapidity of future change may mean that the less mobile species will fail to keep pace. Last but not least, humans have so altered natural habitats that movement is not possible for some, because they would have to cross large areas of already inhospitable land to reach another isolated fragment of suitable habitat (a subject we return to in the next chapter).

Introduced species and diseases

Humans are travellers and have colonised most of the terrestrial surface of the Earth. Along with them, they have deliberately introduced species which are either useful to them as crops or domesticated animals and other species which are familiar to them and aesthetically pleasing, such as garden plants and songbirds. Additionally humans have facilitated the dispersal of many other species that have stowed away and colonised new lands as accidental introductions. Species from both categories have had a devastating impact on the native flora and fauna and this is best illustrated by a series of examples that are given in Chapter 5, but a simple example is that of the introduction of the goat to areas where the flora is not resistant to heavy grazing, particularly tropical and subtropical islands, resulting in the devastation of some unique plant communities.

Overexploitation of resources

The increasing population and per capita demand for energy has resulted in many of our natural resources being directly overexploited. Non-renewable resources, such as fossil fuels, are being used up at rates that will see many of them exhausted by the end of this century. Renewable resources such as water and wild populations such as fish stocks and timber species are not being managed sustainably and many supplies are in danger of being exhausted (see Chapter 6 for examples). The North Sea cod (*Gadus morhua*) a favourite in UK fish-and-chip shops, has recently been classed as endangered by the World Wide Fund for Nature. In many cases overexploitation can be avoided, allowing natural regeneration and providing food, water and materials long into the future (see Chapter 10).

The human impact on species extinctions

The fossil record, although incomplete and often difficult to interpret, shows a gradual rise in the number of species (actually measured in terms of genera or families) through time (see Box 1.1). This is punctuated only by a small number of mass extinction events, five of which are clearly defined and involve the loss of a large percentage of the species extant at that time (Fig. 1.1). An important interpretation of this pattern is that extinctions have always occurred and are a natural phenomenon, but, on average, they have been exceeded by the number of speciation events. We should therefore ask the question 'is the presence of humans accelerating species extinction rates?' This is not as easy a question to answer as might at first seem. Assessing the human impact on species extinction must involve measuring current extinction rates, relative to background natural extinction rates. First, we need a background rate of species extinction from the fossil record. This problem is addressed by May *et al.* (1995). Using average lifespans of species in the fossil record, current estimates of extinction rates since AD 1600, and projected extinction rates based on habitat loss, they concluded that impending extinction rates may be four orders of magnitude higher than background. Although the authors recognise many sources of error in their estimates the scale of the difference makes the message crystal clear. We are in the midst of an extinction crisis.

Patterns of species extinction

If recorded extinctions to date are plotted on a map as is done for birds in Fig 3.10, it is immediately apparent that they are unevenly spread across the globe. Furthermore, they are not concentrated in the most densely populated countries, or those that have the highest biodiversity

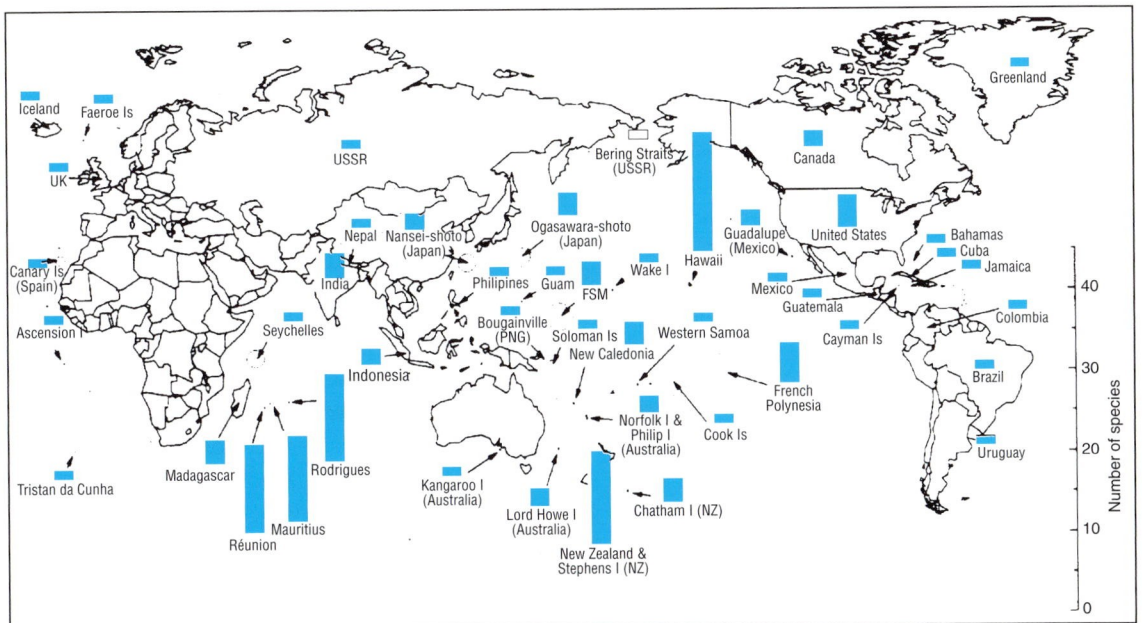

Fig. 3.10 Map of recorded bird extinctions since 1600. Note the high extinction rates on small, isolated oceanic islands. Reproduced from Groombridge (1992) with kind permission of Kluwer Academic Publishers.

(and therefore most to lose). They are clearly concentrated on small oceanic islands. Pimm *et al.* (1995) review the pattern of bird extinctions in the central Pacific and conclude that human colonisation has driven successive waves of extinction. The first colonisation of Melanesia and Micronesia from South-East Asia occurred around 4000 years ago, followed by Fiji and Samoa, with the more remote islands of Hawaii, Easter Island and New Zealand only being first colonised some 1500 years ago. This first wave caused extensive extinctions, but the second wave of colonisations, this time by Europeans, brought further extinctions and continues to the present day (Fig. 3.11).

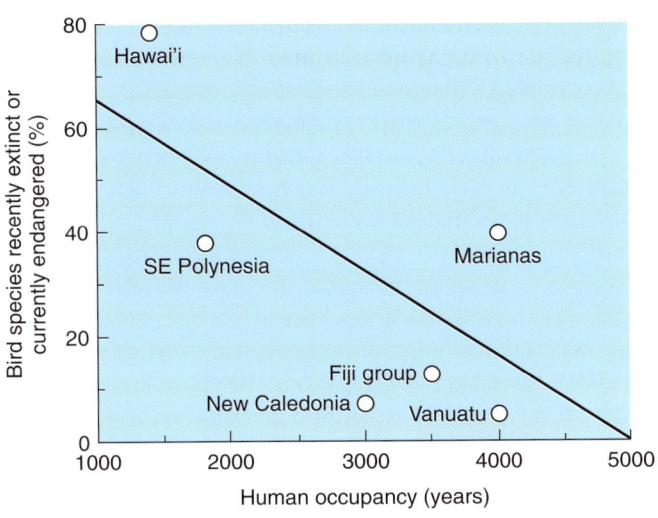

Fig. 3.11 Proportions of Pacific island avifauna that are recorded as recently extinct or currently endangered in relation to the time of human occupancy. The drop in categorised species with time since occupancy suggests that vulnerable species have already been extirpated. Those islands above the line are experiencing current rapid extinction rates due to introduced species. Reproduced from Pimm *et al.* (1995) with kind permission of Oxford University Press.

There are a number of probable reasons for oceanic islands recording so many extinctions:

1. vulnerability due to small population size;
2. the vulnerability of island faunas to human exploitation due to their lack of adaptation to large predators;
3. the vulnerability of island faunas to species introduced by man deliberately (e.g. cats, dogs, goats) or accidentally (e.g. rats, mice), again due to lack of adaptations to cope with predation and competition;
4. the failure to have recorded many species (mainly invertebrates) of large continental land masses before their extinction.

Whatever the specific reason or reasons it is apparent that species are now disappearing from islands and continents alike due directly and indirectly to human activity.

Summary

1. Human population size has recently shown an explosive exponential increase.

2. Humans evolved as hunter-gatherers, who were much like any other large mammal in their role in the ecosystem. Key advances such as use of tools and fire allowed humans to become a dominant influence over their environment, fundamentally changing it. These same advances allowed humans to spread out over the earth changing ecosystems as they went.

3. The industrial revolution and associated technological advances increased resource use per capita, enabled explosive population growth and brought with it new scales of environmental impact.

4. The influence of the developed world on the developing world has had an additional negative impact on the environment, hastening habitat destruction.

5. We now have good statistical evidence that humans are having a negative impact on biodiversity through habitat destruction, habitat disturbance and overexploitation of natural resources. There is also increasing evidence that our activities threaten to drive rapid changes in our climate, in turn causing further negative impacts on natural systems and ourselves.

Discussion points

- What were the major advances in human evolution and technological development that enabled greater impact on the environment?
- To what extent do you think that the spread of humans across the globe immediately caused extinctions of vertebrate species?
- Is desertification increasing due to human or natural causes?
- To what extent can human population growth be directly blamed for the conservation crisis?

Further reading

Bowman, D.M.J.S. (1998). The impact of aboriginal landscape burning on the Australian biota. *New Phytologist* **140**, 385–410.

Conacher, A.J. & Sala, M. (eds) (1998). *Land degradation in mediterranean environments of the world*. Chichester: Wiley.

Goudie, A. (1996). *The earth transformed: an introduction to the human impact on the environment*. Oxford: Blackwell.

Lawton, J.H. & May, R.M. (eds) (1995). *Extinction rates*. Oxford: Oxford University Press.

Stuart, A.J. (1991). Mammalian extinctions in the late Pleistocene of northern Eurasia and North America. *Biological Reviews* **66**, 453–562.

Web sites

International Union for the Conservation of Nature (IUCN): www.iucn.org

Organization for Economic Co-operation and Development (OECD) frequently requested statistics: www.oecd.org/std/fas.htm

United Nations Environment Programme, Meta Data Directory: www.grid.unep.ch/mdd/ home.htm

World Conservation Monitoring Centre: www.wcmc.org.uk

World Wide Fund for Nature: www.panda.org

Earth Trends: earthtrends.wri.org

Chapter 4

Effects of habitat destruction

In the last chapter we saw that human activity is leading to significant levels of destruction of natural habitats. We can and did put some figures on the levels of destruction. In this chapter we consider the effects that these levels of destruction might have on populations, species and communities.

By reading this chapter students will gain an understanding of the effects of habitat destruction and fragmentation on communities of species, on populations, and on genetic diversity within populations. They will gain understanding of how fragmentation of habitat decreases the species diversity and increases the probability of species extinction at the site and landscape scales.

Introduction

There is an intimate and complex relationship between a species and its habitat and the former has certain requirements for persistence: either abiotic (e.g. microclimate) or biotic (e.g. food or symbionts) that their habitat provides. In some species, habitat requirements are much more specific than others (some are specialists and some generalists), but there are usually definable elements that are vital, even for generalists, especially for successful reproduction. If a species has been sufficiently well studied, its presence or absence can often be predicted on the basis of presence or absence of key habitat features, and it follows that if these key features are removed the species will disappear also.

Deterministic versus stochastic effects of habitat loss

The scale of destruction described in the previous chapter means that the habitats of some species have been lost completely. In the absence of human intervention (in the form of *ex situ* conservation, see Chapter 11), no species can survive when the habitat to which it is adapted is suddenly and totally removed. This is a foreseeable or predictable effect of total habitat destruction and we can therefore describe it as **deterministic extinction**. No habitat – no species.

In fact, cases of extinction are rarely as simple as this and fortunately there are few cases of total habitat destruction that have been recorded.

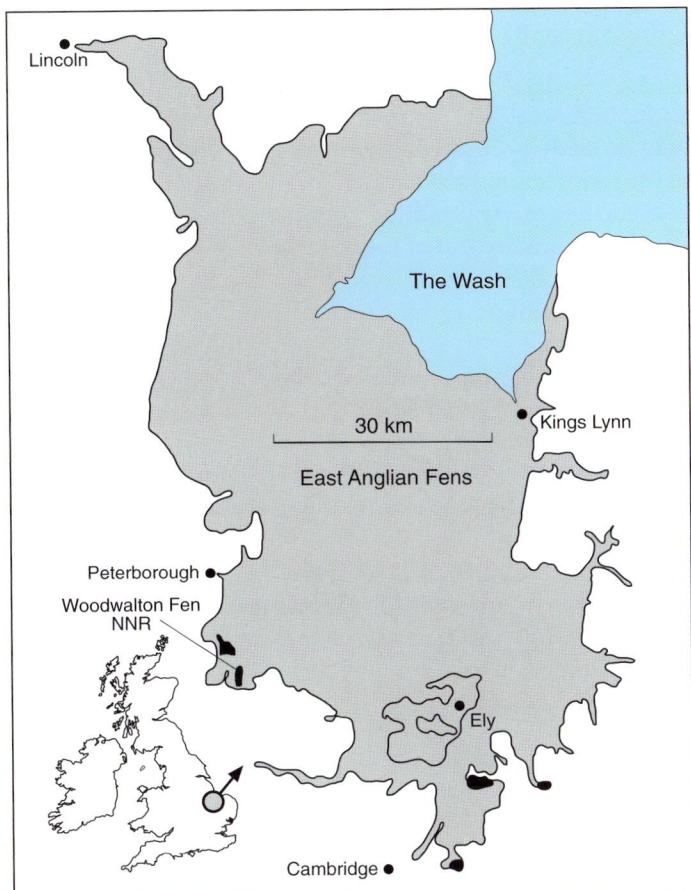

Fig. 4.1 Former distribution of the large copper butterfly, *Lycaena dispar dispar* in the East Anglia region of the UK, showing extent of wetland habitat destruction. This subspecies went extinct around 1860.

Usually, one or two fragments remain in which the species may persist for some time (see below). One example that is close to deterministic is the extinction of the British subspecies of the large copper butterfly, *Lycaena dispar dispar* in eastern England. This species was found across a substantial wetland area called the East Anglian Fens stretching from the city of Lincoln down to the city of Cambridge (Fig 4.1). This area was extensively drained for agricultural use from around 1600 up to the middle of the nineteenth Century. At the end of this period only a few fragments of fen remained and these were substantially altered due to the change in hydrology caused by the extensive drainage works. The large copper was discovered in this area in 1749 and was last seen in 1848, less than 100 years later (Webb & Pullin 1997).

If habitat destruction is only partial, whether or not a species survives, and for how long, is dependent partly on chance events and processes in the future such as weather and population fluctuation in other species. Since there is considerable uncertainty in this process it is termed **stochastic extinction** (stochastic means governed by the laws of probability). In these circumstances we can only state the probability of future extinction. It is these future variables and their probabilities that form the main body of this chapter.

Patterns of habitat destruction

Fortunately natural areas are not usually completely destroyed in one phase of human activity. The detailed pattern of destruction varies greatly, but the result is almost always the fragmentation of continuous habitat into smaller parts. **Habitat fragmentation** is the process whereby a large continuous area of habitat is both reduced and divided into two or more fragments. As a large patch of habitat is eroded by destruction, the remaining fragments differ from the original habitat in four important ways:

1. the total area remaining is smaller;
2. the proportion of edge in relation to the total area is greater;
3. any given point within the fragment is on average closer to the edge than before;
4. on average each fragment is more isolated from other fragments than before.

Each one of these, as we shall see, has a profound effect on communities, species and their populations. The fragmentation process can occur in a number of different ways (Fig. 4.2). Destruction may occur in a wave across the landscape or occur in patches. Linear features such as

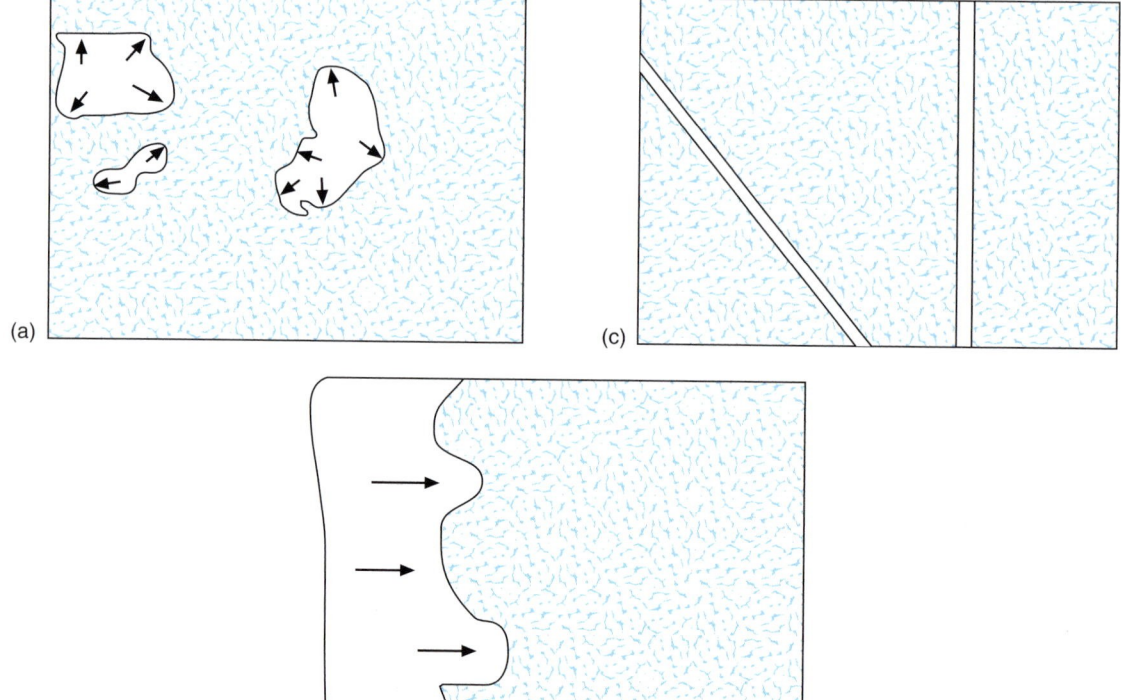

(a) (b) (c)

Fig. 4.2 a–c Some different patterns of habitat destruction and fragmentation. Destruction can occur in patches within a habitat (a) or in a wave across it (b). Linear features such as roads and power line routes can cut habitat into smaller sections (c).

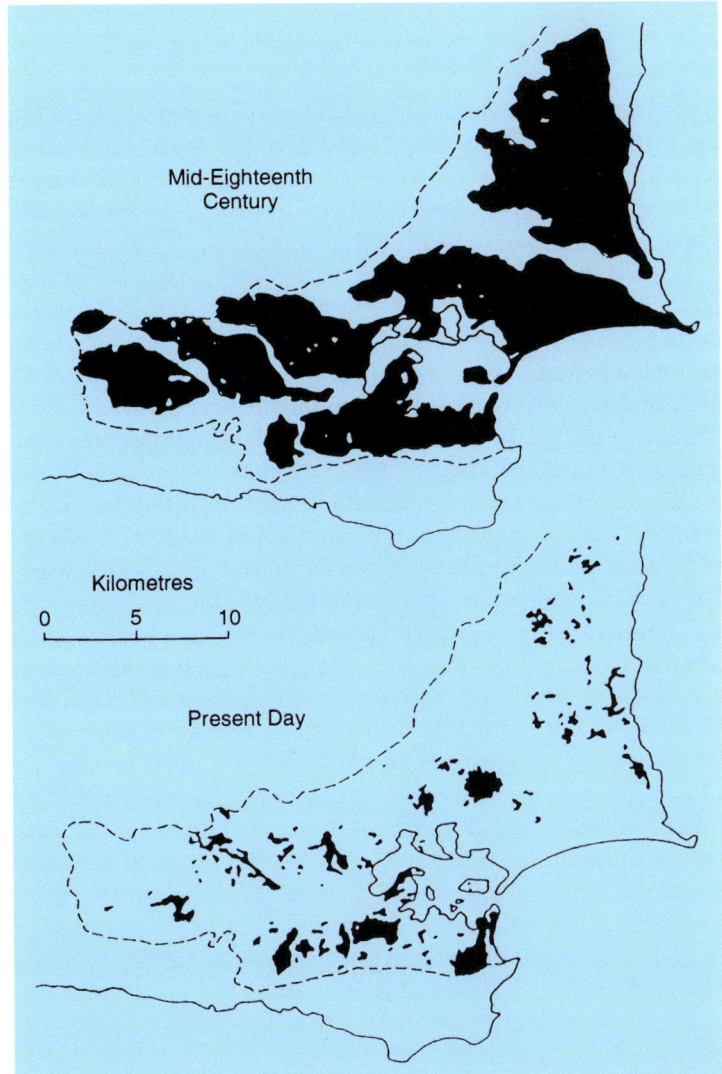

Fig. 4.3 Change in the extent and pattern of fragmentation in heathland in Dorset, UK over the last 250 years. Reproduced from Webb (1997) with kind permission of Cambridge University Press.

roads and power lines may cut through and divide habitat patches into smaller units.

In cases where old maps are available and have been periodically updated, we can clearly see progressive fragmentation of habitats taking place. The heathland habitats in Dorset, UK have been extensively mapped and studied, revealing a picture of fragmentation in to ever smaller and more isolated patches (Fig. 4.3). An area of 40 000 hectares existed in the mid-eighteenth century, fragmented only by river valleys. This has been reduced to less than 6000 hectares today and is split into 141 fragments. In this case the driving forces were agricultural intensification and urbanisation (Webb 1997). Despite different causal factors, the same basic pattern can be seen in many ecosystems such as North American temperate forests, European wetlands and in the tropical forests of Central America.

Biotic effects of habitat fragmentation

The fate of the species in remaining fragments of habitat has been the subject of much conservation study and effort. But even where some areas of habitat have been protected, as national parks or nature reserves, the very species they were set up to conserve are still being lost. Why is this?

Community-level effects of fragmentation

The effect of patch size and isolation on diversity and richness of species was first recognised in the communities inhabiting oceanic islands. Fauna and flora of offshore islands is generally poorer compared with nearby mainland areas and the former are usually a subset of the latter. The mechanism underlying this phenomenon and the general relationship of species richness to area was measured empirically by MacArthur & Wilson (1967). They found that the numbers of species on islands could be predicted on the basis of the differing size and isolation (e.g. distance from mainland) of those islands. By measuring the number of species of chosen taxonomic groups on each of a cluster of islands, such as the reptiles and amphibians of the West Indies, they noticed that if island area and number of species were plotted against each other on a logarithmic scale, a straight line of increasing species number with increasing island area would be obtained (Fig. 4.4). This relationship can be expressed mathematically as $S = CA^z$, where S is the number of species, A is the area, C is a constant given by the intercept with the y axis, and z is the slope of the line. Further studies on other taxa and islands confirm that this relationship generally holds, although C and z will vary among different taxa. This is a basic rule of MacArthur and Wilson's **theory of island biogeography** that seeks to explain the relative numbers of species found on different islands.

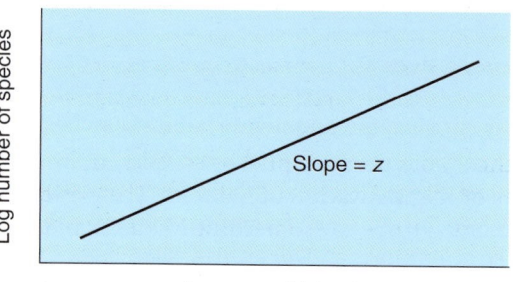

Fig. 4.4 The generalised relationship between species richness and land area.

So what is happening biologically to produce this relationship? MacArthur & Wilson noted that although the number of species varied on islands of different sizes, it was not always predictable which species would occur on each island. It seemed to be partly a matter of chance and they saw the community on islands as being dynamic, with some species colonising an island whilst others go extinct. If an island is stable with respect to species number then the rate of colonisation must

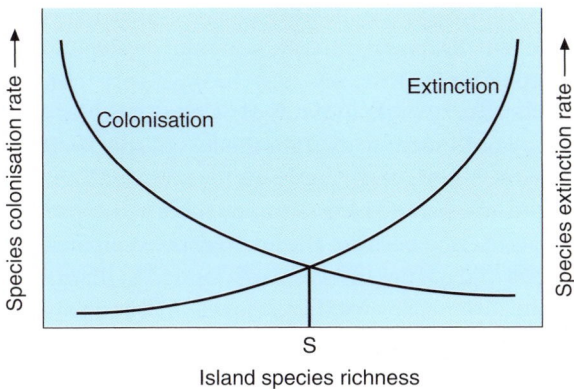

equal the rate of extinction and it could be said to be in equilibrium (Fig. 4.5).

The probability of colonisation by any given species will be a function of island size and isolation. The larger the island and the closer it is to other land, the higher the rate of colonisation will be as more individuals are likely to reach it by chance. Extinction however, will not be so closely related to isolation, but more to island size. Small islands will only have the carrying capacity (defined as the maximum population that can exist in equilibrium with average conditions of resource availability) for small populations and these are more likely to go extinct than large ones, purely by chance (see below under population effects). The dynamics can be shown graphically as in Fig. 4.5. The shape of the curves in Fig. 4.5 and their intersections predict the equilibrium number of species for an island of given size and isolation. In addition, because extinction rates are higher on small islands, they will also experience a greater proportional rate of turnover of species. In other words the species composition on small islands will change more rapidly than on large islands. It has also been argued that large islands can hold more species because they are likely to have a greater diversity of habitats. Whilst this is probably true, it does not appear to be necessary for the relationship to hold. Large uniform islands still have more species on them than small uniform islands.

Island biogeography theory has been adopted by conservationists to explain the consequences of fragmentation of habitats. The presumption is that a habitat fragment will operate something like an island. For example, a patch of forest surrounded by converted agricultural land can effectively be viewed as equivalent to an island surrounded by ocean. As a patch becomes smaller and more isolated from other patches it will lose species as its equilibrium species richness falls. The full consequences of this process may not be immediately apparent, because there is a time lag between the creation of the habitat fragment and the decrease in species richness to equilibrium level. This lag is termed the **relaxation time**. If a patch of forest is suddenly formed through destruction of the forest around it then it will still contain the vast majority of species it formally had. However, over time more species will go extinct than will colonise as the species richness sinks to the new equilibrium state. Some will disappear quickly, some slowly, depending on their resource needs. Top carnivores may be lost very quickly through emigration, whereas a single individual of a tree species may persist for decades. This would seem to explain the loss of species from protected areas that are fragments of formerly more extensive habitat.

However, the application of island biogeography theory to conservation problems has been criticised because the analogy between oceanic islands surrounded by sea and nature reserves surrounded by disturbed land is not perfect. In the latter case overall species richness can rise as a patch gets smaller and more isolated because new species can invade (particularly at the edges) from the surrounding landscape. The surrounding landscape is simply not as different from the remaining fragment as the sea is from an island. Herein lies a limitation of the theory. It simply considers overall species richness not which species compose the community and whether these are representative of the habitat island. In conservation, which species are present is usually more important than the total number.

The Biological Dynamics of Forest Fragments Project in Amazonia is a long-term study of the effects of fragmentation of tropical forest on the communities of species that they contain. A range of different fragment sizes from 1 to 100 hectares in area has been created through clear felling of forest north of Manaus, Brazil. This has enabled the study of tree recruitment (newly established trees achieving 10 cm diameter at breast height) into forest fragments of varying size compared with continuous forest. Results so far, over a 13 year period (Laurance *et al.* 1998), suggest that tree recruitment increased as fragment size decreased, contradicting the predictions of island biogeography theory (Fig. 4.6). It seems that early successional (pioneer) tree species that are effective at colonising disturbed areas were able to invade the edge of the fragments, and since the smaller the fragment the larger the proportion of edge, small fragments were most vulnerable to colonisation. But in addition, because the smaller fragments were experiencing a higher proportional recruitment of early successional rather than old-growth trees, the composition of small fragments was changing rapidly. This is consistent with the higher turnover rate on small islands predicted by the theory.

Edge effects

Earlier in the chapter we noted that habitat fragmentation results in an increase in the proportion of edge in relation to the total area, and that any given point within a remaining fragment is on average closer to the edge than before. Why is this significant?

Since edges of habitat are often different in character to interiors, they are often unsuitable for some species that subsequently become confined to an ever smaller interior or core of unchanged habitat. Evidence that edges are different from the interior is provided by the work of Williams-Linera *et al.* (1998) who investigated species composition at the edge, compared with both the interior, and the surrounding pasture of fragmented tropical rainforest. Of the 244 plant species

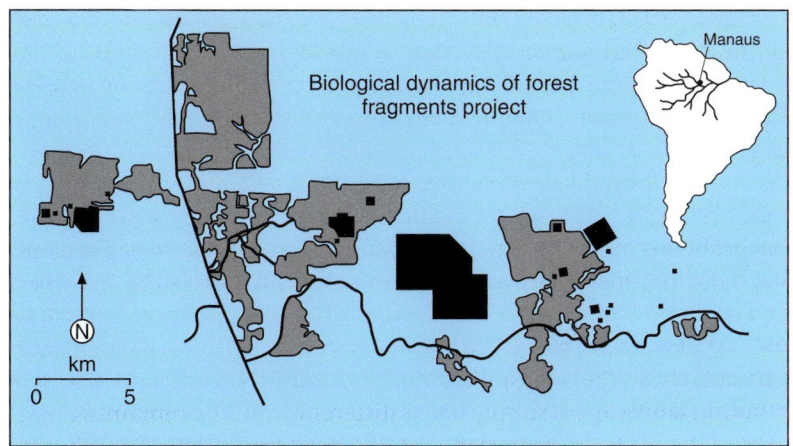

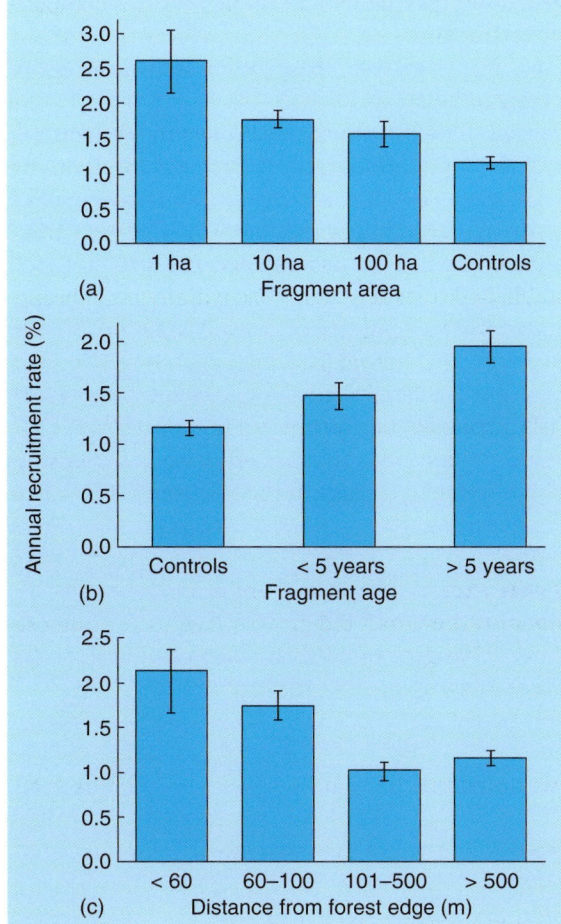

Fig. 4.6 Effects of fragment size, and proximity of edge to annual tree recruitment in tropical forest. Reproduced from Laurance *et al.* (1998) with kind permission of Blackwell Science.

recorded, only two occurred in all three habitats. Exclusively interior species numbered 44, whereas exclusively edge species totalled 26.

The reasons for edges containing different communities from the interior are numerous, but the main ones follow:

ALTERED CLIMATE The climate/microclimate of the surrounding area might be quite different to that inside the patch. For example, in the case of a woodland patch surrounded by grassland, the grassland receives much more sunlight to the ground and much more air movement (wind), thus affecting humidity. If the woodland patch is small and the edge proportion large then these microclimatic factors penetrate most of the patch and this can change the flora substantially, also having knock-on effects for dependent species. Similarly the edge of a wetland surrounded by drained land may become drier than the core, leading to invasion by competitive generalist plant species and disappearance of wetland specialists.

In tropical forest many species that struggle for light in a closed canopy thrive at the edges created by human disturbance. Typical of these species are the lianas, woody climbers that can completely engulf the trees at the edges of the forest, changing the community dramatically. Many small forest fragments in areas such as at the Atlantic Coast of Brazil and in West Africa are seriously degraded by this aggressive weedy growth (Fig. 4.7).

Fig. 4.7 Lianas thriving in the light at the edge of a remnant forest patch in Jamaica. The natural forest vegetation is smothered, completely changing the habitat.

INCREASED INCIDENCE OF ENVIRONMENTAL CATASTROPHES In some cases edges are more likely to be exposed to environmental agents such as high winds and fires, as a result of their proximity to surrounding habitat. This is particularly true of edges of forest surrounded by dry grassland where fires are frequent. The altered climate, noted above, means that forest edge is drier and more easily burnt than the moist interior. Their exposure also makes trees prone to being blown down by high winds coming from the open side (Fig. 4.8). Both of these examples also result in destruction of the original edge, creation of a new edge and consequent reduction in size of the patch and the core area.

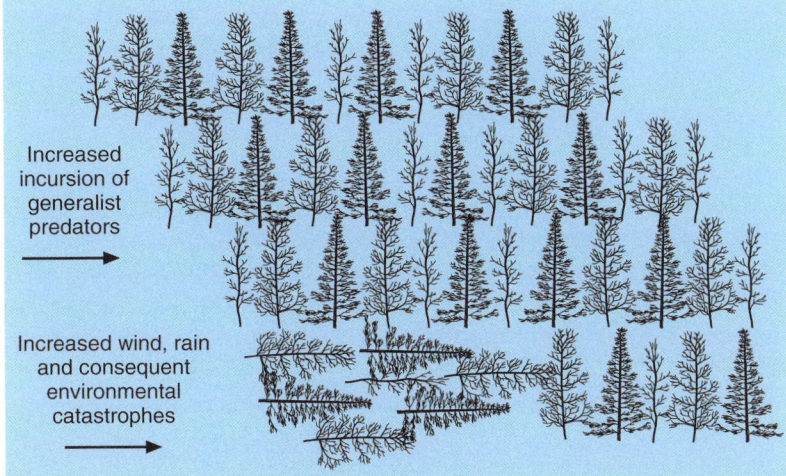

Increased
incursion of
generalist
predators

Increased wind, rain
and consequent
environmental
catastrophes

Fig. 4.8 Some typical climatic and biotic effects at the edge of a forest.

INCREASED INCURSION OF PREDATORS AND COMPETITORS Species that cannot live permanently in the habitat but can forage within it, may become serious competitors to resident species. Analysis of data from a number of experimental studies suggests that bird nest predation rates increase with decreasing forest cover, which may be due to increasing edge effects allowing intrusion of predators such as small mammals in to forest areas (Hartley & Hunter 1998).

INCREASED CHANCE OF PASSIVE EMIGRATION FROM THE HABITAT The fact that a given point within the habitat patch is on average closer to the edge as fragmentation progresses adds another problem: many species are constantly on the move, either as individuals, in groups or as propagules (e.g. plant seeds). In a large habitat this movement, which may largely be random, is unlikely to take them to the edge or out of their habitat, but in a small patch many more individuals may reach the edge and leave purely by chance (Fig. 4.9). Some animal species will have the behavioural capacity to return, others, and plant seeds, will not and are likely to perish in a hostile environment.

Population-level effects of fragmentation

When considering the fate of single species, a major consequence of habitat fragmentation is that populations also get fragmented into smaller units. No patch of habitat is a limitless resource, and the

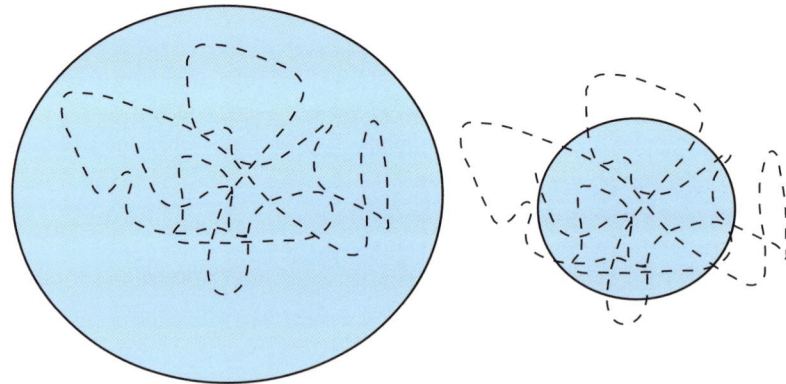

Fig. 4.9 Individuals of some species appear to move randomly through their habitat and are more likely to encounter the edge and leave their habitat in a small compared with a large patch.

– – – Hypothetical random movement of individual

numbers of individuals of each species that any patch can sustain on average (its carrying capacity) will usually be area-related, such that the smaller the habitat patch the smaller the carrying capacity. So as habitat is fragmented into smaller units so are populations. This is a key concern in conservation because small populations are at greater risk of extinction than large ones. Four factors are thought to increase the probability of extinction in small populations relative to large ones:

1. demographic stochasticity: random variation in birth and death rates;
2. genetic stochasticity: random loss of genetic variation and inbreeding;
3. environmental stochasticity: random variation in normal weather patterns;
4. natural catastrophes: volcanic eruptions, fires, floods, etc.

Demographic effects

Populations fluctuate in size and change in age structure from one time period to another (e.g. a year) purely as a result of chance variation in the ratio of births to deaths. This is termed **demographic stochasticity**. In a large population these chance variations are likely to cancel each other out and the fluctuations will only be minor relative to the population size. In contrast, if the population is small, fluctuations can be relatively large and may be large enough to threaten extinction. A theoretical illustration of this is presented in Fig. 4.10. A real example illustrating demographic stochasticity is not readily available because its effects are not easily separated from environmental effects on populations (referred to below). Over time, the cumulative probability that a population will go extinct due to demographic stochasticity can be so high that it is doomed in the long term, but it may not be chance alone that threatens extinction. Having reached a low population size by chance, other factors related to low density can then make it difficult for the population to recover to its carrying capacity. In fact the population size may be driven downward to extinction in what has been termed an extinc-

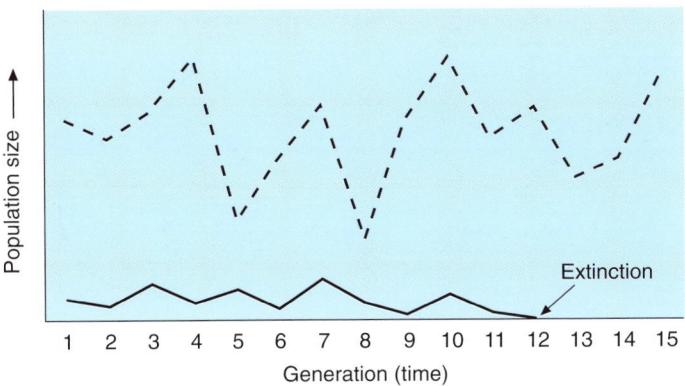

Population size

Generation (time)

Extinction

Fig. 4.10 Theoretical effects of demographic stochasticity on large and small populations. Both populations fluctuate due to random demographic effects, but the small population is more likely to go extinct just by chance.

tion vortex; the decreasing ability to recover at low population densities may be due to lowered individual fecundities and an overall depression in the population's capacity for increase. This downward spiral to extinction is also termed the **Allee effect** after Warder C. Allee who first brought to attention the positive relationship between individual fitness and population size. In other words, at low population size, individual capacity to survive and produce offspring is lowered. Possible contributing factors to this phenomenon include:

- Difficulty in mate location: the population density may become so low that individuals fail to find mates and reproduce. For example, grizzly bears (*Ursus arctos horribilis*) in the Swan Mountains of Montana, USA, exist at a population density of 1.6 bears/100 km^2 (Mace & Waller 1998).
- Reduced group defence against predators: many species, such as lapwings (*Vanellus vanellus*) can efficiently defend themselves against predators in large groups, but small groups are vulnerable.
- Reduced group foraging efficiency: many species rely on group foraging, such as hunting in packs (e.g. African wild dogs, *Lycaon pictus*, see below). If these packs are small the efficiency of foraging can be reduced.
- Breakdown of social integration: many social species live in large groups, such as pack hunters, flocks of birds and grazing herds and survival and reproduction are reduced when group size is small. The now extinct passenger pigeon (*Ectopistes migratorius*) was probably a victim of this process.
- Chance inequality in sex ratio can mean that many individuals are excluded from reproduction, particularly if there is a surfeit of males.

The Allee effect can be seen as part of a dynamic relationship between population size and per capita growth rate (Fig. 4.11). The graph in Fig. 4.11 illustrates that the Allee effect can be so strong that the per capita growth rate becomes negative at low population size and extinction is therefore inevitable. This may be the current situation facing the African wild dog that has shown a population decrease throughout its range. This species has a complex social structure and probably requires a minimum pack size to maintain stable numbers. Possible

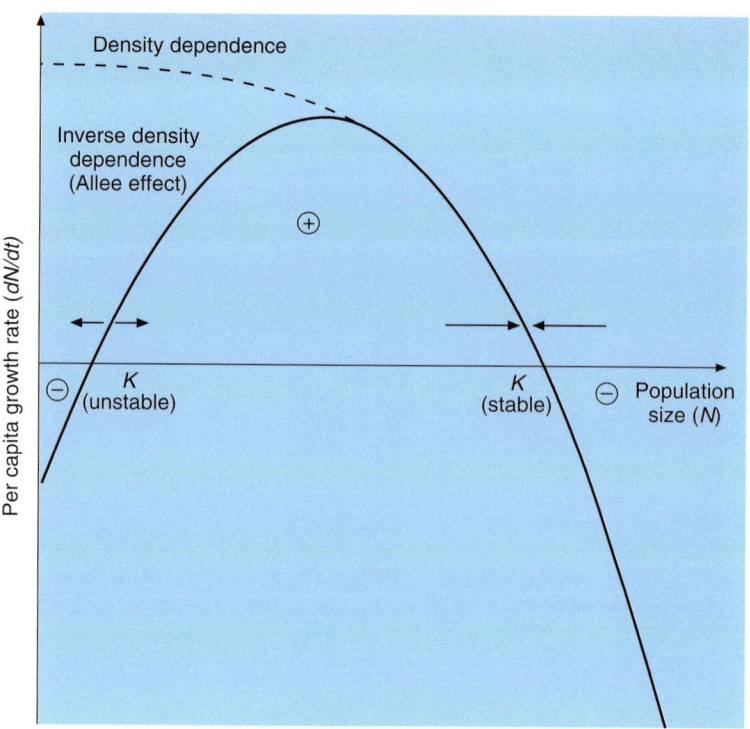

Fig. 4.11 Theoretical illustration of the influence of population size on per capita growth rate incorporating the Allee effect. Not only does density dependence drive down growth rate at high population size, but some factors act in an inversely density-dependent fashion to drive down growth rate at low population size. Reproduced from Courchamp *et al.* (1999) with kind permission of Elsevier Science.

reasons for this include sufficient numbers of individuals being needed for efficient capture of prey, for defending prey from hyenas and for successful rearing of young where the sole breeding female has up to 20 pups and requires help from pack members in feeding and protecting them. Recent survey and status reports on behalf of the IUCN suggest that a minimum of four pack members is required for successful reproduction.

Genetic effects

A parallel stochastic phenomenon in populations is the chance fluctuation in allele frequency that is termed **genetic drift**. Alleles are different forms of a gene and are the basis of much of the genetic diversity found within a species. In the absence of migration (e.g. in isolated populations), new alleles can only be introduced through mutation and lost through natural selection or genetic drift (see Box 4.1 for background explanation). In the absence of selection, the frequency of alleles at any given locus (site on a chromosome where the gene occurs) can vary between generations. This results from two chance events:

1. differential reproductive success, where individuals carrying one allele reproduce more successfully than those carrying an alternative allele simply by chance;
2. heterozygotes (individuals carrying two different alleles) passing on one allele in greater frequency than the other.

In large populations, genetic drift is insignificant in its effect since, as in demography, the fluctuations tend to cancel each other out over the population as a whole. For example, it is unlikely that all the

Box 4.1 | Loss of genetic variability: why is it a problem?

All environments are challenging to survival. The genotype of individuals and the gene pool of populations are an evolutionary response to this challenge. Just as the environment constantly forces selective changes on genotypes from generation to generation, the total gene pool must also change. The ability of populations to cope with this challenge depends on their capacity to adapt to their changing environment. All genetic variation ultimately arises through mutation, but this is a slow process and some of the variation it produces must be maintained in the population to enable it to cope with relatively rapid environmental change. If the variability is lost the flexibility to adapt is reduced.

There is a well-documented positive relationship between population size and genetic variability. In a large population the loss of alleles through genetic drift is balanced by the appearance of new alleles through mutation. In a small and isolated population, rate of loss of alleles through drift increases and the probability of new alleles arising through mutation decreases so that these populations will progressively lose genetic diversity.

In a generalised case of an isolated population with two alleles at each gene locus the expected drop in heterozygosity per generation (ΔF) for an adult population size of N is given by Wright's formula (Wright 1931)

$$\Delta F = 1/2N$$

Thus a population of 50 breeding adults would suffer a loss of 1/100 or 1% of heterozygosity per generation. A population of 5000 breeding adults would only suffer a loss of 1/10 000 or 0.001% of its heterozygosity per generation.

Lacy (1987) looked at this phenomenon using computer models that simulate the probability of loss of alleles from populations of different sizes. By randomly generating changes in allele frequency from generation to generation the models produce individual scenarios which can then be averaged to produce a likely scenario for each population (Fig. 4.12). The model shows that a population which remains

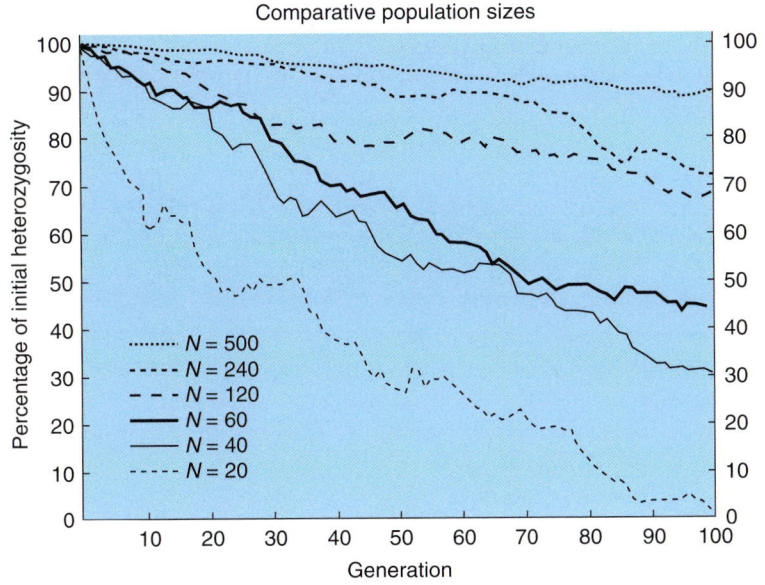

Comparative population sizes

Percentage of initial heterozygosity — *Generation*

Legend:
- $N = 500$
- $N = 240$
- $N = 120$
- $N = 60$
- $N = 40$
- $N = 20$

Fig. 4.12 The effect of population size on the rate of loss of diversity through genetic drift. Reproduced from Lacy (1987) with kind permission of Blackwell Science.

Fig. 4.13 The effects of (a) mutation rate and (b) immigration on the rate of loss of diversity through genetic drift. Reproduced from Lacy (1987) with kind permission of Blackwell Science.

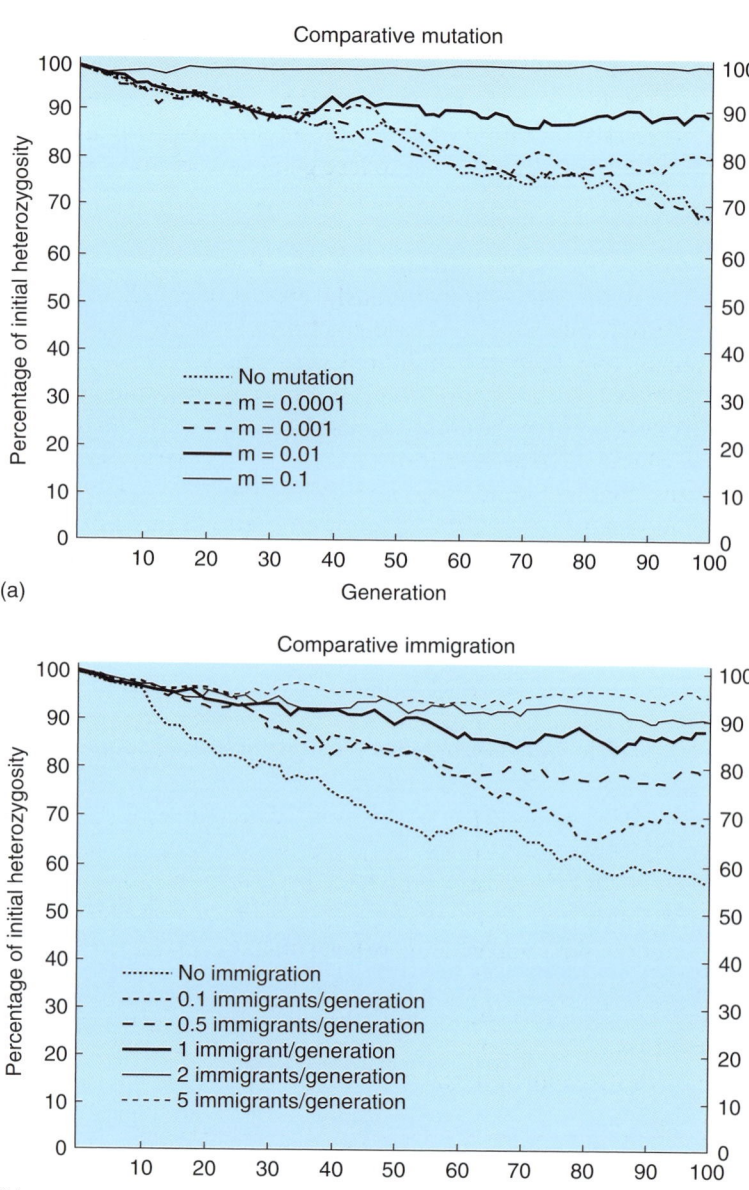

stable at 20 individuals will lose over 50% of its genetic variability in around 20 generations. In contrast a population of 500 would retain more than 90% after 100 generations.

Lacy (1987) then looked at the effects of immigration and mutation on loss of genetic diversity (Fig. 4.13). Immigration at as low a rate as one individual every 10 generations reduces loss of diversity in a population of 120 individuals, and a rate of one immigrant per generation or above virtually negates the loss. In contrast mutation rates of 1% or greater, far above naturally measured rates, are required to counteract loss of genetic diversity in the same-sized population. Thus gene flow between small populations may be crucial to their long-term survival.

individuals carrying one allele in a large population would reproduce more successfully than all individuals carrying an alternative allele, just by chance. In contrast, small populations can lose rare alleles at a rate far in excess of the rate at which mutation can replace them (see Box 4.1). Thus small populations tend to lose genetic diversity and with it the capacity to adapt to environmental change.

INBREEDING IN SMALL POPULATIONS Population gene pools contain recessive alleles (continuously arising through mutation) which are usually deleterious if expressed (when homozygous) in individual phenotypes. In large populations with random mating, they are rarely expressed since they occur at very low frequency and are therefore unlikely to occur in the homozygous state. However, in smaller populations where relatives are more likely to mate with each other (inbreeding) there is an increased probability of such alleles occurring in the homozygous state (relatives are more likely to share a rare allele than two unrelated individuals) and so being expressed. When extensive inbreeding occurs there is likely to be a depression in average fitness of the population, as an increasing number of individuals suffer from genetic abnormalities. This can seriously threaten populations that are probably already declining due to other factors. Inbreeding depression of fitness is commonly observed in many captive populations and there is growing evidence for its existence in isolated small populations.

The Florida panther (*Felis concolor coryi*) is a relict subspecies of the puma or mountain lion that was once more widespread but is now confined to the Florida peninsula (Fig. 4.14). Less than 50 animals survive today and inbreeding is known to be a potential problem because several father/daughter matings have been observed in this closely monitored population. In addition, abnormally low sperm counts have been recorded in captured males, with up to 95% of sperm in each ejaculate being malformed. A congenital cardiac abnormality has also been discovered in captive individuals.

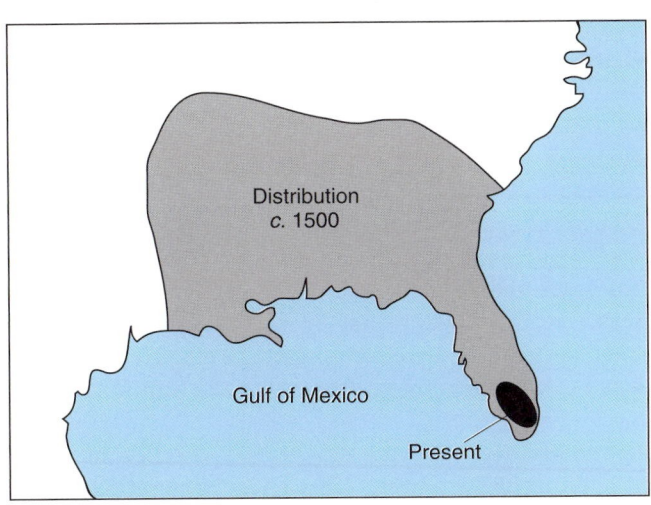

Fig. 4.14 Past (shaded) and present (black) distribution of the Florida panther, *Felis concolor coryi*.

Distribution
c. 1500

Gulf of Mexico

Present

Although examples of inbreeding causing depression of fitness are common in the literature, it is difficult to show that this actually causes extinction of populations. However, Saccheri *et al.* (1998) studied the effect of inbreeding on local extinction in populations of the Glanville fritillary butterfly (*Melitaea cinxia*) and found that the probability of extinction increased significantly with increasing severity of inbreeding, as measured by decreasing heterozygosity. Several components of fitness such as adult longevity were adversely affected by inbreeding, suggesting it was acting directly on the population. Eldridge *et al.* (1999) found very low levels of genetic variation in an island population of the black-footed rock wallaby (*Petrogale lateralis*) causing significant reduction in fitness (reduced female fecundity, skewed sex ratios and increased levels of fluctuating asymmetry) through inbreeding compared with mainland populations. They suggest that since the effective population size is small and the population has been isolated for around 1600 generations, inbreeding may bring as great a threat of extinction as demographic or environmental factors.

However, inbreeding may only be a temporary phenomenon, as the deleterious alleles will be selected out of the population as they are expressed. Providing the population survives the severity of the initial inbreeding depression, its effects should decline over time. This can lead to a rather counterintuitive situation where loss of genetic variability is accompanied by increase in average fitness. But in terms of long-term ability to adapt to changing environmental conditions, this increase in fitness is probably only temporary (Box 4.1). The northern elephant seal (*Mirounga angustirostrus*) may have gone through such a period of inbreeding following a bottleneck caused by hunting, but has now recovered in number despite continued low genetic diversity (see Box 10.2).

It is likely that decreasing heterozygosity will be a symptom rather than a cause of population decline. Many species have been recorded as going through bottlenecks followed by subsequent recovery with no apparent genetic affects. Whether the loss of genetic diversity will subsequently pose problems for that population's long-term recovery is uncertain. This is particularly relevant in the context of *ex situ* conservation strategies that will be covered in Chapter 11.

OUTBREEDING DEPRESSION The opposite of inbreeding, outbreeding at its extreme, is what is frequently termed hybridisation, the mating of individuals of different species. Just as with the crosses between horses and donkeys producing mules, many hybrids are sterile. However, a less extreme case of fitness depression can arise when individuals from the same species but widely divergent populations are allowed to interbreed. Outbreeding has been studied extensively in plants and many species may have an optimal outcrossing distance where the effects of inbreeding and outbreeding are minimised (Fig. 4.15).

Outbreeding can produce offspring that are of low fitness in either of the different habitats of the parents. This arises because individual

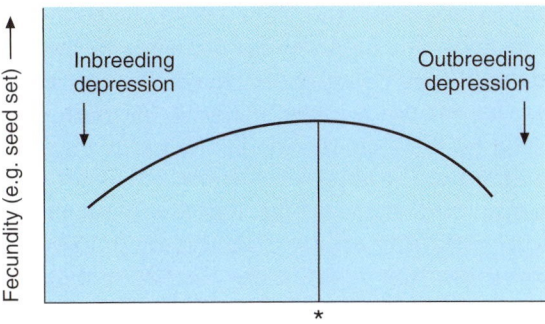

Distance between crossbreeding plants ⟶

Fig. 4.15 Some plants show an optimal outcrossing distance (asterisk) at which fecundity is maximised. Reproduction between plants closer together results in inbreeding depression, but reproduction between those further apart also results in reduced fecundity due to outbreeding depression.

populations can be locally adapted to their own environments, whereas offspring arising from interbreeding will have elements of both gene pools but poor adaptation to either environment.

Outbreeding depression can be a serious problem when translocation and reinforcement of populations is considered (see Chapter 11). It may seem advantageous to combine remaining small populations in order to maximise genetic diversity, but in doing this there may be a risk of losing locally adaptive traits. Similarly by reinforcing a population with individuals from elsewhere local adaptation may be reduced by the introduction of inappropriate genes for the habitat. This is currently of concern with some large mammals such as the black rhinoceros (*Diceros bicornis*) where captive breeding, translocation and reinforcement are significant elements of recovery plans.

SELF-INCOMPATIBILITY IN PLANTS Many plant species have a genetically based physiological mechanism to prevent self-fertilisation (and therefore inbreeding). As a result, closely related individuals will generally not be compatible and will fail to set seed if pollen is not received from an individual from outside that self-incompatibility system. This can lead to depression of average fitness in a small population where few self-incompatibility systems exist and therefore a large proportion of the population cannot interbreed. This is illustrated by the problems of founding new populations of the Hawaiian Mauna Kea silversword (*Argyroxiphium sandwichense*) as part of a recovery programme. The majority of individuals in three surviving newly founded populations appear to have been descended from the same female parent and as a result carry the same self-incompatibility allele. As a consequence, seed set is typically less than 20% (Rieseberg & Swenson, 1996).

GENETIC SWAMPING Species can not only be threatened with extinction through loss of individuals, they can also be threatened through loss of genetic identity. This is possible when a rare species or subspecies comes into contact with a much commoner close relative leading to hybridisation. The genes defining the rare species simply become overwhelmed or swamped by the sheer numbers of the commoner species' genes and can eventually be completely lost. Efforts to conserve the red wolf (*Canis rufus*) in the USA are threatened by the tendency for hybridization with the much commoner coyote (*Canis latrans*) (see Box 10.4). The white-headed duck (*Oxyura leucocephala*) a native of south-west Europe is now threatened by the introduction of the ruddy duck (*O. jamaicensis*) from North America. The latter was introduced to the UK in the 1950s as an ornamental bird; it has subsequently spread to continental Europe where it is hybridising with *O. leucocephala* and threatening its genetic identity. See also the plight of the Catalina mahogany (*Cercocarpus traskiae*) in Chapter 10.

Environmental effects

All populations respond to changes in the climate, both short and long term. Year-to-year fluctuations in the weather, termed **environmental stochasticity**, are chance events in normal weather patterns that affect small populations more than large. A spell of unfavourable weather causing 90% mortality will bring a population of 1000 down to 100, from which it may be able to recover, but it will bring a population of 50 down to 5! Environmental stochasticity operates in both time and space. In a large population, chance unfavourable weather conditions at particular places and times are likely to even out so that a proportion of the population always survives in areas that escaped the worst weather. Small populations confined to small areas are much more vulnerable as any unfavourable weather is likely to affect the whole population and only has to have a small negative influence on the population to drive it to extinction.

The environment also sometimes becomes abnormal (as opposed to fluctuations within the normal range involved in environment stochasticity above) due to catastrophic phenomena such as floods, fire and volcanic activity. These **natural catastrophes** are usually localised and a large widespread population will survive in unaffected areas. However, small populations may be unlucky and get completely wiped out.

All of the above stochastic events can potentially combine and contribute to the dynamics of populations. The three examples in Fig. 4.16, showing changes in populations of three insect species over time, all show occasions when the population drops to a very low level. The insects, with their rapid generation times and large capacity for increase, are known for their variation in population size. It is not always easy to understand the reasons for these fluctuations and detailed ecological studies are often required, but it is likely that a combination of the above factors is behind the dynamics of these populations and it is probably only because these insect populations are normally large and widespread that they can survive.

Isolation of populations

The relative influence of habitat loss and patch isolation on population persistence differs as the percentage of land area that is available habitat decreases in the landscape (Wiens 1997a). As habitat is destroyed the initial effects are due to loss of area alone because popu-

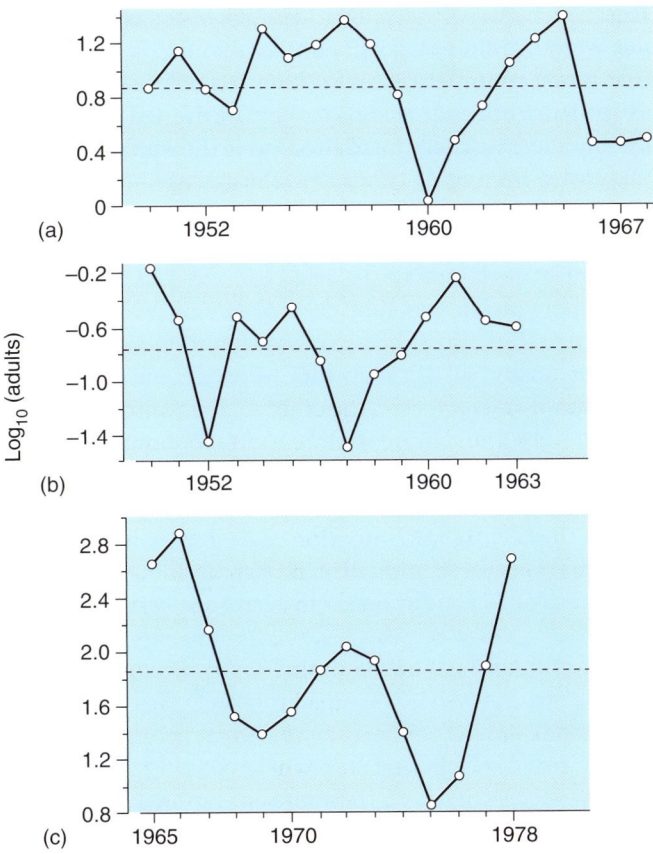

(a)

(b)

(c)

Log₁₀ (adults)

Fig. 4.16 Natural fluctuations in population size in three species of insect: (a) winter moth (*Operophtera brumata*), (b) pine looper (*Bupalus piniarius*) and (c) the carabid beetle (*Calathus melanocephalus*). All show considerable fluctuations due largely to density-independent processes such as the weather. Reproduced from den Boer (1998) with kind permission of the Royal Entomological Society.

lations are still relatively contiguous, but at a critical point in the fragmentation process, dependent on the mobility of the species, isolation of patches leads to local population isolation and extinction without recolonisation. This relationship is shown graphically in Fig. 4.17.

Research in population ecology has shown that some species can persist in a complex of patches where within-patch populations are continually going extinct, but overall persistence among the patches is

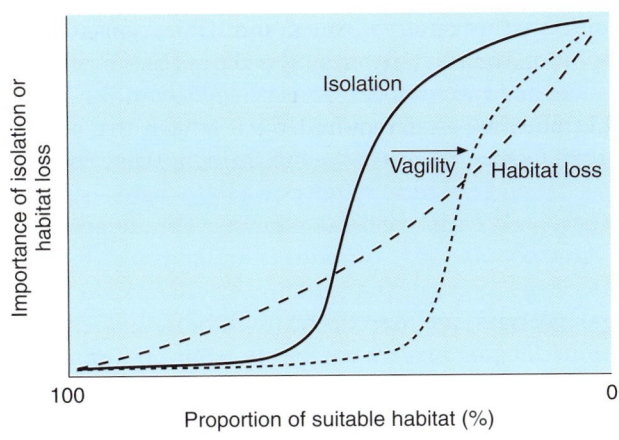

Importance of isolation or habitat loss

Isolation

Vagility → Habitat loss

Proportion of suitable habitat (%)

Fig. 4.17 Hypothesised relationship between the importance of habitat loss and patch isolation, for population persistence. Isolation does not become important until a significant proportion of the habitat is lost, but at some point, dependent on the vagility of the species, isolation increases rapidly in importance. Reproduced from Wiens (1997a) with kind permission of Academic Press.

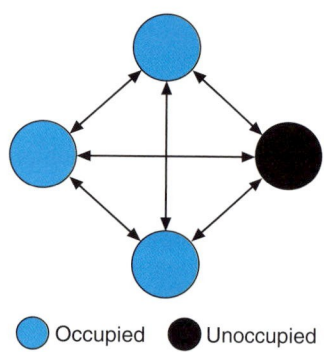

Occupied Unoccupied

Fig. 4.18 Representation of the Levins metapopulation model in which all patches are the same size and equidistant from each other. At any point in time, only a proportion of the patches will be occupied.

enabled by migration between them. This complex of connected populations, each of which could not persist on its own but is viable as a whole, is termed a **metapopulation**. In metapopulations each population is discrete in space, but connected to others by limited migration, in contrast to completely isolated populations at one extreme or populations with extensive mixing at the other. The metapopulation can persist as long as population extinctions are balanced by new populations being founded through colonisation of empty patches. The latter are a characteristic feature of metapopulations.

The term metapopulation was first used by Levins (1969). He put forward a simple model in which a space was separated into suitable and unsuitable patches and all of the former were of equal size, shape and isolation as shown in Fig. 4.18. Of course, such a uniform system does not occur in nature, but do any species occur in situations which even approximate to this model?

Hanski (1997) proposed four conditions that should be met if a true metapopulation of the Levins type is to exist:

1. suitable habitat should occur in discrete patches;
2. even the largest local population should have a substantial risk of extinction;
3. habitat patches should not be so isolated as to prevent recolonisation;
4. local populations should not have completely synchronous dynamics.

There are only a few species in which these conditions are known to be met. One example is provided by the Glanville fritillary butterfly (*Melitaea cinxia*), which exists in a complex of habitat patches of varying size and isolation with significant migration of adults between patches (Hanski *et al.* 1994, Fig. 4.19). At any one time there is a complex of occupied and unoccupied habitat patches. The overall percentage of suitable habitat occupied is greatest where patches are relatively large and close together (Hanski *et al.* 1995). The persistence of the metapopulation as a whole relies on the dynamics of extinction and colonisation, which in turn relies mainly on the size and distribution of patches. The dynamic fluctuations in population size are illustrated in Fig. 4.19b.

It has been pointed out that the Levins model has significant limitations when considered in the conservation context. It does not take into account variability in habitat quality among patches that may influence population size, nor variation in the permeability of the inter-patch spaces and its effect on species mobility. The consequent search for reality in metapopulation theory has led to the use of models with patches of unequal size and isolation. Often one habitat patch is much larger than the others and dominates the dynamics of the metapopulation because the large population it contains is unlikely to go extinct and produces most of the migrants that colonise smaller patches. The so-called mainland–island model describes this situation where the persistence of populations in smaller patches is reliant on migrants from the larger 'mainland' population.

Some of the most detailed 'mainland–island' metapopulation

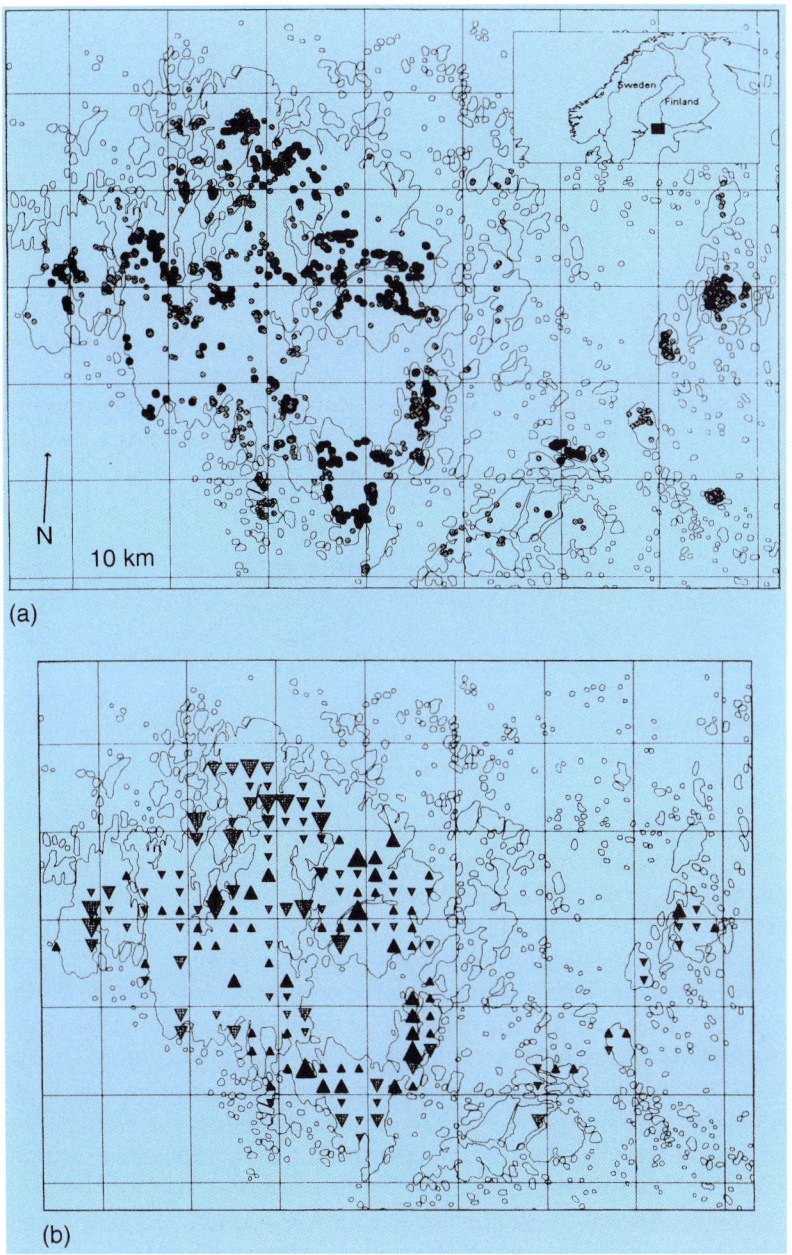

(a)

(b)

Fig. 4.19 (a) Map showing the location of habitat patches on the Åland Islands, Finland, suitable for the Glanville fritillary (*Melitaea cinxia*). Occupied patches in summer 1993 are shown as black dots. (b) Map showing the observed magnitude of population change in each patch between 1993 and 1994. Size of black triangles shows the magnitude of positive increase in population size and grey triangles show decreases in the same way. Reproduced from Hanski (1997) with kind permission of Academic Press.

studies have been carried out on another butterfly, the bay checkerspot (*Euphydryas editha bayensis*) of California. A complex of populations of this species (Fig. 4.20) was studied using mark-release-recapture techniques and revealed that migration was occurring between patches, but was limited. Some 97% of individuals remained within their local population or patch (Ehrlich 1984). Small populations are most likely to go extinct but the empty patches can be rapidly recolonised if a large population occurs less than 5 km away (Harrison *et al.* 1988; Harrison 1989). In this case one 'mainland' population appears to be operating as a

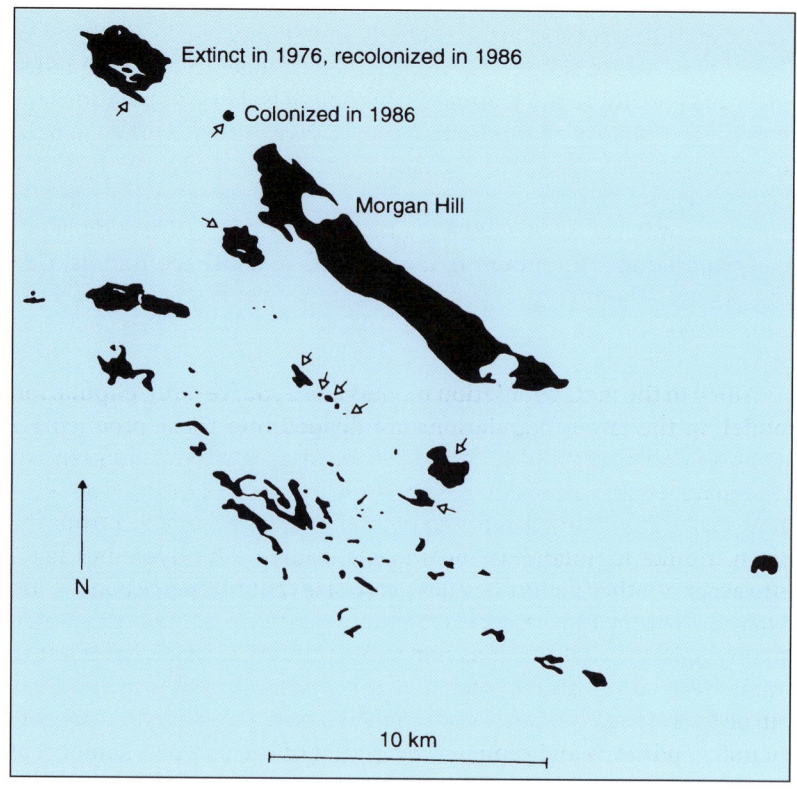

Fig. 4.20 Distribution of habitat patches for the checkerspot butterfly (*Euphydryas editha*) at Morgan Hill, California. This is thought to be a good example of a mainland-island type metapopulation where the persistence of the species is reliant on the persistence of the largest habitat patch. Reproduced from Harrison *et al.* (1988) with kind permission of University of Chicago Press.

source of individuals for surrounding patches, giving the impression of a metapopulation structure. However, this is not a true 'Levins' type metapopulation because (as stated above) even the largest population should have a substantial risk of extinction.

An important conservation aspect of metapopulation theory is that it predicts that colonisation of patches through migration will decrease as patches are removed from an area (through habitat destruction), whilst extinction rates in the remaining patches will stay the same. There will be a point when so many patches have been removed that the metapopulation will collapse and the species, with time, will disappear from every patch without recolonisation occurring. This may explain cases where some species have been recorded as going extinct from their habitats, even though the habitat itself has not changed significantly for many years. The collapse of a metapopulation may take some time depending on the average persistence time of the species in each patch. This is a worrying scenario, since it suggests that many populations of rare and endangered species may be the remnants in the process of metapopulation collapse. Isolated and not self-sustaining, they are what Hanski (1997) terms the 'living dead'.

This scenario seems to fit very well with the rapid decline in populations of several related species of fritillary butterflies in the UK. Monitoring studies on UK butterflies have shown a clear decline in six species of fritillaries starting in the east of England and progressing toward the west. Many populations have apparently gone extinct in the last 30 years despite the fact that the habitat has not radically changed. This may be due to subtle and unidentified changes in habitat quality, but could equally be the gradual extinction of isolated populations following the collapse of the metapopulation structure. Earlier habitat loss, through intensification of agriculture, is probably the ultimate cause, but the long-term effect may be far worse than it currently appears. Similarly, Trine (1998) studied wood thrush (*Hylochicla mustelina*) populations in remaining forest tracts in southern Illinois, USA and found that even the largest existing patches appear to be net population sinks and that even larger patches are needed for this species to persist.

Allied to the metapopulation models is the **source–sink population model**. In the latter, populations are divided into those producing a surplus of offspring and therefore acting as a source of colonisers for other patches, and others that are deficient in offspring and act as a sink in receiving more immigrants compared with emigrants lost from the patch. Unlike mainland–island models, source–sink dynamics takes into account other factors besides patch size that influence population dynamics within a patch, such as habitat quality. In general, larger high-quality habitat patches act as net source of individuals in contrast to small low-quality habitat patches that are net sinks. But some patches can be sinks in one year and sources in another, dependent on environmental conditions and temporal dynamics of the patches. Removal of net source populations may threaten the persistence of the species in the area, but the effect of removal of net sinks is not necessarily negative.

Contraction in species range

As habitat becomes fragmented, populations and metapopulations collapse and the species' range inevitably contracts. It has been argued that populations are most likely to disappear from the edge of the range because conditions here are not optimal. Populations at the edge of a species range tend to be at lower density and experience greater demographic fluctuation than populations at the core of the range. Therefore edge-of-range populations are more likely to go extinct and less likely to be rescued by immigration. Consequently it has been predicted that when fragmentation is experienced throughout its range a species will tend to contract its range towards the core. This hypothesis was tested by Channell & Lomolino (2000) who compared the historical and current ranges of 245 species across a range of taxonomic groups. In contrast to the above prediction most species contracted toward the edges of their range. One explanation for this is that patterns of habitat destruction and other factors such as introduced species (see Chapter 5) are not even but spread along a front in a wave pattern. Species consequently contract as the driving force of population extinction spreads across the landscape. This may explain the fritillary butterfly range contraction from east to west of the UK mentioned above. Habitat destruction and fragmentation has been much greater in the east of the country, whereas the west represents an edge of their range in Europe.

Summary

1. There is an intimate relationship between species and habitat such that if the latter is completely destroyed the former will inevitably go extinct.

2. As a large patch of habitat is eroded by destruction the total area remaining is smaller, the proportion of edge in relation to the total area is greater, any given point within the fragment is on average closer to the edge than before, and on average each fragment is more isolated from other fragments than before. Each one of these has a profound effect on communities, species and their populations.

3. As fragments get smaller the proportion of the habitat that is at the edge increases. Edges contain different communities from the interior because they experience an altered climate, increased incidence of environmental catastrophes, increased incursion of predators and competitors and increased chance of passive emigration from the habitat.

4. The theory of island biogeography predicts that as fragments become smaller and more isolated, species extinctions will be more frequent and colonizations less frequent leading to loss of species richness in remaining habitats.

5. As populations get smaller, the influence of demographic stochasticity (random variation in birth and death rates), genetic stochasticity (random loss of genetic variation and inbreeding), environmental stochasticity (random variation in normal weather patterns) and natural catastrophes (volcanic eruptions, fires, floods, etc.) becomes greater. All of these factors operate to increase the extinction rate of small populations relative to large ones.

6. Metapopulation theory predicts that species can persist as a number of populations connected by limited dispersal between habitat patches provided the probability of extinction is balanced by the probability of colonisation in the complex of patches. Many recent declines in species distribution can be explained by collapse of metapopulation structure.

Discussion points

- What is the most destructive element of habitat fragmentation in terms of its effect on communities of plants and animals?
- Is habitat fragmentation always destructive of biodiversity?
- What are the similarities and differences between the island biogeography and metapopulation theories?
- What is the most important factor causing stochastic extinction?

Further reading

Hanski, I. (1999). *Metapopulation ecology*. Oxford: Oxford University Press.

Laurance, W.F. & Bierregaard, R.O. Jr. (eds) (1997). *Tropical forest remnants: ecology, management and conservation of fragmented communities*. Chicago: University of Chicago Press.

MacArthur, R.H. & Wilson, E.O. (1967). *The theory of island biogeography*. New Jersey: Princeton University Press.

Mallet, J. (1996). The genetics of biological diversity: from varieties to species. Pp. 13–47 in *Biodiversity: biology of numbers and difference*, ed K. Gaston. Oxford: Blackwell.

Web sites

World Wide Fund for Nature: www.wwf-uk.org/

World Conservation Monitoring Centre: www.wcmc.org.uk/

United Nations Environment Programme, Earth Report: www.one-world.Net/tve/earthreport/

Chapter 5

Effects of habitat disturbance

Even when a habitat or ecosystem is not directly destroyed it can be degraded or disturbed as a result of human activities. Our increasing influence over the environment is such that few corners of the earth or depths of the oceans remain that can truly be classified as undisturbed. Disturbance takes many forms; we concentrate here on chemical pollution, introduction of exotic species and diseases, and most recently, genes.

By reading this chapter students will gain an understanding of the range of agents that cause disturbance to natural systems, the mechanisms of disturbance, and be introduced to examples illustrating the variety of impacts disturbance has on species and communities.

Introduction

Ecosystems and the communities they contain can be disturbed by human activity in a variety of ways. The term disturbance is used here to mean the alteration of the natural dynamics of systems. It is distinct from destruction, in that the system remains recognisable, although the level of degradation may be severe. Agents of disturbance include chemical pollutants, introduced species, diseases and genes, each of which are considered below. Disturbance is also manifest on very different scales. Some air pollutants are distributed globally, whereas some heavy metals cause much more localised pollution events. Some species including pathogens have colonised virtually the whole of the land surface along with humans, whilst others have been specifically introduced to small islands with disastrous consequences. Most recently we have the prospect of genetically modified organisms being released into the environment with, as yet, undetermined consequences.

Chemical pollution

Human activity is changing the chemistry of the environment. Chemicals are turning up in places where they do not naturally occur and in concentrations higher than they are naturally found. This is what we normally think of as pollution.

There is a vast amount of data on pollution and pollutants that is beyond the scope of this book. We must therefore confine ourselves to the evidence that pollution is a conservation problem. There is ample evidence that many organisms are affected by pollutants and some examples will suffice to illustrate the general situation.

Example: air pollution and lichens

Lichens are found in some of our harshest natural environments, such as rock surfaces, bare soil and tree trunks. The key to their persistence is that they are not single organisms at all but a partnership between a fungus and an alga. The alga is able to photosynthesise and therefore provides a source of carbon for the fungus that forms the main body of the lichen. Air pollution in cities during the early part of the industrial revolution brought about the first observations on the adverse effects of pollutants on wildlife. Among these was the observation that lichens once common in the centre of cities were rapidly disappearing. However, detailed research and monitoring only started in the 1950s when the effects of heavy industrial pollution were reaching their peak, nevertheless mapping has since shown that there is a well-established correlation between the distribution and diversity of lichens and the concentration of airborne pollutants. The most significant pollutant is sulphur dioxide arising from the combustion of fossil fuels. This reactive chemical is generally toxic to plants but lichens appear extremely sensitive and are adversely affected at sulphur dioxide concentrations of 0.05 parts per million or even lower. Interestingly studies on the establishment and age of lichens were made possible by studies of their distribution on gravestones that are conveniently distributed in cemeteries throughout urban areas. The relationship between sulphur dioxide pollution and lichen occurrence is so strong that the lichens have themselves been used as measures of air pollution. Since different species show different sensitivities to sulphur dioxide (mostly in the range 30–170 (g/m^3), the presence or absence of particular species can indicate recent sulphur dioxide levels (Ferry *et al.* 1973). Lichens have recently been used as indicators of air pollution to correlate the latter with the incidence of lung cancer in humans in the Veneto region of Italy (Cislaghi & Nimis 1997). This is a chilling reminder that many pollutants that harm wildlife also harm us (Fig. 5.1).

Example: acid rain and lake pollution

Natural rainwater is mildly acid ($\sim$ pH 5.6) as a result of the combination of carbon dioxide and water in the atmosphere forming carbonic acid. However measurements of rainwater acidity around industrial areas of Europe and North America have recorded pH values below 4.5, giving rise to the commonly used term 'acid rain'. The cause of increasing acidity is the increased release of sulphur dioxide and nitrogen oxides into the atmosphere from the combustion of fossil fuels. These substances tend to combine with water in the atmosphere using the energy from sunlight to form sulphuric and nitric acid. Acid rain has

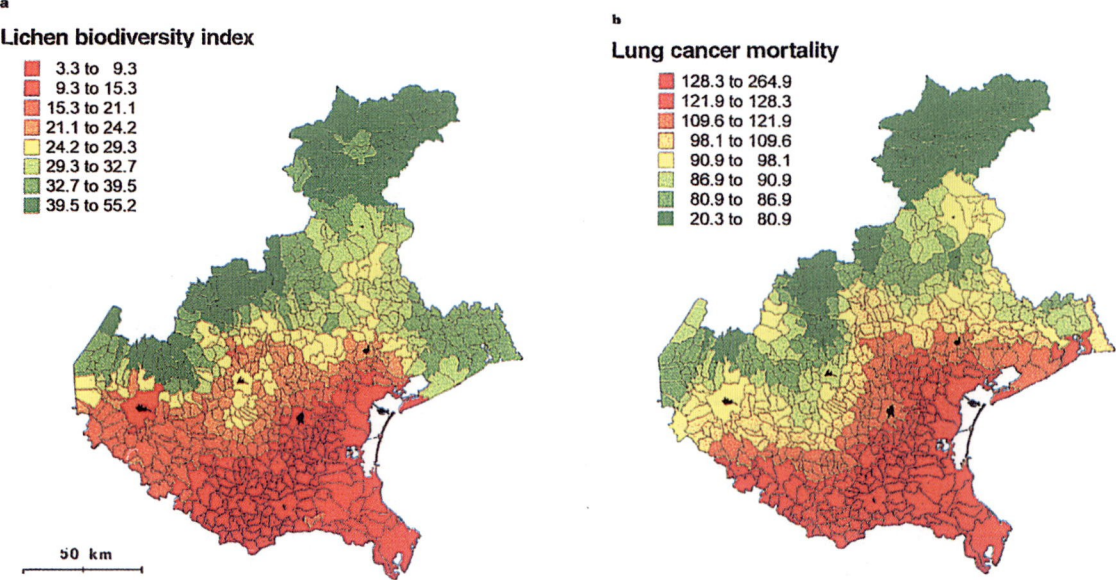

a

Lichen biodiversity index

- 3.3 to 9.3
- 9.3 to 15.3
- 15.3 to 21.1
- 21.1 to 24.2
- 24.2 to 29.3
- 29.3 to 32.7
- 32.7 to 39.5
- 39.5 to 55.2

50 km

b

Lung cancer mortality

- 128.3 to 264.9
- 121.9 to 128.3
- 109.6 to 121.9
- 98.1 to 109.6
- 90.9 to 98.1
- 86.9 to 90.9
- 80.9 to 86.9
- 20.3 to 80.9

Fig. 5.1 Comparison of the distribution of diversity among lichens and the distribution of the incidence of lung cancer in young male residents in the region of Veneto, northern Italy. Reproduced from Cislaghi & Nimis (1987) with kind permission of the authors and Macmillan Magazines Ltd.

had a dramatic effect on lake systems downwind of industrial sources on a global scale (Fig. 5.2). One of the worst affected areas is Scandinavia, which has experienced widespread acidification of its lakes. The lowered pH has both direct and indirect effects on the lake ecosystem that can be difficult to separate, but the overall ecological effects are most important. Probably the most damaging is the increased solubility of some metals at low pH. Aluminium, iron, copper, zinc, nickel, lead and cadmium are all leached out of surrounding soils by acidic runoff and accumulate to toxic concentrations in the lake water. The planktonic organisms in lakes are particularly pH sensitive and the dominant species quickly change as the pH goes down and thus community structure can be fundamentally altered. Most fish disappear at pH values of less than 5.0 and the widespread loss of fish from Scandinavian lakes has been the most obvious result of this phenomenon. Over the last 40 years, some 20 000 lakes have lost their fish in Sweden alone.

Example: organochlorine pesticides and biomagnification

The enormous advantages of the use of effective pesticides in agriculture and public health led to their widespread acceptance in crop protection and pest control. Their use spread rapidly during the middle of the twentieth century, bringing about rapid declines in the incidence of insect-borne diseases such as malaria and playing an integral part in the agricultural revolution, which saw dramatic increases in crop yields. Initial signs that these gains were to be short-lived were quickly noted in the rapid rise in insect resistance to the pesticides, and this necessitated ever increasing dosages being used to gain the same effect. Malaria came back and so did the crop pests.

Public awareness of the impact of pesticide pollution on wildlife was only raised after the publication of Rachel Carson's book, *Silent Spring* in

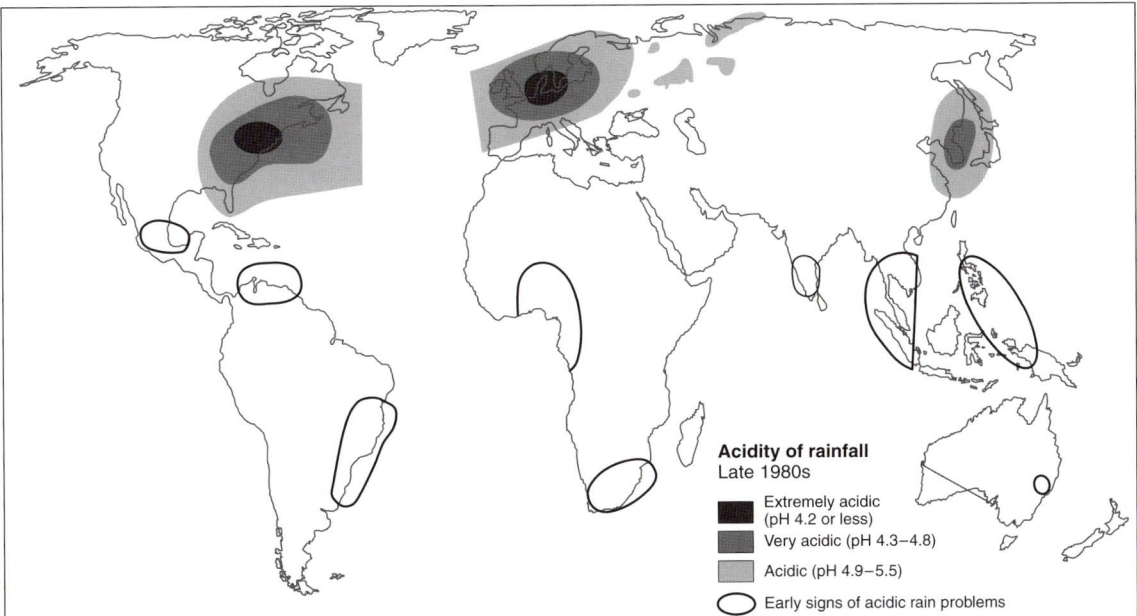

Fig. 5.2 Global distribution of acid rain showing clear relationship with major areas of industrialisation. Source: *The State of the Environment Atlas*, Penguin Books, 1995.

1962. Carson used the image of springtime without birdsong to put over concerns caused by early evidence that the use of organochlorine pesticides in agriculture and in control of insect vectors of disease was threatening bird populations by its transfer through the food chain. In other words, birds were being poisoned through eating insects (or their predators) containing organochlorines. The first organochlorines to be used, such as DDT (dichlorodiphenyltrichloroethane), are very effective killers of insects, but they are also toxic to other animals (non-target species). Most organochlorine compounds share four features that, although originally thought to make them effective pesticides, account for their dangerous status as environmental pollutants:

1. their chemical stability, which means they persist in the environment for long periods (DDT has a half-life of 10–15 years);
2. their high mobility in the environment; DDT is found in measurable quantities in rainwater and in prevailing winds;
3. their high solubility in lipids (including animal fats), which means that animals readily take them up and store them in fatty tissue (DDT is probably measurable in your body fat);
4. their toxicity and biological activity.

One of the best known examples of the devastating side-effects of organochlorine use arose from the application of a closely related pesticide, DDD to control midges that have aquatic larval stages. Midges were regarded as a nuisance at Clear Lake, California (a popular recreational area) and DDD was added directly to the water at 14 parts per billion (ppb) to kill the aquatic larvae in 1949. This was highly successful, reducing the midges by 99%, but they came back and treatment was repeated in 1954 at 20 ppb. Following this, 100 grebes (fish-eating birds) were found dead on the lake. The treatment was repeated again in 1957 and more grebes were subsequently found dead. An investigation in to the link between these events found that the body fat of the grebes contained 1600 parts per million (ppm) of DDD, 80 000 times greater than the concentration applied to the water.

Animals at the top of the food chain are now known to be particularly vulnerable to organochlorine poisoning because of the combined effects of bioaccumulation (the accumulation and concentration in tissues of a substance from the physical environment) and biomagnification (concentration of a substance in tissue through ingestion and transfer up through the food chain). Organochlorines are stored in the fat tissue of animals and will accumulate as the animal eats its contaminated prey. A top predator, such as a bird of prey will in turn eat prey items that already carry high doses of pesticides and so accumulate even higher concentrations. It is not surprising, therefore, that the first effects of organochlorines on bird populations were seen in these top predators.

However, the levels of the organochlorine pesticides such as DDT that accumulated during their widespread use were often not high enough to kill birds of prey outright, but instead they affected their breeding performance. During the 1960s a decline in numbers of some species of birds of prey was detected, and found to be due to a failure of breeding pairs to produce young. A species that underwent one of the most dramatic declines was the peregrine falcon (*Falco peregrinus*). Reports of declining numbers of this species came simultaneously from many countries, including Britain, Sweden, Germany, Poland and the USA. Ecological study revealed that many nests were found to contain broken eggs. Subsequent analyses of eggs of a related species, the sparrowhawk (*Accipiter nisus*), from museum collections showed a consistent eggshell thickness until 1946 after which there was a marked decline (Fig. 5.3). This phenomenon has subsequently been linked with organochlorine accumulation (Newton 1979).

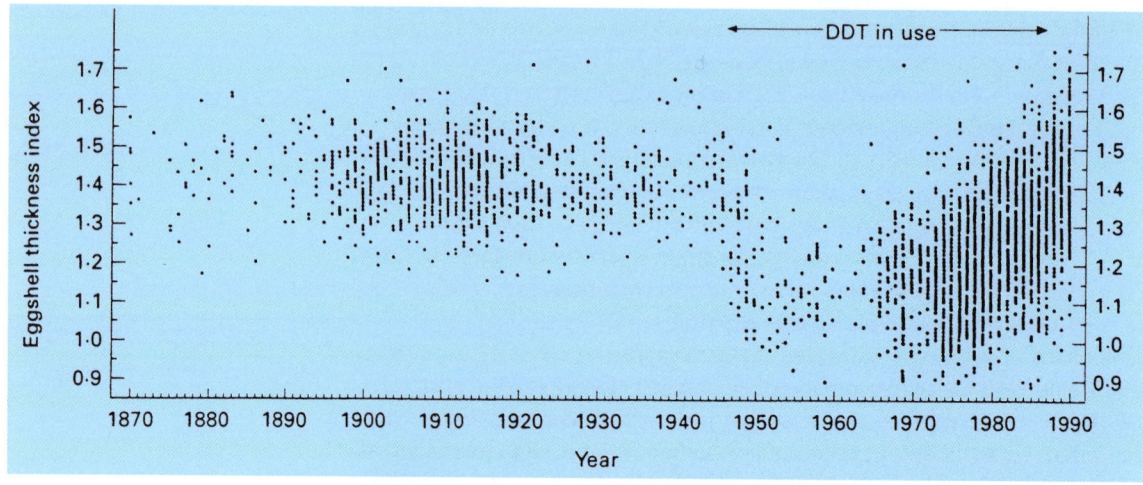

Fig. 5.3   Change in eggshell thickness in British sparrowhawks (*Accipiter nisus*) over the period 1870–1990. Note the rapid drop in thickness during the 1940s when organchlorines entered common use and the subsequent gradual recovery from 1970s following increasing restriction on use. Redrawn from Newton (1986) with kind permission of T. & A. D. Poyser.

Experiments with various birds of prey and insecticide-treated prey, showed that there was a relationship between the concentration of insecticide in the diet and the thickness of eggshells. The eggs were simply getting accidentally broken causing high chick mortality.

The sublethal effects of pesticides on organisms may yet be causing profound changes in populations worldwide (Box 5.1).

Box 5.1 | What is causing worldwide amphibian decline?

Biologists studying amphibians (herpetologists) have noticed a marked decline in populations of many species at a number of sites worldwide. This has led to speculation that some global human-mediated factor is threatening amphibian survival. The declines are most clearly evident in upland areas of the tropics in sites as widely dispersed as Australia, Costa Rica, the Andes, and the Atlantic coast of Brazil. Following a 5-year study of amphibian populations in Las Tablas, Costa Rica, Lips (1998) drew together data from studies going on at other sites and examined the evidence for different causes of decline.

Habitat destruction had undoubtedly been a factor in past declines, but was apparently unrelated to the rapid local declines that were being experienced. Introduced fish species have been suggested as a cause, but declines in amphibians that were safe from fish predation (such as those that breed in fish-free water bodies like bromeliad stems or isolated forest pools) had been recorded as equally severe as those susceptible to predation. Mortality due to disturbance by the researchers counting the amphibians was also ruled out for a similar reason; those being handled or disturbed had not declined at a faster rate than those not handled or disturbed. Although both ultraviolet radiation and water acidification have been shown to affect amphibian survival, there was no evidence for either being the cause of decline in the field. Changes in the pattern or seasonality of rainfall was also ruled out because the groups of species one would have expected to have been most affected (those breeding in seasonal pools) were affected less than those breeding in streams.

There are two possible causes for which there seems to be some circumstantial evidence. First, environmental contamination by agrochemicals is known to affect amphibian reproduction (they are particularly efficient at absorbing chemicals from the environment since they have permeable skin) and the use of pesticides is so widespread that all amphibians are likely to be exposed. Second, some form of pathogen outbreak is supported by the fact that many of the recorded declines appear to have occurred in waves, as if an agent was being passed through the community. These two possibilities may be acting synergistically, such that exposure to chemical pollutants lowers the immunity of amphibians to infection by pathogens. Further work is urgently needed to enable appropriate conservation action to be taken.

Even when pesticides are not directly toxic to species they may have an indirect impact on populations by removing their food supply. The grey partridge (*Perdix perdix*) is a ground-dwelling species of arable ecosystems. As adults, they feed mainly on seeds, but the chicks require higher-protein diets and feed extensively on insects. The removal of these insects through the widespread use of insecticides in arable systems has led to high chick mortality through starvation and a consequent rapid decline in grey partridge numbers in the UK from 25 down to 5 pairs/km^2 over 30 years (Potts 1986).

Example: eutrophication of water bodies

Freshwater rivers and lakes have not only been assaulted by toxic chemical inputs, they have also received increasing levels of nutrients through sewage discharge and fertiliser runoff from agricultural fields. Many of our lakes and rivers are naturally oligotrophic (nutrient poor) and the communities they sustain are characteristic in having limited biomass as a result of the paucity of nutrients. This can change dramatically if nutrient inputs are increased, completely changing the dominant species present at all trophic levels, from bacteria and algae up to the flowering plants and fish. The two major nutrients responsible for eutrophication are nitrogen and phosphorus in the form of nitrates and phosphates respectively. The latter is particularly responsible for the rapid growth of blue-green algae (cyanobacteria) in some water bodies, leading to so-called algal blooms that discolour the water and, in some cases, render it toxic to animals using it as drinking water, as well as causing allergic reactions. Another major problem with eutrophic water bodies is that the increased biomass leads to an increased demand for oxygen, which can cause anoxic conditions in the water resulting in widespread fish kills. A direct result is the decline of many species characteristic of oligotrophic water.

Small water bodies are most at risk and can rapidly change in nutrient status threatening the native flora and fauna. But even very large water bodies such as the Great Lakes Erie and Ontario are experiencing measurable eutrophication. It is even possible that recent algal blooms being reported in our oceans are a direct result of increasing nutrient loads.

Introduction of exotic species

As we saw in Chapter 3, Humans have spread across the globe and have, either deliberately or accidentally, carried with them a wide range of species. The introduction of exotic species into some areas has had a devastating impact on the native biodiversity. Native species most vulnerable to the impact of exotic species introductions are those which have evolved in isolation from high levels of competition and predation. If we re-examine the global pattern of species extinction considered in Chapter 3 (Fig. 3.10), it is evident that the majority of recently extinct species inhabited small isolated oceanic islands. Some of these, such as the dodo (*Raphus cuculatus*), were early targets for sailors as much-needed protein, but many more, particularly smaller flightless birds, were victims of species introduced by man, accidentally or deliberately. Some are opportunist predators such as rats or cats, and others competitors such as pigs and goats that would have fundamentally changed the ecosystem. Before colonisation, the island of Mauritius supported a minimum of 23 species of endemic (species confined to a given area such as an island) land birds, 12 reptiles and two fruit bats, today these numbers have been reduced to nine, five and one respectively.

Deliberate introductions

The deliberate introduction of domestic pets such as cats and dogs and farm animals such as pigs and goats, to islands with few or no comparable natural predators and competitor herbivores, has led to the decline of much of their native fauna and flora. Small mammals and birds may have no fear of such predators and plants have no defensive mechanisms against voracious herbivores. They are effectively naïve of the threat to them and are often referred to as 'naïve prey'. A significant proportion of recorded oceanic island extinctions is probably due to such deliberate introductions. It isn't just small isolated islands that are at risk as some of the following examples illustrate.

Example: introduction of goats to St Helena

The island of St Helena is one of the most isolated in the world being located in the mid-Atlantic, almost equidistant from Africa and South America at 15° south of the equator. It was strategically important in the early days of exploration and for trade by sailing ship and it was colonised at this time. Goats were introduced in 1513 and quickly became semi-wild, ranging across the whole island, providing a ready source of food for the residents and regular seagoing visitors. Unfortunately botanists did not reach the island until 300 years later when the flora had already been radically altered. Even so, 46 species endemic to the island were recorded, of which seven are now extinct. We will never know how many others were driven to extinction before they were recorded. Goats have caused similar damage on many other oceanic islands and are good candidates for second place behind humans as agents of biodiversity loss.

Example: introduction of rabbits and foxes to Australia

The deliberate introduction of rabbits for food and foxes for sport hunting (and to control the rabbits) has presented the native marsupial fauna with both a formidable competitor and an efficient predator, of which they were completely naïve. The result of this has been a rapid spread of rabbits across the country to the extent that they are now serious pests that require highly expensive control measures including mile upon mile of fencing. Foxes have tended to follow, and many of the ground-dwelling marsupials have proved easy prey and consequently declined dramatically. Some, such as the burrowing rat kangaroo (*Bettongia lesueur*), to the extent that they are now found only on offshore islands that are free from these introduced species (Fig. 5.4).

Example: introduction of Nile perch and water hyacinth to Lake Victoria

Perhaps the most dramatic and best-documented negative effect of an introduced species on an indigenous fauna is the case of the deliberate introduction of the Nile perch (*Lates nilotica*) to Lake Victoria in East Africa. Lake Victoria is the world's largest tropical lake (69000 km^2). Until recently the cichlid fishes of the lake formed a highly diversified community of 300+ species, 99% endemic, showing remarkable

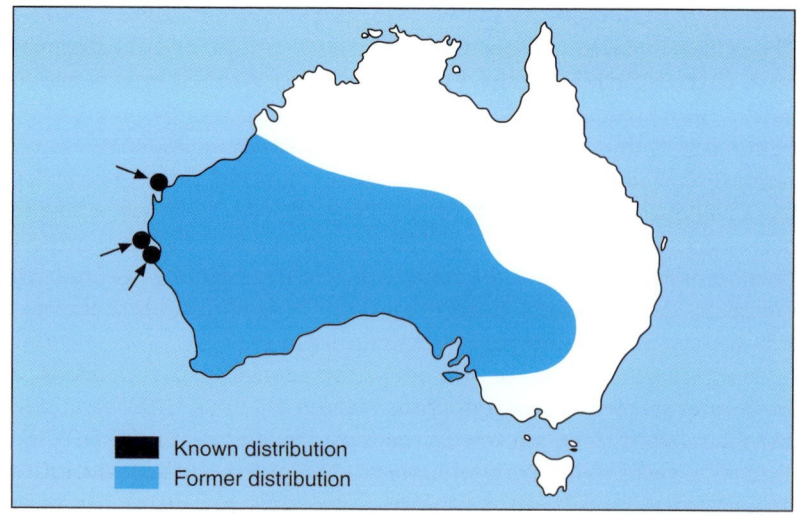

Fig. 5.4 Many marsupials such as the burrowing rat kangaroo (*Bettongia lesueur*) have been driven to extinction on mainland Australia by introduced predators and competitors. They now survive only on offshore islands that are free from such introductions.

Known distribution
Former distribution

adaptive radiation into different forms filling many ecological roles (Witte *et al.* 1992*a*). Nile perch are large predatory fish and were introduced to the lake in the 1950s and 60s because of their value to fisheries. Only in 1980s was a population explosion of the species noted and its impact on the native fishes recorded (Goldschmidt *et al.* 1993). Subsequent studies have shown that the Nile perch was eating the cichlid fish, reducing their density a thousand-fold and driving an estimated 200 species to extinction (Witte *et al* 1992*b*). But the truth is probably not as simple as this. Many of the native fish feed on algae and benefit from the frequent algal blooms that occur in the lake. A reduction in the number of algae-eating fish, together with progressive eutrophication of the water due to increasing human activity around the lake, increased the frequency of algal blooms and decreased the oxygen levels in deep water. This may have caused further declines in deep-water cichlids. The subsequent introduction of the water hyacinth (*Eichhornia crassipes*) from South America, as an attractive ornamental plant, enabled its explosive spread across the surface of the nutrient-rich water to the extent that many bays are completely covered in the weed, making them unsuitable as breeding areas for many native fish.

Accidental introductions

At the same time as the deliberate introduction of many of our most favourite species, humans have also managed, quite accidentally, to introduce some of our least favourite wherever we have been. The most successful vertebrates among these are probably the rats (*Rattus* sp.), which have long been transported around the globe on ships and found suitable habitat in most ports of call. Rats are efficient opportunist omnivores and have undoubtedly had a profound impact on the fauna and flora of islands in particular, both through competition and predation. They are well adapted to survival among human habitation and in disturbed ecosystems, but they are also able to venture into the edge of natural habitats and exploit food sources such as the eggs and chicks of ground-nesting birds.

Introduced species do not have to be malicious predators to be a danger to the native species, they can equally be effective competitors for resources as the following examples illustrate.

Zebra mussels in North America

Amongst the most serious accidental introductions currently occurring are those caused by the transfer of organisms in the ballast tanks of ocean-going ships. To provide stability, ships can take on large quantities of water together with its flora and fauna in one harbour, sail halfway around the world and eject it into another. This has no doubt led to considerable homogenisation of coastal marine communities. However, one of the most dramatic examples of this mode of transport concerns a freshwater species. The introduction of the zebra mussel (*Dreissena polymorpha*) to North America was first recorded in the Great Lakes in 1988. These freshwater molluscs attach themselves to hard surfaces and cause major disruption of water supply because of their habit of attaching themselves to the insides of pipes and blocking them. The first invaders were most probably transported in ballast from a ship leaving a European freshwater port. Given favourable conditions the zebra mussel can multiply rapidly and colonise areas, forming dense beds, changing the relative abundance of the native benthic fauna and potentially changing the dynamics of the ecosystem by consuming large quantities of the phytoplankton (Nalepa & Schloesser 1993). They are now spreading rapidly around the Great Lakes area threatening the water supply and the native freshwater communities (Johnson & Padilla 1996).

Africanized bees in South and Central America

As a result of the poor performance of European honeybees (*Apis mellifera ligustica*) at producing honey in South America, African honeybees (*A. mellifera scutellata*) were imported in to Brazil in 1956 for an experiment to try and produce a successful honey-producing tropical strain. The aggressive nature of the African bees was already well known and they were confined to hives in screened cages for experimental breeding trials. However, where an accident can happen it usually does and sure enough, on one occasion the next year the screens were inexplicably removed and a number of queens escaped.

The African bees soon began to interbreed with local colonies of the European honeybee producing an aggressive strain that quickly spread from the point of release. The africanized bees, or 'killer' bees as they have come to be known, are very aggressive in defence of their hives, with victims of attack experiencing 10 times more stings than from European honeybees. Africanized bees also swarm more often and commonly settle close to human residences. Consequently, the incidence of bee attacks on humans and domestic livestock has risen significantly as these bees colonise new areas. For example, 38 human deaths have been documented in Mexico since africanized bees entered the country in 1986.

The phenomenal spread of this strain has continued at an average rate of 400 km per year across the continent and up into Central America (Fig. 5.5). The first record of migration into the USA came in 1990 in Texas, although they had already accidentally been brought in

Texas

Sonora
Baja California
Chihuahua
Durango
1991
1990
1989
1988
1987
Y
C QR
Belize
1986
1985
Honduras
Chiapas
Guatemala
El Salvador
Nicaragua
Costa Rica
Panama
1984
1983
1982 1980
1979
1978
1976 Guyana
Surinam
1975 French Guiana
1974
Venezuela
1982
1983
1982
1981
1971
Equador
1980
1979
1978
1980
Colombia
1968
1967
Peru
Bolivia
Brazil
1966
1957
1965
1963
Paraguay
Argentina
1980 1975
1983
Uruguay
Chile

30°
15°
0°
15°
30°

Fig. 5.5 Spread of africanized bees since their accidental release in Brazil. Reproduced from Krebs (1994) with kind permission of Harper Collins.

to California by ship in the mid 1980s! Beside the danger the africanized bees pose, they have also wiped out established bee colonies and decimated the honey-producing industry. How much farther north they will spread will probably depend on a number of factors including their cold tolerance. How much damage they will do to the honey-producing industry and to the efficient pollination of crops is unknown. The USA harvests an estimated $9.3 billion in pollinated crops and some $200 million in beeswax and honey each year. What is arguably much more serious from a conservation point of view is the potential negative effect on pollination of wild species in the megadiverse area of the Neotropics. If the africanized bee is outcompeting and displacing some more specialised native bee species many plants may be at risk.

Grey squirrel in the UK

The UK has only one native species of squirrel, the red squirrel (*Sciurus vulgaris*), which formerly occupied most types of woodland throughout mainland Britain. At the beginning of the twentieth century the alien grey squirrel (*Sciurus carolinensis*) was deliberately introduced from North America, but it was never intended that it should spread throughout the UK. The original location into which it was introduced and from which the invasion began was probably Woburn Abbey, about 40 miles north of London. The grey squirrel was able to exploit efficiently the broadleaved woodlands and parkland of the area, which is similar to its native habitat, and rapidly spread throughout England and Wales and up to southern Scotland. At the same time the native red squirrel has drastically declined in distribution to a few scattered locations in upland England and Wales, some offshore islands such as the Isle of Wight where the grey squirrel is still absent, and to its stronghold in Scotland where the woodland is dominated by Scots Pine (*Pinus sylvestris*). Despite the coincident timing of the invader's spread and the native's decline there has been surprising controversy over whether this is really cause and effect. A study by Reynolds (1985) on the geographical replacement of the red squirrel by the grey in eastern England, concluded that the interaction between the two species could only provide a partial explanation for the red's decline. In some areas reds disappeared before greys were recorded and in others the two species coexisted for up to 16 years. Additionally, a poxvirus disease which infected the red but not the grey squirrel was put forward as an alternative (but not mutually exclusive) hypothesis to that based on competition, explaining the geographical replacement. A later study by Okubo *et al.* (1989) showed that the changes in range of the two species were consistent with a simple diffusion–competition model that suggests that as the grey squirrel increases in abundance and moves into new habitats it is competing with the red and causing local extinction. It is now widely accepted that the grey is outcompeting the red directly by reducing juvenile red survival and/or indirectly through differential disease resistance in the broadleaved woodlands, but that the red is holding its own in purely coniferous forests. Interestingly, in North America, both species also occur and live in separate niches, the grey in broadleaved forests and the red in coniferous forests and their ranges rarely overlap. UK conservationists now accept that the red squirrel will not recover its former range whilst the grey remains and that there is no prospect of the grey ever being eliminated.

What sorts of species are successful invaders?

Not all species that get transported to new areas will successfully invade and establish themselves as the examples above have. There are a number of characteristics of species that make them good invaders:

1. species with a high reproductive rate that can quickly build up a large population size under favourable conditions;
2. generalist species with broad habitat requirements and diet that are likely to be able to find somewhere suitable to live and something suitable to eat;

3. good dispersers that can travel across the new area and find suitable habitats.

What types of places are likely to be invaded?

Not all places are equally vulnerable to invasion. There are a number of characteristics of places that may make it easier for introduced species to become established:

1. early successional areas or disturbed areas with empty niches tend to have resources that are unexploited and available for immigrating species with little or no competition;
2. remote islands with low taxonomic diversity are vulnerable because few species have been able to colonise naturally and communities and food webs are often simple with potential empty niche space to be exploited;
3. remote islands with no predators and naïve prey (including plants poorly adapted to herbivory) providing an easily exploited food source.

Hawaii: islands under siege

According to the above criteria, small oceanic islands such as the Hawaiian group are most vulnerable to invading species (they are both remote and often have disturbed, early successional habitat due to volcanic activity); so do the facts support the theory? Vitousek (1988) reviewed the effects of introduced species on the native fauna and flora. There are an estimated 1765 species of vascular plant native to Hawaii and 94–98% of them are endemic. More than 4600 species of vascular plant have been introduced to the islands, some 700 of these have naturalised and are maintaining wild populations. Approximately 200 endemic species are already extinct and a further 800 are endangered. An estimated 86 species of land birds were present on Hawaii 2000 years ago and 68 of these were endemic passerines (songbirds). Shortly after this, when the Polynesians colonised the islands, around 45 species went extinct and a further 11 have been driven to extinction since European colonisation in the eighteenth century. At least 50 alien passerines have been introduced and established on the islands since 1780.

The most diverse taxa have not escaped either. There are 5000 recorded species of Hawaiian arthropods and probably an equal number of undescribed species. Over 3200 alien species have been introduced, most accidentally, but many are still being introduced for use as 'environment friendly' biocontrol agents. Some 2500 of these aliens have become established residents, but their impact is less easy to assess than for the better known taxonomic groups (Howarth 1990). Many native invertebrate species are known to be declining and it is certain that many native species have been lost without ever being described. Englund (1999) has shown that the introduction of a variety of alien fish to the island of Oahu has led to the extirpation of the native damselfly fauna (*Megalagrion* sp.) from most lowland streams. The larvae of these damselflies are naïve to predators such as the introduced fish and tend to swim to the surface when disturbed, making them easy targets. The invasion of Hawaii has been so complete that most low-elevation areas are now dominated by alien flora and fauna.

Invasion and establishment patterns

Invasions usually start with just a few individuals and the probability of survival of such a small population in a new environment is very small. They are much more likely to go extinct due to environmental, demographic and genetic stochasticity. If the population does survive it will first go through an establishment phase in which population size increases but is very little in terms of range expansion. Once established, individuals may emigrate from their natal patch to form new populations in what is called the expansion phase. This then continues until all the available habitat is colonised and the species enters a saturation phase. Shigesada & Kawasaki (1997) recognised three types of establishment phase shown in Fig. 5.6. The first is simple linear

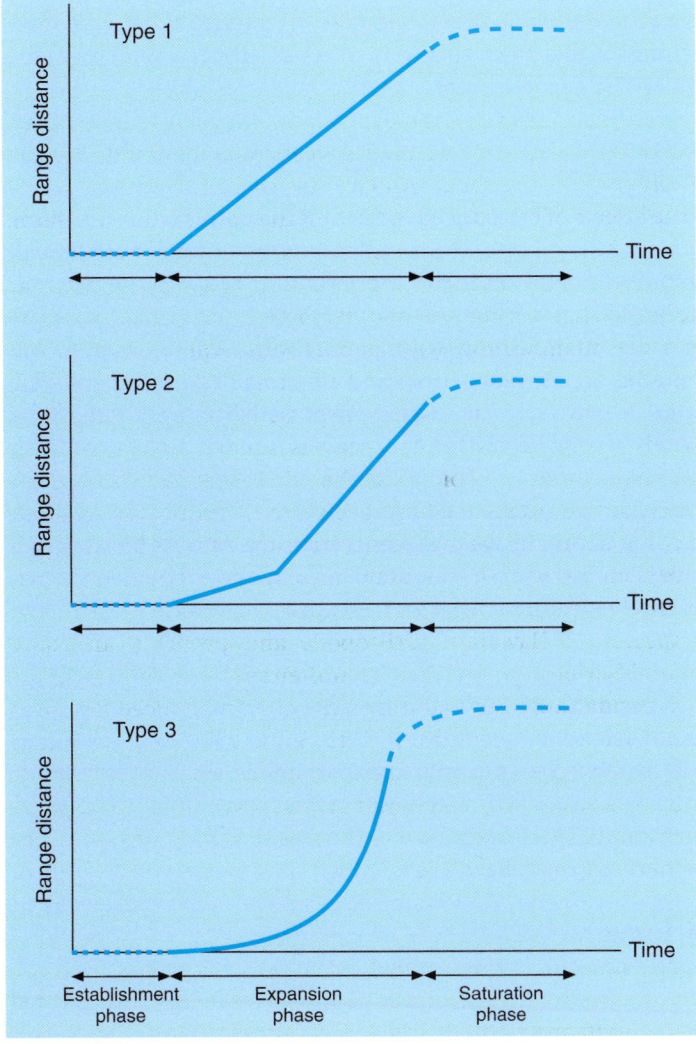

Fig. 5.6 Three hypothesised patterns of range expansion pattern. Each has an establishment and saturation phase (dotted lines), but they differ in their expansion patterns. Type 1 shows linear expansion; Type 2 is biphasic with a switch from a lower to higher rate of expansion; Type 3 shows a continually accelerating rate of expansion. Reproduced from Shigesada & Kawasaki (1997) with kind permission of Oxford University Press.

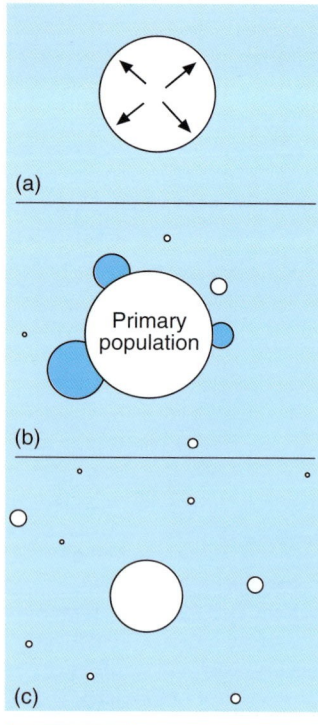

Fig. 5.7 a–c Three possible spatial patterns of range expansion. (a) Continual expansion at the margins of the original founder population. (b) Founder population expansion with satellite populations founding and coalescing. (c) Founder expansion with long-range dispersal and independent expansion of subsequent founder populations. Reproduced from Shigesada & Kawasaki (1997) with kind permission of Oxford University Press.

expansion where the range expansion continues at a constant rate; this pattern was followed by the muskrat (*Ondatra zibethica*) when introduced to Europe from North America in 1905. The second has two phases of expansion, the first relatively slow and the second fast, as exhibited by the European starling (*Sturnus vulgaris*) when introduced to the USA in the 1880s. The third shows a rate that is continually increasing with time, a pattern followed by cheatgrass (*Bromus tectorum*) introduced to the western USA during the late nineteenth century. The differences in these patterns may be explained by the dispersal characteristics of the species concerned (Fig. 5.7). The linear expansion may be the result of species always settling near the home range of their parents in which case the range gradually expands its boundaries as in Fig. 5.7a. Biphasic expansion may result from the same phenomenon, with the addition of some individuals that undergo longer-range dispersal to set up separate colonies that eventually merge with the founding population. A continually increasing rate of expansion may be explained by species with individuals that undergo long-range expansion to set up new colonies essentially independent from the founders, that in turn act as a source of further emigrants to disperse further afield.

Difficulties in eradication of invaders: the example of the Norway rat

Norway rats (*Rattus norvegicus*) have been very successful in following humans around the globe and have colonised many small islands. This species colonised Frégate island in the Seychelles in 1995 (Thorsen *et al.* 2000). The island has a unique fauna, including the critically endangered Seychelles magpie-robin (*Copsychus sechellarum*). An attempt was made to eradicate the newly arrived and expanding rat population during the following year, using poison baits and rat traps. Unfortunately several Seychelles magpie-robins died due to secondary rodenticide poisoning and the eradication attempt had to be abandoned. Rats have been eradicated from islands as large as 1965 hectares in size, but it is clearly an intensive operation that has its hazards. Not surprisingly, Thorsen et al. recommend priority should be given to prevention of invasion rather than cure.

Introduction of disease

A subset of the species we introduce are pathogens, such as some fungi, bacteria and viruses, which can have a devastating impact on native species that may have no resistance to them and quickly succumb. The following serve as examples.

Example: chestnut blight

The American chestnut tree (*Castanea dentata*) was formerly common and locally dominant in the forests of the eastern USA and formed almost continuous cover from Maine to Georgia (Newhouse 1990). This large, relatively fast-growing hardwood tree was a good source of timber

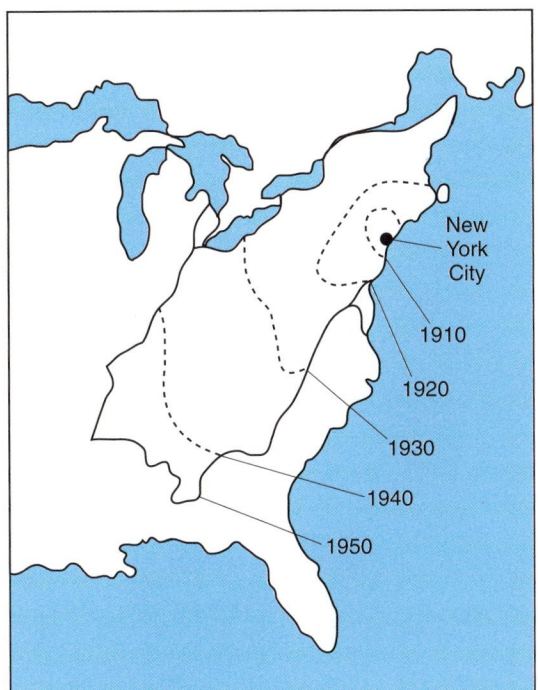

Fig. 5.8 Spread of chestnut blight through the forests of eastern USA Reproduced from Newhouse (1990) with kind permission of Gabor Kiss.

and firewood, and was important for the ecology of the region in being host to a number of specialist insect herbivores and providing seasonal food in the form of nuts to many vertebrates. In 1904 a fungal disease called blight was noted on trees in the New York Zoological Park. The fungal pathogen, which was identified as *Cryphonectria parasitica*, enters the tree through wounds in the bark, spreads and eventually kills the tree. The American chestnut has no defence against the disease, which rapidly spread, and had been recorded throughout the entire range of the tree by 1950. Virtually the entire species, numbering millions of trees, was wiped out (Fig. 5.8).

An epidemiological study of the pathogen discovered that it was originally imported on timber from Asian chestnut trees. Asian species appear to be resistant to the fungus suggesting that they have been exposed to it for a long period of time. Despite the best efforts of plant pathologists to try and find some way of conferring resistance to the disease in the native trees, the American chestnut is now confined to a few specimen trees outside of its natural range. Unfortunately this incident happened too early for the impact of the complete removal of a key species on the ecosystem to be monitored.

The chestnut blight fungus subsequently infected European chestnut trees (*C. sativa*) being first recorded in Italy in 1938. The spread of chestnut blight in Europe has been less extreme because the European chestnut appears to be more resistant to the disease.

Example: Dutch elm disease in the UK

Dutch elm disease infects trees of the genus *Ulmus* and is caused by a microscopic fungus *Ceratocystis ulmi*. The fungus is spread passively by

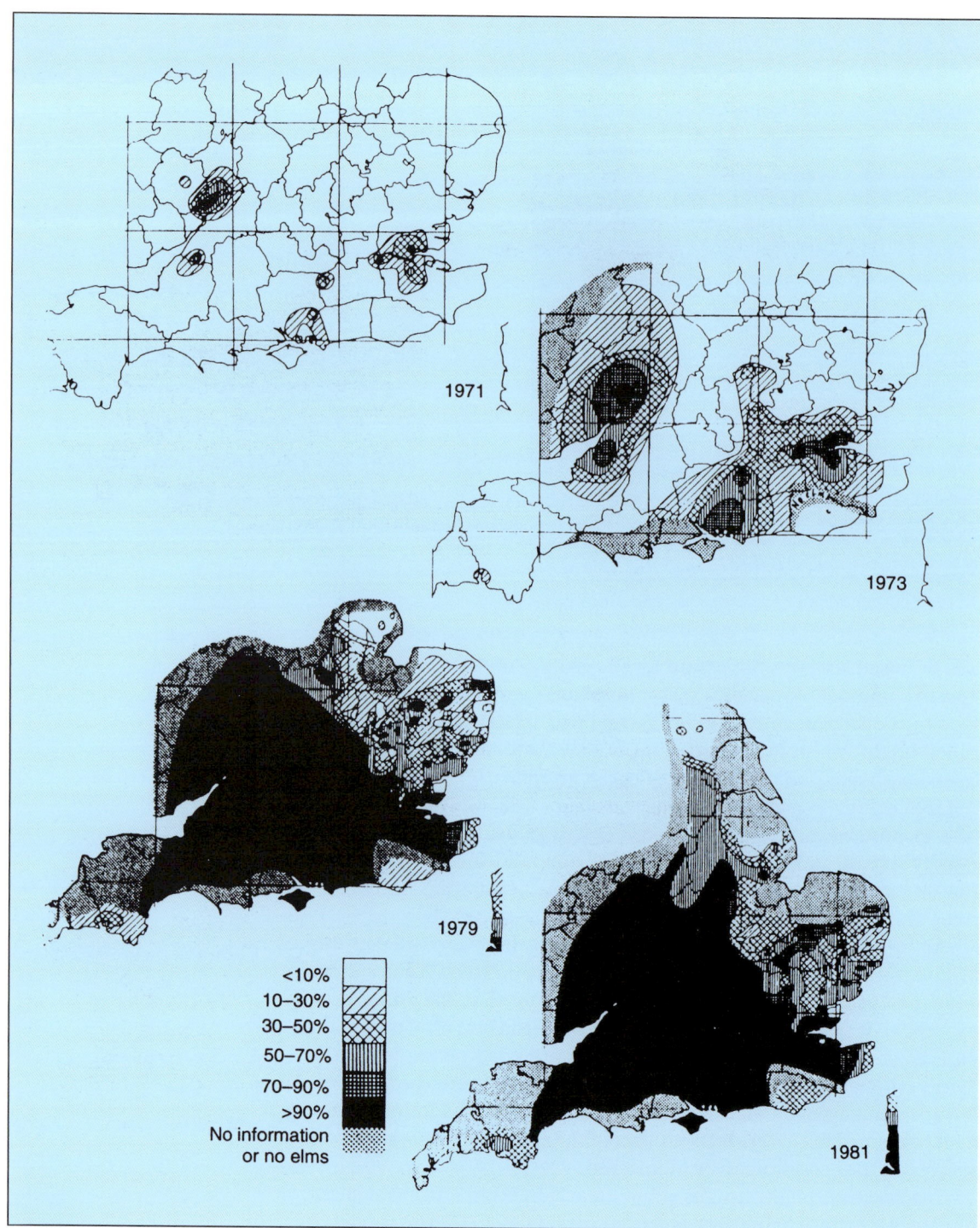

Fig. 5.9 Spread of Dutch elm disease in the UK. Reproduced from Rackham (1986) with kind permission of J.M. Dent & Sons.

two species of elm bark beetle (*Scolytus scolytus* and *S. multistriatus*). They carry spores attached to their body from one tree to the next where the fungus infects the outer wood of larger trees. The latest epidemic of the disease in the UK started in 1965 around the town of Tewkesbury and spread rapidly during the 1970s so that elms suffered a massive decline

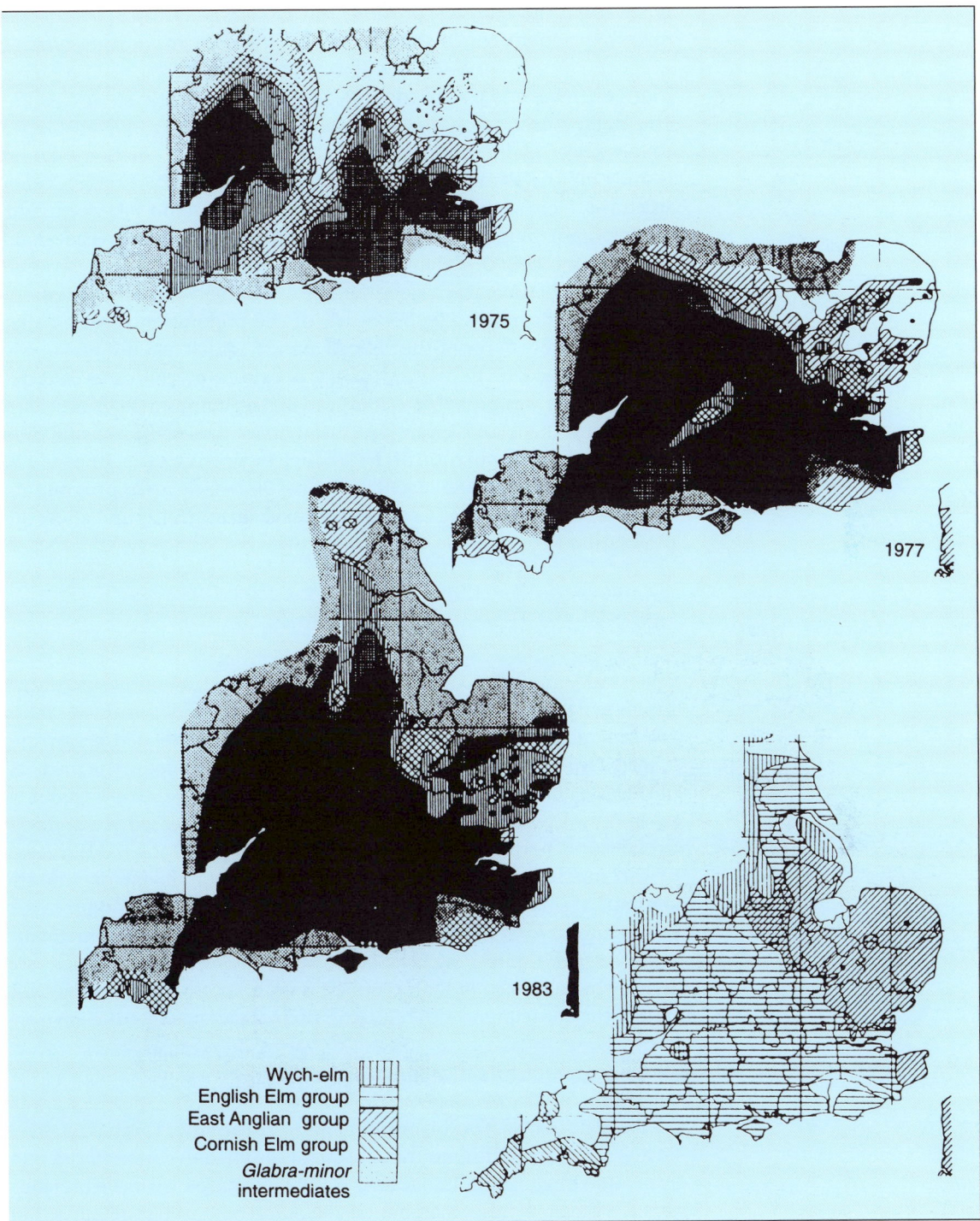

1975

1977

1983

Wych-elm
English Elm group
East Anglian group
Cornish Elm group
Glabra-minor
intermediates

over large areas of lowland Britain (Fig. 5.9; Rackham 1986). The disease gets its name from the research work that was carried out on it in the Netherlands after a similar outbreak there.

There are records of outbreaks in the UK earlier this century and the disease may date back far earlier than this, even as early as 6000 BP (see

Box 3.1). It is therefore not possible to attribute the spread of the disease to human activity conclusively, as it is with American chestnut blight.

Mange threatens the Madnyi Arctic fox

The Madnyi Arctic fox (*Alopex lagopus semenovi*) is a distinct subspecies that has been isolated on the island of Madnyi, one of the Commander Islands off the Kamchatka peninsula of Russia in the Pacific Ocean, since the Pleistocene. Their abundance on the island has been commented upon in many historical accounts and a fur farm on the island was able to take 300–400 foxes a year between 1922 and 1962. Between 1975 and 1977 there was a steep decline in numbers linked with a sharp rise in cub mortality. Further study of the population revealed that many cubs were dying of the disease mange, which had not previously been recorded on the island. Mange is caused by the mite *Otodectes cynotis*, which was probably introduced on the domestic dogs of seafarers visiting the island. From past numbers of between 1000 and 2000 individuals, the population of the Madnyi Arctic Fox had declined to 120 in 1978 and by 1994 had reached a low of 90. A treatment programme has now been introduced to try and reduce cub mortality and allow the population to recover (Goltsman *et al.*, 1996).

Genetically modified organisms

Genetically modified organisms (GMOs) present a unique potential threat to natural biodiversity that is as yet largely undetermined. GMOs are organisms that have had genes from other unrelated organisms inserted into their genomes using transgenic technology. The purpose of this is usually to produce traits in the GMO that are advantageous to agricultural production. This may be through increased yield, nutritional value, herbicide resistance or toxicity to pests. The modification of the nutritional composition (e.g. protein, starch, fat or vitamin content) of some crop species has already been achieved and promises great benefits for human health in poorer nations. However, genetically modified (GM) crops, such as some soya (*Glycine max*) varieties, are already being grown in many countries without any long-term evaluation of the consequences of releasing such organisms into the environment.

One common modification to crops is to insert a gene taken from the bacterium *Bacillus thuringiensis* that enables the plant to produce a substance toxic to insect herbivores that damage the crop. This has enabled farmers to reduce the amount of pesticide applied to cotton in the USA by around one million kilograms in 1999 compared with the previous year (US National Research Council 2000). The potential problem is that this toxin is effective against many different insects. A recent study showed that the toxin is expressed in the pollen of GM maize and reduces survival of the monarch butterfly (*Danaus plexippus*) when larvae feed on its milkweed food plant that has pollen from the maize on its surface. Pollen from such GM crops could travel large distances and therefore be toxic to insects far removed from the targets. However, this experiment was undertaken in the laboratory and may not reflect realistic levels of pollen deposition in the field.

A second modification to crops is to insert a gene that renders them resistant to glyphosate herbicide. The advantage here is that the farmer can spray the field and kill competitive weeds even whilst the crop is growing. The potential problem is that this change in farming practice and efficient eradication of weeds will have a knock-on effect along the food chain, removing the food of many insects and therefore many birds in agricultural landscapes. A research project looking at this problem has just been commissioned by the UK government but it is unlikely that any definitive answers will be produced before more extensive research has been undertaken.

Another potential problem with this technology that requires investigation is that genes conferring advantageous traits, such as resistance to herbicides or salt tolerance, could escape into wild relatives, leading to expansion of their niche, producing races of 'superweeds' that would outcompete native plants and reduce biodiversity. Recent experiments with cabbage varieties and relatives have suggested that this is unlikely, but the possibility remains.

There is no doubt that genetic modification of species for commercial use is set to become an increasingly important issue in conservation biology. The potential of the technology to disrupt natural ecosystems is huge, but as yet there is little evidence either way. There could be substantial benefits to conservation if yields can be increased on existing agricultural land, thus decreasing pressure for even more land to be brought into agricultural use. As with a lot of other potential environmental hazards, the proof may not exist until it is too late. Once novel gene combinations have been released in to the environment it may be difficult, if not impossible, to eradicate them if they are shown to be harmful. This is a direct parallel with the experience of introduced species above. Effective risk assessments are being called for by many governments before commercial use of GMOs, but few are likely to use the precautionary principle (where evidence is lacking either way, refuse permission to proceed rather than grant it).

Physical disturbance of ecosystem dynamics

The scale of human engineering is such that we can influence the dynamics of entire ecosystems, not just through the destruction we cause but also by the constructions we create. The most conspicuous of these are the many dams built recently to provide hydroelectric power. These cause destruction immediately upstream by flooding, sometimes vast areas, but they also disturb the natural dynamics of the river ecosystem downstream.

Many rivers contain fish and invertebrate species that migrate either from one part of the river system to another or out to sea and back (amphidromy). Damming of rivers has the potential to disrupt completely these natural movements. Holmquist *et al.* (1998) investigated the interruption of fish and shrimp migration in Puerto Rico by comparing dammed and undammed streams. Amphidromy is obligate for most of the native fauna and dammed streams without spillways (water released over the sloping surface of the dam) eliminated all native fish and shrimp species from upstream areas. Damns with spillways significantly reduced but did not eliminate native populations upstream. The Atlantic sturgeon has suffered in the same way from damming of rivers along the Atlantic coast of the USA.

Footnote – Is disturbance always bad?

It is important that this chapter does not give the impression that all forms of disturbance have a negative impact on ecosystems. There is good evidence that in ecosystems dominated by late successional communities, such as forests, small amounts of natural disturbance can increase diversity (see Chapter 1). This is simply because it allows pioneer species to gain a foothold and remain part of the system, rather than being totally eliminated by late successional species. This level of disturbance has always occurred through the actions of natural phenomena such as storms, fires, flood and fluctuations in species abundance. The scale and frequency of the disturbance is crucial in determining its effects. Human activity most commonly causes excessive disturbance tipping the balance toward biodiversity loss by favouring a relatively few pioneering species and eradicating highly diverse late successional systems. Interestingly, humans have also reduced the frequency of small disturbance events, for example by suppressing natural fires, similarly resulting in biodiversity loss. Conservation therefore, involves management rather than eradication of disturbance, informed by a knowledge of what is a natural level of disturbance in any ecosystem.

Summary

1. Besides destroying some habitats, humans have also disturbed others by altering their natural dynamics through pollution, introduction of alien species and diseases and, most recently, genes.

2. Chemical pollution causes direct disturbance through effects such as acid pollution and acid rain, pesticide application and eutrophication.

3. The introduction of alien species has been both deliberate and accidental. The effects have been greatest on isolated islands due to the lack of competitive ability and naivety of their native flora and fauna, but larger land masses are also vulnerable to generalist, competitive, invasive species.

4. Introduced diseases have devastated populations of native species that have no natural immunity.

5. Genetically modified organisms pose a new potential threat to native biodiversity and their impact should be studied carefully following the precautionary principle, before they are released in to the wild.

Discussion points

- Is there a clear difference between habitat destruction and habitat disturbance?
- Compare and contrast different agents of chemical pollution. Which are the most damaging to biodiversity?
- Can alien species and diseases be seen as pollutants in the same way as chemicals?
- Are alien genes a threat to biodiversity?

Further reading

Carson, R. (1962). *Silent spring.* Boston, MA: Houghton-Mifflin.

Lockwood, J.L. & McKinney, M.L. (2001). *Biotic homogenization.* New York: Kluwer.

Mason, C.F. (1996). *Biology of freshwater pollution,* 3rd edn. Harlow: Longman.

Newton, I. (1998). Pollutants and pesticides. Pp. 68–89 in *Conservation Science and Action,* ed. W.J. Sutherland. Oxford: Blackwell Science.

Shigesada, N. & Kawasaki, K. (1997). *Biological invasions: theory and practice.* Oxford: Oxford University Press.

Web sites

IUCN/SSC Invasive Species Specialist Group: www.issg.org/

UK Environment Agency: www.environment-agency.gov.uk/

US Environmental Protection Agency: www.epa.gov/

Chapter 6

Non-sustainable use

In this chapter the fate of those species that have been directly exploited for human use, either as food, materials, pets or status symbols is considered. The reasons for use, patterns of exploitation and the reasons why the harvesting has often been non-sustainable are discussed. A series of examples and case studies are used to illustrate the wide range of species that are threatened in this way.

By reading this chapter students will gain an understanding of what is meant by sustainable and non-sustainable use of natural resources; gain a knowledge of the extent of exploitation of wild species and of the different types of trade that result in exploitation.

What is sustainable use?

The concept of sustainable use has different meanings in different contexts, for example, it would have different interpretations in economics and ecology. In conservation terms it generally means the use of species or natural communities in such a way that ensures they will remain in a 'healthy' state and be available for use by subsequent generations. The United Nations Conference on Environment and Development held in Rio de Janeiro in 1992 (commonly known as the 'Earth Summit'; see Chapter 7) brought the idea of sustainable development to the centre of the world political agenda. Central to the idea of sustainable development is the sustainable use of natural resources, including wild populations of animals and plants. We saw in Chapter 3 that human societies and economic systems still operate under the 'Frontier Ethic': 'there's always more and its all for us'. We have a long way to go to achieve sustainable use of resources, as the following examples illustrate.

Overexploitation of wild populations

Despite our sophisticated and intensive agricultural systems, the harvesting of wild plants and animals is still a major human activity. For instance, most of the fish we eat are still taken from wild populations.

As we saw in Chapter 3, the first humans were hunter-gatherers who exploited the living resources around them, but their population size was small in relation to the overall resource. From time to time some of these resources may have been overexploited so that individual species disappeared, but only at a local level. Human populations may have fluctuated in response to this and a nomadic existence was probably partly a response to this problem. However, as humans became more numerous and widespread they started to kill species faster than those species could replace themselves, either through reproduction or immigration from elsewhere. When North America and Australia were invaded by humans, large herbivores were abundant and naïve of the human threat. Many were rapidly extirpated leaving only bones as evidence of early overexploitation (see Chapter 3). Humans may not have had the knowledge or the organisational ability to think in terms of sustainable utilisation at this time; we have no such excuse today, but unfortunately we still continue to practise such short-term exploitation. Non-sustainable use of wildlife has continued and accelerated along with the growth in human population. The exploitation of wildlife is monitored by a number of organisations including the IUCN and the World Conservation Monitoring Centre, from where much of the information in this chapter originates.

To understand what we mean by non-sustainable use we need to consider some basic population dynamics. When conditions are favourable all populations will tend to increase toward a carrying capacity. Population increase will tend to be rapid at moderately low densities (but not so low that the Allee effect starts to operate: see Chapter 4) but slow down as the carrying capacity is approached and density-dependent regulators (factors such as food availability, which have an increasingly inhibitory effect on population growth as the population density increases) begin to limit population growth.

In its simplest sense, the non-sustainable use of a species occurs when it is harvested at a level that cannot be compensated for by the capacity of the population for increase through reproduction. To understand this we must examine a simple model of population growth. The equation most often used to describe population growth with limited resources is the logistic equation:

$$\frac{dN}{dt} = rN\left(\frac{K-N}{K}\right)$$

where dN/dt is the change in population size over time, r is the capacity of the population for increase through reproduction, N is the population size, and K is the carrying capacity. The equation gives us the growth curve shown in Fig. 6.1. The sigmoidal pattern of the curve is produced by the population growth rate declining as the population size tends towards the species carrying capacity in a given habitat.

If harvests consistently remove individuals from the population at a greater rate than they can be replaced, even when the population can achieve its maximum rate of increase (r), then the population will crash (a point elaborated on in Chapter 10). This is an all too familiar scenario,

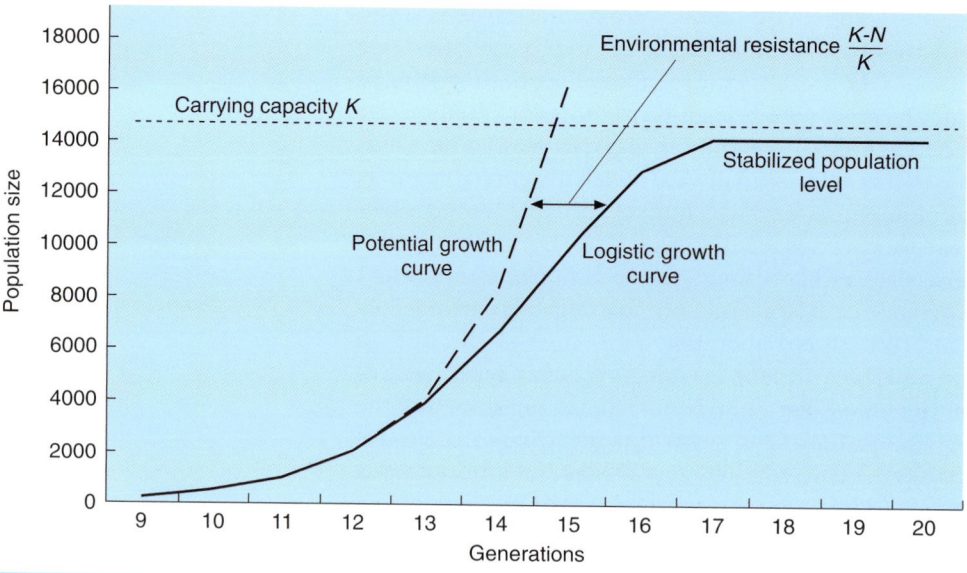

Fig. 6.1 All populations have the potential to increase in size exponentially (dashed line) but they are ultimately limited by the resources available in their environment so that they will tend toward a carrying capacity following a sigmoid growth curve (solid line).

even today. The vulnerability of species to overexploitation is partly predicted by their capacity for increase (r). The values of r for many commonly hunted large mammals are low. Their populations are therefore easily depleted by overhunting and take a long time to recover even if the hunting ceases. But even when the capacity for increase is high, such as in many of the fish we eat, the market demand and the efficiency with which they are caught are such that harvests far outstrip replacement

The general scenario of exploitation is similar across a whole range of examples. A species is harvested on a local scale and a market is established, providing profit. Others then become interested in exploiting the species to get a share of the profit. As the stocks start to decline and become difficult to harvest, raising prices for the consumer and competition among the harvesters, there may then be a drive for greater efficiency that further depletes the stocks. At this point activity often switches to other areas or related species that become profitable due to the dwindling supply of the primary target. These stocks in turn are overexploited and either the market eventually collapses or some form of controls are enforced, which may or may not allow some recovery of stocks.

The inevitability of overexploitation can also be seen from another point of view that is frequently referred to as 'the tragedy of the commons'. If a renewable resource, such as wild species or an area of land is made available to a community, you might expect that each of the interested parties could take an equal share and the resource could be managed sustainably for the benefit of all. But history tells us otherwise. If there aren't sufficient controls to stop individuals taking more than their share then most will opt to take as much as they can before everybody else does. When this practice becomes widespread the resource will dwindle due to overexploitation, often causing a vicious downward spiral as no individual is willing to stop for the sake of the community. An early example of this process is the overexploitation of common grazing lands. In a situation in which all commoners (joint 'owners' of the land) had the right to graze livestock on the 'common' it would be sensible to agree on a number of livestock that each could graze and the land could sustain. What actually happened in many cases was that each commoner kept as many livestock as possible with overgrazing being the inevitable consequence. It is easy to think as an individual that one extra head of livestock will not make a significant difference, but if everybody thinks that way, the 'tragedy' ensues. Of course everyone then blames everybody except themselves.

A different form of overexploitation arises from the opportunities provided by the global market economy. If you owned a valuable resource, such as a forest, and wished to make a profit from it, you could either manage it sustainably and take an annual profit or you could capitalise the full value of the resource straight away by clear felling the forest and selling the land for agricultural use, or some other form of development. The latter would allow you to invest money elsewhere and would almost certainly mean a much greater income, at least in the short term. This incentive of short-term profit through cashing in on your capital has led to the overexploitation of renewable resources such as timber and has contributed to the high rates of deforestation that were noted in Chapter 3.

Example: the whaling industry

Our largest animals, the whales, have been the object of commercial hunting since the ninth century when fishermen of the Basque region of western Europe hunted biscayan right whales just offshore in the Bay of Biscay, for their meat and oil as well as other materials. For many centuries there was probably little impact on populations as hunters were few and weapons were primitive, consequently catch rates were low. Whales were so plentiful off the shores of Massachusetts at Nantucket that they often entered the harbour and ships did not have to lose sight of shore in capturing all the whales they needed. But by the nineteenth century the availability of both steam-powered whaling ships and harpoon guns resulted in a sharp increase in catches and in profits. Some whale populations close to shore were quickly depleted and ships sailed ever farther to open oceans and distant shores in search of their quarry. By the early twentieth century the use of organised whaling fleets, complete with factory ships to process the carcasses whilst at sea, greatly increased the efficiency with which whales could be caught. In the year 1930–31 the harvest peaked at 3.6 million tons. The number of whales caught per year did not peak until 1960–61, when 90 000 individuals were taken. This discrepancy reflects the decreasing size of whales taken as the populations were depleted; a characteristic of overexploitation. The impact of whaling has affected different whale species at different times as species after species have declined and others have replaced them as targets, often starting with the largest and working down in size as in the case of successive exploitation of blue , fin, sei and

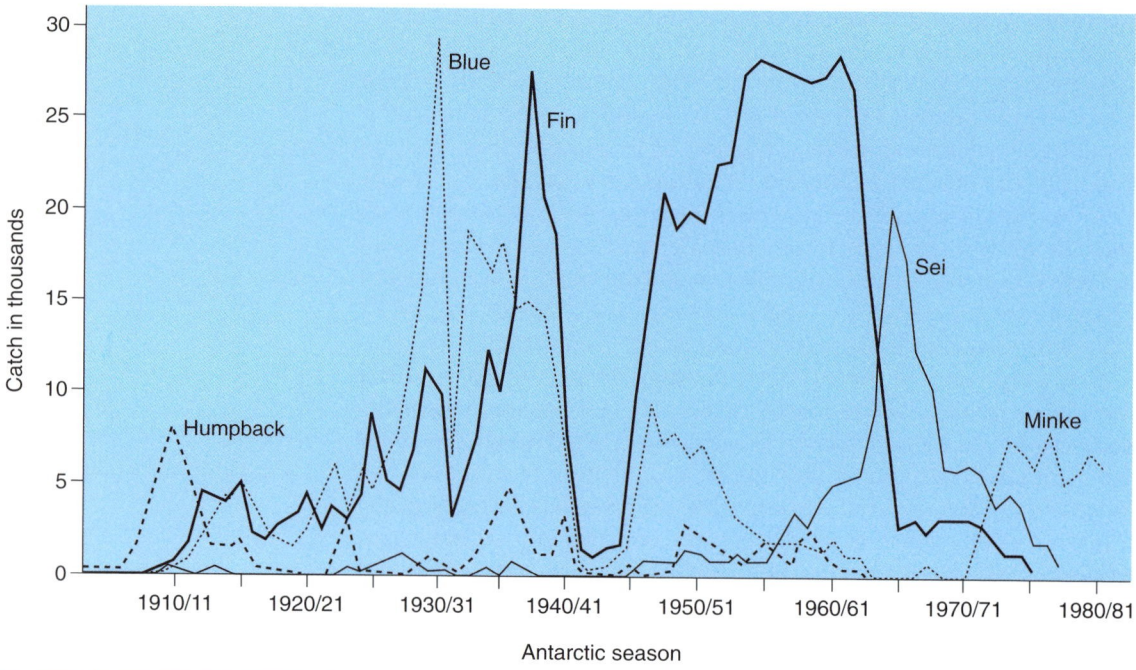

Fig. 6.2 Exploitation of whale stocks in the southern hemisphere 1900–1980. Note the progressive exploitation of species, from large to small. Reproduced from Evans (1987) with kind permission of Academic Press.

minke whales (*Balaenoptera* sp.) (Fig. 6.2). The bowhead (*Balaena mysticetus*) which inhabits Arctic and sub-Arctic waters, has been hunted commercially since the 1600s, but had been harvested long before that by the Inuit peoples indigenous to this area. This species was one of the first whales to be seriously depleted in numbers, having been reduced in European waters from 25 000 to under 100 individuals by the end of the nineteenth century. In contrast, the blue whale (*Balaenoptera musculus*) is an inhabitant of the open sea and was rarely caught in any numbers until modern whaling techniques were available. Subsequently, populations were rapidly depleted as large catches were recorded, peaking in 1930–31, when approaching 30 000 blue whales were slaughtered. The effect of this overexploitation on the Antarctic population was to reduce numbers from an estimated 500 000 to less than 1000.

In response to the peak in harvest and concerns over falling profits, the International Whaling Commission (IWC) was set up in 1946. This included most whaling and some non-whaling nations and one of its key functions is to set quotas for each species and country. The realisation of continuing decline in many species has led to zero quotas for all whales except in certain special circumstances, such as traditional Inuit whale hunts. This has been largely adhered to, with a few exceptions such as Iceland, Norway and Japan who claim their continued whaling is solely for scientific purposes. However there is ongoing pressure from these whaling nations to lift the ban and resume commercial whaling of some species, which seem to have made some recovery. It is arguable whether sustainable use of these creatures should include a return to some hunting or if more profit can be gained through the tourist industry. An increasing number of people wish to see whales in their natural environment and it is an increasing source of income for some communities.

Example: overfishing

World fish catches have increased greatly over the last 50 years from around 30 million tonnes per annum to over 100 million tonnes today. Fish and shellfish contribute 70 million tonnes of edible animal protein annually. Greater demand for protein and greater efficiency in fishing methods has allowed larger and larger catches to be landed. It is hard not to think of our vast oceans as having limitless resources, but in fact only restricted areas are highly productive. A report from the United Nations Food and Agriculture Organization (FAO) using figures from 1992 stated that 44% of the world's fisheries were heavily exploited, a further 16% were overexploited, 6% depleted and 3% recovering from overexploitation. The demand for fish, the efficiency of modern trawlers and their ability to sail large distances and store large catches has caused a crisis in the world fishing industry. Today, a complete ban on fishing has been necessary in some areas, such as the Grand Banks off Newfoundland, in order to allow recovery of fish stocks of such species as Atlantic cod (*Gadus morhua*) and haddock (*Melanogrammus aeglefinus*). The same depletion is also occurring off the North Atlantic coast of Europe.

Fishing is a highly valuable commercial industry. The vested interests are high and the methods have been developed for efficiency and maximisation of yield rather than conservation and sustainable use. Control over fisheries is difficult because of lack of data on population dynamics and in many cases a lack of understanding of the species' basic ecology. This ignorance has effectively been used as an excuse for the continued exploitation of remaining stocks. Depletion of fish stocks has often been extraordinarily blamed on other species such as seals, which themselves have been ruthlessly culled as competitors to the fishermen. Fisheries are often remote and difficult to police. Laws may be well founded, but enforcement is weak and sustainability often becomes a remote theoretical concept.

The rapidity with which overexploitation can lead to serious depletion of populations is illustrated by the following example of Antarctic fisheries. The oceans around the Antarctic are sufficiently remote to have escaped commercial fishing until recently. Commercial fishing started off the shores of South Georgia in the South Atlantic in 1969–70. The major fishing nation in this region was the former Soviet Union taking 92% of the total catch of over 1.6 million tonnes between 1969 and 1990. The reported catch of the main species, *Notothenia rossii* was 399 704 tonnes in the first year and 101 558 in the second. Thereafter the catch of this species dropped precipitously to approximately 2000 tonnes in the next year. Subsequent catches were mainly composed of other species such as *Lepidonotothen squamifrons* and *Champsocephalus gunnari* (Fig. 6.3). The total catch was thereafter maintained by increasing effort and by switching to alternative species as previous targets declined. Belatedly, in 1984 the Convention on the Conservation of

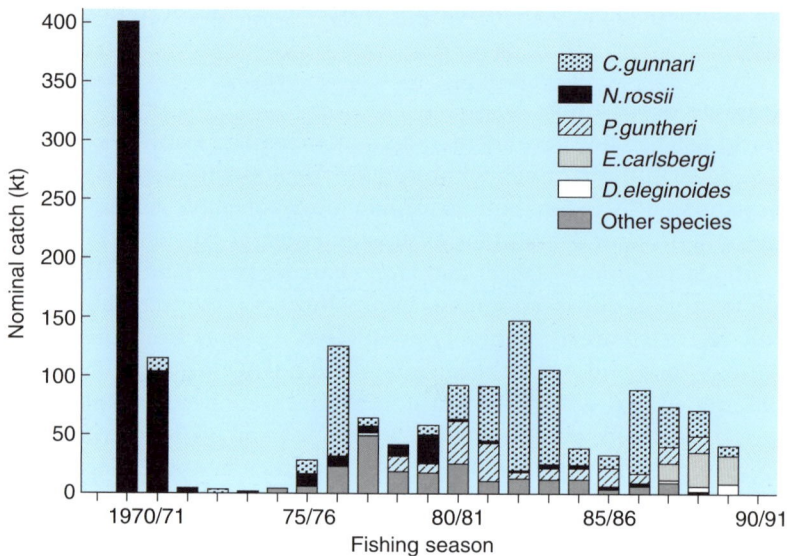

Fig. 6.3 Fish catches in the Antarctic from 1970 to 1990. Reproduced from Kock (1992) with kind permission of Cambridge University Press.

Antarctic Marine Living Resources prohibited fishing for 12 miles around South Georgia and enforced minimum net mesh sizes, thus allowing smaller, younger fish to escape.

Overfishing has also seriously depleted many coral reefs, which are particularly alarming victims of non-sustainable use due to their high diversity and vulnerability (see Box 6.1)

Box 6.1 | Exploitation of coral reefs

Coral reefs, some of our most diverse ecosystems, are formed from the calcareous skeletons of corals (colonial animals related to jellyfish and sea anemones) and other organisms. The corals rely on a symbiosis with a unicellular algae that in turn requires sunlight for photsynthesis and such reefs are thus limited to depths of less than about 50 m. They are also limited to waters that maintain a temperature above 18 °C, roughly between the tropics of Capricorn and Cancer. Their extent is therefore limited, but still covers about 600 000 km², about 0.18% of the total ocean area. They are among the most productive ecosystems, producing 1–5 kg carbon m^{-2} per year, and support a striking diversity of fish and macroinvertebrates. Large numbers of fish use them as both feeding and breeding grounds.

Positioned as they are just off the coast in shallow waters, they are easily accessible from the shore and are being overfished at an alarming rate. Ault *et al.* (1998) estimate that of the coral reef fish in the Florida Keys, 23 of 35 species of groupers, snappers, wrasse and grunts are below numbers set by the US federal overfishing standards. The situation is probably far worse in many other areas. The estimated annual global catch on coral reefs is 6 million tonnes. Many target species such as spiny lobster (*Panulirus*) are widely overexploited. Additional problems are caused by the non-specific fishing methods that are used; trawling with nets and use of explosives and poisons, not only kill many non-target species, they also do considerable damage to the reef.

Beside food, fish are also caught for the pet trade and the aquarium market is currently valued at around $50 million annually, involving about 1000 species of fish as well as some invertebrates. Coral itself is a valued commodity and can be sold along with shells in local markets and exported far from its place of origin. It is also very slow growing and therefore vulnerable to even low levels of exploitation. Many reefs are popular with recreational divers and the tourist industry is putting increasing pressure on some areas with consequent damage, much of which is unintentionally caused by simply standing on the coral (Fig. 6.4).

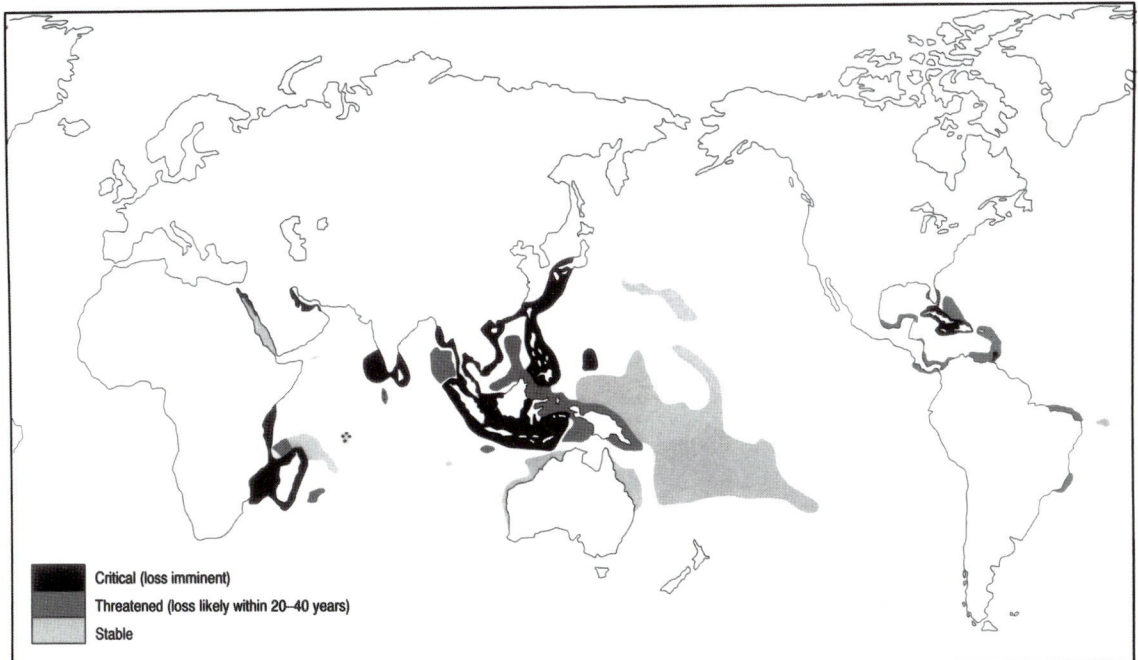

Critical (loss imminent)
Threatened (loss likely within 20–40 years)
Stable

Finally, coral is also mined for use in construction of buildings and roads. The Maldives in the Indian Ocean have become a popular tourist destination, causing demand for hotels and associated infrastructure. Over 111 000 m³ of coral have been mined from local reefs and their structure so completely destroyed that there is little sign of regeneration. The cost to these small islands may be great as they rely on reefs as natural coastal defences (increasingly important in times of rising sea levels) and the tourist industry relies on the presence of beautiful reef and beach systems to attract visitors so they are in danger of ruining the very systems on which their new found industry depends.

Fig. 6.4 The state of the world's coral reefs. Large areas are critically endangered through overexploitation and pollution. Reproduced from *The State of the Planet Environment Atlas* with kind permission of Penguin Books.

The pet trade

The demand for unusual and exclusive pets is increasing, particularly in Western countries and this has placed significant monetary value on species that can be collected from the wild and traded for profit. This is a source of income that many people in the developing world find irresistible, the inevitable result being overexploitation. Many live animals, including primates, are traded each year, legally and illegally, with little assessment of the effects on wild populations. The most serious problem with this type of exploitation probably concerns the parrots. During the 1980s, over 2 million parrots are known to have been exported from South America and many more illegal exports have certainly occurred. As a result, many species are now on the brink of extinction. The blue-throated macaw (*Ara glaucogularis*) is known only from the north and east of Bolivia. Its original rarity has made it a prized and valuable pet, and therefore local trappers can trade this species for significantly more money than other local species directly as a result of the pet trade. It is probably now one of the world's rarest parrots with around 100 pairs remaining in the wild. Many parrots face the twin dangers of habitat destruction, through the activities of loggers and settlers in their forest habitat, and the trapping for the pet trade that the settlers indulge in for valued income. Spix's macaw (*Cyanopsitta spixii*) known only from gallery forest along the Río São Francisco in northern Brazil, has been reduced to just one wild male through habitat destruction followed by illegal trading. A captive breeding programme is under way and a female has been reintroduced to join the male, but the species will clearly only have a future if the illegal trade is stopped.

Trade in ornamental plants

The international market in ornamental plants is fast growing and runs in to tens of millions of dollars annually. The majority of those traded are artificially propagated in nurseries but a significant proportion is still harvested from the wild. The demand for some plant groups such as orchids and cacti has led to their overexploitation and illegal trade in some countries. Approximately 6% of the 30 000 known orchid species and 38% of the 1500 known cacti are currently threatened, mostly though overexploitation. Mexico alone exports over 50 000 cacti annually and a high proportion of these are wild collected and illegally exported. A similar illegal trade in bulbs of various species (mainly snowdrops, winter aconite, anemone, and three species of cyclamen) exists in Turkey where exports of many species have been banned.

Trade in animal parts

Many charismatic vertebrate species, either because of their large size or famed ferocity have been hunted for trophies, such as heads, skins and claws that are traded and proudly displayed as status symbols by some. Other species are sources of ornaments such as ivory dagger handles, which signal wealth and status in some countries, and chess pieces that appeal to some collectors. Still others are demanded for their body parts that are thought to have medicinal uses as cures for everything from dandruff to impotence. This trade has resulted in some of the most dramatic and exasperating overexploitation of populations.

The tiger (*Panthera tigris*) is suffering from this type of illegal hunting or poaching and exploitation, to the extent that this is a greater threat to its survival than is loss of its remaining habitat (although the latter is not insignificant). The total number of tigers at large in the nineteenth century was probably around 100 000. Today the total wild population is down to less than 7000 individuals and it is now categorised by the IUCN as an endangered species. The Bali (*Panthera tigris balica*), Caspian (*P. t. virgata*) and Javan (*P. t. sondaica*) subspecies are now extinct. In the past the tiger has declined because of human population pressure causing destruction of its habitat, through poisoning by farmers as the big cats become a threat to livestock, and through hunting for sport. Today however, most of its remaining habitats are protected and managed, and sport hunting has largely ceased. The threat to tigers today is illegal poaching fuelled by the value of its various body parts for status symbols and for forms of traditional medicine practised in many Asian countries. There is considerable demand as evidenced by a survey of 88 retail outlets in northern Sumatra that found tiger products on sale (mostly bones, claws and teeth) in 10 of them (Plowden & Bowles 1997). Perhaps most sadly, a body part in great demand is the penis as a claimed treatment for male virility problems.

Many other species are currently threatened by this activity. For example, recent evidence suggests that populations of seahorses, pipefishes and pegasid fishes (sea moths) are currently overfished for sale in Chinese markets (Vincent 1997). The latter has only been used for such purposes in the last few decades, but already millions are sold each year and trade has expanded to the Phillipines, Indonesia and Vietnam.

The poaching problem has perhaps been greatest in the demand for ivory. The African elephant (*Loxodonta africana*) was once widespread across the continent, but the demand for ivory has played a large part in its geographical decline to the extent that it is now rarely found outside of protected areas. The trade in ivory was widespread in Africa during the 1980s (Fig. 6.5) and poaching of elephants was increasing rapidly, even within national parks. Local poachers could receive large sums of money for a pair of elephant tusks and the incentives were high, as were the risks. But the real profits were made by the 'middle-men' who sold on the ivory in the lucrative markets of the Far East. There is currently an international ban on ivory trading, but this is unlikely to be a long-term solution, as many African countries want to gain profits from legal trade. The latter opportunity arises because some areas are thought to have too many elephants and a proportion have been culled, providing legal ivory. Indeed in April 1999 international sales of raw ivory resumed in Botswana, Namibia and Zimbabwe under tight controls.

The effects of hunting and illegal poaching on rhinos have been even worse. A long history of exploitation, involving killing for sport, trophy hunting and trade in rhino horn has reduced both rhino species (the white rhinoceros, *Cerantotherium simum*, and the black rhinoceros, *Diceros bicornis*) to fragmented populations in protected areas. During the 1970s the trade in rhino horn for use in dagger handles as status symbols for Yemeni men increased as the standard of living in Yemen increased with their trade in oil. The price of a rhino horn increased 21–fold and the poaching problem became acute. This was made worse by the increase in demand for rhino horn for use in traditional Asian

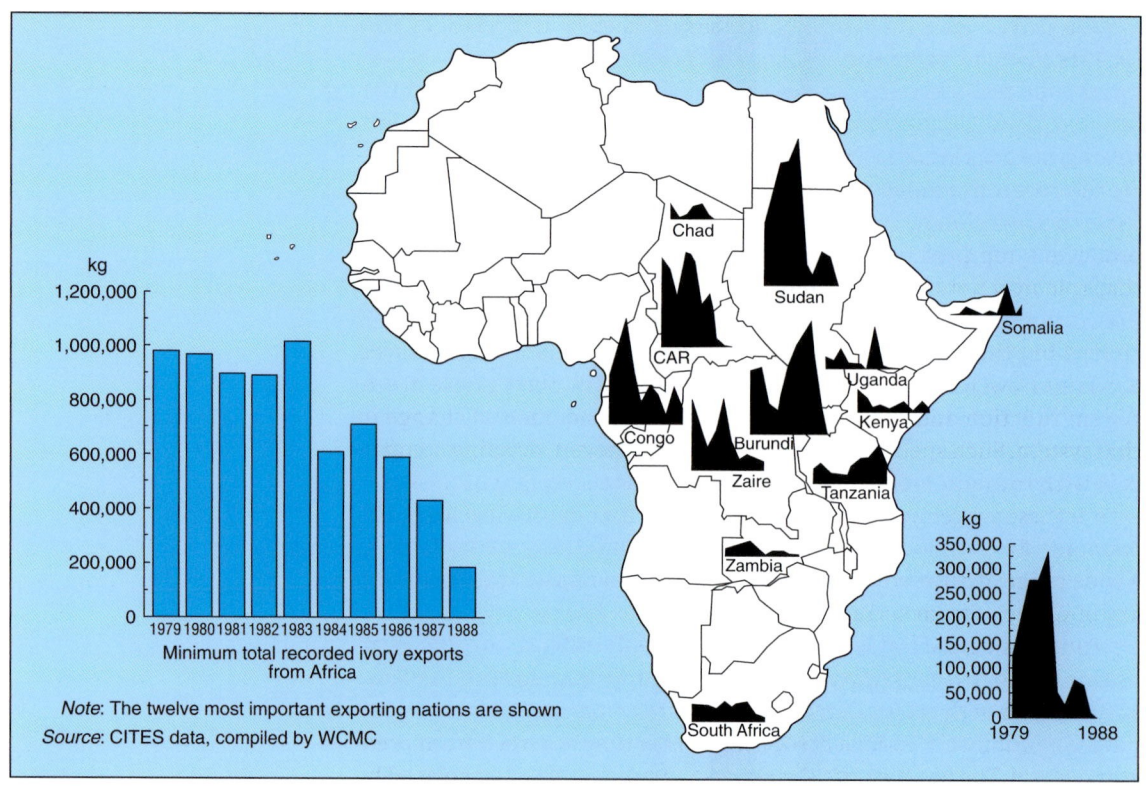

Fig. 6.5 The extent of legal ivory exploitation during the period 1979–1988 leading up to the ban on trade. Reproduced from Groombridge (1992) with kind permission of Kluwer Academic Publishers.

medicine (as a treatment for epilepsy, fevers, strokes and AIDS). The price of a rhino horn in countries such as China, Taiwan and South Korea was recently estimated at around US$60 000. The overexploitation of rhino populations resulted in a 95% decrease in black rhino numbers between 1970 and 1994 (Kemf & Jackson 1994). This decline is only now being halted by unprecedented levels of protection for reserves, including the employment of armed guards who operate a shoot-to-kill policy.

The Convention on International Trade in Endangered Species of Wild Fauna and Flora (CITES) came into force in 1975. Its purpose is to protect wildlife from overexploitation through international trade in live animals and plants or their body parts. To this end a list of protected species is agreed between participating countries and their trade is banned, other species are protected through restricted trade. The list is periodically updated and the Convention currently covers 145 countries. The convention has been criticised for having serious weaknesses in its approach of banning and restricting international trade. First, it is one thing to pass legislation but quite another to enforce it. Significant resources are needed in many of the world's poorest nations to adequately police trade. CITES has often failed to have the desired impact due to lack of resources in key areas. Second, since trade in wildlife is not the only threat, the situation is often complex and there may be cases, such as ivory, where controlled trade may help prevent habitat destruction and a wholesale ban can make the situation worse. Regular updating of CITES agreements is necessary to keep pace with the changing international situation.

Indirect effects of overexploitation

Apart from the threat to a species that is being directly exploited, there are indirect consequences for the communities and ecosystems to which these species belong. All species play a role within ecosystems (as primary producers, top predators, detritivores, pollinators, etc.), but for many that role may not be unique and if they were removed by overexploitation, other species would fulfil the same role. Thus the composition will change but the community will remain, though perhaps with reduced diversity. However, some species play a unique and important role in ecosystem function and their removal results in a fundamental change in that system. Such species are termed **keystone** species, drawing comparison with the large stones in buildings that bear the weight of the structure. If these are removed the building is likely to collapse. Species can be keystones for a number of different reasons; because they are the food for a wide range of different species or because they are predators that keep any one species from becoming too abundant.

Thus, beside the concern that fish stocks will collapse through overfishing, ecologists fear that removal of many top predator fish that constitute much of the current catches will disrupt marine ecosystems and have major impacts on lower trophic levels as they are freed from predator control. The biomass of fish removed may effectively be replaced by increased biomass of organisms from lower down the food chain, potentially causing large changes in ecosystem dynamics, and knock-on effects for many species and biodiversity as a whole. The removal of whales from the Antarctic Ocean seems to have allowed the abundance of Antarctic Krill (*Euphausia superba*) to increase significantly, but the knock-on effects of this are yet to be evaluated.

Impact of overexploitation of non-living resources

Some non-living resources are also used in a non-sustainable manner. An obvious example is fossil fuel such as oil, which has indirect effects on wildlife through pollution and climate change that are discussed elsewhere. Another important resource from a conservation viewpoint is probably freshwater. In many areas of the world, where the surface water supply is insufficient to meet demand, freshwater is pumped from groundwater aquifers (natural underground reservoirs). Groundwater aquifers can be seen as reserves of water that are slowly replenished from the surface. If water is abstracted at too high a rate the groundwater reserves will become depleted and lower the water table.

Overabstraction of water has had a major influence on the ecology of some wetland areas. Lowering the water table has led to a progressive drying out of the surface of fens and marshes allowing rapid succession to woodland and loss of diverse early successional wetland communities. Effects can most easily be seen in small wetland areas such as

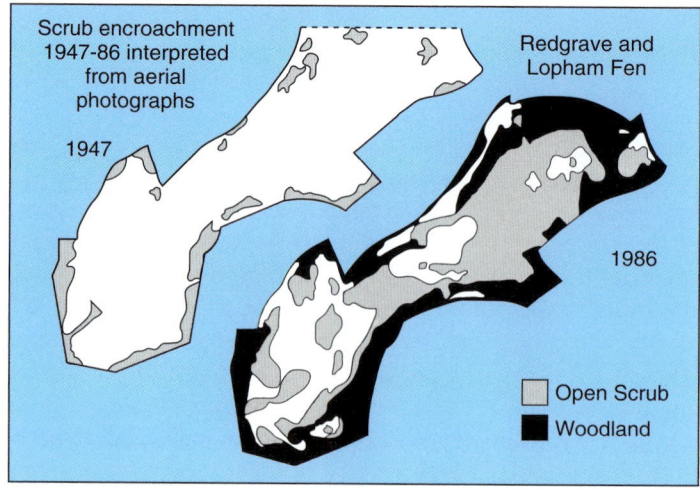

Fig. 6.6 The extent of scrub encroachment at Redgrave and Lopham fen between 1947 and 1986 largely due to lowering of the water table following water abstraction. Reproduced from Harding (1994) with kind permission of English Nature.

Redgrave and Lopham Fen in England, a 125 hectare wetland system on the border between the counties of Norfolk and Suffolk which was designated as a nature reserve in 1961. At the same time, just 100 metres from the reserve boundary, a water abstraction borehole was established which was used to extract 3600 cubic metres of water per day. The fen was entirely dependent on groundwater springs that kept the peat waterlogged and the pH high due to the underlying chalk. As water abstraction began, the peat surface dried out, the specialised plant community disappeared, and scrub invaded (Fig. 6.6). Fortunately agreement has been reached with the water authorities to relocate the borehole and restoration of the fen and its conservation value is under way (Harding 1994).

Summary

1. Many populations and species are being threatened through over-exploitation for food, materials, the pet and ornament trade and trade in animal parts.

2. Unregulated commercial hunting has caused serious depletion of whale populations and fish stocks throughout the world.

3. The demand for exotic pets and ornamental plants has led to the illegal trade that has endangered particular taxa such as parrots, cacti and orchids.

4. Trade in animal parts for trophies, status symbols and alternative medicines has led to the endangerment of populations through poaching and illegal trade of species such as tigers, elephants and rhinos.

5. Overexploitation of particular keystone species can have a knock on effect on the whole ecosystem.

6. Overexploitation of natural resources such as timber and freshwater lead to direct destruction or disturbance of habitats (see also the previous two chapters).

Discussion points

- Is there a clear definition of sustainable use?
- Can overexploitation be controlled by legislation?
- Is sustainable use appropriate in cases such as trade in animal parts?
- How can sustainable use be incorporated in environmental policy of commercial companies?

Further reading

Cherfas, J. (1989). The hunting of the whale: a tragedy that must end. Harmondsworth: Penguin.

Sugg, I.C. & Kruet, U.P. (1994). Elephants and ivory: lessons from the trade ban. London: Institute of Economic Affairs.

Web sites

Convention on International Trade in Endangered Species of Wild Fauna and Flora: www.cites.org/

International Whaling Commission: ourworld.compuserve.com/home-pages/iwcoffice/

Cetacean Society International: elfi.com/csihome.html

Project Tiger, India: envfor.nic.in/pt/

Part 3

Chapter 7

The rise of conservation biology

Conservation biology is a young science that is still establishing its own boundaries and relationships with other disciplines. In this chapter we explore the development of conservation from the first ideas about its relevance through the first actions and on to the development of the science. The boundaries of the subject and relationship with the non-scientific aspects of conservation are also considered.

By reading this chapter students will gain a basic understanding of the origins of the conservation ethic; understand how conservation biology developed from more established scientific disciplines; and understand the relationship between conservation biology and related disciplines relevant to conservation action.

Introduction

To understand the rise in conservation biology as a science we must first briefly consider the development of conservation awareness; the realisation that conservation is an important undertaking for society. This was not initially based on science but eventually led to the need for scientific enquiry to provide the evidence on which to base action (although this is far from always being the case even today, as we shall see in later chapters).

From an historical viewpoint, many world religions have viewed humans as above nature, and the natural world as a resource for humans to exploit; a God-given resource which humans should restrain and improve for our own good. This view has subsequently been reflected in many Western philosophies and scientific works, along with the belief that it is possible for humans to control nature for their own benefit. The rise of the industrial economy has reflected this exploitative and adversarial view, as noted in Chapter 3 (Chiras's 'frontier ethics').

We have considered evidence in the previous chapters that clearly illustrates the decrease in natural areas on earth and the increasing negative impact of human activity on biodiversity. One of the earliest writers to recognise the ability of humans to upset the balance of nature was the physical geographer, Mary Somerville (1858) who stated that 'the works of the Creator are nicely balanced, and man cannot infringe his laws with impunity'. Perhaps the most influential early work was that of George Perkins Marsh (1864) who wrote in his *Man and Nature* of the profound way in which the woods and streams of Western Europe were being changed forever by human activity.

Early conservationists

Some notions of conservation can be found in the very same religions that encourage exploitation of the natural world, particularly those of the far east. However, whether or not the beliefs and actions of any early societies reflect any sort of conservation ethic is largely a matter of interpretation.

Tracing the origins of conservation action is complex and if we go back too far the evidence of motive is poor. For example, the royal families and nobility of Europe created many preserves during the Middle Ages, most notably the 'royal forests'. These areas, and the game within them (typically deer and wild boar), were protected solely for the recreational use (hunting and stalking) of a privileged few. This was in some ways fortuitous, because some of these are now among Europe's finest nature reserves, but was it conservation action?

Early ideas of the advantages of natural resource management are evident in the reports from the colonies of many Western nations. Colonial rulers were concerned to maintain newly acquired supplies of timber and protect watersheds and rainfall for adjacent agricultural land. As a consequence, reserves were set up under colonial law, but this was not strictly an action for the conservation of wilderness or wildlife.

Nineteenth century collectors started to ask questions about the distribution and abundance of species, leading of course to the evolutionary theory of Darwin and Wallace, but also to the discipline of biogeography. Extensive collections brought back by expeditions and deposited in museums hinted at immense diversity in tropical areas, and the interest of amateur naturalists, resulting in the publication of their records, led to early realisation of species loss.

Comparative progress in Europe and the USA

The earliest designation of nature reserves and national parks for the good of the nation came almost simultaneously in Europe and North America during the nineteenth century (see Chapter 8). Concern grew at this time about the ethics of natural resource exploitation, fuelled by the near extinction of many once-numerous species on which humans depended for food such as the European and American bison (*Bison bonasus* and *B. bison*). In the USA the extinction of the passenger pigeon (*Ectopistes migratorius*) through overexploitation, and in the UK the extinction of the large copper butterfly (*Lycaena dispar*) through drainage of its wetland habitat, brought attention to the consequences of human impact on the environment at the end of the nineteenth century. These early losses lent ammunition to movements wishing to conserve species by designating reserves for their protection.

Toward the later part of the nineteenth century, conservation action was beginning to increase in the UK as a result of the formation of a number of societies such as the National Trust for England and Wales, the Society (later Royal Society) for the Preservation of Birds (RSPB), and later, the Society for the Promotion of Nature Reserves. Their collective concern over the loss of many valued wild places led to the formation of many protected areas throughout the country. Areas known by naturalists to be of particularly high value for their wildlife, particularly plants and birds in the first instance, were purchased or leased and declared nature reserves. There was no grand plan in this undertaking except the idea that putting a fence around an area and declaring it a reserve would in some way protect the habitat and species contained within it. At the same time the subject of ecology was developing, with active research on the dynamics of plant communities and animal populations. Key elements of future conservation biology such as the interdependence of species, vegetation succession and ecosystem dynamics were appearing in scientific journals, particularly those of the newly founded British Ecological Society.

Conservation ethics developed in North America in the late nineteenth and early twentieth centuries through the writings of John Muir, Gifford Pinchot and Aldo Leopold. The latter wrote of the conservation ethic as the gradual evolution of the idea that it is antisocial to exploit and destroy natural systems. Leopold's writings were inspired by the destruction and degradation of land in the midwestern USA during a time of economic depression in the 1930s. He also drew on his historical knowledge to make the case that the progress of civilisation has depended heavily on whether occupied areas of land were able to remain productive under the pressure of human abuse. This is still true, despite advances in technology, and was certainly true at the time of his writing when widespread soil erosion was driving many farmers from their land in the so-called dustbowl of the Midwest (see Box 3.2).

Protected areas continued to be the main focus of conservation action throughout the twentieth century with a steady increase in designation of all forms of national parks and nature reserves in the USA and Europe. This was also the case in many colonies, where ruling nations were able to plan land use with little regard to the local people. This resulted, for example, in the significant national park network we see today in East Africa. The legacy of this and other enforced national park networks is that local people feel disenfranchised and are disinclined to support the park system. Giving the control of the land back to local people has enabled continued protection for some parks, provided they are a source of income. Such important socioeconomic aspects of conservation are outside the scope of this text but further reading is suggested at the end of this chapter.

New legislation passed in the later decades of the twentieth century, most notably the US Endangered Species Act (ESA), have helped set clear targets for conservation and directed much of the conservation action. This powerful legislation has also created significant political controversy when it is used and may give conservation a negative image. Considerable friction can be created between the conservation and economic lobbies as evidenced by the northern spotted owl (*Strix occidentalis caurina*) versus logging battle in the north-western USA. This species is dependent on substantial tracts of old-growth forest to maintain territories and breeding areas. These same forests are being logged on an industrial scale resulting in a rapid decline of the owl. The ESA has been used to restrict logging activities, an action that has greatly angered the logging communities in the area.

The emergence of conservation biology as a science

Conservation biology as a science in its own right emerged almost imperceptibly from ecology. Early ecologists frequently commented and provided theories on which to base conservation practice, but they did not call themselves conservation biologists.

The coming together of organisations that practise conservation and scientists investigating causes of decline took a surprising amount of time (and is still largely lacking) and new solutions to problems were often slow to be implemented. In post-Second World War Europe nature conservation was (and to some extent still is) largely a matter of leaving areas to 'return to nature' or continuing 'traditional' forms of land management. The practitioner took little notice of the scientist and was more concerned with practical issues such as manpower and equipment to carry out the prescribed management. Few studies at this time monitored and evaluated any management in order to produce evidence of its efficacy.

Increasing environmental awareness during the 1960s brought to light a new generation of scientists who applied their knowledge directly to environmental problems, including species and habitat loss. At the same time the new medium of television brought wildlife into people's homes and increasingly exposed them to stories of destruction and extinction. Campaigns led by new non-governmental organisations such as the World Wildlife Fund (now called the World Wide Fund for Nature) began to demand information and action that only scientific study could effectively provide. Scientists in universities worldwide began to embark on conservation-based research programmes and to offer degree programmes in conservation. This spawned a further generation of scientists eager to join in research. By the late 1970s scientific journals such as *Biological Conservation* emerged to cater for the growing number of scientific papers being produced on the subject, closely followed by scientific societies, such as the Society for Conservation Biology, devoted to the promotion and pursuit of the science of conservation biology.

Conservation biology as a crisis, value-laden discipline

The relationship of conservation biology to ecology is rather like that of emergency surgery to health care or that of war to political science. It is a crisis discipline in which action must be taken despite lack of sufficient knowledge. Because to wait would mean certain destruction (Soule 1985).

Conservation biology is often called a value-laden science. The sorts of values referred to were summarised by Soule (1985) in an article entitled 'What is Conservation Biology?'. He proposed four postulates that characterise value statements if conservation biology is to be viewed as a worthwhile discipline:

1. diversity of organisms is good and extinction and degradation of diversity is bad;
2. ecological complexity is good and simplification of ecosystems by humans is bad;
3. evolution is good;
4. biotic diversity has intrinsic value.

However, one could argue that all applied science is value laden (e.g. medicine). Any goal has an element of value. Conservation biologists must accept that if they are to have a real impact on their discipline they must be willing to defend these values.

Today, conservation biology is still in a very active period of growth. There remain many challenges to face and many questions to answer, as I hope this book will make clear. The number of scientific papers being published per year and the number of research projects undertaken is still rapidly increasing. The current challenge is perhaps to ensure that the scientific information produced is used effectively in conservation practice, a subject to be returned to in the final chapter.

As you might expect, ideas have developed during the short time in which conservation biology has been a recognised science, to the extent that some foundations on which the subject was built have crumbled, to be replaced by new constructs. Two examples should suffice to illustrate this.

The 'balance of nature' paradigm

Early ecological theories suggested that the process of successional change (the change in community composition as it matures from a pioneer stage to a stable 'climax' state) is of central importance to conservation. All environments had their successional stages and climax communities, to which they would return if perturbed, and which would persist indefinitely in the absence of intervention. So, during the early development of conservation biology, the prevailing view of ecosystems was that left alone they reach an equilibrium or a climax state.

One of the biggest controversies in ecology at that time was to what extent ecosystems really form some sort of superorganism in which individual species have coevolved to form a functioning unit. The ultimate expression of the superorganism idea is the Gaia hypothesis which was put forward by James Lovelock (Lovelock 1979). He suggests that the biosphere is one big functioning system with a certain level of self-regulatory capacity. According to Pickett *et al.* (1992) the conservation implications of the equilibrium view of ecosystems are:

1. a particular unit of nature in equilibrium is conservable by itself in a reserve;
2. such units will maintain themselves in a stable and balanced configuration;
3. after disturbance, the system will return to its former, balanced state.

One can understand that given these views, nature reserves would seem to be the answer to most conservation problems. This seductive idea has largely been refuted by current research on ecosystems, which suggests they are dynamic and chaotic systems that have little capacity for self-regulation and may be very prone to change even on a global scale. Over the last two decades, research in community ecology has shifted our view towards a paradigm in which there is no true climax community or equilibrium state. The conservation implications of this non-equilibrium hypothesis are quite different:

1. a particular unit of nature is not easily conservable as a reserve in isolation from its surroundings;
2. reserves will not maintain themselves in stable and balanced configuration;
3. reserves will experience natural disturbances (as well as human disturbances) and are likely to permanently change their state as a result.

As a consequence of this shift in thought, emphasis has also shifted from the concept of reserves to a more regional landscape-based approach. This shift is progressively reflected in the rest of this book as we move from consideration of conservation action which has predominated in the past, with emphasis on protected areas and single species, to the conservation of the future which emphasises the importance of natural processes and landscape scales.

Reserves and their management are certainly not ignored, since the reality is that most of our conservation effort is still directed toward the reserves we have and the species they contain, and their relevance will remain high. However, emphasis now is on heterogeneity among dynamic patches and how to maintain this through management (Wiens 1997b). Looking forward we need to address the new challenge of conservation in the wider landscape and the research that is required to achieve this.

Population dynamics

A long running debate in ecology has centred on the question of how population size is regulated. One school of thought maintains that only factors acting in a density-dependent fashion (such that their negative impact on the population in terms of increasing death rate or decreasing birth rate increases as the population grows) can regulate population size (the Biotic School, e.g. Nicholson & Bailey 1935). Examples cited are biotic factors such as competition for food, predators, parasites or disease. Abiotic factors were thought to act independently of the population density. A second school proposed that all factors, biotic and abiotic, were capable of acting in a density-dependent fashion and thus regulating populations, but in any case populations were rarely influenced in this way and were far more commonly limited by environmental conditions, particularly weather (the Climate School, e.g. Andrewartha & Birch 1954). Some early work on this debate suffered from having too simplistic a view of populations, in regarding their dynamics as being primarily controlled by changes in birth and death rates. Subsequent research has shown that many populations are heavily influenced by immigration and emigration, and that the dynamics of movement between local populations can be much more significant to overall species persistence than previously thought (see also Chapter 4). This has had profound implications for our view of maintaining isolated populations in nature reserves (see Chapter 9) and opened up a whole new area of research on landscape scale conservation (see Chapter 12).

The Rio Summit and Biodiversity Convention

The term biodiversity arose as a shortening of 'biological diversity' as mentioned in Chapter 1. It appears to have first been used by Walter G. Rosen in 1985 for the first planning meeting of the US National Forum on Biodiversity held in 1986. This resulted in a proceedings volume entitled 'Biodiversity' that brought the term into popular use (Wilson & Peters 1988). While the science of conservation biology has been developing, environmental politics has added to the challenges the subject faces by setting agendas for action which should be clearly informed by the science. The rise of environmental issues on the political agenda was reflected in a call for a summit of world leaders to discuss environmental problems and agree on actions and targets for sustainable development. This was manifest in the United Nations Conference on Environment and Development (often referred to as the 'Rio Summit' or 'Earth Summit') held in Rio de Janeiro, Brazil in 1992. This meeting discussed many broad environmental issues, but for conservation biology the most important aspect was the convention on biodiversity, which requires signatory countries to take action to protect biodiversity and use it sustainably (see below). As a consequence of signing up to this convention, many countries have produced their own action plans for both habitats and species. This has simultaneously increased conservation activity and exposed areas of ignorance that require urgent research, such as species about which we know very little but where nevertheless we have to take some action. Unfortunately, governments have been less enthusiastic about providing money for these programmes to be carried out. There have now been a number of follow-up meetings where progress has been reviewed and the convention is likely to remain a major driving force for conservation action in the foreseeable future.

Conservation biology and the conservation movement

It is relevant here to consider the relationship between conservation biology as a science and what we can loosely call the conservation movement. The latter is a political lobby that has grown rapidly in recent years out of the concern for the damage humans are doing to natural habitats and species. This is now a powerful lobby containing many large non-governmental organisations (NGOs) funded through members' subscriptions and charitable donations and committed to carrying out conservation activity on a number of fronts. These, along with some governmental organisations, can be seen as the campaigners and practitioners. Many NGOs own substantial areas of land and manage it for conservation, as well as employing conservation biologists.

There are many things that influence actions taken by the conservation movement, beside the science. The role of conservation biology is to provide the scientific basis for action and a vital role of the conservation biologist is to effectively communicate the science to enable appropriate action to be taken. As a scientific discipline, conservation biology should stand apart, and independent from the politics, ethics and economics. As individual conservation biologists, we may not want, and do not need to stand aside from these issues, but the distinction between the discipline and the opinions of the individual practising it is important. However, the direction of research within conservation biology should and must be influenced by social needs, and frameworks to facilitate this must be sought (see Chapter 15). A key concept likely to drive the direction of research in the new century is that of sustainability (Lubchenco 1998). There is an urgent need, as we have seen from Chapter 6, to change our use of the earth's living resources from a non-sustainable, exploitative pattern, to a sustainable platform, which ensures that future generations will not be left to solve the problems caused by our own.

Summary

1. Early philosophies and religions all contain some ideas on conservation but largely place the human race above the rest of the living world with an ability to control and a right to exploit it.

2. Early conservation efforts were largely taken to secure natural resources not biodiversity.

3. Conservation ethics developed following the realisation that species and habitats as well as fertile land were being lost through short-term exploitation.

4. The science of conservation biology grew as an applied arm of ecology during the twentieth century, but has only been recognised in its own right during the last 30 years.

5. The Convention on Biodiversity, agreed in 1992, has provided

focus for conservation producing an ever greater demand on the production of good science to underpin conservation action.

Discussion points

- Can a distinction be made between the science of conservation biology and the wider conservation movement?
- What are the practical conservation implications of the alternative views of the 'balance of nature' paradigm?
- Should the science of conservation biology drive the practice or should the need for action dictate the direction of research (you could view this as a top-down or bottom-up debate)?

Further reading

Evans, D. (1992). *A history of nature conservation in Britain*. London: Routledge.

Leopold, A. (1949). *A Sand County almanac and sketches here and there*. New York: Oxford University Press.

Pickett, S.T.A., Ostfeld, R.S., Shachak, M. & Likens, G.E. (eds) (1997). *The ecological basis of conservation*. New York: Chapman & Hall.

Sheail, J. (1998). *Nature conservation in Britain: the formative years*. London: The Stationery Office.

Web sites

The British Ecological Society: www.demon.co.uk/bes/
Society for Conservation Biology: conbio.net/scb/
Convention on Biological Diversity: www.biodiv.org
UK Government's Conservation Organisation for England: www.english-nature.org.uk
US Environmental Protection Agency: www.epa.gov/
Royal Society for the Protection of Birds: www.rspb.org.uk/
UK Wildlife Trusts: www.wildlifetrust.org.uk/index.htm
World Wide Fund for Nature: www.panda.org

Chapter 8

Selecting protected areas

Conservation activity is still largely concerned with the concept of protected areas. Areas of high conservation value are set aside from the ravages of habitat destruction (Chapter 4) in order to preserve remnants of natural systems. If this approach is to be efficient we must examine the current protected area system to see to what extent it conserves biodiversity and explore how we might identify where new areas should be designated. Any weaknesses with the protected area approach also need to be considered.

By reading this chapter students will gain an understanding of the history of protected area designation, the range of methods that have been employed to select areas for protection and some of the challenges and limitations of protecting areas.

Introduction

The dominant conservation action to this day is to identify valuable natural and semi-natural areas and protect them, with the assumption that in so doing one also protects the species and communities they contain. This seems logical as one could argue that the only effective way of conserving biodiversity in the long term is to protect intact ecosystems. However, the size of these protected areas ranges from a few hundred square metres to the Greenland National Park at $972\,000\ km^2$. The largest areas encompass whole ecosystems and are essentially functioning natural systems with minimal human influence. In contrast, many smaller protected areas, particularly in developed countries, are only fragments of once much larger ecosystems and their dynamics have fundamentally changed. As a consequence, they require intensive management to retain the characteristic communities and species that they were established to conserve. This chapter considers the criteria by which we might select new areas for protection in order to maximise opportunities for conservation of biodiversity and the potential problems with the protected area approach.

What is a protected area?

The definition of a protected area adopted by the International Union for the Conservation of Nature (IUCN) is:

> an area of land and/or sea especially dedicated to the protection and maintenance of biological diversity, and of natural and associated cultural resources, and managed through legal or other effective means.

Protected areas vary greatly in their status and there are many different reasons for designation of areas and many different levels of protection, largely dependent on the country to which they belong. The IUCN has produced a list of categories of protected areas with a justification and rationale for each (see Box 8.1). These are of necessity very general and every country has its own legislation, terms and definitions of protected areas.

Box 8.1 | **IUCN categories of protected area and their definitions (IUCN 1994a)**

CATEGORY Ia. Strict Nature Reserve: protected area managed mainly for science
Definition: area of land and/or sea possessing some outstanding or representative ecosystems, geological or physiological features and/or species, available primarily for scientific research and/or environmental monitoring.

CATEGORY Ib. Wilderness Area: protected area managed mainly for wilderness protection
Definition: large area of unmodified or slightly modified land, and/or sea, retaining its natural character and influence, without permanent or significant habitation, which is protected and managed so as to preserve its natural condition.

CATEGORY II. National Park: protected area managed mainly for ecosystem protection and recreation
Definition: natural area of land and/or sea, designated to (a) protect the ecological integrity of one or more ecosystems for present and future generations, (b) exclude exploitation or occupation inimical to the purposes of designation of the area and (c) provide a foundation for spiritual, scientific, educational, recreational and visitor opportunities, all of which must be environmentally and culturally compatible.

CATEGORY III. Natural Monument: protected area managed mainly for conservation of specific natural features
Definition: area containing one, or more, specific natural or natural/cultural feature which is of outstanding or unique value because of its inherent rarity, representative or aesthetic qualities or cultural significance.

CATEGORY IV. Habitat/Species Management Area: protected area managed mainly for conservation through management intervention
Definition: area of land and/or sea subject to active intervention for management purposes so as to ensure the maintenance of habitats and/or to meet the requirements of specific species.

CATEGORY V. Protected Landscape/Seascape: protected area managed mainly for landscape/seascape conservation and recreation
Definition: area of land, with coast and sea as appropriate, where the interaction of people and nature over time has produced an area of distinct character with significant aesthetic, ecological and/or cultural value, and often with high biological diversity. Safeguarding the integrity of this traditional interaction is vital to the protection, maintenance and evolution of such an area.

CATEGORY VI. Managed Resource Protected Area: protected area managed mainly for the sustainable use of natural ecosystems
Definition: area containing predominantly unmodified natural systems, managed to ensure long-term protection and maintenance of biological diversity, while providing at the same time a sustainable flow of natural products and services to meet community needs.

Fig. 8.1 Three contrasting national parks designated for different reasons and managed with different objectives: (a) Yellowstone Park, USA; (b) Lake District, UK; (c) Tikal, Guatemala. (see overleaf)

(a)

(b)

History of protected area designation

As noted in the previous chapter, the first national parks were designated almost simultaneously in the USA and Europe in the mid-nineteenth century. A characteristic of the development of national parks on both continents is that they were not originally designated for their nature conservation value. Most, such as the Yellowstone National Park in the USA, were designated for their geological features or their historical context. A century later, UK national parks were designated for their natural beauty and amenity value (Fig. 8.1). In both cases designation was made easier by their marginal value as agricultural land. This explains the conspicuous lack of national parks in lowland, flat fertile areas.

If we look at a graph of the trend in foundation of protected areas (Fig. 8.2) it is apparent that designation accelerated throughout the twentieth century reflecting the growing concern for conservation during this time. A somewhat false peak is apparent around 1980 due to the designation of two very large areas, the Greenland National Park and the Australian Barrier Reef Biosphere Reserve, but the flattening off thereafter probably reflects the lack of new areas remaining for consideration. From figures published in 1996 by the World Conservation Monitoring Centre (WCMC), there are currently 9869 protected sites covering 9 317 874 km^2. This is around 6.3% of the earth's land area. These figures can differ considerably depending on the method of calculation.

Fig. 8.1 (cont.)

(c)

For example these WCMC figures only take in to account areas greater than 1000 hectares in size. Many small nature reserves typical of Western Europe will therefore not be included. For example, the average size of national nature reserves in England is about 400 hectares. Many European countries have complex patterns of small reserves, many of which are privately owned and have only partial protection through weak legislation, such as sites of special scientific interest (SSSI) in the UK. If these are included the proportion of the land area protected increases significantly (Table 8.1).

It seems unlikely given the extent of human population pressure that much more than 8% of the earth's land surface will eventually be set aside especially for biodiversity conservation. This inevitably means that we will have to ensure that conservation is effective within cur-

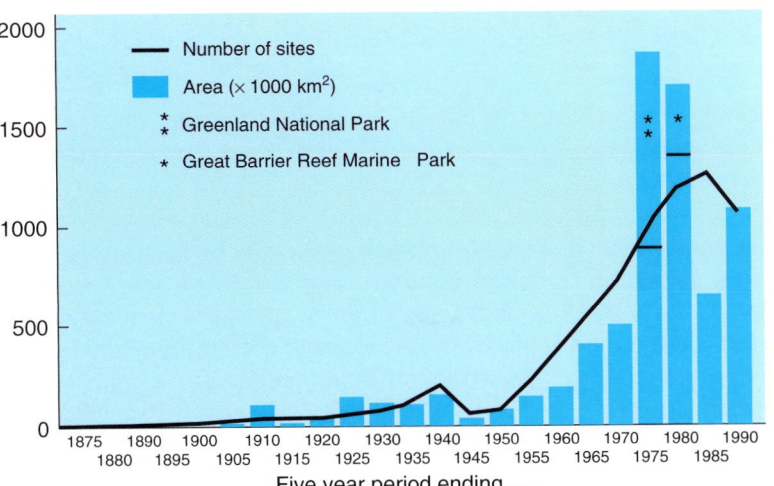

Fig. 8.2 The growth in global protected area since such areas were first designated in the mid-nineteenth century. Reproduced from Groombridge (1992) with permission of Kluwer Academic Publishers.

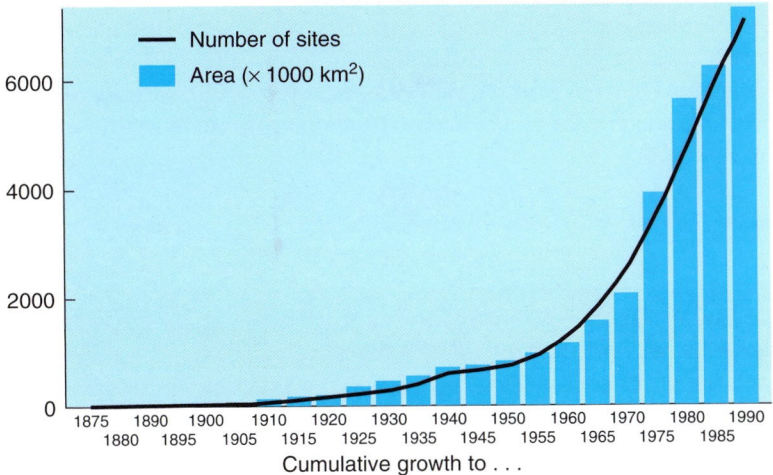

Table 8.1 Number and total area of protected terrestrial sites in the UK. These are divided in to Sites of Special Scientific Interest (SSSI) with lesser protection and National Nature Reserves (NNR) with greater protection

Protected area status	Total area (ha)	Total number	Mean area (ha)	Proportion of land area
SSSI	1 985 148	6045	328	8.1%
NNR	189 540	304	623	0.8%

rently protected areas as well as ensuring that any new protected areas are carefully selected on scientific grounds (see below). In addition, there is an increasing tendency to give areas that have other primary economic functions, such as agriculture, some secondary protected status. The objective being that their use should be compatible with landscape conservation, or more recently, that the land use should be sustainable in the long term, not exploitative (see Chapter 12).

Criteria for measuring conservation value of areas

Conservation will always have to compete with other land uses and there are only limited resources available to protect areas and their biodiversity. Conservationists are forced to be selective. So which areas should we protect? We have seen above that historically, reserves have not always been selected on the basis of their biodiversity. Not surprisingly, protection is uneven, countries vary greatly in their total designated area and habitat types vary in the level of protection afforded to them. Criteria and approaches are required to select areas for conservation before they are designated for other land uses as human demand for land grows.

The challenge is to find objective criteria by which to identify areas most in need of designation and protection. This is not as easy as it sounds. We have already noted in Chapter 1 that we still know very little about some of our richest ecosystems. Most species are still undescribed. If we waited until we had a full understanding of an area, it is more than likely that the area would have been destroyed before we take the decision to protect it. Short cuts have to be taken, as rapid measures of value are required.

How can we estimate biodiversity?

Species diversity indices

We saw in Chapter 1 that biodiversity is normally considered at the species level, and that the species diversity of an area is a measure of both the number of species present and their relative abundance. From a theoretical point of view there are a number of equations that allow us to convert raw data on species number and relative abundance in to an index of species diversity. For example, three commonly used indices of species diversity are:

Simpson's index

$$D = 1/\Sigma \; (p_i)^2$$

Shannon–Wiener index

$$H = -\Sigma \; (p_i)(\ln p_i)$$

In both of these p_i is the fraction of the total sample made up by species i. (The term e^H is sometimes used as it converts H back from a logarithmic scale and makes it directly comparable with D)

Margalef's index

$$I = (S-1)/\ln N$$

Where S is the number of species and N the number of individuals.

Examples of the figures produced by these indices are given in Table 8.2. The indices differ in the relative importance they give to species richness (Shannon–Weiner), relative abundance or eveness (Simpson's) and total sample size (Margalef's). Nevertheless, in all cases, those areas with few species, of which a small number are very common or dominant,

Table 8.2 Comparison of three diversity indices Simpson's (D), Shannon–Weiner (H) and Margalef's (I)

Number and Proportion of sample (pi) represented by each species				Diversity values		
Species 1	Species 2	Species 3	Species 4	D	H (e^H)	I
12 (0.33)	12 (0.33)	12 (0.33)	0 (0)	3.00	1.10 (3.00)	0.56
9 (0.25)	9 (0.25)	9 (0.25)	9 (0.25)	4.00	1.39 (4.00)	0.84
11 (0.31)	11 (0.31)	11 (0.31)	3 (0.08)	3.39	1.29 (3.64)	0.84
20 (0.56)	10 (0.28)	5 (0.14)	1 (0.03)	2.42	1.06 (2.89)	0.84

have a low diversity score. Examples of this are extreme environments such hot springs, and intensive agricultural landscapes. Those areas with many species, none of which is common or dominant, have high diversity. This is true of tropical rain forests and coral reefs and, interestingly, of some less intensively managed agricultural landscapes. These indices reflect what we actually might perceive if we looked at these areas. Just by observation we would get an impression of low diversity if most of the individuals we saw were of one or two dominant species. In contrast if we saw a lot of individuals, all of which were of different species, we would get an impression of high diversity. There are three types of species diversity that can be measured in this way:

1. alpha diversity: the diversity measured within a unit area (e.g. a patch of woodland, or a lake);
2. beta diversity: the diversity gradient measured by sampling across an ecotone (e.g. from savanna to forest, or along an environmental gradient);
3. gamma diversity: the rate at which diversity changes with increasing area.

Alpha diversity is the most frequently used in conservation as it is site-based and enables comparison of alternative areas and the mapping of the distribution of diversity on a regional scale. Although these indices provide a fairly simple way of processing data on diversity, we are still left with the problem of how to collect the data. The species diversity approach to prioritising areas for protection often stalls at the first step because preliminary classification of the biodiversity present is easy to ask for, but usually very difficult to obtain. An absolute measure of all species is a formidable task and even simply counting the number of species is beyond our capacity for the vast majority of areas.

Surrogate measures of biodiversity

In the real world, limited resources and time dictate that short cuts are necessary to estimate biodiversity. The most popular short cut to measuring and comparing biodiversity among sites at the regional scale has been the use of **indicator taxa**. A taxonomic group that is easy to sample and is well studied usually forms the focus of a survey, and the patterns in its biodiversity then used as an indicator or a **surrogate** of overall biodiversity. Many efforts to do this have used well-studied groups such as birds, mammals, or flowering plants. The assumption here is that an area that is highly diverse for one taxonomic group is also highly diverse for other groups. Since some taxonomic groups are much better known than others or more easily sampled, they are a convenient solution to the problem and they have been extensively used.

The second short cut that is generally used is to simplify species diversity down to just species richness (as mentioned in Chapter 1). This means that species simply have to be recorded as present rather than their relative abundance measured. This can even negate the need for fieldwork if extensive collections have been made in the area before. But are these short cuts at the cost of accuracy?

Choosing indicator taxa

Often it is simply the most familiar and easily surveyed group that is chosen as an indicator. Birds, mammals and flowering plants often present the easy solution to assessment because extensive databases on their distribution already exist and therefore decisions can be made quickly and cheaply. But this may be at the cost of accuracy. Which indicator taxa you use could be a crucial factor in the feasibility and accuracy of biodiversity assessment. Greater objectivity in the selection of indicator taxa has been advocated by Pearson (1994), who proposed seven criteria that can be used in the selection of an indicator group as follows:

1. well-known and stable taxonomy;
2. well-known ecology and natural history;
3. readily surveyed;
4. occurs over a broad habitat and geographical range;
5. some species specialised to each habitat type;
6. patterns observed in indicator taxa are reflected in other taxa;
7. should have potential economic importance.

In practice it is rare that all of these are satisfied, some are not easily measurable, whilst the last has no biological relevance. Most problematic is the criterion that patterns of biodiversity observed in the chosen indicators should reflect the patterns of biodiversity of other taxa (see below).

Is information for one taxonomic group also good for others?

As we considered above, the logic behind the use of indicator taxa requires that they are adequate surrogates for other taxa of concern. This problem has been the subject of a number of studies, one of which was undertaken by Prendergast *et al.* (1993) who asked two specific questions.

1. Are habitats that are species rich for one taxon also species rich for others?
2. Do rare species occur in, and therefore benefit from, the conservation of species-rich habitats?

To address these questions they analysed the distribution of five different taxa (birds, butterflies, dragonflies, liverworts and aquatic plants) within the UK, a country that has particularly good distributional data for a wide range of taxa and so is ideal for such a study. They divided the

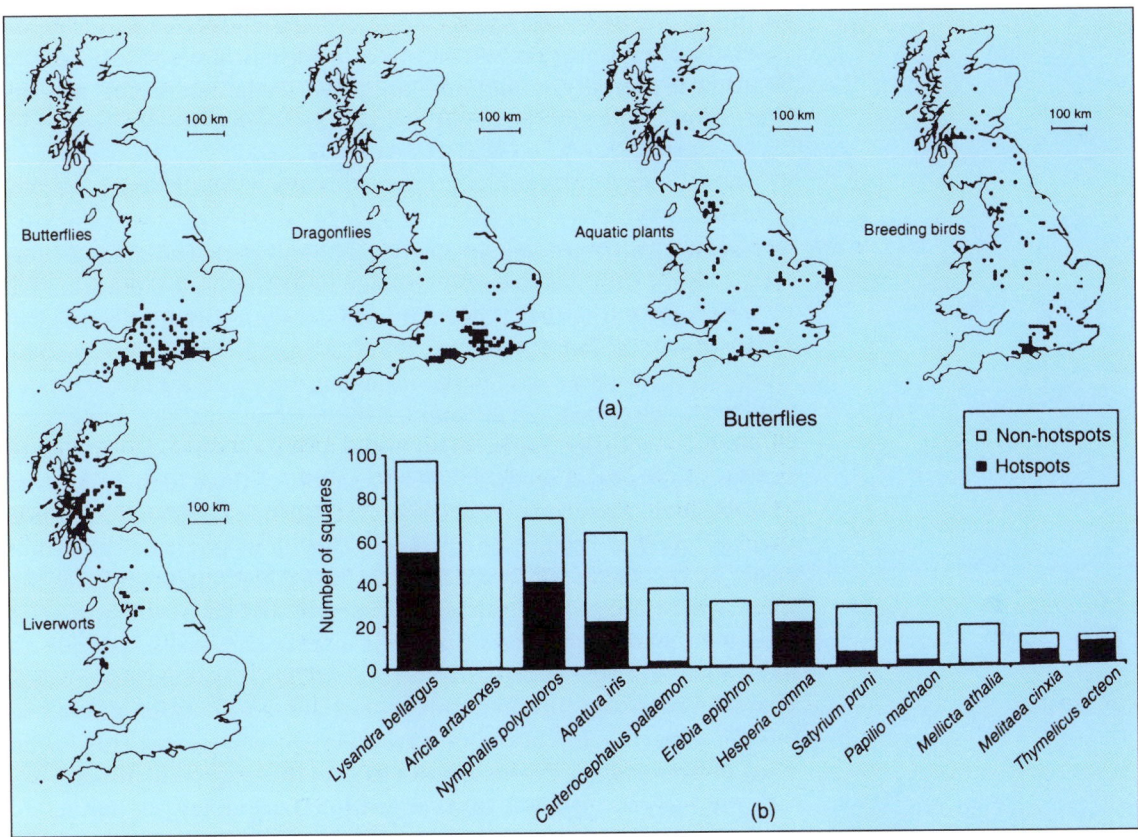

Fig. 8.3 (a). Top 5% of UK 10-km squares chosen on basis of species richness for five selected taxa. Note the markedly different distribution of these squares among the taxa. (b) The total number of squares and the proportion that have been identified as hotspots occupied by threatened species of butterflies. Reproduced from Prendergast et al. (1993) with permission of authors and Macmillan Magazines Ltd.

country into 10-km squares and compared the distribution and overlap of the richest 5% of squares for species in each group (Fig. 8.3). A glance at the maps suggests that some groups would probably be good surrogates for others, but that no group is a good surrogate for all. Species-rich areas for different taxa do not generally coincide. However, their data covered a wide range of habitats within the UK and considered taxa as diverse in their habitat requirements as butterflies (generally most diverse in the hottest, driest parts of the UK) and liverworts (generally most diverse in the mildest, wettest parts of the UK). It is not surprising therefore that a lack of correlation was found. For two taxa with similar climatic requirements, the butterflies and dragonflies, the correlation was greater and diversity of one may well be an adequate indicator of diversity in the other even though one is totally terrestrial and the other partially aquatic.

In relation to the second question, the study showed that rare species are not always found in species-rich habitats. Conserving the top 5% of areas in terms of species richness for butterflies did not protect some of the rarest species, which are confined to specialised, but relatively low-diversity habitats; this is a problem we shall return to.

Several other studies have also questioned the use of single indicator groups to predict overall biodiversity and for predicting changes in biodiversity resulting from habitat modification, including a study by Kerr (1997) which tested the hypothesis that reserves selected on the basis of mammal diversity would also be effective for conserving invertebrate diversity. He found that setting up a hypothetical reserve system to protect the diversity of mammalian carnivores did not protect invertebrate diversity any more effectively than randomly selecting areas.

The multi-taxa or 'shopping basket' approach in biodiversity assessment

In response to the problem of one taxon being an inadequate indicator for all others, the use of a suite of taxa has been proposed. The advantage of this approach is that a diversity of taxa with different ecological requirements is more likely to reflect the patterns of diversity as a whole. This seems a particularly promising approach for invertebrates where a range of taxa can be sampled in the same way.

Kremen *et al.* (1993) argued for the use of arthropod taxa as indicator groups of terrestrial biodiversity on account of their higher diversity and abundance relative to other taxa and the wide ranges of functional niches that they occupy. The problem they draw attention to is that many such taxa are poorly studied and have a high taxonomic impediment (there are many undescribed species and few taxonomists to describe them). Given this situation it might take years to provide an assessment of an area's diversity during which the area may have disappeared. A possible solution to this problem of taxonomy, or lack of taxonomic expertise, has been put forward by Oliver & Beattie (1993) who used morphological characteristics to rapidly group individuals into 'morphospecies' without use of conventional taxonomy (see Box 8.2).

Box 8.2 | The use of morphospecies for rapid biodiversity assessment

Assessing patterns of biodiversity for the setting of conservation priorities is a difficult task with the resources that are normally available. In some ecosystems where species diversity is very high, the taxonomy is poorly developed and the simple identification of specimens is a formidable task which could take so long (even if the expertise is available) that the opportunity for conservation is lost.

Oliver & Beattie (1993) proposed a method for the rapid assessment of biodiversity that does not rely on a high level of taxonomic expertise. Thus it is useful for assessment of biodiversity in lesser known but speciose groups such as invertebrates and lower plants. Their approach is to sort specimens based on their major morphological characteristics, rather than their strict taxonomy. They named this type of pseudotaxonomy the morphospecies approach. Their argument is that this allows much more rapid sorting of specimens, yet the results reflect diversity patterns sufficiently to be an effective tool in biodiversity assessment.

To test this assertion, they used non-expert students to sort samples of a range of taxonomic groups, including spiders, ants, polychaetes and mosses. The non-experts were given a few hours training in taxonomy so they could recognise key morphological features and then allowed to sort specimens, using these features, into what appeared to them to be separate taxa, termed Recognisable Taxonomic Units (RTUs), equivalent to species.

Results showed a significant correlation between RTUs estimated by non-experts and species richness estimated by experts. The RTUs identified were not the same as the true species and there were cases where similar species were lumped together as one RTU and cases where one species was split into two because of polymorphism or sexual dimorphism. However, the levels of lumping and splitting were similar in most cases and therefore cancelled each other out.

This approach is controversial because of the potential for error, but is increasingly being used, especially in invertebrate biodiversity assessment.

Kotze & Samways (1999) sampled a range of ground-dwelling invertebrate taxa, landhoppers (Amphipoda), spiders (Araneae), ground beetles (Carabidae), rove beetles (Staphylinidae) and ants (Formicidae), in a range of montane forest habitats in South Africa. Only the two beetle taxa showed any correlation in diversity pattern and clearly no one taxa would be an effective indicator of the others. However, taken together, all taxa indicated significant differences in assemblage structure among the forest patches that would be potentially useful in setting conservation priorities. It looks likely that this approach will be more commonly used than single indicator taxa in primary biodiversity assessment.

Is diversity the only criterion for identifying areas for protection?

We saw from the study by Prendergast *et al.* (1993) earlier in the chapter that designating areas of high diversity does not necessarily protect the rarest species. Many rare species are highly specialised and have restricted geographical ranges, and many of our most threatened species are confined to one area or island and are said to be **endemic** to that area.

Conservation priorities must reflect both diversity and endemism

Due to their history and biogeography, some areas have a large number of endemic species whilst not being particularly diverse. Oceanic islands, such as the Hawaiian Islands, are the most prominent of these. They have relatively low species richness compared with the nearest mainland, but because of their isolation they have many endemics that have evolved *in situ* through adaptive radiation since their ancestors first arrived. Some mainland areas also have high levels of endemicity, which often coincides with high diversity, but not always. The Cape region of South Africa has around 8600 vascular plant species recorded, of which nearly 6000 are endemic (68%) in an area of just 90 000 km². In terms of overall diversity this area would not rate very highly, but when you consider that over 2% of the earth's vascular plants are endemic to this small area, its conservation priority is clear.

The extent of overlap, or lack of it, between diversity and endemism is not always as clear as in exceptional areas like the Cape region. Nott and Pimm (1997) compared species richness and endemism in two groups of North American birds, the icterids (blackbirds and orioles) and warblers (Fig. 8.4). They found that not only did species richness and endemism of the two groups not coincide spatially, but additionally,

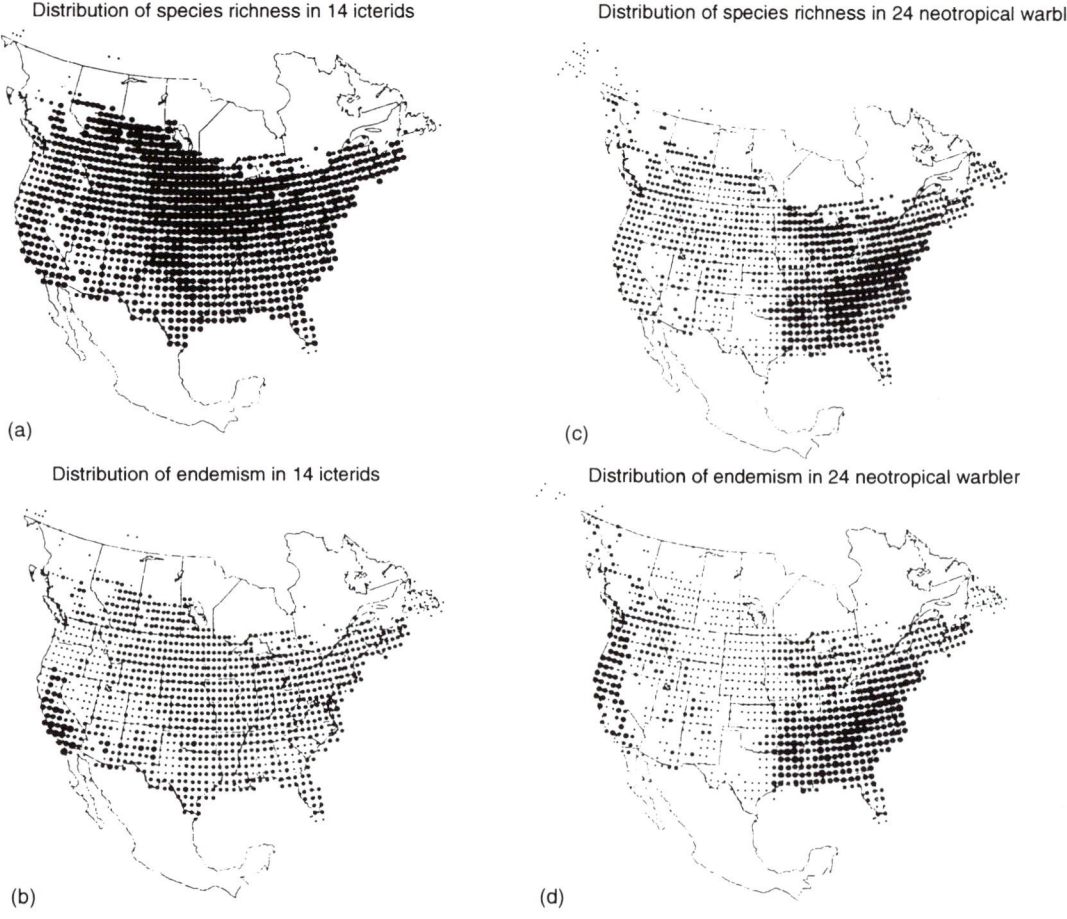

Distribution of species richness in 14 icterids

Distribution of species richness in 24 neotropical warbler

(a)

(c)

Distribution of endemism in 14 icterids

Distribution of endemism in 24 neotropical warbler

(b)

(d)

Fig. 8.4 Distribution and overlap of hotspots for species richness and endemism in two groups of passerine birds (icterids and neotropical warblers) in North America. The size of the filled circles reflects the magnitude of species richness or endemism. Reproduced from Nott & Pimm (1997) with kind permission of Kluwer Academic Publishers.

species richness and endemism hotspots did not coincide within each of the groups. We are therefore left with the problem of how to weight the importance of species richness and endemism in selection of conservation areas.

Taxonomic distinctiveness as a component of biodiversity

Another variable that may be considered important in prioritising areas for conservation is the presence of species that are unrelated to others and therefore taxonomically distinct. These are often species considered to be evolutionary relics; the sole survivors of largely extinct taxonomic groups sometimes referred to as living fossils. Candidates for this are species such as the coelacanth (*Latimeria*), a sea fish found off the south-east coast of Africa whose nearest relatives died out in the cretaceous period (>60 million years ago), and the tuatara (*Sphenodon*) from New Zealand, a primitive reptile which looks superficially like a lizard, but is a relic from the early beginnings of the reptiles in the Triassic. It has been proposed that such species should be given special priority on the grounds of their scientific importance, but others have argued against this on the grounds that such species have little evolutionary potential; they are evolutionary dead ends.

Clarke & Warwick (1998) used an index of taxonomic distinctiveness (Δ^+) which is based on the average taxonomic distance (number of taxonomic steps back to common ancestor) between any two organisms chosen at random from the chosen sample taxon and the average phylogenetic distance between any two individuals from different species. Taxonomic distinctiveness can be calculated from simple species presence/absence data and therefore has a number of advantages over simple species richness and species diversity indices (Fig. 8.5):

1. it is not reliant on sampling effort;
2. it can be compared across studies and sites;
3. it appears to be more sensitive to environmental degradation than species richness estimates, which can show initial increases as generalist species move in (Warwick & Clarke 1998).

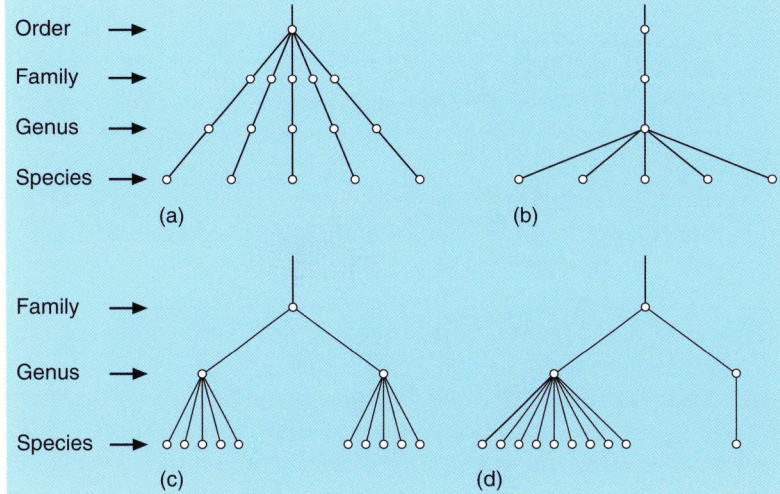

Fig. 8.5 Four hypothetical taxonomic trees resulting from presence/absence data. Standard diversity measures would not distinguish a from b or c from d. Taxonomic distinctiveness, based on average path lengths back to a common ancestor, ranks them from highest to lowest in the order a (3.0), c (1.56), d (1.2), and b (1.0). Reproduced from Clarke & Warwick (1998) with kind permission of Blackwell Science.

A study by Polasky et al. (2001) compared the use of taxonomic distinctiveness with simple taxonomic richness as criteria for choosing priority sites in a conservation network for North American birds. Distinctiveness was based on genetic distances calculated for 147 genera using DNA hybridisation techniques. The two methods produced markedly similar results with 12 of the 15 or 16 sites selected by each of the methods respectively. The authors concluded that, although taxonomic distinctiveness deserves recognition, given the practicalities of use, simple taxonomic richness would appear to be a good surrogate in this case.

There is still much to learn and debate about biodiversity assessment and it is likely that consensus will never be reached on the relative values of contrasting natural areas. The results in terms of areas selected for protection will depend on the criteria used, and judgement of the best method is to some extent based on the relative values given to different elements of biodiversity and not purely on scientific evidence. With this problem in mind we move on to consider practical ways in which the results from the above methods can be used to select areas for protection.

Practical approaches to protected area designation

Once criteria for measuring conservation value of areas have been selected and used to produce a data set, how can this be used to select specific areas as priorities for protection? A number of practical methods have been devised.

Gap analysis

Burley (1988) produced a simple approach to establish conservation priorities within a country or region. Assuming that some protected areas already exist, the logic is that information is gathered on biodiversity and gaps in the protected area system identified.

The method normally progresses as follows:
1. a preliminary classification of biodiversity present is made (as in the previous section);
2. the existing system of protected areas and other land use systems is mapped;
3. gaps in the protected area system where elements of biodiversity are not adequately protected are identified by comparison of 1 and 2 above;
4. priorities for action to fill gaps are set;
5. progress is reviewed periodically and priorities revised if necessary.

Example: gap analysis in remnant patches of lowland fynbos in South Africa

Sometimes detailed analyses are possible, as was the case with a study of remnant patches of lowland fynbos vegetation in South Africa (Huntley 1988). The fynbos vegetation of the Cape region is an exceptionally species-rich heathland-type community that has been shaped by frequent summer fires. A 3-year study achieved step one by ranking sites according to rarity of vegetation type, habitat diversity, species richness, number of threatened plants species present and sites were also weighted by size and shape, isolation and degree of disturbance. A total of 153 sites identified as being of conservation value were recorded. Ratings ranged from 13 to 80 out of a possible 100. Only five of the 32 sites with a rating above 50 were protected at that time. A case for protection of other sites was therefore made. This was a very detailed study with a large resource input the like of which is unlikely to be available to most other studies, but it does serve to illustrate how inadequate some current reserve systems may be.

Example: prioritising forest areas for conservation in Parà, Brazil

Parà is an eastern state of Brazil that surrounds the mouth of the River Amazon. Over 90% of the area is naturally forested and deforestation has only removed some 12% of this. However, the potential for deforestation is high and a state-wide plan is required to ensure the conservation of the area's highly diverse rainforest ecosystem. Veríssimo *et al.* (1998) put forward a plan for the state, incorporating areas for timber extraction with protected areas for conservation. To achieve this they used Geographical Information Systems (GIS) to undertake a spatial analysis of the forest areas to produce and combine the following information:

1. the extent of legally protected areas where logging is prohibited or restricted, including national forests, nature reserves, buffer areas, ecological stations, Indian lands and military lands;
2. priority areas for conservation (protected or unprotected) as defined by a previous scientific meeting in which criteria such as species richness, rarity and endemism were used;
3. the maximum geographical extent of profitable timber extraction using criteria of accessibility and value of timber in each area.

As a result they were able to produce a map of proposed zonation of logging and designation of protected areas (Fig. 8.6). Most of the areas produced by the analysis were large and so few problems of reserve size or landscape fragmentation should arise (see Chapter 9). The challenge from here is to get the state's authorities to accept and police such a plan.

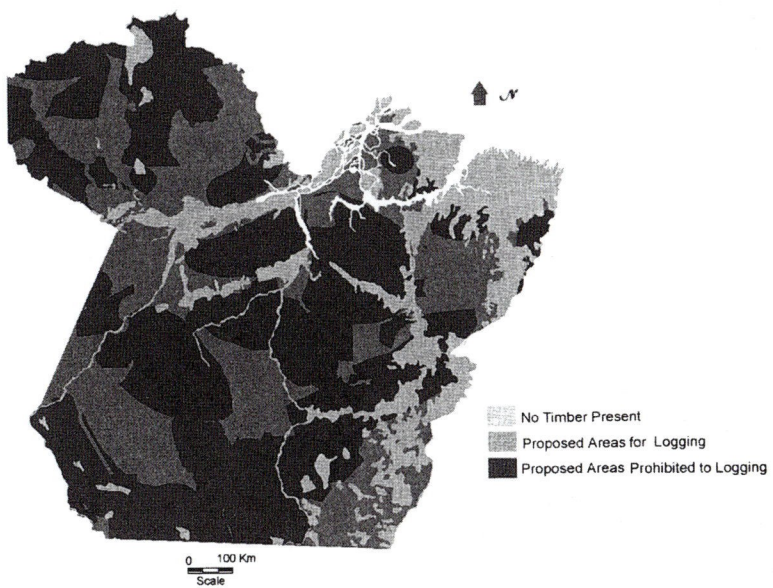

Fig. 8.6 Zonation of land use between timber extraction and forest conservation in Pará, Brazil. Reproduced from Veríssimo *et al.* (1998) with kind permission of Blackwell Science.

No Timber Present
Proposed Areas for Logging
Proposed Areas Prohibited to Logging

0   100 Km
Scale

The representation approach

Despite the problems posed above, large databases have been accumulated on species distributions and habitat types on a global scale. This has enabled some ambitious efforts at identifying a list of areas that would best represent the earth's wildlife resources and therefore be a priority for protection.

An example of this method uses endemism of indicator taxa (flowering plants and vertebrate species) combined with degree of threat, measured by loss of 75% or more of their original vegetation. From this approach Mittermeier *et al.* (1998) drew up a list of 24 terrestrial hotspots which covered only 2% of the earth's land surface but which they estimate contain approximately 50% of all terrestrial biodiversity (Fig. 8.7a).

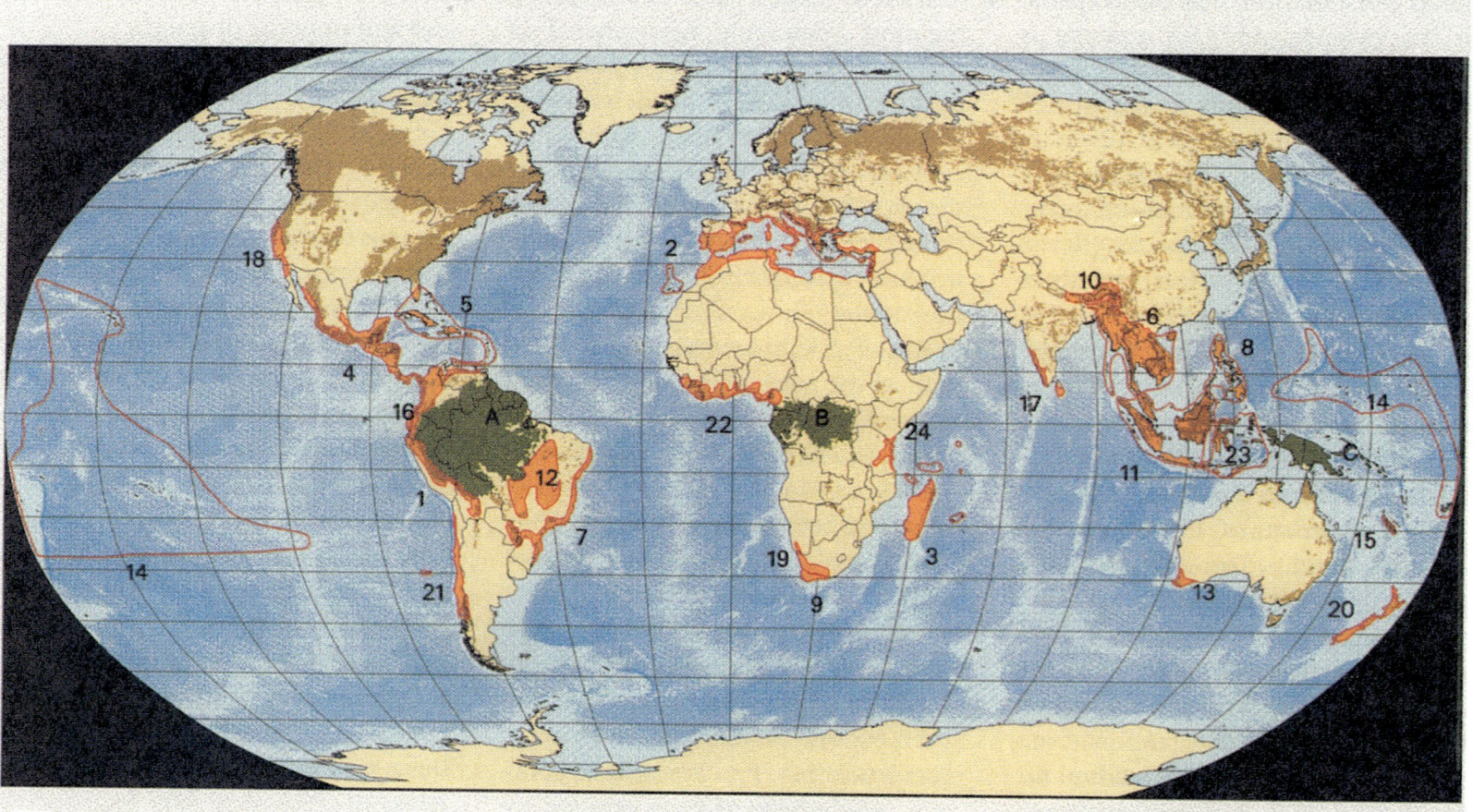

GLOBAL BIODIVERSITY HOTSPOTS
AND MAJOR TROPICAL WILDERNESS AREAS

(a)

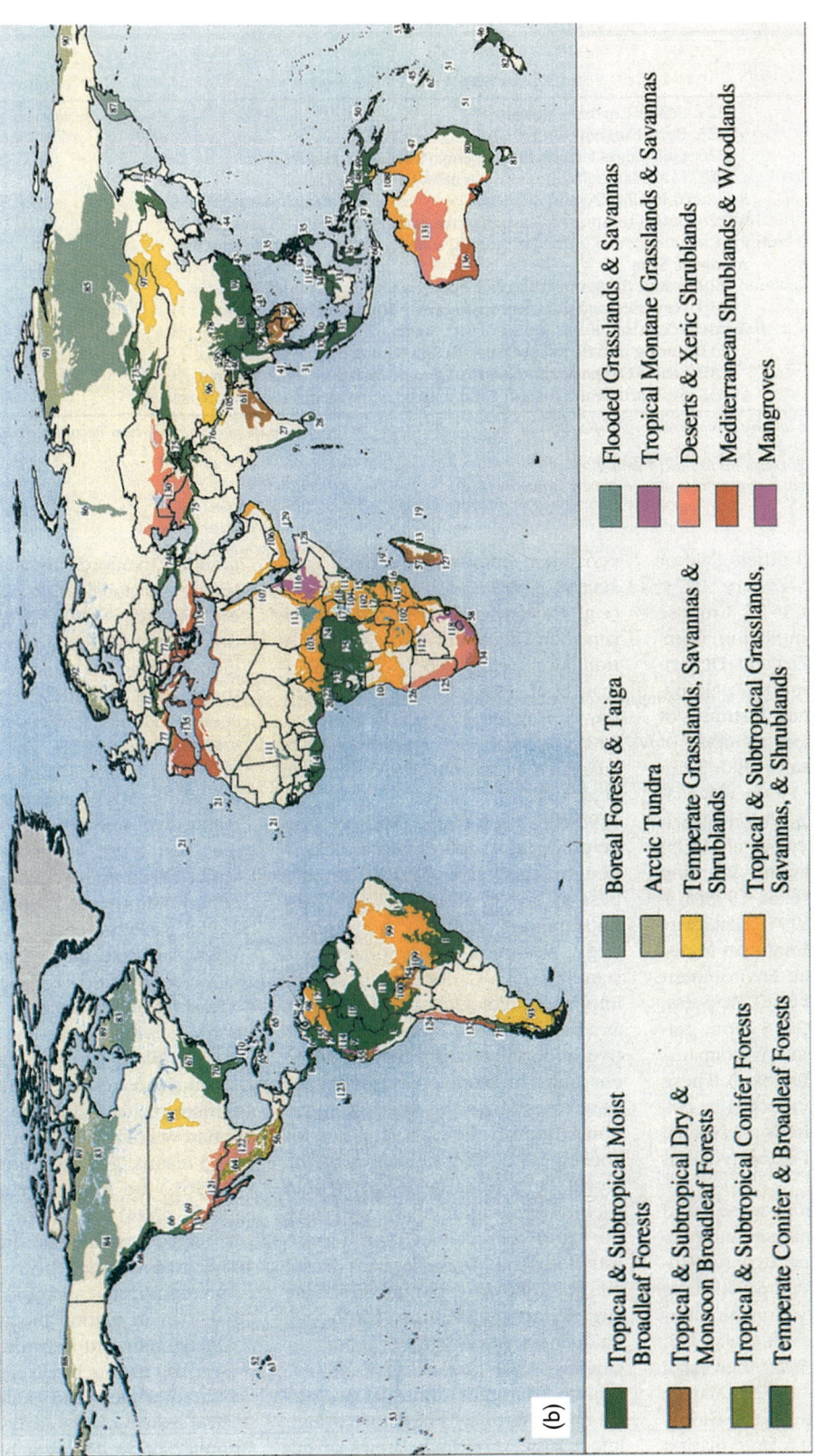

Fig. 8.7 (a) Global hotspots for biodiversity identified by Mittermeier *et al* (1998) and (b) Top 200 terrestrial sites identified by Olsen and Dinerstein (1998), using the representation approach. Reproduced with kind permission of Blackwell Science.

Olsen and Dinerstein (1998) have compiled a list of 200 priority conservation areas (the Global 200) by first dividing the world up in to realms (marine, freshwater, terrestrial) and by major habitat types or biomes (tropical moist forest, temperate grasslands, arctic tundra, etc.). They then further subdivided these by biogeographical realms (Neotropical, Australasian, Palearctic, etc.) and then into ecoregions within each realm that contain the most distinctive examples of biodiversity. Final selection within these subdivisions was made using a range of criteria as shown below:

1. species richness;
2. endemism;
3. taxonomic uniqueness;
4. unusual ecological or evolutionary phenomena;
5. global rarity of the major habitat type.

This analysis produced a list of 233 areas of highest priority for conservation (Fig. 8.7b)

The complementarity approach

This method is closely allied to the representation approach and progresses by dividing the area of concern in to spatial units of set size to produce a grid. A focal taxon or group, whose species composition and distribution is well known, is used and complementary sets of spatial units are sought (by computer analysis) in which each species is represented at least once. The aim is usually to produce the most space-efficient protected area system by identifying the smallest group of spatial units which contains all species. This can then be seen as the minimum set of areas required for the conservation of that taxon.

In a study using British breeding birds, Williams et al. (1996) compared three methods of choosing priority areas for conservation. The top 5% 10×10 km grid squares were chosen by

1. selecting the 5% richest in species (richness method);
2. selecting the 5% richest in species with restricted ranges (taken as the 25% of species with most restricted ranges in Britain; rarity method); and
3. selecting the 5% with the greatest combined species richness (complementarity method).

The richness method produced a set of areas that contained only 89% of all British bird species; the rarity method produced a set that covered 98% and the complementarity method covered all species (Fig. 8.8). The complementarity method is also efficient at identifying areas that supplement the existing conservation network by adding more species to the list of those within protected areas. Whilst this may be effective within a given taxonomic group, as we saw earlier in this chapter, there is no guarantee that any group will be a good surrogate for others. This assumption was tested by Jaarsveld et al. (1998) using data from South African plants and animals and found little overlap among complementary sets derived from different taxonomic groups. Therefore the complementarity approach also requires a 'shopping basket' approach, which involves the use of a range of taxonomic groups.

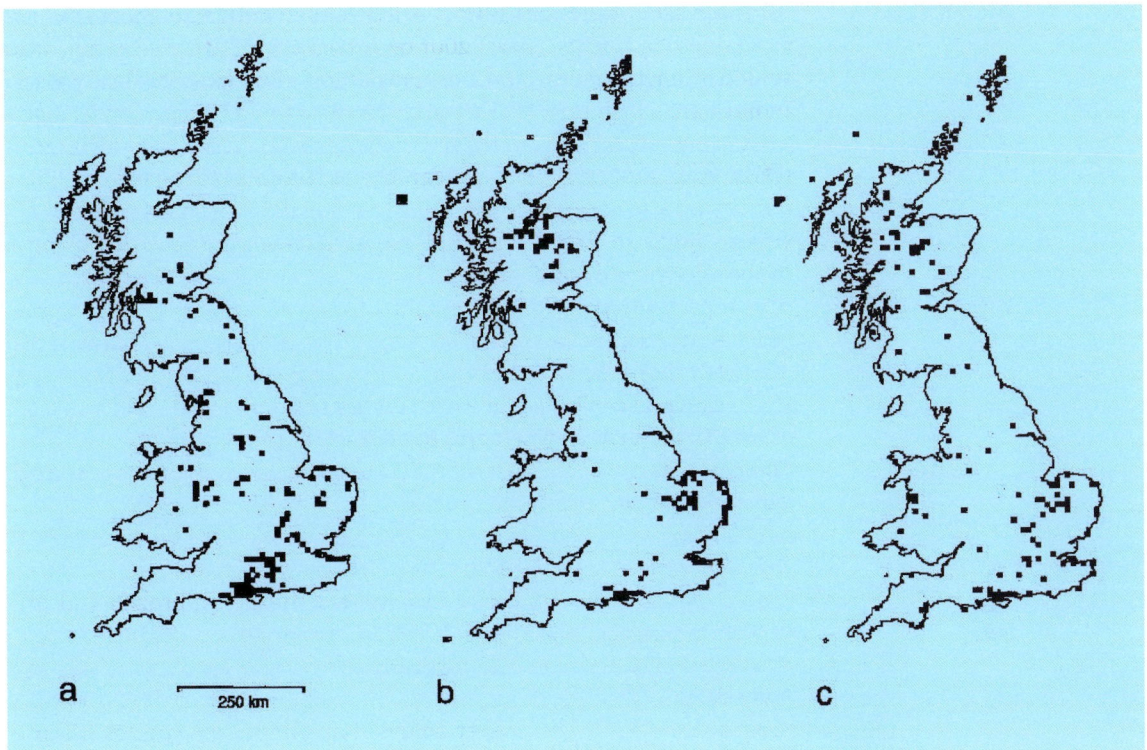

a   250 km   b   c

Habitat-based approaches

An alternative to the problem of dealing with number and relationships among species is to prioritise habitat types for protection. This approach has been developed by English Nature (1994). In order to draw up a list of priority habitats, a set of criteria was devised with a scoring system for each as shown in Table 8.3. Using these criteria produced top priority for terrestrial habitats such as chalk cliffs and lowland neutral meadow and pasture, and aquatic habitats such as brackish lagoons and mesotrophic standing waters. This type of approach relies heavily on good quality information and the ability to

Fig. 8.8 Distribution of top 5% grid cells using (a) the richness method, (b) the rarity method and (c) the complementarity method for British birds. Reproduced from Williams *et al.* (1996) with kind permission of Blackwell Science.

Table 8.3 | Criteria used by English Nature to categorise habitats according to their need for protection

Criteria	Score: 0	1	2	3
International importance (NW Europe)		England holds <10% total	10–40%	>40%
% GB total in England		<20%	20–60%	>60%
Area (ha)	>100000	10000–100000	1000–9999	<1000
Loss since 1940	Area increased	<10%	10–40%	>40%
Threat (source)		Low	Medium	High
Threat (area)	<10%	10–40%	41–60%	>60%
Naturalness		Artificial	Semi-natural	Natural
Fragmentation		Relatively unfragmented	Fragmented	Highly fragmented

estimate accurately qualitative variables such as threat. These are only available in a limited number of countries. More detailed criteria for selecting Special Areas for Conservation on a European scale are given in Box 8.3.

Box 8.3 | Selection of Special Areas for Conservation

The designation of Special Areas for Conservation (SACs) has been the subject of a European Community (EC) directive (European Commission Habitats Directive 92/43/EEC (1992)) and each member state has drawn up a list of priority habitat types and species for the designation process. The following is modified from the policy of the Joint Nature Conservation Committee (JNCC) of the UK government.

The EC process and criteria for site selection

The process that member states and the Commission must follow in drawing up the list of SACs is broken down into two stages:

Stage 1. Assessment of the relative importance of sites containing examples of the individual habitat types and species in each Member State.

Stage 2. Assessment of the overall importance of the sites in the context of the appropriate biogeographical region and the EC as a whole.

The criteria to be employed can be summarised as:

For habitats:

a. degree of representativity;
b. area;
c. degree of conservation of habitat structure and function and restoration possibilities;
d. global assessment of the site (i.e. the overall assessment, based on a–c above).

For species:

a. proportion of the total national population at the site;
b. degree of conservation and restoration possibilities of the features of the habitat that are important for the species;
c. degree of isolation of the population;
d. global assessment (i.e. overall assessment, based on a–c above).

In addition, member states are required to classify sites on their national lists according to their relative value for each habitat type and species and to identify which of the sites in their national lists are selected for priority habitat types and species.

The criteria used in Stage 2 are intended to be used to assess the sites at the level of the six biogeographical regions of Europe and the EC as a whole. The Stage 2 criteria may be summarised as:

a. relative value of the site at national level;
b. relationship of the site to migration routes or its role as part of an ecosystem on both sides of one or more Community frontiers;
c. total area of the site;
d. number of priority habitat types and species present;
e. global ecological value (i.e. overall assessment, based on a–d above) of the site at the level of the biogeographical region and/or EC as a whole.

Site selection principles in the UK

In preparing the UK national list, eleven main factors have been employed on the basis of the above requirements.

For habitats:

Representativity
Area of habitat
Conservation of structure and function

For species:

Proportion of UK population
Conservation of features important for species survival
Isolation of species populations

General:

Priority/non priority status
Rarity
Geographical range
Special UK responsibilities
Multiple interest

The process of site selection as a whole in the UK has been one of considering, in respect of the relevant principles above, the relative value of the sites in relation to the whole national resource of each habitat type and species.

All the above methods of selection, despite their promise, could lead to the creation of isolated areas of protection. Some of the tools to combat this problem are design, management and monitoring, which are considered in the next chapter.

Summary

1. Protected areas vary greatly in their status. There are many different reasons for designation of areas and many different levels of protection, largely dependent on the country to which they belong.

2. Although biodiversity can be measured in sophisticated ways (including the use of species diversity indices) if the information is available, it is more often measured as the species richness in a limited taxonomic group because of constraints on resources. Biodiversity is therefore estimated and is subject to error.

3. Indicator taxa have commonly been used as surrogate measures of overall biodiversity in reserve selection. The assumption that diversity in one taxon is an accurate indicator of diversity in others has been repeatedly refuted by experiment. Consequently more complex multi-taxa indicator groups have been advocated.

4. Protected area selection must reflect both diversity and endemism. Due to their history and biogeography, some areas have a large

number of endemic species whilst not being particularly diverse. Tropical oceanic islands are the most prominent of these.

5. The following are key challenges for conservation of biodiversity in protected areas; the most diverse areas (in Third World tropical countries) are among the most weakly protected; the areas of highest diversity are to some extent dependent on the taxonomic group measured; the majority of diversity is composed of those groups least understood and least appreciated; centres of high diversity do not completely equate with centres of endemism.

6. Practical approaches to selection utilising data on both diversity, endemism and taxonomic distinctiveness can be used to select the most critical areas for protection. However, this may lead to the creation of isolated reserves and approaches are needed to avoid diversity loss as a result.

Discussion points

- What are the strengths and weaknesses of the protected area approach to conservation?
- Does the surrogacy approach to biodiversity assessment really work?
- How should we balance the value of diversity and endemism (and perhaps taxonomic distinctiveness) when prioritising sites for protection.

Further reading

Groombridge B. (ed) (2000). *Global biodiversity: earth's living resources in the 21st century*. Cambridge: World Conservation Monitoring Centre, Hoechst Foundation.

Heywood, V.H. (1995). *Global biodiversity assessment*. Cambridge: Cambridge University Press.

Sutherland, W.J. (2000). *The conservation handbook: research, management and policy*. Oxford: Blackwell Science.

Web sites

International Union for the Conservation of Nature (IUCN): www.iucn.org

World Conservation Monitoring Centre: www.wcmc.org.uk

Information on biodiversity in central and eastern Europe: www.grida.no/enrin/biodiv/ index.htm

Chapter 9

Design and management of protected areas

Once an area has been identified for protection the next steps are to design the reserve system and to put in place a plan for the management of the area(s) that will ensure protection and conservation of its biodiversity. Equally as important are the monitoring of outcomes of the management and the assessment of its effectiveness. This chapter continues from the previous one in responding to the problems of habitat destruction and fragmentation covered in Chapter 4.

By reading this chapter students will gain an understanding of the ways in which reserves can be designed to optimise their value, an understanding of the need to manage reserves and a knowledge of the range of different management approaches to different habitat types. Lastly they should gain an understanding of the vital importance of monitoring to assess the effectiveness of a management plan.

Designing protected areas

We have seen that in the past most protected areas have been set up in a random fashion more dependent on opportunity than design. However, a growing body of literature has developed on the optimal design of protected areas. The principles owe much to the theory of island biogeography and more recently to the concept of metapopulations, both of which were introduced in Chapter 4. Let us now look at some factors that could be optimised in the theoretical design of a protected area.

Shapes and sizes

It is generally agreed that the optimal shape for a protected area is circular (Fig. 9.1) because circles have minimum edge to area ratio therefore minimising marginal areas and edge effects. Additionally, the centre of the reserve will be further from the edge than for any alternative shape of the same area. Obviously most protected areas are of irregular shape, but a roughly circular shape should be aimed for. Discontinuities and constrictions that may inhibit movement of species should be avoided. This includes the building of roads or similar linear

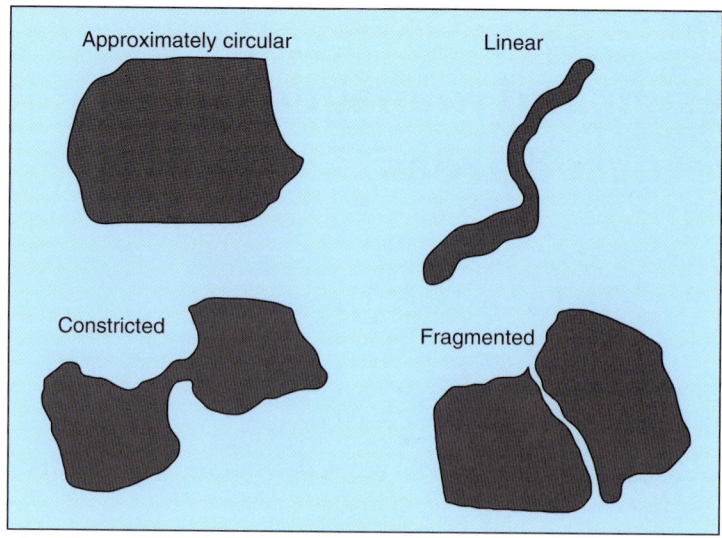

Fig. 9.1 Some common shapes of protected areas. Approximately circular areas are best in theory because they minimise edge to area ratio.

structures through the reserve. Many species are reluctant to cross even the narrowest of gaps in their habitat, whilst others may suffer increased mortality in doing so. Roads and other linear features also allow incursion of predators and effectively create another edge.

The obvious answer to the question of optimum size is the bigger the better, but in a situation where every hectare has to be fought for and subsequently protected, the question becomes more one of minimum viable size. This question is obviously linked to those species that demand the largest areas (usually large vertebrate carnivores). If the carrying capacity of the protected area is below the minimum for a viable population (see Chapter 10), it isn't big enough unless movement is possible to and from neighbouring reserves. Newmark (1987) was able to show that mammalian extinctions in western North American parks were inversely proportional to park size (Fig. 9.2). The smaller parks were losing many larger species, presumably because they could not maintain viable populations in isolation.

It seems clear from the available evidence that most protected areas, particularly those in Europe, are too small to maintain viable populations of larger species. One strategy to combat this problem could be to acquire surrounding land and enlarge the area, but this is usually not possible and many parks are already under pressure at their borders and the appropriate habitat is no longer there. The alternative is to acquire land that is nearby in order to try and form a network of protected areas in which populations can be linked by movement of individuals reducing probability of extinction (see Chapter 12).

Pickett & Thompson (1978) argued that protected areas should be large enough to contain the complete range of habitat heterogeneity of the area being represented and to accommodate the disturbance dynamics of the system. This would allow natural process to be maintained and such areas would require minimal management. Related to this point, it is obviously better that the reserve encompasses entire

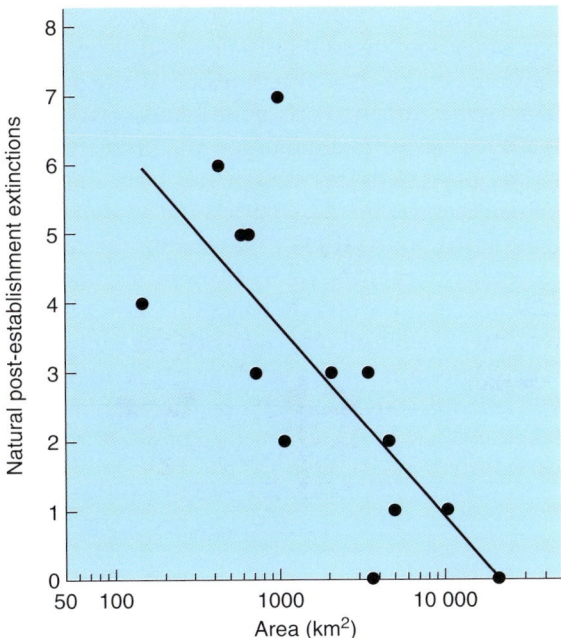

Fig. 9.2 Relationship between the size of protected areas in western North America and the number of known species extinctions recorded in those areas. Reproduced from Newmark (1987) with kind permission of the author and Macmillan Magazines Ltd.

metapopulations so that species are self-sustaining at the reserve level. However, habitats are often fragmented for a variety of reasons and the opportunities to designate protected areas as large as the ecosystem are few. This has led to a debate on the optimisation of reserve space. Is it better to have one large reserve encompassing both optimal and suboptimal areas or to have several small reserves (amounting to the same area) focused on optimal habitat? This has been called the Single Large or Several Small (SLOSS) debate. It may be that single large is best for most species whose populations would be isolated and below viable population size in small areas, but some species may survive equally well in several small areas in some situations. To some extent this question is dependent on the scale at which habitats occur in a heterogenous landscape and the mobility of the species concerned, which determines whether they are isolated within habitat patches or can move freely among them. It is also sometimes the case that several well-placed reserves will conserve a greater diversity of species than one large reserve. This may be particularly true for plants that are distributed in a naturally patchy environment. The rich flora of the South African Cape is very patchily distributed and in theory, several small, well-placed reserves would protect more diversity than a single large one (unless it covered the entire area), but whether the small populations are viable in the long term is not known.

Design of marine reserves

Design of reserves to conserve marine biodiversity presents particular challenges because of the different spatial and temporal processes that operate in marine systems and our general ignorance of the structure of marine communities. Marine ecosystems may have no obvious boundaries and their dynamics may operate over much larger scales than terrestrial ecosystems. The fauna may well be very transient dependent on the dynamics of ocean currents. Added to this is the issue of ownership (or lack of it), which is often a barrier to designation and protection.

A proposal for marine protected area design has been made by Hooker *et al.* (1999) in which they use the distribution and abundance of marine cetaceans to delimit the boundaries of a reserve off the coast of Nova Scotia, Canada. They found that the cetaceans were significantly more abundant in a gully area of the Scotia shelf up to 100 km in length and up to 2000 m deep. They therefore proposed that the gully area, with a 10-km buffer zone, be designated as a marine reserve, to protect it from the oil and gas production activities which are currently increasing on the shelf (Fig. 9.3).

Fig. 9.3 Proposed marine reserve off the coast of Nova Scotia, Canada. Reproduced from Hooker *et al.* (1999) with kind permission of Blackwell Science.

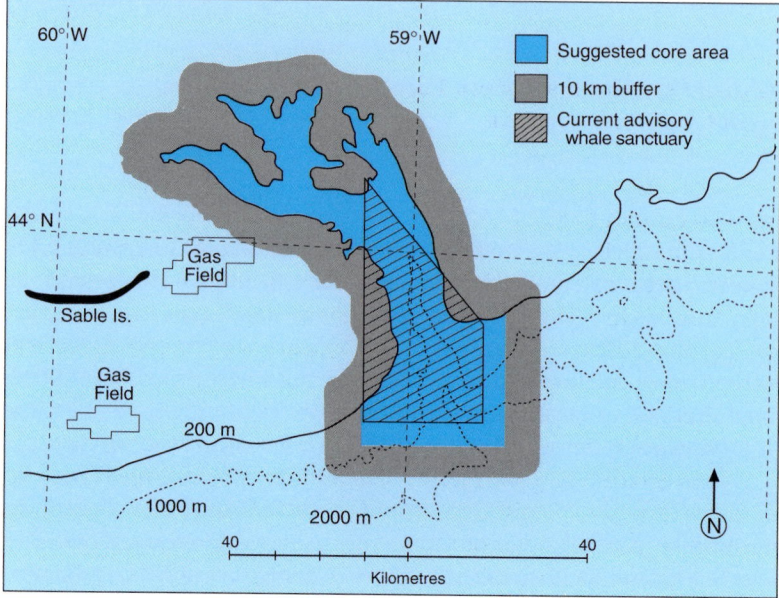

In summary, beyond the accepted logic of the optimal shape and size of reserves, their optimal design depends greatly on the type of ecosystem and landscape and the objectives for the reserve; designing a reserve for perennial herbs may require very different criteria to a reserve for a large predatory mammal.

Managing protected areas

Once a protected site has been designated it may be that it is large enough to continue to function as a truly natural ecosystem without significant human intervention, like the Greenland National Park, which covers 972 000 km². More realistically though, the majority of protected areas are too small and heavily influenced by human activity to be left alone. The natural dynamics of many areas have been radically altered such that leaving the area alone would result in rapid community change and possible loss of biodiversity value. Active management is often necessary and it is essential to plan the management of the site in order to maintain or enhance its biodiversity.

The management of reserves in its widest sense (including resources, labour, social and political issues) is outside the scope of this text. Here we consider to what extent practical management is based on knowledge of the ecology of systems. In the final chapter we will consider how to improve further the scientific evidence on which management is based.

When and why is management necessary?

Almost all protected areas are influenced by or under threat from human activity. Management is required to compensate for or counteract this activity in order to conserve biodiversity. The level of management that is required depends on the nature of the ecosystem to be conserved and the past level of human involvement in its processes. For example, a grassland system in southern Europe which has developed following hundreds of years of grazing by domestic livestock (e.g. sheep, cattle or goats) may require intensive management to retain its semi-natural communities. A large tropical rainforest reserve that has experienced minimal human impact in the past may need little in terms of management (although it will need protection) in the future. In general though, protected areas can require management for the following reasons:

1. their communities are the result of long-term human activity;
2. they are small fragments of the former ecosystem and therefore cannot support many of the species that formerly occurred there;
3. they are isolated from other natural areas and the dynamics of colonisation and extinction may not favour persistence of many species;
4. remnant areas will not experience the former frequency of natural disturbance, such as fires or floods;
5. they are surrounded by a different, and usually fundamentally altered ecosystem, which may threaten the integrity of the area through pollution or other disturbance.

Management aims and objectives

The type of management entered into is entirely dependent on the objectives for the reserve. Each reserve will have its priority communities and species that may, or may not, have been the reason for its original selection (see Chapter 8). The objectives should form the focus for management and only when these are clear can the management plan be constructed.

A common objective for large areas is to maintain the natural processes and interactions present in the community or ecosystem. The community of organisms present on a reserve is a reflection of the ecological processes that shape the system. There will often be key processes that dominate and therefore must be maintained, e.g.

hydrological regimes, grazing, or fire. Some species may also have a keystone role (see Chapter 6) and have to be managed accordingly, e.g. large herbivores, carnivores, ants or trees.

Activities surrounding the reserve may require a management response. Negative influences such as disturbance and pollution may have to be combatted directly. In many cases the conservation manager will need to work with the owners of land surrounding the reserve to reduce negative impacts of their land-use practices. In areas where there is significant human pressure, efforts should be made to encourage use of the reserve for educational and perhaps recreational purposes to raise the value of the reserve to the local community.

Included within the objectives of many reserves, particularly in Europe, is the critical factor of past human land use. The biodiversity present may depend heavily on traditional management practices that were not aimed at conservation. In this case, certain aspects of the traditional land use may need to be retained and other factors refined. However, just because a management practice is traditional doesn't necessarily mean it is good for conservation or the best option, a subject we will explore below and in Chapter 15.

Management of semi-natural communities

Intensive management of protected areas is most highly developed in the small nature reserves of Europe. Here many of the management practices are based on the traditional management of the land that created the characteristic communities. Below we explore a number of examples of this, largely taken from the UK.

Woodland management

Woodland is the natural climax community over much of Europe but little of the original natural cover remains (see Fig. 3.7). Some woodland may be left relatively unmanaged as 'high forest', however most semi-natural woodland has a history of management of some kind. Rackham (1986) lists six basic situations in which trees have remained in the UK landscape:

1. wildwood: land on which trees have arisen naturally but may be managed to provide timber, etc.;
2. wood-pasture: trees in a pastoral landscape managed for grazing animals;
3. plantation: afforested land, usually of one or few introduced species. Could be on land which was clear of trees for a considerable time;
4. non-woodland: single trees in hedgerows and fields;
5. orchards: plantations of trees managed for fruit production;
6. ornamentals: planted specimen trees in gardens and streets.

The first is closest to the original forest cover and thus of high conservation value. Points two to four are also of importance to conservation because they provide habitat for a variety of species. The remaining two are of low conservation value.

Coppice management

People have traditionally made use of the self-renewing power of trees by practising a rotational cropping system. Many native European hardwoods will regrow from stump or root systems allowing a woodland patch to be cut one year and left to regrow whilst other patches are being cut in subsequent years on a rotational basis; a practice called coppicing (Fig. 9.4). This is an efficient way of obtaining poles for construction of huts and fences, etc. A common form of this practice is called 'coppice with standards', in which some mature trees are left to provide structural timber and the underwood is coppiced.

Coppicing is usually carried out on a rotational basis in woodland (over a 5–30 year period depending on species), so that each year a section is cut. This forms a shifting mosaic of open and closed woodland in different successional stages. Mobile species can move around with

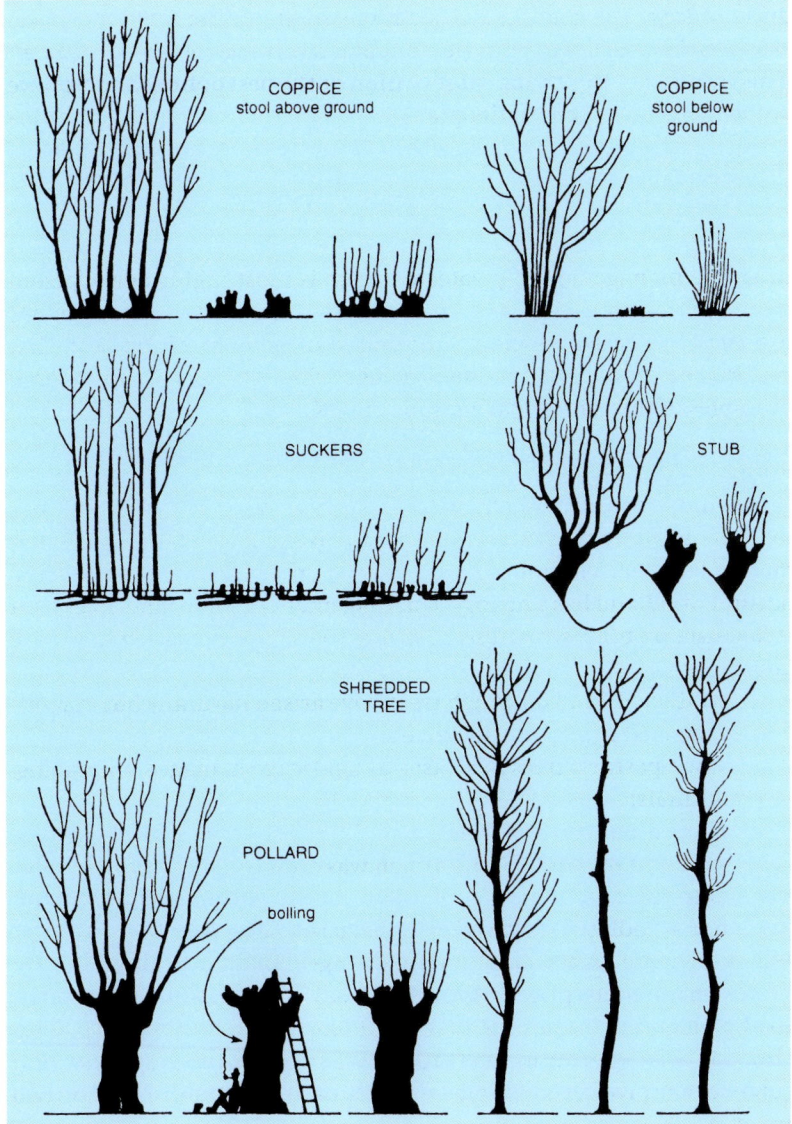

Fig. 9.4 Common traditional forms of woodland management in the UK. Reproduced from Rackham (1986) with kind permission of Cambridge University Press.

the cycle and exploit the suitable areas. Many plants can survive in vegetative or seed form until the right conditions return for flowering. The problem is that coppicing requires an annual input of labour, for which the returns have been diminishing in modern times. Coppice woodland has therefore become increasingly neglected this century and the result has been a more uniform closed structure. Many species that rely on the periodic clearings have therefore been lost.

The consequences of the neglect of coppicing in woodland were demonstrated in an experiment at Monks Woods National Nature Reserve. This is a medium to large mixed deciduous woodland in Cambridgeshire, traditionally managed as coppice with standards. When taken over by the Nature Conservancy Council, Monks Wood had a fauna and flora which was rich for eastern England, at a time when intensive agriculture was beginning to decimate large areas of this region. A decision was made to leave large areas of the wood unmanaged and to record the changes in the fauna and flora. The wood inevitably became more enclosed with the canopy maturing and rides closing up. This resulted in the disappearance of many of the species for which the wood was originally designated a reserve. This included such sun-loving groups as the butterflies, from which 11 species were lost in the space of 20 years (Table 9.1).

Table 9.1 Disappearance of butterfly species from Monks Wood NNR since it was managed as a nature reserve

Date of disappearance	Species
1957	*Hamearis lucina* (Duke of Burgundy)
Late 1950s	*Argynnis aglaja* (dark-green fritillary)
1962	*Argynnis adippe* (high brown fritillary)
1963	*Boloria euphrosyne* (pearl-bordered fritillary)
1966	*Thecla betulae* (brown hairstreak)
1969	*Erynnis tages* (dingy skipper)
	Argynnis paphia (silver-washed fritillary)
	Aricia agestis (brown argus)
Early 1970s	*Callophrys rubi* (green hairstreak)
1971	*Carterocephalus palaemon* (chequered skipper)
1976	*Melanargia galathea* (marbled white)

Source: Data from Thomas (1991).

Realisation of this situation led to a revised management plan involving the maintenance of open space within the woodland. Research at Monks Wood and elsewhere has suggested that sheltered but sunny patches are of vital importance to many woodland invertebrates because they provide warmth as well as nectar sources and larval food plants. A management practice other than traditional coppicing that has been successful in creating such areas is the cutting of wide rides leaving herbaceous vegetation at each side, with intersections

Fig. 9.5 Woodland ride management for conservation. Reproduced from Kirby (1992) with kind permission of JNCC.

between rides that act as periodic clearings. A ride with a width roughly 1.5 times the height of the bordering trees is needed to ensure that at least part will remain sunny through the hours of daylight. Creation of a band of coppice along the rideside may facilitate this (Fig. 9.5). Any ride management e.g. mowing or cutting is done on a rotational basis to provide a mixture of sward and scrub heights.

Species conservation in coppiced woodland

The heath fritillary butterfly (*Mellicta athalia*) suffered a substantial decline in the UK during the second half of the twentieth century. The main larval food plant throughout much of its range is common cow wheat (*Melanpyrum pratense*) which relies on coppice clearing for growth, exploiting the open areas in which to flower and set seed. Blean Woods National Nature Reserve in Kent contained a large heath fritillary population when it was designated in 1950s, but this had dropped to just a few individuals in 1980. This decline was thought to be the result of a break in the coppice cycle between 1970 and 1974 so that its food plant became scarce during this time (Warren 1991). Since 1980 the reserve has been managed specifically for the butterfly. A substantial area is now coppiced in small plots of 1–5 hectares on a rotation of 15–20

Fig. 9.6 Response of the heath fritillary butterfly (*Mellicta athalia*) to coppice management in Blean Woods National Nature Reserve, UK. Shaded areas indicate distribution of adults and dates refer to year of coppicing. Reproduced from Warren (1991) with kind permission of Elsevier Science.

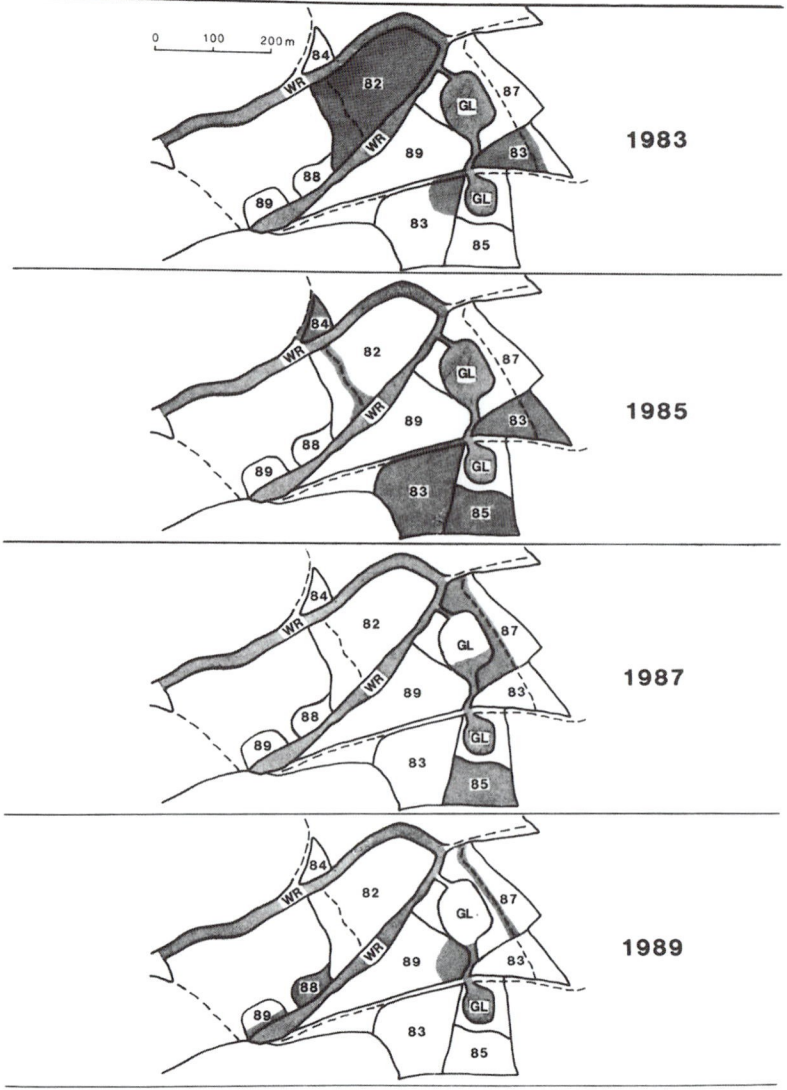

years and the plots have been connected by a series of rides and permanent glades (Fig. 9.6). The butterfly has subsequently recovered in numbers and similar management practices are being implemented in other sites where the species has been reintroduced.

The decline of the nightingale (*Luscinia megarhynchos*), a migratory warbler renowned for its beautiful song, has probably been partly caused by neglect of coppiced woodland. Research by Stuttard & Williamson (1971) has suggested that the distribution of this species is strongly correlated with a particular stage in the coppice cycle. They established this by recording the number of singing males in a range of coppiced woodland and concluded that coppice 4–8 years after cutting was required for the persistence of the species in Kent (Fig. 9.7).

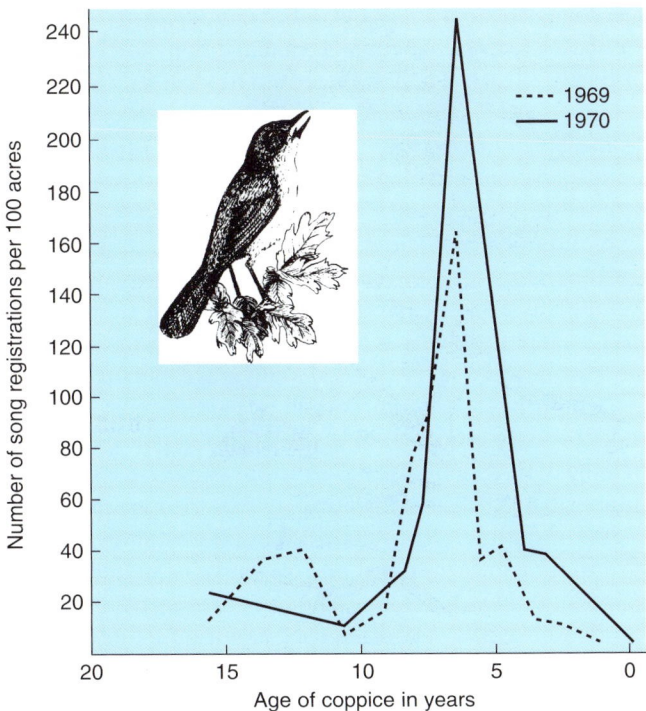

Fig. 9.7 Response of the nightingale (*Luscinia megarhynchos*) to the coppice management cycle. Reproduced from Stuttard & Williamson (1971) with kind permission of the British Trust for Ornithology.

Presumably the shrub layer at this age affords protection to singing males from predation and provides suitable nesting sites. A more general study of the effect of coppice management on songbirds shows that most species select areas of coppice between 3 and 10 years old and this is explained by changes in the density of the shrub layer as the trees recover (Fuller & Henderson 1992).

Among the mammals, the dormouse (*Muscardinus avellanarius*) is strongly associated with coppice with standards management in the UK. This species feeds predominantly on hazelnuts (*Corylus avellana*), a major component of the coppiced understorey. Dormice are almost entirely arboreal in their activity and consequently have limited dispersal capacity. Maintenance of viable populations and interchange between subpopulations is thought to depend heavily on maintenance of substantial woodland areas with established coppice management.

Despite these examples of the importance of coppicing to certain species, there is significant controversy over the use or overuse of the practice within woodlands. Not all species benefit from coppicing and there is some evidence that species associated with ancient late-successional woodland may be threatened by it. These include species dependent on old and decaying wood such as saproxylic insects and fungi as well as some birds such as woodpeckers. A number of rare forest grasses in southern Sweden appear to have been eradicated by coppice management and are reliant on ancient beech forest persisting without disturbance (Brunet 1993). It has been argued that less charismatic species such as these make up the majority of woodland biodiversity and they may be threatened by overuse of coppice management to conserve a charismatic minority. Clearly a balance needs to be struck.

Wood-pasture and parkland management

Wood-pasture and parklands are open canopy woodland areas traditionally maintained by grazing animals such as sheep, cattle or deer. The artificially maintained high density of grazers prevents growth of sapling trees and therefore after natural tree mortality and/or selective felling what remains is a landscape of scattered mature trees with a grass-dominated understorey, which forms the familiar parkland still found on some European country estates. Many parklands date from medieval times when they were maintained as part of royal hunting forests or parts of country estates. Beside the hunting, poles were harvested from trees by periodic pollarding, a similar system to coppicing, but the cut is higher, 2.5–3.5 m above ground, so that the new shoots are out of reach of grazing animals, thus maintaining the established trees (Fig. 9.4). Pollarding is also carried out on rows of trees in hedges and along riverbanks (e.g. willows, *Salix* spp.). The wood was used for fuel and construction whilst the leaves were often used as winter fodder for livestock. This practice can be very significant in increasing tree longevity and in provision of dead-wood habitats (see below).

Grazing of wood-pasture was widespread in Europe up to the nineteenth century but changes in agricultural and forestry practice have severely reduced the amount of this habitat. The parklands that remain contain largely over-aged trees in an advanced state of decay. Long-term maintenance of wood-pasture requires selective planting and protection of young trees that will eventually replace the old, and maintenance of grazing at the correct intensity. In some cases, as in Hatfield Forest in Essex, UK, the practice of pollarding has been neglected and the trees (hornbeams, *Carpinus betulus* and oaks, *Quercus robur*) have become top heavy with regrowth and are in danger of falling. Pollarding was reinstated, but many of the trees were apparently unable to cope with the removal of such large branches and many failed to regrow or suffered dieback (Wisenfeld 1995).

Many old parkland trees provide an important habitat for a diverse community that live on and actively decompose dead wood (the saproxylic community). Dead and rotting wood is an extremely important and neglected habitat for a high diversity of saproxylic invertebrates and fungi. Managers of parkland have traditionally cleaned up dead wood, both to keep the parkland tidy and to prevent the spread of disease among trees. This is a good example of where traditional management is not appropriate for conservation aims. Conservation management in this case is to allow dead wood to remain and decay where it is. Large pieces of timber are most valuable and best placed in partial shade where they remain damp and cool. Very old trees should be carefully managed to preserve decaying parts. Most controversial is a management policy of damaging young healthy trees to bring on premature senility. Pollarding is a good way of 'damaging' trees providing sites for invasion of fungi and the start of decay. The trees can then be inoculated with spores of wood-decaying fungi. Another strategy is to plant shorter-lived trees but which support similar dead-wood communities, for example, sweet chestnut (*Castanea sativa*) rather than oak. Creation of wood piles from felling operations is also thought to be a good way of creating habitat. All of these strategies involve complex management and none as yet have been the subject of full scientific experimentation and monitoring of results.

Grassland and heathland management

Grassland is a very broad term disguising a very diverse set of habitats, heavily influenced by geology and soil structure. Grasslands are normally broadly classified according to soil conditions as calcareous, neutral or acidic. Other less common special types are also of conservation importance, such as salt-marsh grassland, sand-dune grassland and cliff-top grassland.

In Europe, grasslands have largely been created by man's activities following clearing of forest. Two common traditional management practices for grassland maintenance are grazing, producing pastureland and cutting for hay, producing meadow. Pastureland types are very diverse depending partly on the management. For example, the nature of pasture will depend on whether the sward has been sown and/or fertilised with periodic ploughing (improved pasture), or is self-seeding and unploughed and is only fertilised by the dung of the grazing animals (high conservation value). Additionally, the intensity and timing of the grazing practised will influence its floristic diversity and its invertebrate fauna.

Traditional grazing practices may have partly compensated for the loss of large wild herbivores and their impact on natural systems in highly populated areas such as Europe. This may have enabled the persistence of many species that were dependent on natural disturbance in the emerging human-dominated landscape. The decline of these traditional practices may therefore have a greater negative impact on biodiversity than it might first appear (Pykala 2000).

Grazing of traditional pastures has decreased for economic reasons and the last 100 years has seen a significant shift from grazing in many areas of Europe. Typical traditional distributions of grassland in the southern counties of the UK are exemplified by my home county of Wiltshire. On a map made in 1794 (Fig. 9.8) one can see areas of pasture that would have supported cattle on relatively fertile neutral grasslands on clay soils. The downs are calcareous grassland which were used for sheep grazing, and water meadows would have been used for hay production with grazing on the regrowth. There was relatively little woodland as it had already been largely cleared by this time. All of these semi-natural systems have been altered by modern farming practices. The clay pastures have been improved, and ploughed for arable production in many cases. The chalk downlands were ploughed and heavily fertilised for arable production at a time when the economic situation was suitable. Water meadows have fared the worst; these are situated along

Fig. 9.8 Map of the county of Wiltshire, UK in the late eighteenth century, showing the major land use types. Reproduced from Duffey *et al.* (1974) with kind permission of Kluwer Academic Publishers.

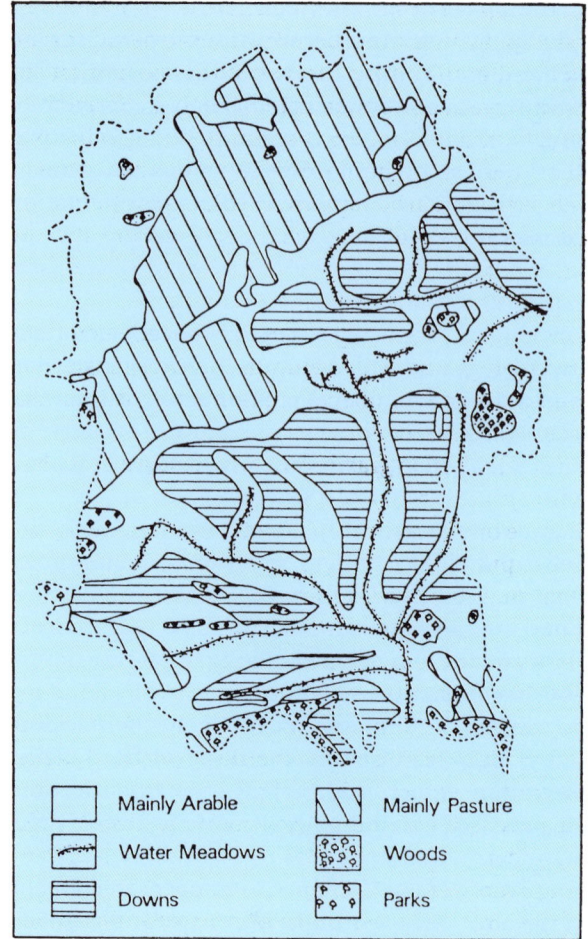

riverbanks and are flooded in the winter using the water as a source of fertiliser. They have declined dramatically over the last 50 years, as they are in flat low-lying areas. The increase in drainage technology and management of water courses has enabled their use as arable land. Consequently the specialist flora and fauna of these areas has similarly declined.

Management of grassland nature reserves is generally dictated by traditional practices. Grassland character can be rapidly altered by changes in management, so consistency is the safest option. For example, hay meadows are cut once a year for their crop and the community is directly related to the timing of cutting. Most are cut during late June and July and this favours spring-flowering plants. The impact of the mowing is so catastrophic that the community is specialised and not necessarily highly diverse. However, the community will change rapidly, and possibly to one of lesser conservation value, if the cutting regime is replaced by any other form of management.

The largest UK colony of an endangered plant, the snake's head fritillary (*Fritillaria meleagris*), occurs at North Meadow in Wiltshire. It is regularly flooded by the upper Thames river in winter and the summer hay crop is divided among local commoners (local residents who have joint rights to the use of the land and joint responsibility for its management). The commoners may then subsequently graze livestock from 12 August each year. This common land arrangement has probably prevented any major 'improvement' of the Meadow and it was designated a National Nature Reserve in 1973. The important point here is that the management regime does not necessarily maximise diversity. But the consistency of management over a long period of time has enabled a specialised community and its associated rare species to survive.

Many nature reserves that were traditionally grazed, now lack grazing stock and so mowing is used to maintain the sward instead of grazing. However, this has led to a number of problems because mowing is different from grazing in a number of ways:

1. mowing is uniform in action, grazing is always selective;
2. mowers cut where grazers pull and rip out vegetation;
3. mowing takes place once or twice a year, grazing is a longer-term lower impact practice;
4. the grazers leave their dung as fertiliser.

The distinction is shown by the example of three areas around Oxford, UK. Port Meadow, has a history of grazing and no cutting (therefore is pasture, not meadow) since 1086, whereas Pixey and Yarnton Meadows have been cut for hay and the aftermath grazed. Of the 95 species of plants that have been recorded in these areas, 26 were confined to Port Meadow (pasture) and 39 to the hay meadows. Only 30, mostly common, species were found in all, despite very similar soils and geology (Duffey *et al.* 1974). It seems that consistent management is more important on grassland sites than most other habitat types. Therefore, if the traditional management is known this should have a major influence on future management plans in the absence of more scientific evidence.

Some attempts have been made to address the complex issue of association of species with particular grassland management regimes. Walk & Warner (2000) studied the habitat preferences of four grassland songbirds in midwestern USA. A 473-hectare study area was divided into an array of 3-hectare management units providing a range of grassland types including burnt, mown, grazed, undisturbed and an area of arable weeds. Distinct preferences were shown by some of the species. Low intensity late-season grazing was attractive to all species because of the habitat heterogeneity that resulted, whereas recently burnt cool-season grasses were least attractive.

Problems can arise when management for single species conflicts with management for biodiversity as a whole. Grassland management for the silver-spotted skipper butterfly (*Hesperia comma*) requires heavy grazing of its calcareous grassland habitat to produce a very short turf with patches of bare ground with suitable clumps of the hostplant (*Festuca ovina*). Biodiversity of grassland invertebrates as a whole in southern UK is highest in tall grass and lowest in short turf (Morris 2000). This conflict can to some extent be resolved by maintaining heterogeneity, but the sizes of some reserves can make this difficult.

Heathlands occur on sandy soils which are acidic and low in nutrients. They provide a very important invertebrate habitat in northern Europe, being noticeably rich in rare thermophilous species at the northern edge of their range because bare sandy soils of early successional stages can provide a hot microclimate. More than half of the British species of spiders, dragonflies and true bugs are found in this habitat. Sandy soils are particularly suited for ground dwelling and burrowing species, which includes many spiders and solitary wasps.

As with grassland there are communities associated with every successional stage from bare ground to scrub and woodland, and management should therefore aim to maintain examples of all stages, but, in Europe, it is early successional heathland dominated by heathers (*Calluna vulgaris* and *Erica* spp.) that is generally regarded as having the highest conservation value. Past management has a profound influence on the flora and fauna they contain. As with grasslands, the traditional management has been grazing and without this the habitat is quickly colonised by later successional species such as bracken (*Pteridium aquilinum*) and invasive scrub and trees.

Maintaining early successional heaths requires careful management of grazing stock. Stocking density is generally much lower on heathland than more productive grassland. In principle, any grazing animal that can tolerate heathland can be used to provide management. Cattle often produce better results than sheep as their greater weight produces more effective ground disturbance and can suppress bracken growth. In addition they are more patchy grazers than sheep and will produce a more varied vegetation structure in grass-dominated areas. However, overgrazing by cattle can damage mature heather. Rabbits are generally encouraged on heathland reserves because it is thought that their digging and scraping as well as grazing produces a mosaic of vegetation structures, but large populations can cause extensive damage. The effects of grazing are very complex and a review of grazing as a management method in UK lowland heaths could not reach any firm conclusions on cause and effect (Bullock & Pakeman 1997).

Heather (*Calluna vulgaris*) a major component of European heaths, is managed on a rotational basis usually by burning. Webb (1986) has described its life cycle as consisting of four distinct growth phases: pioneer 3–10 years; building 7–13 years; mature 12–30 years; and degenerate >30 years. The pioneer phase is good for species that require hot sunny habitats, whilst more mature stands are good for web-building invertebrates and ground-nesting birds. Some species require more than one phase. Typical management is on a 15–20 year rotation, which avoids allowing the heather to degenerate too much and prevents too much scrub encroachment.

Burning has been widely used as a management tool to clear accumulated litter and expose bare soil, facilitating heather regeneration from seed. However, its use is controversial as it can damage the invertebrate community and may spread beyond the designated area. If it is used, only small areas should be burnt at any time and it should not be done when the litter is very dry and precautions should be taken to ensure that it doesn't spread. Sedlakova & Chytry (1999) were able to show that burning was more effective than turf cutting or mowing at encouraging heather regeneration in a central European dry heathland. Mowing appears to encourage the spread of grasses and does not remove the accumulated litter that covers the bare ground (removing litter may be resource intensive). Mowing also produces a more uniform habitat. The process of deliberately disturbing small areas by scraping can be beneficial in taking the habitat back to an early successional stage, but it also provides opportunities for establishment of scrub and tree species.

Bracken (*Pteridium aquilinum*) encroachment into heathland is an interesting problem since bracken does have some value as a habitat, but also can invade and wipe out heathland or grassland communities if uncontrolled. This species was used in the past in a similar way to straw as bedding for livestock, and was also valued as a fuel. Some insects feed solely on bracken whilst others exploit plants within bracken stands. Bracken invasion is associated with increased soil nutrient concentrations and once established it can be very difficult to control; some nature reserve managers resort to use of herbicides or cutting several times during the summer to control it. Both are expensive options. If it is not allowed to get out of hand in the first place, cattle grazing is suitable since bracken is intolerant of trampling.

The future of the Dartford warbler (*Sylvia undata*) in southern England is closely tied to the maintenance of sufficient heathland habitat. It reaches the northern limit of its range in southern Britain and its stronghold is the Dorset heath. It suffers in cold winters, being a resident insectivore, but in favourable periods it does expand its range and colonise small isolated patches of heath. In bad times it contracts in range back to the largest patches. Research by Bibby (1979) suggests this species is specialised to the scrubland habitat that gorse (*Ulex europeaus*) and mature heather provide. It usually nests in mature heather stands but the gorse is used primarily in foraging as it contains a denser invertebrate fauna (Fig. 9.9). Gorse is often found at low density, which limits

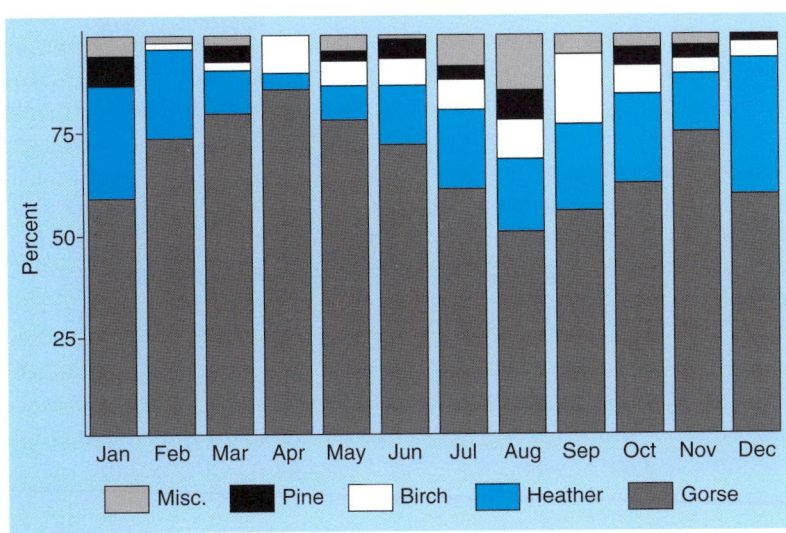

Fig. 9.9 Proportion of time Dartford warblers (*Sylvia undata*) spent feeding in different vegetation types during a year. Reproduced from Bibby (1979) with kind permission of the Zoological Society of London.

the warbler population, but is highest near to roads, which account for a significant amount of adult mortality. Additionally, uncontrolled burning can destroy the scrubby habitat, which takes a long time to recover. Increased visitor pressure is likely to increase the frequency of fires and road kills, so management for this species is concentrating on providing the right mix of scrubby species away from the roads.

Wetland management

Examples of management on two different types of wetland, raised bogs and fens, will suffice to illustrate the diversity of management required in this broad habitat category.

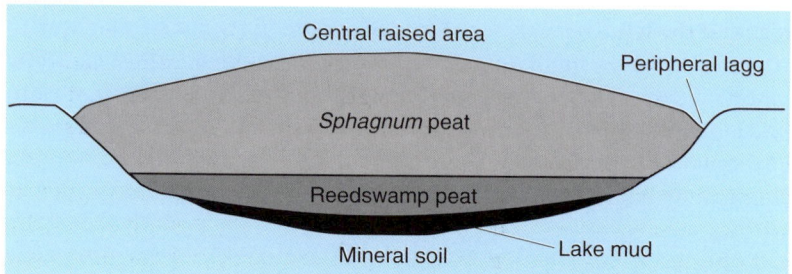

Fig. 9.10 Cross-section of a typical raised bog showing succession from lake through reedswamp to *Sphagnum* bog.

Raised bogs are composed of a convex lens of peat, normally developed in a basin over an initial marsh or lake (Fig. 9.10). Such bogs can be many square kilometres in extent, and would have once occurred all over northern Europe and North America, mostly in natural basins left after the last glaciation. The bog forms in high-rainfall areas as a result of a type of vegetation succession starting from open water, called a **hydrosere**; as vegetation invades the edge of a lake, litter and eventually peat accumulates forming a marsh-type habitat, at this stage dominated by sedges and reeds. The edge of the marsh can be invaded by wooded plants, but the middle continues to accumulate peat and when it reaches the height limit of winter flooding it becomes nutrient poor, no longer being under the influence of groundwater. Instead it is influenced by rainwater, which is naturally acidic. As a result, the community changes to acid bog, dominated by *Sphagnum* mosses. Initially species of *Sphagnum*, which are most tolerant of base-rich, nutrient-rich conditions dominate, but other species invade as the conditions change to being acidic and nutrient poor. In the latter conditions the *Sphagnum* grows more rapidly at the centre of the bog than at the edges and the profile becomes raised and dome-shaped. Since the peat is acidic, fully saturated and low in nutrients, scrub encroachment is not a problem.

The major threat to raised bogs is their use for commercial peat cutting. This not only causes the lowering of the surface as the peat is removed, but also causes desiccation due to the associated drainage practices. The first step in the process of mechanised peat cutting is to dry out the surface by digging drainage ditches so that the cutting machines can gain access. Most raised bogs have some history of peat digging and have suffered from drainage to some extent. Additionally, the infiltration of nutrient-rich groundwater can be a problem, but is usually secondary to desiccation. Desiccation of the bog allows invasion of scrub and trees such as birch and pine. Management of raised bogs for conservation commonly involves hydrological management to restore the water table. Drainage systems removing water from the edge of the bog can be blocked creating a lagg zone around the central dome and surface ditches can be blocked with peat to reduce runoff from the dome itself. Large-scale changes to the hydrology can effect surrounding agricultural land leading to problems with local farmers. In addition, rapid changes in water levels resulting from this type of management can adversely effect some of the characteristic species. Overwintering survival of the large heath butterfly (*Coenonympha tullia*) is significantly reduced when its bog habitat is inundated with water for much of the winter (Joy & Pullin 1999).

Fens can be permanently wet areas over silt, often called marshes, but most commonly they form over significant accumulations of peat. Much of the water comes from runoff from surrounding hills and so can be nutrient rich and often base rich. This makes them very different in character to bogs. However, their origins are very similar and the hydrosere in its early stages can go either to bog or fen, depending on the water table, acidity and supply of nutrients resulting in either bog moss (*Sphagnum*) or common reed (*Phragmites australis*) gaining dominance in the early stages (Fig. 9.11).

Fig. 9.11 Early stages of fen vegetation succession showing presence of both bog moss (*Sphagnum*) and reed grass (*Phragmites*).

Being nutrient-rich habitats, producing a high biomass of plant material, the speed of drying out and vegetation succession may be rapid. The value of fens and marshes for wildlife resides largely in the early successional stages that are characterised by wet open vegetation often dominated by common reed or sometimes sedges. If left alone this vegetation is quickly replaced by scrub, dominated in Europe by willow (*Salix*), birch (*Betula*), alder (*Alnus*) and finally oak or pine, whilst the whole system also dries out to form lowland woodland which, although of conservation value, does not support the specialist wetland species. Consequently, management has to be based around frequent disturbance to prevent scrub encroachment, usually by cutting, grazing and sometimes burning. In the longer term gross disturbance is necessary to prevent desiccation, involving removal of vegetation and lowering of the peat surface to restore open water areas (see Chapter 15 for restoration management of fenland). The fen vegetation is very much dependent on the type of management employed and some examples are given in Box 9.1.

Box 9.1 | Some common fenland management techniques

1. Grazing marshes: summer grazing is a traditional management in some fens and marshes producing a potentially rich and varied flora. If areas are overgrazed, this technique encourages growth of competitive grasses and unpalatable plants such as rushes (*Juncus*) reducing diversity of vegetation and fauna. As with grassland and heathland, the results of grazing depend crucially on the stock used and the stocking density and generalisations are elusive.

2. Reed cutting: winter cutting of reed is a traditional management practice, which maintains high, dense stands of reed, which provide good habitat for a particular community of wetland birds and invertebrates. Winter cutting requires management of the water table by a system of drains and sluices to dry out the surface before cutting.

3. Peat cutting: peat cutting on a small scale has enhanced some wetland areas, such as the Norfolk Broads. This takes succession right back to open water and essentially allows the fen to redevelop. The peat is cut in plots with peat banks being left in between for access and piling up of the cut peat for drying. This creates a patchwork of small pits that flood if not actively pumped. Some banks may then collapse in times of flood and storm to create larger areas of open water.

4. Summer mowing: summer mowing for hay together with removal of the cuttings, creates a more nutrient-poor flora and prevents dominance of reed. The sward tends to be shorter and more dense and favours sedges and herbs, or when particularly nutrient poor, *Sphagnum* moss. The removal of the cuttings is often a problem, particularly in more remote and inaccessible areas. Cuttings are often gathered into heaps and burnt, which creates local patches of high-nutrient levels encouraging invasion of weedy species.

5. Burning: direct burning of standing vegetation is a controversial fen management technique as it may have a negative impact on the fauna, particularly invertebrates. It is not thought to be a traditional activity in most fens but it is convenient and relatively cheap. More research is required on its effects before it is considered for general use.

Illustrations of the type of management undertaken for single species are provided by the following two examples.

The fen violet (*Viola persicifolia*) is confined to the base-rich fens and declined rapidly as they were drained, and also as they were abandoned and succession took many to woodland. A characteristic feature of this plant's ecology is that it germinates from seed after disturbance of the peat surface. In the past it must have relied on small-scale disturbance caused by falling trees or changes in water levels. By the 1970s it was confined in the UK to Woodwalton Fen National Nature Reserve (NNR), but following clearance of an area of scrub at nearby Wicken Fen the plants appeared in thousands. Since the area had not been touched for over 60 years it was clear that the seed must have remained dormant for this length of time. Much attention has been paid to trying to find the right kind of management to retain this species. Work by Pullin and Woodell (1987) suggested that small-scale disturbance on a long rotational basis of around 10–15 years could be beneficial. However, combining this with other priorities in fen management has not been easy.

The bittern (*Botaurus stellaris*), a secretive wetland bird of the heron family, is heavily dependent on open wet reedbed areas. Its food is largely aquatic and it uses the reedbeds, both for hunting and as a safe nesting site. It has declined in recent times because of the general decline in the market for reeds over the last century. This has led to the abandonment of these areas and the encroachment of scrub and alder/oak woodland. A UK national census in 1976 estimated only 45–47 pairs remained, centred on the Norfolk Broads. A survey of 17 reedbed sites used by bitterns for breeding in the UK over the period 1979 to 1994, showed that areas where breeding numbers were decreasing were characterised by scrub encroachment and reduction in the area of reed (Tyler *et al* 1998). This species is now the subject of a species recovery programme and has been the focus of an initiative to restore areas of open reedbed.

This section has been different from many other sections in this book because the information imparted on what is good or bad management is largely experience-based (i.e. it has worked for somebody and so the word has spread). This is a potentially dangerous way in which to spread information, because isolated one-off experiences cannot necessarily be relied upon. Conservation biology requires us to seek sound scientifically based evidence that management regimes are effective. This challenge will be picked up again in Chapter 15.

Monitoring change in protected areas

It is tempting to think that a major management objective should be to keep things as they are, frozen in time, and to combat all external forces for change. But we have seen from Chapter 7 that the view of ecosystems in equilibrium has been replaced by a dynamic view that systems do not naturally stay as they are. This is a major challenge for management, because effectively the goal posts are constantly moving. An essential element of any management plan is to monitor the effects of external influences and the management actions themselves. A practical consideration of the role of management plans is covered in Chapter 15; more general points are covered below.

Simple surveillance of communities may be carried out at regular intervals to detect changes in relative abundance of species over time, but monitoring differs in that it has specific aims and objectives, focused on testing for a response to change in an identified factor. For example, it may be the effect of a change in grazing regime on the plant community. The null hypothesis is therefore that the change in regime has no effect. When this is the case it is essential that the monitoring is adequate to be able to reject the null hypothesis if it is false. An inadequate sampling regime without proper control plots might fail to show an effect when one really exists. This may lead to inappropriate management decisions.

Monitoring for change may involve basic ecological sampling techniques to test for changes in the composition of communities or in the distribution and abundance of particular species. Sampling techniques such as quadrat sampling, transect counts and mark-release recapture fall within the realm of basic ecology and are covered more than adequately in texts on that subject. It is enough to emphasise here that the appropriate sampling techniques need to be selected to test for the changes that are of most concern.

Stork & Samways (1995) list a number of factors on which successful monitoring depends, as follows:

1. having clear spatial and temporal scales for both the management and the monitoring;
2. setting a clear time limit to the monitoring programme;
3. sampling the appropriate taxa to provide the information needed (see below);
4. using the appropriate methodology, including statistical analysis, to test the hypothesis;
5. standardisation of data collection and analysis (this is vital if different recorders are involved);
6. maintaining voucher collections of the subject organisms (particularly important if the taxa are not well known);
7. using existing data where they are valid so as not to use resources on unnecessary repetition;
8. ensuring that all relevant environmental variables are recorded and tested as possible agents of change.

To be effective, monitoring programmes require limits which, when reached, trigger action. This may involve changing the management when the monitoring clearly indicates that the conservation value of an area is declining. Such limits need to be predetermined to avoid permanent damage to the conservation value of the site.

In the same way that indicator groups can be used as surrogates for the measurement of biodiversity, by repetitive measurement some taxa can be used to monitor ecosystem change. The taxa chosen for monitoring may not be the same as in rapid biodiversity assessment; different qualities may be required. In particular the taxa chosen should be sensitive to possible agents of change, such as pollution. The following are some examples.

Flagships, sentinels and umbrellas

The overwhelming diversity of species present in most communities and ecosystems makes complete species inventories an unrealistic goal. In many situations in which conservation monitoring is urgently required, single species have acted as the focus for assessment of protection and management of reserves. One category of species used are the large charismatic vertebrates, such as tigers, giant pandas or mountain gorillas, which require substantial reserve areas for long-term survival. Species used in this way have been termed **flagships**, because measures taken for their survival and well-being may also benefit the ecosystem as a whole.

In an effort to conserve tiger populations in India, the government initiated a programme called 'Project Tiger' in 1973, which involved the setting up of a network of 20 reserves and the regular monitoring of tiger populations within them (Fig. 9.12). This was initially very successful and led to an increase of tigers in India from around 1900 to 4300 in 1989 (unfortunately this gain has since been undermined by poaching activities in the reserves; see Chapter 6). The presence of the tiger as a flagship and the management of the reserve for its survival have ensured the conservation of a large community of species. Top predators may well make good flagships because they are often the most demanding of space, but they may not necessarily be very sensitive to change. The relative stability of a population of a long-lived species, such as the tiger, may mask subtle changes in their habitat that result in rapid changes in populations of other species.

The 'health' of an ecosystem is difficult to measure, but a combination of threats covered in earlier chapters can lead to loss of species. In this situation some species will be more sensitive than others and respond more rapidly to ecosystem degradation. Where the ecology of a species is sufficiently known and its sensitivity recognised, it can be used as a **sentinel species**, acting as a measure of overall ecosystem health. Thus the monitoring of one sentinel species could suffice as a check for the whole ecosystem.

The white-backed woodpecker (*Dendrocopos leucotos*) is an endangered bird in Finland and Sweden, having declined due to changes in forest composition, particularly the removal of dead and diseased wood. The woodpeckers feed mainly on dead-wood-dwelling insects from deciduous trees, and particularly rely on birch (*Betula* sp.) trees for nesting holes. The populations of these birds are well known in comparison to the many invertebrates and fungi that rely on the same dead-wood habitats and therefore monitoring of the bird as a sentinel can also function as a monitoring strategy for many less conspicuous species (Martikainen *et al.* 1998).

When managing protected areas, it is often necessary to focus on a

Fig. 9.12 Network of tiger reserves in India. Reproduced with kind permssion of Project Tiger.

few species in order to monitor the effects of management. Some species are easier to detect and monitor than others and it is impossible to construct action plans for all species. If a number of complementary groups of species are chosen carefully their needs may encapsulate the needs of the majority of other species. These groups of species may therefore be termed **umbrella groups**, because monitoring their responses to change safeguards other species.

In the same way that indicator groups can be used to measure relative diversity and help prioritise areas for protection (Chapter 8), they can also be used to monitor areas for changes that may be taking place.

However, the same problems of surrogacy apply. A study of the impact of disturbance on biodiversity by Lawton *et al.* (1998) in the tropical forests of Cameroon, measured species richness of eight different taxonomic groups in six areas that provided a gradient of disturbance from primary forest to fallow farm fields cleared of trees. Their results suggest that no one taxonomic group acts as a good indicator of species richness changes in other groups.

Complementary groups of terrestrial arthropods have been suggested as an effective umbrella group by Kremen *et al.* (1993). They argued that many groups of arthropods are good indicators for monitoring because they can respond more rapidly to environmental change than do vertebrates whose long generation times means that their populations respond much more slowly. Also the diversity of taxa means that complementary groups such as ants, butterflies and ground beetles can be used to gain greater coverage of niches and trophic levels.

Summary

1. Protected areas should be as large as possible and should ideally be circular in shape so as to provide as large a core area as possible in relation to edge habitat that is likely to be of lower value.

2. Several small reserves may be as appropriate as single large reserves in cases where habitats are patchy on an appropriate scale, and movement between patches is feasible for species of concern.

3. Almost all protected areas are influenced or under threat from human activity. Management is required to compensate for or counteract this activity in order to conserve biodiversity. The level of management that is required depends on the nature of the ecosystem to be conserved and the past level of human involvement in its processes.

4. Semi-natural habitats often require intensive management in order to retain the characteristics valuable to retention of their biodiversity. These management activities may approximate to traditional management activities not originally undertaken with conservation aims. However, scientific research should seek to test and if necessary improve these techniques.

5. Monitoring of the outcomes of management activities is vital to good conservation practice. This may involve the targeted monitoring of species that act as surrogates for the community as a whole.

Discussion points

- What are the critical factors in deciding whether a single large or several smaller reserves would be the better option?
- To what extent can traditional management practices be relied upon as effective conservation techniques?
- What is the difference between surveillance and monitoring?

Further reading

Goldsmith, F.B. (1991). *Monitoring for conservation and ecology*. London: Chapman & Hall.

Shafer, C. L. (1990). *Nature reserves : island theory and conservation practice*. Washington, D.C.: Smithsonian Institution Press.

Sutherland, W.J. (ed.) (1996). *Ecological census techniques: a handbook*. Cambridge: Cambridge University Press.

Sutherland, W.J. (ed.) (1995). *Managing habitats for conservation*. Cambridge: Cambridge University Press.

Web Sites

Project Tiger, India: envfor.nic.in/pt/pt.html

National Trust, Wicken Fen: www.wicken.org.uk/

World Conservation Monitoring Centre: www.wcmc.org.uk/

English Native Management Handbooks: www.english-nature.org.uk/pubs/handbooks

RSPB: www.rspb.org/wildlife

Chapter 10

Protecting species. I.
In situ conservation

Much of our current conservation activity is directed towards individual species that have come under threat for the range of reasons described in earlier chapters. Species naturally form a focus for conservation because they are recognisable units whose loss can be quantified, but more importantly because the public can relate to species in a more direct way than to ecosystems or to genes. In this chapter we look at how threat to individual species can be assessed and how the theoretical tools of population dynamics and population genetics can be used in the management of threatened species and their populations.

By reading this chapter students will gain an understanding of the basis of assessing threat to species and the system of categorisation, methods of managing species and their constituent small populations so as to minimise the threat of their extinction, and efforts towards the sustainable harvesting of species that are directly exploited.

Commoness and rarity among species

The science of ecology has given us many studies pointing towards an intimate link between species and their habitats. It is evident that species have become adapted through the process of evolution to persist within a restricted range of environmental parameters and many are highly specialised and vulnerable to environmental change. Over time, gene pools track their ever-changing environmental template, some genes becoming rarer or even disappearing, whilst others arise through mutation and may become common in a population. This has continued for millennia with some species going extinct when they have been unable to adapt sufficiently rapidly to track environmental changes, and others arising through speciation. But rapid rates of environmental change imposed by current human activity threaten to tip the balance between these two processes as many more species lack the adaptive capacity to cope and plummet towards extinction.

The constant change in environment that species experience, both abiotic and biotic, leads to variations in each species' distribution and

Table 10.1 Why are some species common and others rare? A combination of geographical range, habitat specificity and population size results in seven ways in which species can be considered rare

Geographical range	Large		Small	
Habitat specificity	Wide	Narrow	Wide	Narrow
Large population size, dominant somewhere	Locally abundant over a large range in several habitats	Locally abundant over a large range in a specific habitat	Locally abundant in several habitats but restricted geographically	Locally abundant in a specific habitat but restricted geographically
Small population size, not dominant	Constantly sparse over a large range and in several habitats	Constantly sparse in a specific habitat but over a large range	Constantly sparse and geographically restricted in several habitats	Constantly sparse and geographically restricted in a specific habitat

Source: Rabinowitz (1981).

abundance over time. Chance changes in the environment can result in a species becoming either very common or very rare. This is manifest at any one period of time, as variation from species to species in commoness and rarity, so that there are species at all points on the continuum. This is a natural phenomenon that we need to distinguish from the human impact on species distribution and abundance. Rabinowitz (1981) recognised that there are a number of distinct ecological reasons for rarity and defined different classes of rarity based on three parameters:

geographical range – species confined to a small geographical range, but may be numerous where they occur;

habitat specificity – a species may be geographically widespread but confined to very specialised habitats;

population size – where a species occurs there may always be only a small population.

A classification of rare species based on combinations of these three parameters is shown in Table 10.1. A species may become rare through changes in any of the above parameters, but the very rarest species are those with a combination of small geographical range, high habitat specificity and low population size.

Assessing and categorising threat to species from human activity

The natural variation in abundance shown above illustrates that it would be inappropriate to base conservation priorities on rarity. Many species are naturally rare, such as cave-dwelling invertebrates, whilst their populations have remained stable for long periods of time. *The most important factor from a conservation viewpoint is the level of threat.* Lists of species that contain an assessment of the threat they are under have been compiled by the International Union for the Conservation of Nature (IUCN) and published in 'Red Data Books'. This is an attempt to categorise species (in terms of threat of extinction) according to the level of threat and therefore prioritise species conservation action on national and international scales.

The original categories of threat at the species level defined by IUCN are as follows:

1. *Extinct* – species that are no longer known to exist in the wild after repeated searches of former localities and other known or likely places;
2. *Endangered* – taxa in danger of extinction and whose survival is unlikely if the causal factors of decline continue operating;
3. *Vulnerable* – taxa believed likely to move to the 'Endangered' category in the near future if the causal factors continue operating;
4. *Rare* – taxa with small world populations that are not at present 'Endangered' or 'Vulnerable' but are at risk;
5. *Indeterminate* – taxa that are known to be 'Endangered', 'Vulnerable' or 'Rare' but where there is not enough information to indicate which of the three categories is appropriate;
6. *Insufficiently known* – taxa that are suspected but not definitely known to belong to any one of the above categories because of lack of information.

The Red Data Books have proved very useful in identifying species requiring action and in allocating resources for species conservation. However, the early methods of categorisation relied upon a qualitative assessment by an expert on the species and as more of the books have been produced a wide divergence in the interpretation of these categories and therefore of the threat to species has become evident. Subjective judgements rely on the availability of expertise and information; this makes it difficult to compare threat across taxa and therefore set broad conservation priorities.

Mace & Lande (1991) suggested a series of semi-quantitative definitions for assessing threat of extinction (Table 10.2). These categories assess the probability and rapidity of extinction of the given species if present trends continue. Notice that each of the main categories has

Table 10.2 Suggested new definitions for IUCN threatened species categories

Category of threat	Criteria for designation
Extinct	As before
Critical	50% probability of extinction within 5 years or 2 generations, whichever is the longer
Endangered	20% probability of extinction within 20 years or 10 generations, whichever is the longer
Vulnerable	10% probability of extinction within 100 years
Insufficiently known	As before

Source: Mace & Lande (1991).

both a probability of extinction and a timescale to which that probability refers. This method relies on the measurement of species decline and on analysis of population viability, two measurements that present formidable problems, as we shall see below. The categories of threat are covered in greater detail in Box 10.1.

Box 10.1	Definitions of IUCN categories of threat and criteria for assigning species to the major categories (reproduced from IUCN 2001)

EXTINCT: a taxon is Extinct when there is no reasonable doubt that the last individual has died. A taxon is presumed extinct when exhaustive surveys in known and/or expected habitat, at appropriate times (diurnal, seasonal, annual), throughout its historic range have failed to record an individual. Surveys should be over a time frame appropriate to the taxon's life cycle and life form.

EXTINCT IN THE WILD: a taxon is Extinct in the Wild when it is known only to survive in cultivation, in captivity or as a naturalised population (or populations) well outside the past range.

CRITICALLY ENDANGERED: a taxon is Critically Endangered when the best available evidence indicates that it meets any of the following criteria (A to E), and it is therefore considered to be facing an extremely high risk of extinction in the wild:

A. Reduction in population size based on any of the following:

1. An observed, estimated, inferred or suspected population size reduction of ≥90% over the last 10 years or three generations, whichever is the longer, where the causes of the reduction are clearly reversible AND understood AND ceased, based on (and specifying) any of the following:
(a) direct observation
(b) an index of abundance appropriate to the taxon
(c) a decline in area of occupancy, extent of occurrence and/or quality of habitat
(d) actual or potential levels of exploitation
(e) the effects of introduced taxa, hybridisation, pathogens, pollutants, competitors or parasites.

2. An observed, estimated, inferred or suspected population size reduction of ≥80% over the last 10 years or three generations, whichever is the longer, where the reduction or its causes may not have ceased OR may not be understood OR may not be reversible, based on (and specifying) any of (a) to (e) under A1.

3. A population size reduction of ≥80%, projected or suspected to be met within the next 10 years or three generations, whichever is the longer (up to a maximum of 100 years), based on (and specifying) any of (b) to (e) under A1.

4. An observed, estimated, inferred, projected or suspected population size reduction of ≥80% over any 10 year or three generation period, whichever is longer (up to a maximum of 100 years in the future), where the time period must include both the past and the future, and where the reduction or its causes may not have ceased OR may not be understood OR may not be reversible, based on (and specifying) any of (a) to (e) under A1.

B. Geographical range in the form of either B1 (extent of occurrence) OR B2 (area of occupancy) OR both:

1. Extent of occurrence estimated to be less than 100 km^2, and estimates indicating at least two of a–c:

(a) Severely fragmented or known to exist at only a single location.

(b) Continuing decline, observed, inferred or projected, in any of the following:

    (i) extent of occurrence

    (ii) area of occupancy

    (iii) area, extent and/or quality of habitat

    (iv) number of locations or subpopulations

    (v) number of mature individuals.

(c) Extreme fluctuations in any of the following:

    (i) extent of occurrence

    (ii) area of occupancy

    (iii) number of locations or subpopulations

    (iv) number of mature individuals.

2. Area of occupancy estimated to be less than 10 km^2, and estimates indicating at least two of a–c:

(a) Severely fragmented or known to exist at only a single location.

(b) Continuing decline, observed, inferred or projected, in any of the following:

    (i) extent of occurrence

    (ii) area of occupancy

    (iii) area, extent and/or quality of habitat

    (iv) number of locations or subpopulations

    (v) number of mature individuals.

(c) Extreme fluctuations in any of the following:

    (i) extent of occurrence

    (ii) area of occupancy

    (iii) number of locations or subpopulations

    (iv) number of mature individuals.

C. Population size estimated to number fewer than 250 mature individuals and either:

1. An estimated continuing decline of at least 25% within 3 years or one generation, whichever is longer, (up to a maximum of 100 years in the future) OR

2. A continuing decline, observed, projected, or inferred, in numbers of mature individuals AND at least one of the following (a–b):

(a) Population structure in the form of one of the following:

    (i) no subpopulation estimated to contain more than 50 mature individuals,

OR

    (ii) at least 90% of mature individuals in one subpopulation.

(b) Extreme fluctuations in number of mature individuals.

D. Population size estimated to number fewer than 50 mature individuals.

E. Quantitative analysis showing the probability of extinction in the wild is at least 50% within 10 years or three generations, whichever is the longer (up to a maximum of 100 years).

ENDANGERED: A taxon is Endangered when the best available evidence indicates that it meets any of the following criteria (A to E), and it is therefore considered to be facing a very high risk of extinction in the wild:

A. Reduction in population size based on any of the following:

1. An observed, estimated, inferred or suspected population size reduction of ≥70% over the last 10 years or three generations, whichever is the longer, where the causes of the reduction are clearly reversible AND understood AND ceased, based on (and specifying) any of the following:

(a) direct observation

(b) an index of abundance appropriate to the taxon

(c) a decline in area of occupancy, extent of occurrence and/or quality of habitat

(d) actual or potential levels of exploitation

(e) the effects of introduced taxa, hybridisation, pathogens, pollutants, competitors or parasites.

2. An observed, estimated, inferred or suspected population size reduction of ≥50% over the last 10 years or three generations, whichever is the longer, where the reduction or its causes may not have ceased OR may not be understood OR may not be reversible, based on (and specifying) any of (a) to (e) under A1.

3. A population size reduction of ≥50%, projected or suspected to be met within the next 10 years or three generations, whichever is the longer (up to a maximum of 100 years), based on (and specifying) any of (b) to (e) under A1.

4. An observed, estimated, inferred, projected or suspected population size reduction of ≥50% over any 10 year or three generation period, whichever is longer (up to a maximum of 100 years in the future), where the time period must include both the past and the future, AND where the reduction or its causes may not have ceased OR may not be understood OR may not be reversible, based on (and specifying) any of (a) to (e) under A1.

B. Geographical range in the form of either B1 (extent of occurrence) OR B2 (area of occupancy) OR both:

1. Extent of occurrence estimated to be less than 5000 km², and estimates indicating at least two of a–c:

(a) Severely fragmented or known to exist at no more than five locations.

(b) Continuing decline, observed, inferred or projected, in any of the following:

    (i) extent of occurrence

    (ii) area of occupancy

    (iii) area, extent and/or quality of habitat

    (iv) number of locations or subpopulations

    (v) number of mature individuals.

(c) Extreme fluctuations in any of the following:

    (i) extent of occurrence

    (ii) area of occupancy

    (iii) number of locations or subpopulations

    (iv) number of mature individuals.

2. Area of occupancy estimated to be less than 500 km², and estimates indicating at least two of a–c:

(a) Severely fragmented or known to exist at no more than five locations.

(b) Continuing decline, observed, inferred or projected, in any of the following:

(i)   extent of occurrence
(ii) area of occupancy
(iii) area, extent and/or quality of habitat
(iv) number of locations or subpopulations
(v)   number of mature individuals.
(c) Extreme fluctuations in any of the following:
(i)   extent of occurrence
(ii) area of occupancy
(iii) number of locations or subpopulations
(iv) number of mature individuals.

C. Population size estimated to number fewer than 2500 mature individuals and either:
1. An estimated continuing decline of at least 20% within 5 years or two generations, whichever is longer, (up to a maximum of 100 years in the future) OR
2. A continuing decline, observed, projected, or inferred, in numbers of mature individuals AND at least one of the following (a–b):
(a) Population structure in the form of one of the following:
(i)   no subpopulation estimated to contain more than 250 mature individuals, OR
(ii) at least 95% of mature individuals in one subpopulation.
(b) Extreme fluctuations in number of mature individuals.

D. Population size estimated to number fewer than 250 mature individuals.

E. Quantitative analysis showing the probability of extinction in the wild is at least 20% within 20 years or five generations, whichever is the longer (up to a maximum of 100 years).

VULNERABLE: A taxon is Vulnerable when the best available evidence indicates that it meets any of the following criteria (A to E), and it is therefore considered to be facing a high risk of extinction in the wild:

A. Reduction in population size based on any of the following:
1. An observed, estimated, inferred or suspected population size reduction of ≥50% over the last 10 years or three generations, whichever is the longer, where the causes of the reduction are clearly reversible AND understood AND ceased, based on (and specifying) any of the following:
(a) direct observation
(b) an index of abundance appropriate to the taxon
(c) a decline in area of occupancy, extent of occurrence and/or quality of habitat
(d) actual or potential levels of exploitation
(e) the effects of introduced taxa, hybridisation, pathogens, pollutants, competitors or parasites.
2. An observed, estimated, inferred or suspected population size reduction of ≥30% over the last 10 years or three generations, whichever is the longer, where the reduction or its causes may not have ceased OR may not be understood OR may not be reversible, based on (and specifying) any of (a) to (e) under A1.
3. A population size reduction of ≥30%, projected or suspected to be met within the next 10 years or three generations, whichever is the longer (up to a maximum of 100 years), based on (and specifying) any of (b) to (e) under A1.

4.   An observed, estimated, inferred, projected or suspected population size reduction of $\geq 30\%$ over any 10 year or three generation period, whichever is longer (up to a maximum of 100 years in the future), where the time period must include both the past and the future, AND where the reduction or its causes may not have ceased OR may not be understood OR may not be reversible, based on (and specifying) any of (a) to (e) under A1.

B.   Geographical range in the form of either B1 (extent of occurrence) OR B2 (area of occupancy) OR both:

1.   Extent of occurrence estimated to be less than 20 000 km^2, and estimates indicating at least two of a–c:

(a) Severely fragmented or known to exist at no more than 10 locations.

(b) Continuing decline, observed, inferred or projected, in any of the following:
   (i)   extent of occurrence
   (ii) area of occupancy
   (iii) area, extent and/or quality of habitat
   (iv) number of locations or subpopulations
   (v)   number of mature individuals.

(c) Extreme fluctuations in any of the following:
   (i)   extent of occurrence
   (ii) area of occupancy
   (iii) number of locations or subpopulations
   (iv) number of mature individuals.

2.   Area of occupancy estimated to be less than 2000 km^2, and estimates indicating at least two of a–c:

(a) Severely fragmented or known to exist at no more than 10 locations.

(b) Continuing decline, observed, inferred or projected, in any of the following:-
   (i)   extent of occurrence
   (ii) area of occupancy
   (iii) area, extent and/or quality of habitat
   (iv) number of locations or subpopulations
   (v)   number of mature individuals.

(c) Extreme fluctuations in any of the following:
   (i)   extent of occurrence
   (ii) area of occupancy
   (iii) number of locations or subpopulations
   (iv) number of mature individuals.

C.   Population size estimated to number fewer than 10 000 mature individuals and either:

1.   An estimated continuing decline of at least 10% within 10 years or three generations, whichever is longer (up to a maximum of 100 years in the future), OR

2.   A continuing decline, observed, projected, or inferred, in numbers of mature individuals AND at least one of the following (a–b):

(a) Population structure in the form of one of the following:
   (i)   no subpopulation estimated to contain more than 1000 mature individuals, OR
   (ii) all mature individuals are in one subpopulation.

(b) Extreme fluctuations in number of mature individuals.

D. Population very small or restricted in the form of either of the following:

1. Population size estimated to number fewer than 1000 mature individuals.

2. Population with a very restricted area of occupancy (typically less than 20 km^2) or number of locations (typically five or fewer) such that it is prone to the effects of human activities or stochastic events within a very short time period in an uncertain future, and is thus capable of becoming Critically Endangered or even Extinct in a very short time period.

E. Quantitative analysis showing the probability of extinction in the wild is at least 10% within 100 years.

NEAR THREATENED: a taxon is Near Threatened when it has been evaluated against the criteria but does not qualify for Critically Endangered, Endangered, or Vulnerable now, but is close to qualifying for or is likely to qualify for a threatened category in the near future.

LEAST CONCERN: a taxon is Least Concern when it has been evaluated against the criteria and does not qualify for Critically Endangered, Endangered, Vulnerable or Near Threatened. Widespread and abundant taxa are included in this category.

DATA DEFICIENT: a taxon is Data Deficient when there is inadequate information to make a direct, or indirect, assessment of its risk of extinction based on its distribution and/or population status. A taxon in this category may be well studied, and its biology well known, but appropriate data on abundance and/or distribution are lacking. Data Deficient is therefore not a category of threat or Lower Risk. Listing of taxa in this category indicates that more information is required and acknowledges the possibility that future research will show that threatened classification is appropriate.

NOT EVALUATED: a taxon is Not Evaluated when it is has not yet been evaluated against the criteria.

Managing small populations

As we saw in Chapter 4, a key consequence of habitat destruction and fragmentation is the reduction of large populations into smaller ones, each of which has a greater probability of extinction than the original due to loss of genetic variability, demographic problems, environmental stochasticity and catastrophes. Naturally small populations also become increasingly vulnerable as human disturbance increases. This section explores the applications of population biology to the problem of conserving such populations. Most conservation efforts have been aimed at small, isolated populations, and on reducing the probability of extinction in the short term.

Populations are dynamic and always have some probability of extinction; the conservation problem is that humans have greatly increased that probability for many populations so that the rate of population extinction has outstripped the founding of new ones. The objective of managing threatened species is to change the prevailing trend that has led to the increased probability of extinction.

Minimum viable population size

The increasing problems of demographic and genetic stochasticity in populations as their size decreases, together with the possibility of Allee effects (extinction vortices) occurring as populations drop below a critical threshold, have led to conservationists thinking in terms of populations having a minimum viable size. Below this size the population is unlikely to recover and will decrease to extinction. However, in reality, there are no certainties about population extinction (until it happens), only probabilities. Therefore, even though **minimum viable population** (MVP) size has seen increasing use as a tool in managing populations, it is an illusive term based on two parameters set by the conservationist; probability of survival that is considered acceptable (100% probability of survival is not achievable) and the time period being considered. For example, Shaffer (1981) suggested that the minimum viable population size for any given species is the smallest population having a 99% chance of remaining extant for 1000 years. These are desirable objectives, but largely unrealistic in the current environment especially considering our ability to accurately calculate a MVP for such a time scale. To be at all accurate the estimation of a MVP requires considerable ecological information on population dynamics, demography and habitat requirements. At the present time the relevant research has not been undertaken for long enough for us to have any idea of the accuracy of MVP estimates over long time scales for any species. Consequently, other more achievable combinations of probability and time have been used, e.g. 95% probability of surviving the next 100 years.

An example of a species where there is sufficient information to give an indication of the minimum viable population size is the bighorn sheep (*Ovis canadensis*). This species has been reduced to isolated populations in open vegetation on mountains in south-west USA. Observations on 120 populations over 70 years show that all populations with 50 or fewer individuals when first recorded went extinct within 50 years, whereas most populations of more than 100 survived (Fig. 10.1a) (Berger 1990). These data suggest that the minimum population size is around 100 or more for this species in its current environment, if survival for a minimum of 100 years is being considered. However, a reanalysis of the data from Californian populations, with the addition of a longer time series (by inclusion of historical size estimates) by Wehausen (1999) suggests that populations smaller than 50 are not so doomed to extinction as Berger's analysis suggests (Fig. 10.1b). Ten populations increased in size from estimates of fewer than 50 to over 100 during the recording period, and of the 27 currently extant populations, 85% were estimated over 50 years ago to number 50 individuals or fewer and therefore should be extinct according to Berger's estimates. Berger (1999) provides an interesting response to Wehausen, emphasising the generality found in both studies that smaller populations are more likely to go extinct, but also how difficult it may be to provide accurate estimates of MVPs and how dependent the estimates will be on the data available.

The challenge of dealing with different levels of probability of survival over different time scales has led to the development of **population viability analysis (PVA).** This method attempts to build models that

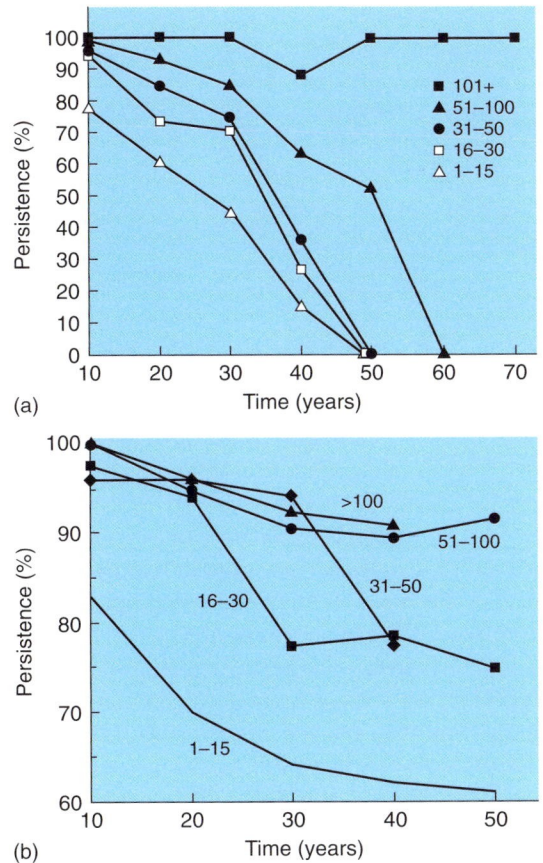

(a)

(b)

Fig. 10.1 a, b Persistence of bighorn sheep (*Ovis canadensis*) populations of different intial sizes in California, USA; (a) an analysis by Berger (1990) showing that only populations of 100 or more are viable; (b) a subsequent analysis by Wehausen (1999) suggesting that some of the smaller populations were persisting longer than predicted in the original analysis. Reproduced with kind permission of Blackwell Science.

predict future population trends based on the relationship between population size (the dependent variable) and the variables that influence it (e.g. weather, disease). This is done through the calculation of the influence of key variables on birth and death rates. A simple model can be used as an example:

Population size at some future time N_{t+1} is dependent on the current population size N_t and the birth and survival rates over the period in between. This can be expressed as follows:

$$N_{t+1} = (N_t \times S) + (N_t \times B \times S)$$

where S is the probability of an individual surviving from t to $t + 1$ and B is the average number of offspring produced per individual in that time. Both S and B will change according to the environmental variables mentioned above. If the relationship between these environmental variables and birth and death rates has been measured in the field, stochasticity can be incorporated in the model by generating random weather events such as wet summers and cold winters. Intrinsic variability in reproductive output (demographic stochasticity) can also be added by assigning a random fecundity value (within a set range) to each individual. Computer-generated projections of survival over specified periods of time can then be produced, as in Fig. 10.2. These can be run a large number of times and generate a probability that a current population will survive

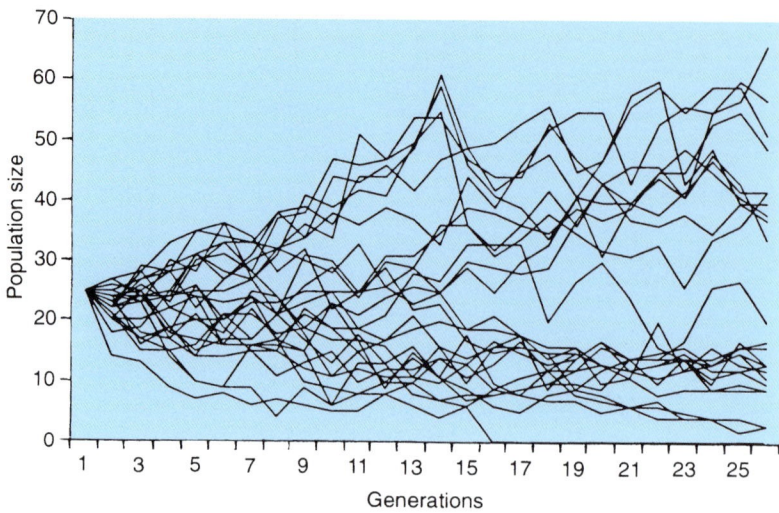

Fig. 10.2 Theoretical computer-projected population viability analysis for a large mammal showing a range of scenarios from the same original population. Note that one of the populations goes extinct after 16 generations.

over a specified period of time. For example, if 95 out of 100 computer simulations show the population surviving for 50 years we could say that the population has a 95% chance of survival over this period.

Although the concept of PVA is seen as useful in assessing population risk and formulating conservation strategies, it has been as yet infrequently used because of the limitations of the models and our inability to adequately measure all the variables involved, recalling the old computer modelling problem of 'rubbish in–rubbish out'. Detailed, long-term studies are required on the species' ecology before the models can be used with any confidence. A PVA analysis on the northern spotted owl (*Strix occidentalis caurina*) was able to model the effect of continuing destruction of its forest habitat and incorporate measures of juvenile and adult mortality, probability of successful dispersal to unoccupied territories, fecundity and environmental stochasticity (Lamberson *et al.* 1992). But the authors stopped short of producing precise figures for population viability or minimum habitat area required because current knowledge of some parameters is insufficient.

Until conservationists can be more confident in the predictions of PVA, it will remain a rather illusive theoretical tool. At present it would seem that constant monitoring of populations and their demography is still necessary to manage them effectively.

Measuring species decline

When we say a species has declined by 50% over the last 10 years, what exactly do we mean and how do we know? Whereas population decline can be measured in terms of actual numbers of individuals, species decline is usually measured in terms of contraction in range or, less frequently, loss of populations. So a decline such as that above usually means that a species has disappeared from half of the area it occupied 10 years ago. This of course is an estimate, based on the estimated distribution of the species at two points in time. Distributions are normally plotted at a

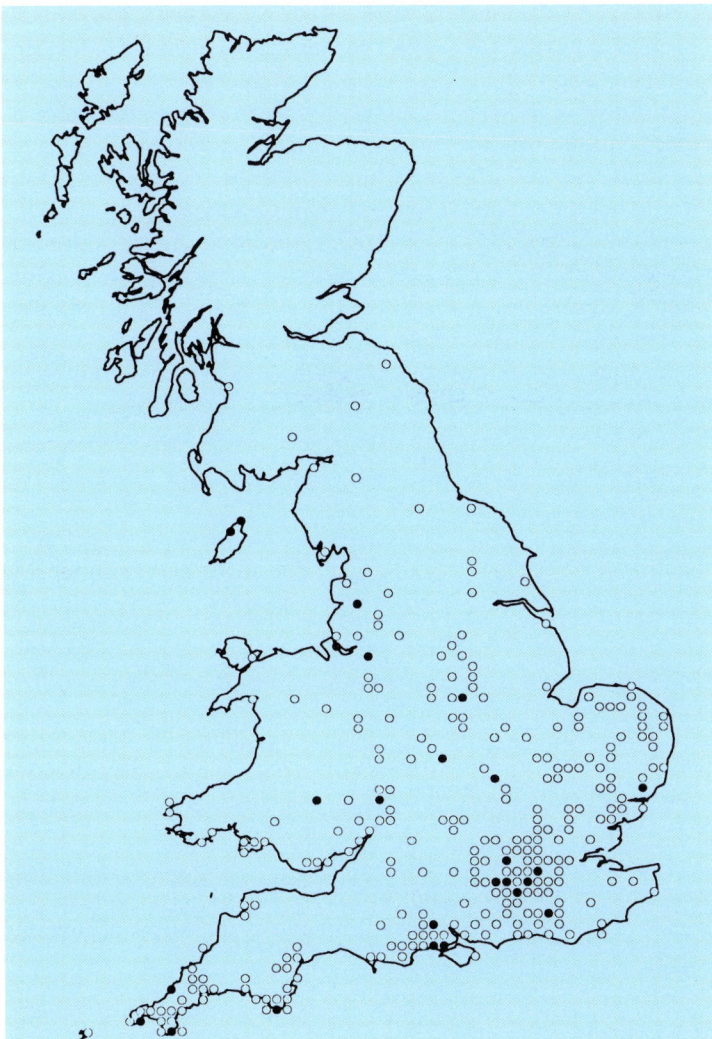

Fig. 10.3 Distribution map showing the decline of pennyroyal (*Mentha pulegium*). Open circles are pre-1990 records and black circles post-1990. Reproduced with kind permission of the Botanical Society of the British Isles Threatened Plant Database.

resolution such as 10 km squares (10×10 km squares or 100 km^2) using records of sightings sent in by recorders or following targeted surveys. The presence of a dot in the square therefore means that the species has been recorded there. Decline (or increase) is then measured by the difference in the number of squares occupied at the two sampling times. Fig. 10.3 shows the distribution of pennyroyal (*Mentha pulegium*) in the UK at two such times giving a visual impression of decline.

There is, however, a serious problem with this method. The resolution of recording (100 km^2) is larger than the habitat occupied by populations of most species, particularly plants and invertebrates, but also many sedentary vertebrates. If we imagine that within a 10 km square five populations of a species occur at time t, but over the period to time $t + 1$ four of those populations go extinct, we would say that the species had declined by 80%, but the species is still registered as present in the square and so no decline is detected on a regional or national scale (Fig. 10.4). This problem has probably led to the underestimation of the

Before

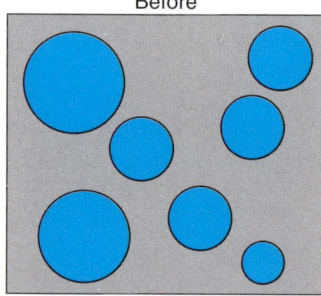

After

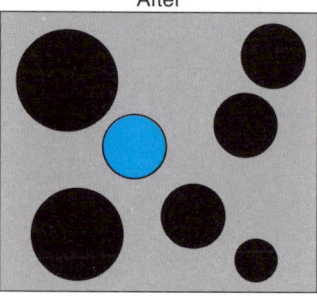

10 km square

● Occupied ● Unoccupied

Fig. 10.4 Recording presence or absence at scales larger than the habitat patch size will underestimate the level of species decline because complete loss from all habitat patches within the unit area is required before any change is recorded on the larger scale. The example shows a 10 km² scale where a species is still recorded as present despite losing all but one population between the two census periods.

decline of many of the more widespread species. A recent study on the decline of British butterflies shows that moderate declines of 15–20% recorded at the 10 km square resolution can mask 80–90% declines at the population level (Cowley *et al.* 1999). This masking effect can be worst among quite common and widespread species, which could undergo massive decline in population number before any significant decline would be evident on national distribution maps.

Future monitoring efforts must strive to record at the scale relevant to the area of population occupancy which, for some species of insects and plants for example, will be much less than 10 km squares. Limitations in resources will prohibit this across the entire range in most cases and this may necessitate sampling intensively in a small number of representative areas whilst sampling at a cruder scale elsewhere.

Genetic management of small populations

The threats of inbreeding and loss of heterozygosity are immediate in small populations as we saw in Chapter 4. The resulting depression of fitness and loss of genetic variability can have both immediate and long-term consequences for population persistence. In order to effectively manage small isolated populations so as to maintain genetic variability we must ask, how many individuals are needed to maintain a healthy outbreeding population? Again, we saw in Chapter 4 (Box 4.1) that small populations lose genetic variability in the absence of migration, in a manner described by Wright's law. In larger populations the lower rate of loss is also balanced by the rate of mutation. Based on these assumptions, Franklin (1980) suggested that a population size of 50 individuals would be an absolute minimum in the short term to avoid rapid loss of variability and inbreeding depression, but that data based on mutation rates in *Drosophila* suggest a population of 500 is required in the long term to allow mutation rates to balance loss of alleles due to genetic drift. This has led to the so-called 50/500 rule for managing small populations. However, these figures are based on relatively little evidence, on a narrow range of species and they have frequently been questioned.

These kinds of estimates of minimum population size are complicated by the fact that we cannot assume that all adults contribute to the next generation. This is very rarely the case in wild populations (mating is not random in real populations) and has led to the use of the term **effective population size** (N_e). In its most simple sense the effective population size is the number of individuals that are at any given time contributing to the next generation through reproduction. Obviously, immature and over-aged individuals do not contribute to this number, but there are also many mature adults that may fail to reproduce and thus not pass on their genes. Effective population size is also viewed in a more complex way than this because there are a number of factors, other than simple individual reproductive failure, that increase the probability of losing genetic diversity from generation to generation. The three most common are described here with the assumption that the population is isolated, sexually reproducing and diploid.

1. Variation in reproductive output

If there is a large variance in the reproductive output of females then N_e will be low since some individual's genes will be disproportionately represented in the gene pool of the next generation.

$$N_e = 4N/(\sigma^2 + 2)$$

Where σ^2 = variance in family size among females

2. Unequal sex ratios

Since unequal numbers of breeding males and females will tend to mean that some are unable to breed, this can cause reduction in N_e. This is particularly true in monogamous species. The relationship between N_e and male:female ratio is as follows:

$$N_e = 4N_m N_f/N_m + N_f$$

where N_m and N_f are numbers of adult males and females respectively. Note from Fig. 10.5 how, as the numbers of males and females become increasingly unequal, so the N_e goes down, so that a distribution of 20:80 males:females in a population of 100 produces an effective population size of 64, a reduction of 36.

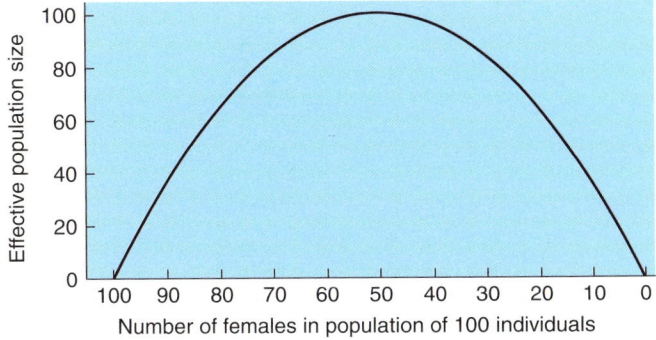

Fig. 10.5 Effect of unequal sex ratios on effective population size (Ne).

3. Population fluctuations

When population size fluctuates over generations and when population size reaches low levels then the N_e is reduced. The effective population size can be estimated over a number of generations of known size by calculating the harmonic mean:

$$1/N_e = 1/t(1/N_1 + 1/N_2 + 1/N_3 + \ldots 1/N_t)$$

where t = time in generations.

Compare two populations, one stable and one fluctuating, that both have an average population size of 50 over 5 years.

Stable population:

$$1/N_e = 1/5(1/50 + 1/50 + 1/50 + 1/50 + 1/50) \text{ so } N_e = 50$$

Fluctuating population:

$$1/N_e = 1/5(1/50 + 1/100 + 1/10 + 1/30 + 1/60) \text{ so } N_e = 34.1$$

Therefore even single generation population crashes should be avoided, as they significantly reduce N_e and therefore genetic variability.

Estimates of N_e based on just a few annual counts in free-ranging animal populations are quite unreliable and even a series of ten annual counts tends to overestimate N_e. This is because short-term counts tend to underestimate the normal extent of fluctuation in population size (Vucetich & Waite 1998).

The effect of population size on genetic variability has also been shown empirically in studies on a number of species, such as the New Zealand coniferous tree *Halocarpus bidwillii* (Fig. 10.6).

Severe loss of genetic diversity can result from crashes in population size. During this process genes are being passed through just a few individuals so that even on recovery much of the variation that was in the former population has been lost due to the majority failing to reproduce. Populations in this case are said to have gone through a **genetic bottle-**

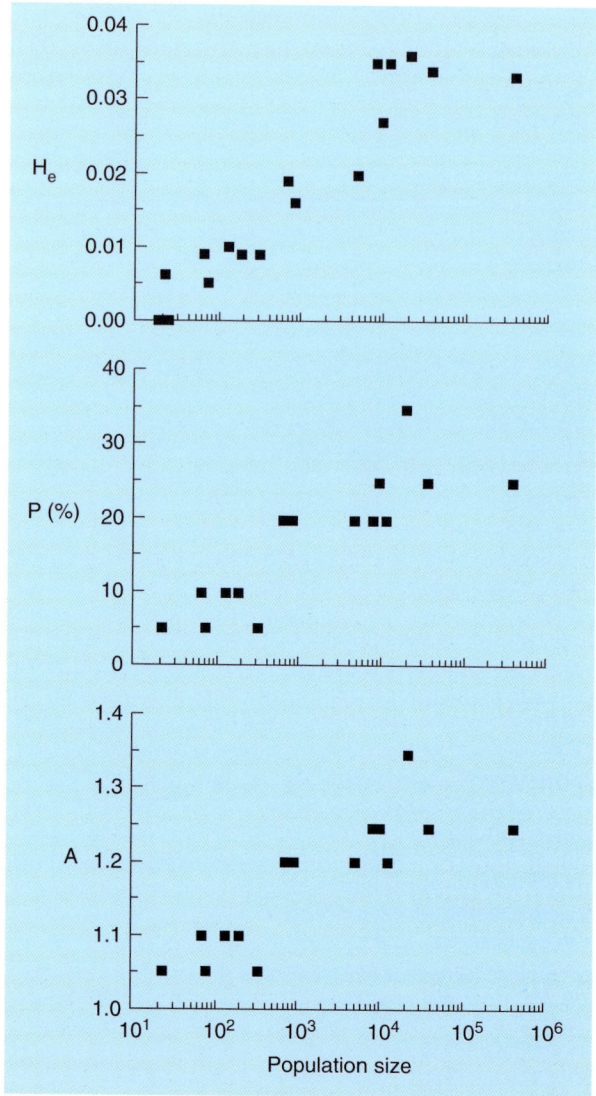

Fig. 10.6 Relationship between population size and genetic diversity (measured as heterozygosity (H_e), number of polymorphic loci (%P) and mean number of alleles(A)) in the New Zealand coniferous tree *Halocarpus bidwillii*. Reproduced from Billington (1991) with kind permission of Blackwell Science.

neck. It is not only the magnitude of the bottleneck that is crucial to the loss of genetic diversity but also its duration, in terms of generations. The longer the population size remains very small, the more diversity is lost. It is therefore crucial to try and manage populations for recovery as quickly as possible. An example of the consequences of a population bottleneck on genetic makeup is provided by the recent history of the northern elephant seal (*Mirounga angustirostrus*) (Box 10.2).

Box 10.2 | Genetic bottleneck in the northern elephant seal

The demography of the northern elephant seal (*Mirounga angustirostrus*) has been particularly well recorded, at first because of the value of their blubber for lamp oil in the nineteenth century and later due to their conservation interest. This species was harvested to the brink of extinction, culminating in a search for remaining populations lasting six years until a small remnant population was found on Isle de Guadalupe off the southern California coast in 1892. Eight individuals were counted at the time and seven of these were killed and taken for collections! Fortunately a small number of others must have escaped detection and the population survived. Subsequent protection for the species has enabled a recovery to numbers in excess of 100 000 individuals today.

The severe bottleneck in numbers has left the resulting population lacking in genetic variation despite the much larger present-day population. Genetic variation has been lost, first through loss of alleles as individuals were harvested from the original population and secondly, through genetic drift while the population is small. Rare alleles are most likely to be lost by this chance process, but commoner alleles may also disappear during a severe bottleneck, resulting in a major shift in gene frequencies. As a consequence the resulting population has low average heterozygosity. Further, the small populations are likely to suffer inbreeding depression and expression of deleterious traits.

The northern elephant seal population today still has no detectable heterozygosity as measured by allozyme analysis. This suggests that only one allele remains for all gene loci and that the population has lost all genetic diversity. In fact DNA analysis has revealed some variation in some regions of the genome. Back calculation using simulation models based on both genetic and demographic data suggests that the bottleneck probably consisted of fewer than 20 individuals.

Since the species has recovered so well it is worth asking whether the genetic effects are really a threat to the species. The northern elephant seal was probably lucky for a number of reasons. First, the restricted genome seems to have been sufficient for survival in the current environment. However, rapid environmental changes may find the population lacking in adaptability. Secondly, the prevalence of inbreeding depression of fitness and developmental abnormalities does not seem to have been sufficient to trap the species in an extinction vortex and the population has been able to recover quickly to more viable numbers.

Founder effects

A natural genetic bottleneck occurs when a small number of immigrants founds a new population. Empty habitats are often colonised by a few individuals and these may be the sole sources of genetic material for subsequent generations. Populations in such circumstances often have very limited genetic variability as a result of this **founder effect**.

This may give them a unique character when compared with their parent populations, such as the blue chaffinch (*Fringilla teydea*) of the Canary Islands, but may also make them vulnerable to extinction, inhibiting expansion into new areas.

Genetic management of species

It is clear from many studies in population and ecological genetics that distinct populations of the same species can differ significantly in their genetic makeup and their genetic diversity (see Box 10.3). Morphological differences between some populations were well recorded even before the discovery of genetics. Old natural history books are replete with descriptions of regional variations in morphology and, with the advent of molecular techniques, substantially more genetic variation has been found within and among outwardly uniform populations.

Box 10.3 | Why do populations differ in their genetic makeup?

This is most easily understood by first considering a single population of a species, within which individuals mate randomly, which subsequently gets split into two smaller populations by the appearance of a geographical barrier (Fig. 10.7). This may occur naturally or be the result of human activity (e.g. habitat destruction). If gene flow (the exchange of individuals and therefore genes between populations) does not occur between these two populations then two things will happen over time.

1. The frequencies of alleles in the populations will change purely by chance as a result of genetic drift; some will increase in frequency at the expense of others and some may be lost completely. These random events will of course differ between the populations and allele frequencies will become increasingly distinct over time.

2. The process of natural selection will differ between populations because they are exposed to different environments. Small differences in such factors as predation pressure, food availability, climate and competition will drive divergent changes in the genetic makeup of the populations.

These two factors may operate over long periods of time to render the gene pools of the populations sufficiently different to be recognised as separate subspecies. But if the barrier disappeared at this stage and the populations came back into contact, they would freely interbreed and become a single population again. Over even longer periods, secondary barriers to reproduction (barriers other than geographical, e.g. behavioural, mechanical, developmental, temporal) may evolve between populations, so that even if they do come back into contact they are unable to interbreed and they are considered separate species.

The pattern of genetic diversity among a group of fragmented populations will therefore be the consequence of four factors:

1. the historical distribution of diversity before fragmentation;
2. the contemporary distribution and size of the fragmented populations;
3. the level of isolation of the populations (rate of exchange of individuals relative to generation time);

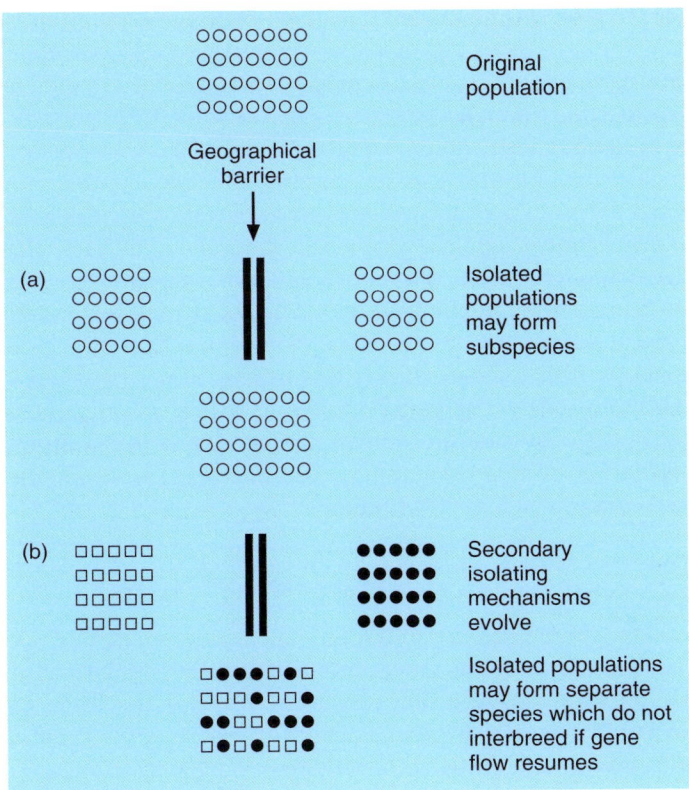

Fig. 10.7 The process of genetic divergence in populations of the same species as they become isolated. (a) The primary isolating mechanism, in this case a geographical barrier, may persist long enough for the populations to become sufficiently distinct to be regarded as subspecies, but if the barrier was removed the populations would be able to interbreed. (b) The primary isolating mechanism may persist for long enough to allow secondary isolating mechanisms to evolve. These mechanisms operate to inhibit reproduction between the populations even if the primary isolating mechanism is removed. In this case the two populations may be regarded as separate species.

4. the reproductive ecology (mating system, dispersal behaviour, etc.).

Changes in the distribution of genetic diversity among populations can be a long-term process and at any one period of time there are species with populations at all possible levels of relatedness. A major problem for conservationists is how to manage species at different stages in this process and, indeed, how to conserve this process at natural rates (see Chapter 13).

So what is the significance of this genetic diversity among populations? First, we could say that the diversity of genes contained within a species is a reflection of that species' adaptation to its ever-changing environment. Since the environment is not constant over time or space, there is no one best combination of genes for a population. Instead, a gene pool ensures that different combinations are available as environmental conditions change. The more diversity is reduced, the less able the species will be to cope with the environmental conditions and perturbations throughout its range and it will become increasingly specialised and sensitive to chance events such as bad weather. Additionally, as a species becomes more restricted and specialised, it may lose its ability to recolonise restored habitats, making recovery and re-establishment increasingly difficult. In short, the more diversity that is lost the more human intervention and resources are needed to conserve the remainder. Secondly, a species is characterised by the genetic diversity that underlies its visible (morphological) variation. When we lose genetic diversity we lose part of the species, equivalent to losing a distinctive geographical race or colour variant and its evolutionary potential is reduced.

An emerging example of genetic management is provided by efforts to conserve the koala (*Phascolarctos cinereus*) in Australia. This species is threatened by habitat destruction and disturbance from exotic species since European colonisation. Many populations have undergone crashes in numbers and exhibit low genetic variation, which may in turn be lowering individual fitness. Sherwin *et al.* (2000) reviewed the results of a range of molecular genetic studies and concluded that significant variation among populations exists across the species range, suggesting local adaptation to ecological conditions. They conclude that conservation efforts should ensure that mixing of genotypes does not occur between widely divergent populations with resulting loss of variation and local adaptation. In contrast, connectivity between neighbouring populations should be maintained or restored to avoid genetic isolation and consequent loss of variation.

How can we use information on genetic diversity in conservation?

The importance of maintaining population size was covered earlier, but most often rare species occur as a measurable number of populations of variable size. We have also seen that conservation of rare species must have maintenance of genetic diversity as a high priority, but that genetic diversity will never be distributed uniformly among all populations and, frequently, that distribution may be very irregular. It is useful to look at the two possible extremes illustrated in Fig. 10.8, in which the genetic diversity within six populations is represented in terms of the letters a to f. These could, for example, be alternative alleles at one locus. In the first example we have six populations all of which contain the total gene pool of the species. In this case the loss of any one population would not result in the loss of overall genetic diversity. Second, a species may exist in a number of populations, all of which have a number of genes that are unique. In this case the genetic diversity is distributed among the populations and the loss of one population will significantly reduce the genetic diversity of the species as a whole.

In practice some populations are likely to be relatively distinct whilst a majority may be closely related and prioritisation of protection can be based on these measurements (among other factors). Some may contain many alleles and others only one; and some alleles may be common to all populations whilst others are rare.

Fischer and Matthies (1998) investigated genetic variation among 11 populations of the rare plant *Gentianella germanica* in the Jura Mountains crossing from Switzerland into Germany. Significant variation was found among populations compared with that found within subpopulations, suggesting that each population was relatively distinct. There was also a significant correlation between genetic variation, population size and the number of seeds produced per plant. They concluded that gene flow between existing populations is very limited and that reduction in population size was eroding genetic variation and plant fitness.

Extreme 1. All alleles found within each population

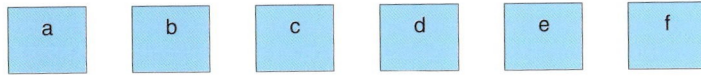

Extreme 2. Each allele found in only one population and each population shows extreme homozygosity

More realistic case where alleles show a mixed distribution, some are more common than others

Fig. 10.8 Possible distribution of alleles from one gene locus among the populations of a species. At one extreme the genetic diversity is found within each population and the loss of any one population would have minimum genetic impact. At the other extreme the genetic diversity is found among the populations and the loss of one population would have maximum genetic impact. The realistic situation is always intermediate, with some populations containing more diversity, and some alleles more frequent and widespread than others. In addition, patterns of diversity will differ from locus to locus.

Detecting centres of diversity

Many species have a history of contraction and expansion caused by climatic cycles such as ice ages. As the climate warmed at the end of the last ice age, each species will have expanded out toward higher latitudes. Since expansion occurs through a series of founder events, populations in areas of expansion have a subset of the genes contained within populations in the areas that acted as refuges during the period of contraction. The location of the refuge and the pattern of expansion are major influences on each species' current phylogeography. In order to conserve genetic diversity within the species we may therefore wish to identify refugial areas that are centres of diversity and concentrate our efforts there. For example, research on a range of tree species in Europe has shown that ice age refugia exist in three Mediterranean areas: the Iberian Peninsula, the Italian Peninsula and the area including the Balkans, Greece and Turkey (see Chapter 13, Fig. 13.3). This is also true for the vast majority of European fauna and flora and it is therefore arguable that in the European context we should be concentrating our conservation efforts in Mediterranean regions.

Detecting isolation and gene flow

At a local level genetic relatedness can indicate levels of gene flow between populations. If a species exists as a number of identifiable populations it is important to know if gene flow is occurring between them. If the genetic relatedness is very high and all populations are genetically uniform then substantial gene flow is probably occurring or has recently occurred. Therefore the loss of any one population is probably recoverable because:

1. the total gene pool of the species has not been eroded;
2. the site may well be recolonised naturally because movement between sites has recently occurred; and
3. if not, the species can be re-established using a donor population that is very similar to the original.

However, if the populations are genetically distinct, indicating lack of gene flow, the consequences of losing a population are much more serious.

1. the total gene pool of the species may be eroded (unique alleles may be lost);
2. natural recolonisation is unlikely;
3. re-establishment attempts will have to use a donor population which differs genetically from the original and is therefore less likely to succeed.

This approach was taken in a study by Hoole *et al.* (1999) of the swallowtail butterfly (*Papilio machaon*) in England. This species is quite common and widespread in continental Europe, but is confined to a small wetland area of eastern England called the Norfolk Broads (Fig. 10.9). Within this area the breeding sites are reasonably well known and are in many cases managed for the butterfly and optimal growth of its larval foodplant, milk parsley (*Peucedenum palustre*). The study used genetic techniques to investigate whether there is significant gene flow between these sites and whether the species exists as isolated populations or as one large but patchy population. The results show no significant differences in genetic composition among the populations and strongly suggest that substantial gene flow exists and the large patchy

Fig. 10.9 Map of the Broadland area, UK, with sites of sampled swallowtail butterfly (*Papilio machaon*) populations associated with the different river valley systems. Reproduced from Hoole *et al.* (1999) with kind permission of Elsevier Science.

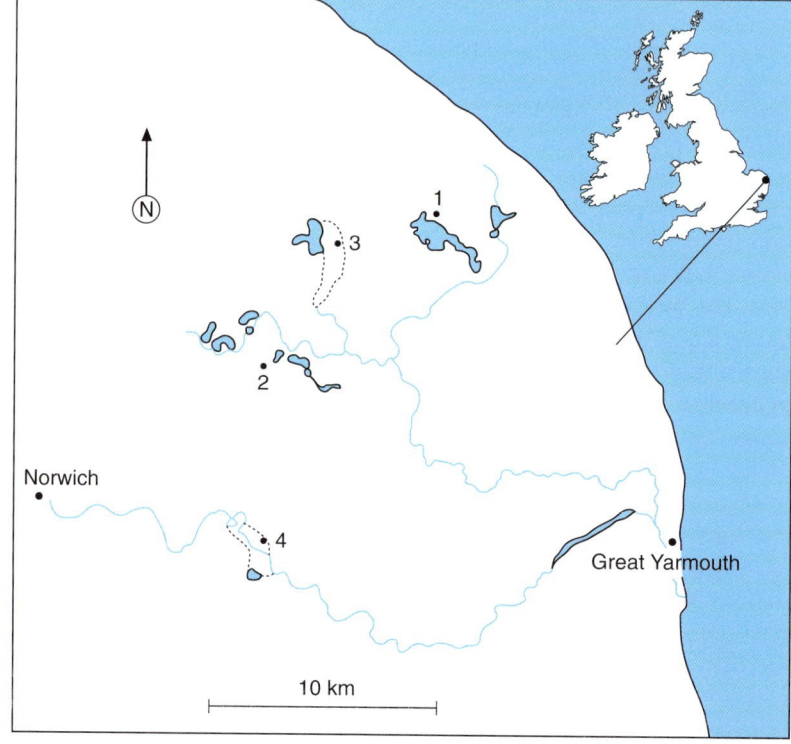

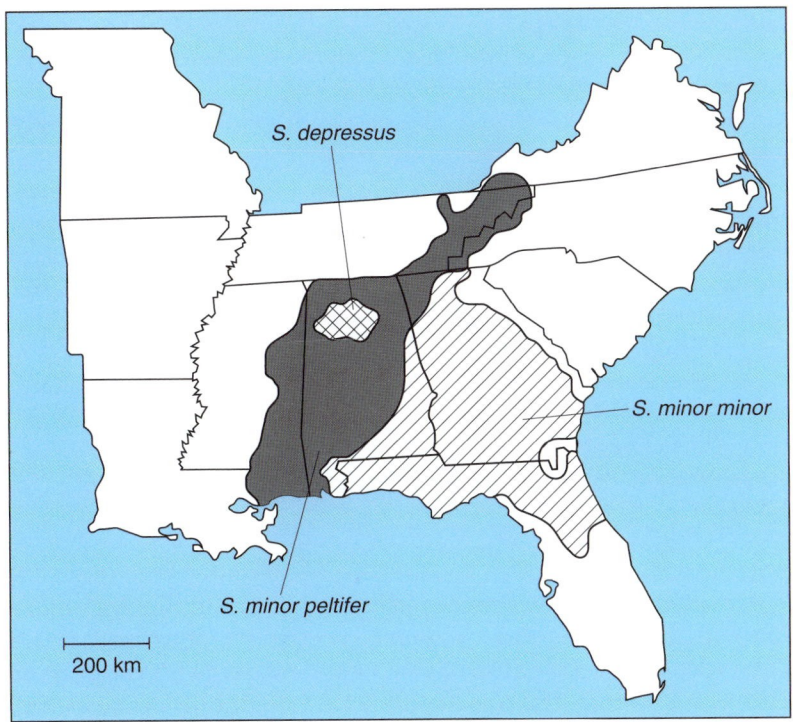

Fig. 10.10 Distribution of the flattened musk turtle (*Sternotherus depressus*) and its sibling species *S. minor* in south-eastern USA. Reproduced from Walker *et al.* (1998) with kind permission of Blackwell Science.

population model is closest to reality. The relevance for the species' conservation is that management should concentrate on providing sufficient high quality habitat at the landscape scale rather than worrying about the fate of individual populations.

Taxonomic recognition

The conservation status of a species dictates the amount of resources that are allocated to it. If there is doubt about the distinctiveness of a taxon, then it is often the case that its plight will be neglected in favour of well-defined taxa. Genetic studies can often be employed to clarify taxonomic status and therefore conservation status. One example is the case of the threatened flattened musk turtle (*Sternotherus depressus*) the distribution of which is nested within the more widespread *S. minor* along the Atlantic coast of the US. Research by Walker *et al.* (1998) has shown that the former is a true species and not a subspecies of *S. minor* as previously thought (Fig. 10.10). This has led to increased conservation status for this federally threatened species. A long-running taxonomic debate of this kind has surrounded the conservation effort for the red wolf (*Canis rufus*; Box 10.4).

Box 10.4 | The red wolf problem

The red wolf (*Canis rufus*) has been the subject of a debate over its taxonomic status and therefore over its conservation status. It is considered by some (e.g. Nowak 1992), including the US Fish and Wildlife Service, to be an endangered species with its natural range in southeastern USA. It was driven to extinction in the wild by 1970 but has since been bred in captivity and reintroduced to North Carolina. This latter action has caused controversy because there is an alternative hypothesis that the red wolf is not a true species, but the result of hybridisation between the grey wolf (*Canis lupus*) and the coyote (*Canis latrans*). The is based on an initial analysis of DNA from all three taxa by Wayne and Jenks (1991). The doubt about its status threatens to undermine conservation action for this species and therefore needs to be resolved. The fact that hybridisation between the red wolf and the coyote has taken place is not in dispute. But this may be a recent phenomenon resulting from human disruption and disturbance of habitat. However, Wayne and Jenks proposed that the red wolf actually originated from hybridisation. The fossil evidence does not support the 'hybrid origin' hypothesis, but further evidence from molecular genetic studies does (Roy *et al.* 1996). This is an interesting example of a problem of conservation status where the morphological data are in disagreement with the genetic data. More detailed genetic studies will hopefully resolve this issue soon.

Some rare species are threatened through hybridisation with more common congeners. One example is the Catalina mahogany (*Cercocarpus traskiae*), a native of Santa Catalina island off the coast of southern California. This tree is confined to a single canyon and a study of its morphology and genetics suggested considerable hybridisation with the closely related *C. betuloides*, a species more widespread on the island. Of the 11 adult trees remaining, five were thought to be of hybrid origin (Fig. 10.11). Now that this situation has been identified, it is a management decision as to whether all hybrids and *C. betuloides* should be eliminated from the canyon leaving a small number of pure *C. traskiae* individuals, or whether to continue to monitor the situation, perhaps only allowing pure seedlings to survive. The primary threat to the species has been from introduced mammals such as goats and pigs. Consequently juvenile mortality is high, but construction of an exclosure resulted in 70 seedlings appearing. Significantly, all of those sampled were pure *C. traskiae*, giving some grounds for optimism (Riesberg & Swenson 1996). See Chapter 13 for a further discussion of the status of hybrids.

Sustainable harvesting of populations

We saw in Chapter 6 that many wild populations of plants and animals are still harvested today for food or materials for building or clothing. Effective conservation of these species and the ecosystems of which they are part requires that they be harvested on a sustainable basis.

General principles of population growth and sustainability

Central to the idea of sustainable harvesting is the concept of the **sustainable yield**. This is any level of harvest that can be taken from a population indefinitely without detriment to the population. Clearly, one

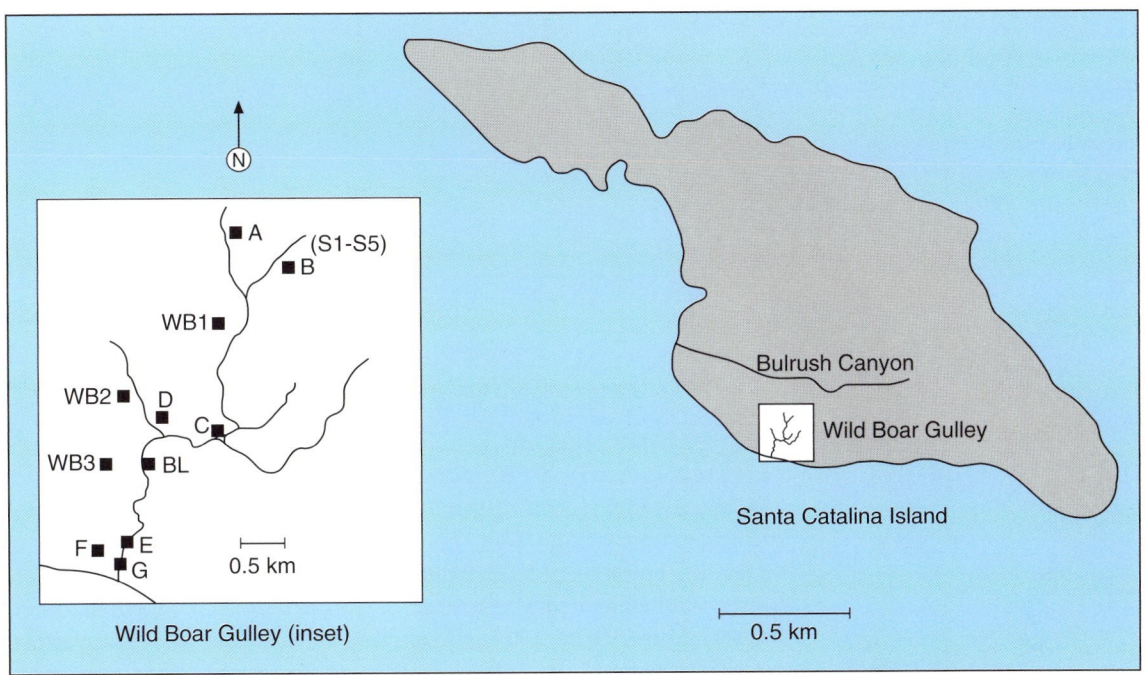

Fig. 10.11 Distribution of *Cercocarpus* trees in Wild Boar Gully, Santa Catalina Island. Trees A–D, WB1, WB2 are Catalina mahogany; trees E–G, BL, WB3 and seedlings S1–S5 are hybrids with mountain mahogany. Reproduced with kind permission of the authors (Riesberg & Swenson 1996).

could be harvesting a small number that has an insignificant impact on the population and this would therefore be sustainable. However, from a commercial point of view the important level of harvest to calculate is the **maximum sustainable yield** (MSY): the greatest level of harvest that can be taken indefinitely.

Mathematical models of harvesting are based around the concept of the **carrying capacity** of the habitat and how populations fluctuate relative to this carrying capacity. Many factors affect population growth, for example, density-dependent processes, such as food availability and predation (which increase in their intensity of action as a population approaches the carrying capacity), will exert greater mortality on large populations than small. The result is that population growth will be high when population density is low and vice versa.

Much of theory relating to sustainable yields is based on the logistic equation (see Fig. 6.1). If a graph is plotted showing the relationship between the change in population size over time dN/dt and the number of individuals in the population N, the result is a dome-shaped curve with a peak halfway between 0 and K (Fig. 10.12). In other words, the population is growing fastest when N equals $K/2$. If exactly that number of individuals is harvested ($rK/4$), the population will not increase, and during the next time interval it will produce this maximum growth again, when it could be harvested once more. This shows that in theory the MSY is possible when a population is at about half its carrying capacity when (according to the logistic equation) it is in a phase of exponential growth. This is fine in theory, but conservation requires us to look for practical solutions.

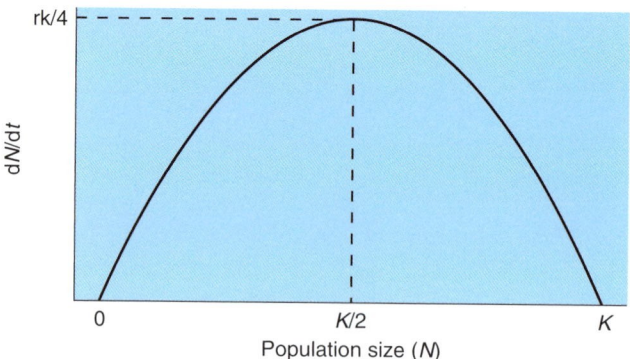

Fig. 10.12 The logistic equation predicts that the rate of growth of a population (d*N*/d*t*) changes with population size such that the maximum rate is achieved when the population size is half of the carrying capacity (*K*).

Techniques of harvesting

There are two common approaches to regulating the level of a harvest:

1. fixed quota per unit time;
2. fixed harvesting effort per unit time.

With a fixed quota system, a fixed amount (e.g. weight or number) of a species will be harvested regardless of the effort (e.g. number of days or labour) required to complete the harvest. With a fixed harvesting effort system a fixed amount of effort in terms of time or labour is permitted, regardless of the amount that is actually removed from the population.

The different impacts of these two harvesting systems can be visualised graphically as in Fig. 10.13. With a fixed quota system, the relationship between the quota and the MSY is crucial. If the quota is fixed at the calculated MSY and the population is greater than $K/2$, then the population will tend to decrease towards $K/2$. However, if the population size is less than $K/2$ the population will tend towards extinction, because the population growth rate is not fast enough to replace the individuals harvested. This system will therefore only work if $K/2$ can be accurately estimated. So how do we know when the population is at half of its carrying capacity? This is not possible for the vast majority of species and so techniques of harvesting are needed that do not rely on such estimates.

The fixed harvest effort acts in a different fashion. If the effort is calculated so that this will result in the MSY being taken when the population is at $K/2$, and if the population size is greater than this, more individuals will be harvested per unit effort and the population will decrease towards $K/2$, as with the fixed quota system. The difference between the two methods is that when the population size is below $K/2$ fewer individuals will be caught per unit effort, allowing the population to recover towards $K/2$. This system is therefore self-regulating in theory. In principle, therefore, this is a sounder approach to harvesting but it still relies on an accurate estimate of the carrying capacity.

In reality these harvesting models make a number of assumptions that are unrealistic when applied to real populations.

1. They assume that all individuals have equal reproductive potential, whereas real populations consist of pre-reproductive and post-reproductive individuals. In fact, in age-structured populations where reproductive potential only occurs in certain age classes, or differs

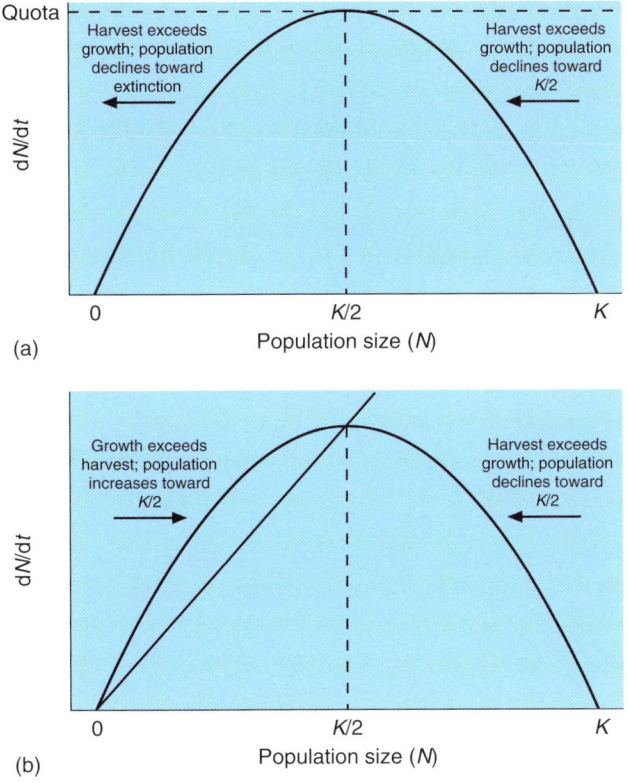

(a)

(b)

Fig. 10.13 (a). The fixed quota method of harvesting risks depletion of populations if the population falls below half of the carrying capacity. (b) The fixed harvest effort method ensures that the population is allowed to recover when it drops below half the carrying capacity.

between age classes, the MSY tends to lie between half and three-quarters of the carrying capacity.

2. They assume that mortality due to harvesting is compensated by reduced natural mortality. There is no evidence that this is the case.

3. They assume that there are no knock-on effects for species that interact with the harvested species, such as predators or competitors, which might change the carrying capacity of the environment for the target species.

Also, they do not take account of age structure, recruitment to the population, body growth rate, natural mortality rate and the harvest rate of individuals of various ages or sizes.

These acknowledged problems have led to the development of more detailed models which describe the numbers or biomass of different age (or size) classes as a function of the different processes (recruitment, natural mortality, etc.), each of which is described by one or more equations. But no matter how detailed the model, there remains the problem of how to predict the outcome of stochastic events for each successive generation to estimate the appropriate sustainable yield.

Considerable efforts have been expended on achieving sustainable yields of fish such as the Atlantic cod, but difficulties in both the scientific estimates of quotas and the acceptance of the economic consequences for local fishing industries has led to continued decline of stocks to the extent that the species is now classed as endangered.

Summary

1. Some species are naturally rare and are not necessarily threatened. Prioritisation for conservation requires estimation of the level of threat in terms of probability of extinction over a given time scale. This method is now employed in the construction of Red Data Books.

2. Populations are dynamic and have a finite probability of extinction. Population viability analyses can be used to assess population vulnerability and set targets for management but their accuracy is limited by lack of data in most cases.

3. As populations become smaller and more isolated, they become more prone to losing genetic diversity which underpins their adaptive ability and therefore their future survival prospects. Recently developed molecular techniques can be used to measure genetic diversity within and among populations and construct genetic management strategies to counteract loss of diversity.

4. Sustainable harvesting of wild populations has a well-developed theoretical basis but is much harder to achieve in practice because of the number of variables that can effect a population besides the impact of the harvest.

Discussion points

- What is the difference between the concepts of rarity and threat in species conservation?
- Is the concept of minimum viable population size practical and useful in species conservation?
- Does genetic diversity really matter in species conservation?
- Can the use of maximum sustainable yield lead to effective conservation of exploited species?

Further reading

Avise, J.C. & Hamrick, J.L. eds (1996). *Conservation Genetics: case histories from nature*. New York: Chapman & Hall.

Groombridge, B. (ed.) (2000). *Global biodiversity: earth's living resources in the 21st century*. Cambridge: World Conservation Monitoring Centre.

IUCN (2001). *International Union for the Conservation of Nature Red List Categories. Version 3.1*. Gland, Switzerland: IUCN.

Maxted, N., Ford-Lloyd, B.V. & Hawkes, J.G. (eds). (1997). *Plant genetic conservation: the* in situ *approach*. London: Chapman & Hall.

Web sites

Species Survival Commission: www.iucn.org/themes/ssc/
Fauna and Flora Preservation Society: www.fauna-flora.org/
World Wide Fund for Nature: www.panda.org/
US Endangered Species Program: www.endangered.fws.gov/
Royal Society for the Protection of Birds: www.rspb.org.uk/
British Butterfly Conservation Society: www.butterfly-conservation.org/

Chapter 11

Protecting species. II. *Ex situ* conservation and reintroduction

When a species reaches very low numbers or its habitat becomes critically endangered the decision may be taken to remove some or all individuals from the wild and attempt to conserve them in captivity. This chapter explores the rationale for the strategy as well as the methods and effectiveness. The ultimate goal must be to reunite species and habitat through reintroduction and we also explore the methods used to achieve this through examples of recent efforts.

By reading this chapter students will gain an understanding of the circumstances in which *ex situ* conservation and reintroduction have been undertaken; the range of methods used in plant and animal breeding; and the advantages and disadvantages of opting for *ex situ* conservation strategies. Additionally, students should gain a knowledge of some of the current *ex situ* programmes and reintroduction projects taking place.

What is *ex situ* conservation and when is it necessary?

The practice of *ex situ* conservation involves the removal of individuals or groups from their natural habitat into captivity, either to breed or to maintain a genetic stock. This is usually done by zoos and aquaria for animals and botanic gardens and herbaria for plants. Such places are increasingly moving from simply exhibitions of species that satisfy public curiosity to organisations with an active role in conservation.

In the previous chapter we have seen how populations can decline to a size where the odds are stacked against their survival, and the probability of extinction is greater than the probability of survival. When such populations are the sole representatives of a species or subspecies then a tough decision may have to be made. Do you attempt to save them by capturing remaining individuals, taking them into captivity and breeding from them to increase numbers, or do you do the best you can to manage the population and its native habitat and leave a lot to chance? In exceptional circumstances of endangerment to populations and species, the drastic step of taking individuals into captivity in order to conserve them is an option used with increasing frequency. The advantages and disadvantages as well as the circumstances under which this course of action is justified are considered here.

The biggest philosophical problem with this action is that conservation can only have real meaning if species are kept in context with their habitat. Conservation is about conserving the whole with its complex interactions, not isolated pieces. So in the long term, captive breeding or *ex situ* conservation cannot be considered conservation by itself, but can only be justified if reintroduction is a primary goal.

Some of the major challenges in captive breeding programmes, as we shall see below, are ensuring that the captive population has a genetic makeup which is representative of the population or populations on which they were founded (this may not be an issue if you are removing all that remains) and ensuring that you are removing individuals in such a way as to minimise the impact on the donor population. Additionally, if you take on the responsibility of captive breeding an endangered species you must have the facilities to maintain it in a healthy condition and retain the possibility of reintroduction.

Ex situ conservation of plants

Plants have been cultivated outside of their natural habitat for agricultural, medicinal and ornamental purposes for many centuries (see Chapter 3). A great deal of the expertise gained from these activities has been put to good use in *ex situ* conservation and documentation now exists on how to keep a large proportion of flowering plant species under cultivation. In addition, modern techniques have enabled new strategies to be followed and some of these are described below.

Seed preservation

One big advantage the plant conservationist has over his animal equivalents is that plants produce seeds. This stage in the life cycle, which reduces life processes to a low level in a small package, yet contains all the genetic information necessary to form the mature plant, is ideal for long term storage. An additional advantage is that many seeds go through natural periods of dormancy that can last many years. This can be exploited and the dormancy period extended further if the conditions for maintenance and cessation of dormancy are understood. The Millennium seed bank project run by The Royal Botanic Gardens at Kew, London aims to collect and conserve 10%, over 24 000 species, of the world's seed-bearing flora, and the entire UK native seed-bearing flora.

Research has shown that many plant species have seeds that respond to broadly the same environmental cues and therefore can be stored under broadly the same conditions. The Food and Agriculture Organization (FAO) has published standard conditions for long-term storage of seeds, including storage at $-18\,^{\circ}\mathrm{C}$ or below and maintaining a seed moisture content of 2–5%. Lower temperatures are desirable, but not always practical in terms of costs and reliability of equipment. Unfortunately, many tropical and some temperate plants possess seeds which loose viability when dried (recalcitrant seeds) and therefore cannot be stored in this way.

Pollen preservation

The preservation of pollen is much less common than of seeds and the techniques are consequently less advanced. Pollen grains are either cryopreserved at -180 to $-196\,°C$ or freeze-dried and stored between $+5$ and $-18\,°C$. The former is only effective up to 6 years and often less. The latter has successfully preserved pollen of some species for up to 12 years. The technique has mainly been used in fruit and forest species. The advantage of pollen over seed preservation is that pollen is immediately available for crossing (Frankel *et al.* 1995), but on the other hand, you need female flowering parts to pollinate.

Tissue preservation

Where seed or pollen storage are not effective (e.g. for those species with recalcitrant seeds), the alternative technique is normally tissue culture. This is particularly effective in those species that exhibit clonal growth and normally reproduce vegetatively. It is also effective for those species that are vegetatively propagated to maintain commercial races (e.g. potato, banana and *Citrus* spp.). The plant tissue can be cryopreserved in liquid nitrogen if suitable protocols have been developed for the species; alternatively, the tissue can be kept under conditions that maintain growth, but at much reduced rates requiring low levels of maintenance.

Collecting material for *ex situ* plant collections

If plant species are to be effectively conserved *ex situ*, it is important that as wide a diversity of genetic material as possible is obtained. The most commonly collected material is seed and a number of guidelines have been produced to try and optimise genetic diversity within collections:

1. samples should be collected from at least five populations (if this many remain) that are as geographically spread as possible throughout the species's range;
2. Seeds should be collected from a minimum of 10 and ideally at least 50 individuals per population to maximise the intrapopulation genetic diversity;
3. The number of seeds taken per individual should be dictated by the viability of the seeds so that enough are taken to ensure that some will be viable;
4. Care should be taken not to remove too many seeds during one collection period, particularly for species with low reproductive output, to minimise possible impacts on the population.

There is clearly a potential conflict between the last two above and some assessment may need to be made in order to reach a compromise between collecting sufficient to ensure viability and leaving enough to ensure that the donor population is not endangered.

Ex situ conservation of animals: captive breeding

A wide range of animals is relatively easily kept in captivity given adequate resources but a major challenge in *ex situ* conservation of animals is to get them to breed. Many species have been kept in captivity for centuries, but have never been the subject of a properly planned breeding programme for conservation purposes. But more recently an increasing number of zoos and wildlife parks are shifting their emphasis from pure exhibition toward conservation by undertaking, or contributing to, captive breeding programmes.

Captive breeding can have clear advantages and disadvantages for conservation of critically endangered animals (Table 11.1). It is obviously a method for increasing the numbers of individuals and therefore decreasing the risk of species extinction, but there are other significant advantages. Many endangered species are poorly understood and captive breeding provides an opportunity greatly to increase knowledge of their biology. Additionally, if the programme does successfully increase numbers so that the captive population becomes self-sustaining, this reduces the need to take remaining individuals (if there are any) from the wild. Last, but not least, the captive individuals can be used to inform the public of the need for conservation of that

Table 11.1 | The advantages and disadvantages of entering into and maintaining a captive breeding programme

Advantages of captive breeding programmes for conservation
1. Building up numbers for re-establishment
2. Enables research on basic biology of species
3. Can eventually reduce need to collect individuals from the wild
4. Captive colonies can be used to educate public about the species and its conservation

Problems in managing a captive breeding programme
1. Initial source of stock: can endanger remaining small wild populations.
2. Facilities in which to do the breeding: zoos and aquaria
3. Maintaining a large enough population size to prevent problems of genetic drift and loss of variability: particular problem with large vertebrates
4. Captive populations may undergo selection, adapting them to their captive conditions and leaving them maladapted to their natural environment
5. Loss of learned behaviour can occur due to unnatural behaviour under captive conditions
6. Susceptibility to disease due to artificially high concentration of individuals
7. It may be difficult to get the species to breed under captive conditions

and other species, gaining support (financial and political) in the process.

Unfortunately, captive breeding also brings with it significant problems. We have already seen that to set up a captive breeding programme we may have to capture all remaining individuals and therefore condemn the species to extinction in the wild. It follows that to take a significant number of an already small and endangered population for captive breeding may increase the danger of extinction for the remaining population. To undertake captive breeding in vertebrates requires a lot of resources in terms of money and space; only a limited number of zoos and aquaria have the appropriate facilities. Usually, only a small number of individuals are used in captive breeding, which may cause significant genetic problems through inbreeding and drift (as mentioned in the context of small wild populations in Chapters 4 and 10). A related problem is the risk of selection that can take place over successive generations in the new captive environment to which populations are exposed. The genetic makeup of the individuals will have been the result of selection for survival in their natural habitat. As soon as captive breeding begins there may be selection for survival in captivity. This will get worse, as the number of generations in captivity increases. This may result in a population that appears very healthy in captivity but is incapable of surviving in the wild. This effect is difficult to demonstrate in terms of cause and effect, but is probably a major reason for the unsuccessful attempts to reintroduce the large copper butterfly (*Lycaena dispar*) to Woodwalton Fen NNR, UK after many years captive breeding in greenhouse conditions. A similar problem may occur in those species where parents teach their young specific types of behaviour, such as foraging or predator avoidance. These behaviour patterns may not be passed on in captivity, rendering subsequent generations ill-equipped to survive in the wild. Keeping populations in captivity usually involves confining them in unnaturally small areas that can have a number of detrimental effects. Some animals can become aggressive when at high density and the incidence of fights can increase leading to injuries, infections and often death. Additionally, the incidence of disease tends to be higher in densely packed captive populations. Diseases can also spread quickly threatening the entire captive stock, a problem illustrated later by the example of the black-footed ferret (*Mustela nigripes*).

Captive breeding technology

The most fundamental problem with captive breeding may simply be getting the animals to breed. Many endangered species are slow breeders and may only reproduce when conditions are right. Complex behaviour may also be involved, including long periods of courtship. Some of our most endangered animals, such as the giant panda (*Ailuropoda melanoleuca*) have been the subject of long-running captive breeding programmes with only limited success because of their apparent unwillingness to breed out of their natural environment. The answer may lie in making the captive conditions more like their natural habitat, but when this is not feasible due to limited space, as with the giant panda the solution probably lies with new advances in reproductive technology.

A range of reproductive technologies now exists to help in circumstances where achieving natural mating has proved difficult. The methods are most advanced in mammals because many of the techniques have come from medical research into treatment of human infertility, although it is not simply a case of transferring the technology as mammalian reproductive biology is very varied. Those interested in the details of the techniques should refer to Holt (1994); it is appropriate to give just short descriptions here.

1. Semen collection. Techniques for collection of semen from males range from using artificial females to induce mating to the stimulation of ejaculation by mild electric shock (electroejaculation)

2. Insemination techniques. This technique simply deposits the sperm obtained from a male in to the female as near to the ovulated oocyte as possible to maximise chances of successful fertilization.

3. *In vitro* fertilisation. Eggs and sperm are removed from their respective donors and fertilisation takes place 'in the test tube' without need for the individuals to mate. The resulting embryo can then either be implanted in the female donor (the mother), implanted in a surrogate mother or stored (see below).

4. Microinjection of spermatozoa. In cases where fertilization of the egg is a problem the spermatozoa can be directly injected in to the egg.

5. Embryo transfer. Embryos from fertile females can be transferred to surrogate mothers for gestation in cases where excess ovulation and fertilisation can be induced using fertility drugs. The surrogates are often females of related common species.

6. Cryopreservation. A common problem with use of reproductive technologies is that of timing, all the necessary materials are not always available at the same time. Fortunately embryos, eggs and sperm can be stored until needed using cryopreservation techniques, although this has only been successful in some species.

All of these techniques offer opportunities but are very resource intensive. Difficult choices will have to be made as to which species warrant such action.

Cloning technology: the future of *ex situ* conservation?

The recent success in cloning of animals such as sheep promises new opportunities for *ex situ* conservation. Not only might it be possible to produce large numbers of clones of endangered species, it also provides the possibility to maintain and even increase the gene pool in living animals, thus overcoming some of the traditional captive breeding problems. For example, genotypes that were becoming rare in a captive population, simply through genetic drift, could be restored by cloning large numbers of key individuals that may be reproductively inactive or even may have recently died! Uneven sex ratios might also be balanced in this way. However, all of this assumes a large input of resources for the technology and monitoring of the gene pool at a level not so far attempted.

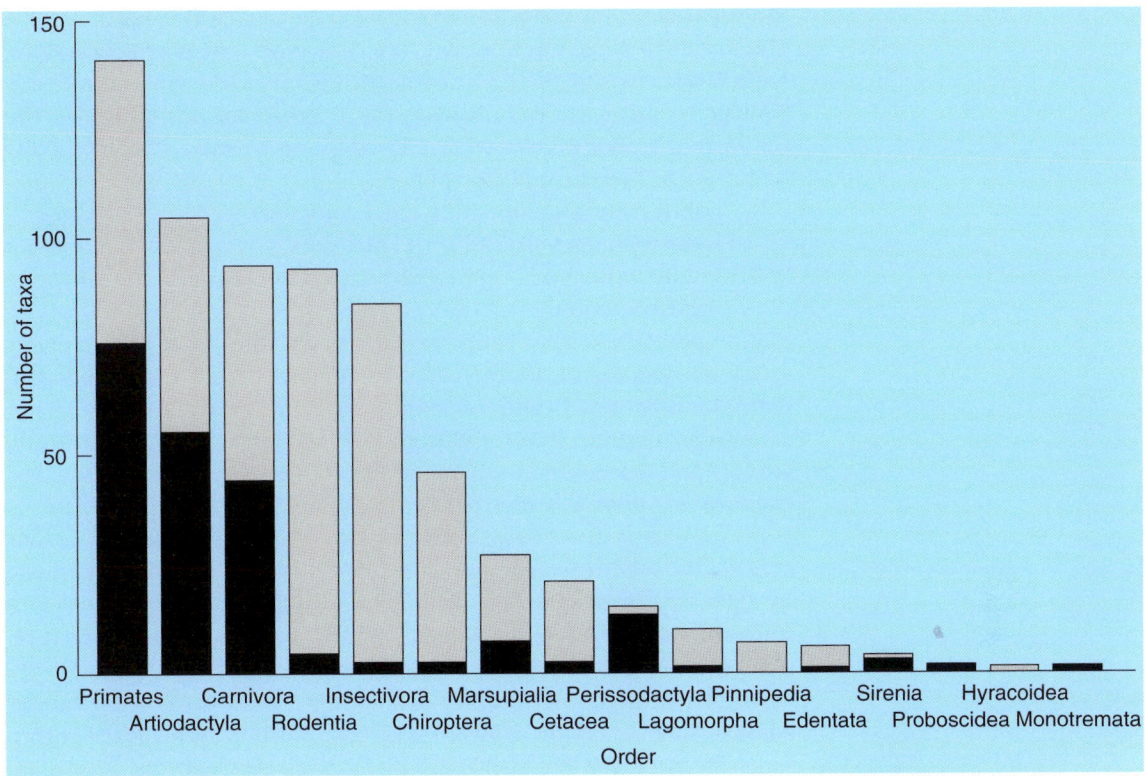

The significance of ex situ animal programmes for conservation

The effectiveness of captive breeding programmes is difficult to measure at this stage. Concerted actions of this kind are new and only time will tell how successful they will be. Even so, captive breeding will only be possible for a very limited number of species and cannot be seen on its own as a significant contributor to the conservation of biodiversity. In the past, captive breeding programmes have concentrated on mammals and birds, particularly birds of prey, but more recently have included increasing numbers of invertebrates.

The potential facilities for captive breeding are large, but zoos have only recently viewed captive breeding as a main aim. Most zoos still largely keep species that are attractive to visitors, but not threatened in the wild. According to the international zoo yearbook (Olney & Ellis 1991), of the world's threatened tetrapod species only around 9% of amphibians, 20% of reptiles, 3% of birds and 34% of mammals are held in captivity. Even within the 34% of threatened mammals, the distribution amongst taxa is very patchy (Fig. 11.1), and the number of individuals held in captivity is often not sufficient to prevent inbreeding depression, even if zoos coordinate their programmes.

Some examples of captive breeding and reintroduction programmes are given later in this chapter and it will suffice here to give one example of a successful captive breeding programme. The California condor (*Gymnogyps californianus*) was widespread in North

Fig. 11.1 Threatened mammal taxa held in captivity shown as the proportion of all threatened species in each Order. Black portion held in captivity. Grey portion not held. Reproduced from Magin *et al.* (1994) with kind permission of Kluwer Academic Publishers.

America before the Pleistocene extinction of megafauna (see Chapter 3). The species's rapid decline over last 100 years has been blamed on habitat destruction, disturbance, shooting and direct and indirect poisoning. Its critically endangered status led to the formation of the California Condor Recovery Team in 1978 and a recovery plan was prepared, with three related elements:

1. habitat studies acquisition and protection;
2. radio telemetry studies with wild birds;
3. establishment of a captive population to produce birds for reintroduction.

Radio telemetry studies confirmed the population to be at a critically low level and recovery of dead birds suggested that being shot and eating contaminated food were the major causes of mortality rather than habitat loss. In 1985 the wild population declined from 15 to 9 individuals and the decision was made to take the rest into captivity. The California condor was then extinct in the wild and the captive populations were kept in only two zoos, San Diego and Los Angeles. The first successful breeding was achieved in 1988 and 49 condors had been bred by 1993. The problem of chicks imprinting on humans and therefore not being sufficiently wary of them on release was overcome by feeding chicks with glove puppets resembling adult condors and humans otherwise having minimal contact. The closely related but more common Andean condor (*Vultur gryphus*) was used both to provide surrogate mothers and to develop methods for releasing captive birds.

Releases began in 1991 using both species (two of each). Birds were acclimatised by keeping them on site in aviaries for 3 months. The programme is continuing but, although the captive breeding has undoubtedly been successful, it is too early to measure the success of the reintroduction. The true measure of the success of *ex situ* conservation is whether it contributes to conservation in the wild through re-establishment of wild populations. This process is considered in the next section.

Species reintroduction

A major limitation of captive breeding is that it is futile if there is no prospect of eventually reintroducing the species into the wild. The legitimate objective of all captive breeding programmes must be to reintroduce species to their natural habitat in a way which provides a good chance of establishing self-sustaining (viable) populations. Therefore captive breeding is not effective in isolation; it must be used in tandem with habitat conservation and/or habitat restoration to enable eventual reintroduction. Reintroduction is only possible if the original reasons for endangerment or extinction in the wild have been removed. For example, it is no good reintroducing rhino to an area where they have just been extirpated through poaching if the threat from poachers has not been removed.

Reintroduction is defined by the IUCN (1998) as 'an attempt to establish a species in an area which was once part of its historical range, but from which it has been extirpated or become extinct'. Reintroduction of endangered species to the wild is often an attention-grabbing exercise and can raise awareness of conservation issues. Consequently there is a temptation to carry out reintroductions in the hope rather than a well-found expectation that they will succeed. Even more serious is the possibility that reintroduction will be resourced at the expense of conservation of remaining wild populations and may adversely affect conservation efforts. A number of conservation organisations have produced guidelines for reintroduction to try and limit the incidence of poorly planned efforts. The IUCN guidelines are given in Box 11.1 as an example. The practice is becoming increasingly common with some 217 species being the subject of current programmes registered in the IUCN *Reintroduction Practitioners Handbook* and many more unregistered. In most countries there are no effective restrictions on reintroduction attempts and many go unrecorded.

Box 11.1 | IUCN Guidelines for reintroductions (IUCN 1998)

Aims and objectives of reintroduction

Aims

The principle aim of any reintroduction should be to establish a viable, free-ranging population in the wild, of a species, subspecies or race, which has become globally or locally extinct, or extirpated, in the wild. It should be reintroduced within the species's former natural habitat and range and should require minimal long-term management.

Objectives

The objectives of a reintroduction may include: to enhance the long-term survival of a species; to re-establish a keystone species (in the ecological or cultural sense) in an ecosystem; to maintain and/or restore natural biodiversity; to provide long-term economic benefits to the local and/or national economy; to promote conservation awareness; or a combination of these.

Multidisciplinary approach

A reintroduction requires a multidisciplinary approach involving a team of persons drawn from a variety of backgrounds. As well as government personnel, they may include persons from governmental natural resource management agencies; non-governmental organisations; funding bodies; universities; veterinary institutions; zoos (and private animal breeders) and/or botanic gardens, with a full range of suitable expertise. Team leaders should be responsible for coordination between the various bodies and provision should be made for publicity and public education about the project.

Pre-project activities

Biological

Feasibility study and background research
• An assessment should be made of the taxonomic status of individuals to be reintroduced. They should preferably be of the same subspecies or race as those which were extirpated, unless adequate numbers are not available. An investigation of historical information about the loss and fate of individuals from the reintroduction area, as well as molecular genetic studies, should be undertaken in case of doubt as to individuals' taxonomic status. A study of genetic variation within and between populations of this and related taxa can also be helpful. Special care is needed when the population has long been extinct.
• Detailed studies should be made of the status and biology of wild populations (if they exist) to determine the species's critical needs. For animals, this would include descriptions of habitat preferences, intraspecific variation and adaptations to local ecological conditions, social behaviour, group composition, home range size, shelter and food requirements, foraging and feeding behaviour, predators and diseases. For migratory species, studies should include the potential migratory areas. For plants, it would include biotic and abiotic habitat requirements, dispersal mechanisms, reproductive biology, symbiotic relationships (e.g. with mycorrhizae, pollinators), insect pests and diseases. Overall, a firm knowledge of the natural history of the species in question is crucial to the entire reintroduction scheme.
• The species, if any, that has filled the void created by the loss of the species concerned, should be determined; an understanding of the effect the reintroduced species will have on the ecosystem is important for ascertaining the success of the reintroduced population.
• The build-up of the released population should be modelled under various sets of conditions, in order to specify the optimal number and composition of individuals to be released per year and the numbers of years necessary to promote establishment of a viable population.
• A Population and Habitat Viability Analysis will aid in identifying significant environmental and population variables and assessing their potential interactions, which would guide long-term population management.

Previous reintroductions
• Thorough research into previous reintroductions of the same or similar species and wide-ranging contacts with persons having relevant expertise should be conducted prior to and while developing reintroduction protocol.

Choice of release site and type
• Site should be within the historic range of the species. For an initial reinforcement there should be few remnant wild individuals. For a reintroduction, there should be no remnant population to prevent disease spread, social disruption and introduction of alien genes. In some circumstances, a reintroduction or reinforcement may have to be made into an area which is fenced or otherwise delimited, but it should be within the species's former natural habitat and range.

• A conservation/ benign introduction should be undertaken only as a last resort when no opportunities for reintroduction into the original site or range exist and only when a significant contribution to the conservation of the species will result.

• The reintroduction area should have assured, long-term protection (whether formal or otherwise).

Evaluation of reintroduction site

• Availability of suitable habitat: reintroductions should only take place where the habitat and landscape requirements of the species are satisfied, and likely to be sustained for the forseeable future. The possibility of natural habitat change since extirpation must be considered. Likewise, a change in the legal/political or cultural environment since species extirpation needs to be ascertained and evaluated as a possible constraint. The area should have sufficient carrying capacity to sustain growth of the reintroduced population and support a viable (self-sustaining) population in the long run.

• Identification and elimination, or reduction to a sufficient level, of previous causes of decline: could include disease; over-hunting; over-collection; pollution; poisoning; competition with or predation by introduced species; habitat loss; adverse effects of earlier research or management programmes; competition with domestic livestock, which may be seasonal. Where the release site has undergone substantial degradation caused by human activity, a habitat restoration programme should be initiated before the reintroduction is carried out.

Availability of suitable release stock

• It is desirable that source animals come from wild populations. If there is a choice of wild populations to supply founder stock for translocation, the source population should ideally be closely related genetically to the original native stock and show similar ecological characteristics (morphology, physiology, behaviour, habitat preference) to the original subpopulation.

• Removal of individuals for re-introduction must not endanger the captive stock population or the wild source population. Stock must be guaranteed available on a regular and predictable basis, meeting specifications of the project protocol.

• Individuals should only be removed from a wild population after the effects of translocation on the donor population have been assessed, and after it is guaranteed that these effects will not be negative.

• If captive or artificially propagated stock is to be used, it must be from a population which has been soundly managed both demographically and genetically, according to the principles of contemporary conservation biology.

• Reintroductions should not be carried out merely because captive stocks exist, nor solely as a means of disposing of surplus stock.

• Prospective release stock, including stock that is a gift between governments, must be subjected to a thorough veterinary screening process before shipment from original source. Any animals found to be infected or which test positive for non-endemic or contagious pathogens with a potential impact on population levels, must be removed from the consignment, and the uninfected, negative remainder must be placed in strict quarantine for a suitable period before retest. If clear after retesting, the animals may be placed for shipment.

- Since infection with serious disease can be acquired during shipment, especially if this is intercontinental, great care must be taken to minimise this risk.
- Stock must meet all health regulations prescribed by the veterinary authorities of the recipient country and adequate provisions must be made for quarantine if necessary.

Release of captive stock
- Most species of mammal and birds rely heavily on individual experience and learning as juveniles for their survival; they should be given the opportunity to acquire the necessary information to enable survival in the wild, through training in their captive environment; a captive-bred individual's probability of survival should approximate that of a wild counterpart.
- Care should be taken to ensure that potentially dangerous captive-bred animals (such as large carnivores or primates) are not so confident in the presence of humans that they might be a danger to local inhabitants and/or their livestock.

Socioeconomic and legal requirements

- Reintroductions are generally long-term projects that require the commitment of long-term financial and political support.
- Socio-economic studies should be made to assess impacts, costs and benefits of the reintroduction programme to local human populations.
- A thorough assessment of attitudes of local people to the proposed project is necessary to ensure long-term protection of the reintroduced population, especially if the cause of species's decline was due to human factors (e.g. over-hunting, over-collection, loss or alteration of habitat). The programme should be fully understood, accepted and supported by local communities.
- Where the security of the reintroduced population is at risk from human activities, measures should be taken to minimise these in the reintroduction area. If these measures are inadequate, the reintroduction should be abandoned or alternative release areas sought.
- The policy of the country to reintroductions and to the species concerned should be assessed. This might include checking existing provincial, national and international legislation and regulations, and provision of new measures and required permits as necessary.
- Reintroduction must take place with the full permission and involvement of all relevant government agencies of the recipient or host country. This is particularly important in reintroductions in border areas, or involving more than one state or when a reintroduced population can expand into other states, provinces or territories.
- If the species poses potential risk to life or property, these risks should be minimised and adequate provision made for compensation where necessary; where all other solutions fail, removal or destruction of the released individual should be considered. In the case of migratory/mobile species, provisions should be made for crossing of international/state boundaries.

Planning, preparation and release stages

- Approval of relevant government agencies and land owners, and coordination with national and international conservation organizations.

- Construction of a multidisciplinary team with access to expert technical advice for all phases of the programme.
- Identification of short- and long-term success indicators and prediction of programme duration, in context of agreed aims and objectives.
- Securing adequate funding for all programme phases.
- Design of pre- and post-release monitoring programme so that each reintroduction is a carefully designed experiment, with the capability to test methodology with scientifically collected data. Monitoring the health of individuals, as well as their survival, is important; intervention may be necessary if the situation proves unforeseeably unfavourable.
- Appropriate health and genetic screening of release stock, including stock that is a gift between governments. Health screening of closely related species in the reintroduction area.
- If release stock is wild-caught, care must be taken to ensure that: (a) the stock is free from infectious or contagious pathogens and parasites before shipment, and (b) the stock will not be exposed to vectors of disease agents which may be present at the release site (and absent at the source site) and to which it may have no acquired immunity.
- If vaccination prior to release, against local endemic or epidemic diseases of wild stock or domestic livestock at the release site, is deemed appropriate, this must be carried out during the 'Preparation Stage' so as to allow sufficient time for the development of the required immunity.
- Appropriate veterinary or horticultural measures as required to ensure health of release stock throughout the programme. This is to include adequate quarantine arrangements, especially where founder stock travels far or crosses international boundaries to the release site.
- Development of transport plans for delivery of stock to the country and site of reintroduction, with special emphasis on ways to minimise stress on the individuals during transport.
- Determination of release strategy (acclimatisation of release stock to release area; behavioural training, including hunting and feeding, group composition, number, release patterns and techniques, timing).
- Establishment of policies on interventions (see below).
- Development of conservation education for long-term support; professional training of individuals involved in the long-term programme; public relations through the mass media and in local community; involvement where possible of local people in the programme.
- The welfare of animals for release is of paramount concern through all these stages.

Post-release activities

- Post-release monitoring is required of all (or a sample of) individuals. This most vital aspect may be by direct (e.g. tagging, telemetry) or indirect (e.g. spoor, informants) methods as suitable.
- Demographic, ecological and behavioural studies of released stock must be undertaken.
- Study of processes of long-term adaptation by individuals and the population.
- Collection and investigation of mortalities.

- Interventions (e.g. supplemental feeding, veterinary aid, horticultural aid) when necessary.
- Decisions for revision, rescheduling, or discontinuation of programme where necessary.
- Habitat protection or restoration to continue where necessary.
- Continuing public relations activities, including education and mass media coverage.
- Evaluation of cost-effectiveness and success of reintroduction techniques.
- Regular publications in scientific and popular literature.

Prior to the consideration of reintroduction initiatives, it is essential that the full weight of conservation measures are already being applied to arrest the species' decline, particularly the implementation of action plans, recovery programmes, or effective management procedures. Reintroduction programmes are expensive and it would be unwise to use up scarce resources on such relatively risky ventures without considering how effectively the same money could be used on *in situ* conservation.

Ironically, one of the biggest problems with captive breeding can be that it is sometimes too successful and surplus stock is produced. Some of this stock can be dispersed around other zoos and institutions, but there is also a temptation to reintroduce as a solution to this problem, even though the habitat has not improved and the individuals are likely to perish. Reintroductions should not be carried out merely because captive stocks exist, nor should they be a means of disposing of surplus stock.

Examples of species captive breeding and reintroduction

There are a number of well-recorded cases where captive breeding has been used in a crisis situation where the species concerned has gone, or was about to go, extinct in the wild. Many of these make good conservation stories, but from a scientific point of view it is best to use examples that illustrate the challenges involved and the problems encountered.

Arabian oryx (*Oryx leucoryx*)

This species of antelope was once widespread in the deserts of the Arabian Peninsula, but due to overexploitation by hunters was exterminated from the wild by 1972. Fortunately, this event was anticipated and a captive population had previously been established, and through captive breeding, a reintroduction programme was made possible. The first oryx were reintroduced into the wild in Oman in 1982. Despite the individuals being several generations removed from the wild, they survived well. Since 1990, 72 individuals have been released on a continuous basis in the Mahazat as-Sayd Protected Area in Saudi Arabia. A genetically diverse group has been selected and initially released in to a 200-hectare enclosure before being released into the larger reserve, which itself has been fenced to exclude livestock that had previously degraded the vegetation. This population was monitored on a continuous basis and by the beginning of 1998 numbered 350 individuals (Fig.

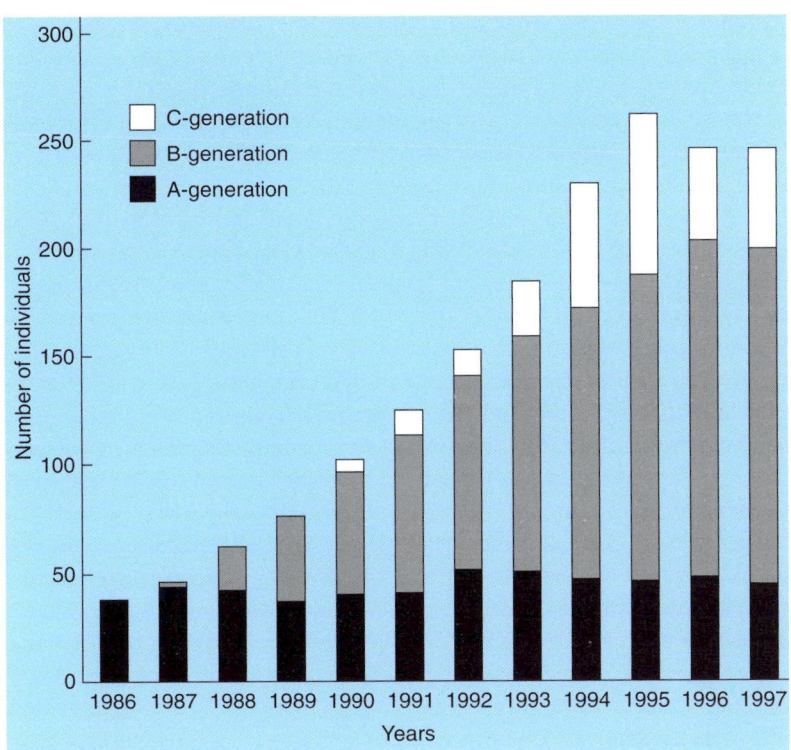

Fig. 11.2 Increase in the number of captive bred oryx (*Oryx leucoryx*) at the National Wildlife Research Centre of Taif, Saudi Arabia, since 1986. Reproduced from Ostrowski *et al.* (1998) with kind permission of Blackwell Science.

11.2). The initial success of this reintroduction is evident from the reproductive rate of the population and has encouraged a further reintroduction into the Uruq Bani Ma'arid Protected Area to the south. The long-term prospects are good and are in part due to careful genetic management of the captive stock and the policy of maintaining a large captive herd above the minimum viable population size of 250 (taken as the size required to conserve 90% of the genetic polymorphism after 200 years). Unfortunately, renewed poaching in recent years threatens a second extinction in the wild. Longer-term survival in the wild will require reintroduction to more sites and the formulation of a metapopulation structure, continued protection from hunting and a resolution of the problem of livestock overgrazing, which continues to threaten oryx habitat (Ostrowski *et al.* 1998). This is a good example of a reintroduction programme that relies primarily on the reversal of human pressure on the species and its natural habitat for its success.

Black-footed ferret (*Mustela nigripes*)

This well-documented and long-running reintroduction programme illustrates a range of the most common problems associated with the technique. The black-footed ferret is a native of North America, inhabiting the Great Plains area from southern Canada down to Texas. Its range probably matched that of its prey, the prairie dog (*Cynomys* spp.). Its rapid decline was first noted in the 1960s and was followed in 1970 by the establishment of a recovery team. The cause of decline was identified as a decline in prairie dogs to about 5–10% of former numbers, largely due to destruction of habitat for agricultural development and associated poisoning campaigns by farmers who considered them as pests, but also due to the introduced disease, sylvatic plague. A captive breeding effort was initiated using nine ferrets captured between 1972 and 1974. Two litters were born but the colony subsequently failed.

At that time only one free-ranging ferret population had been studied, but a further colony was discovered in 1981. This colony was doing well and 128 individuals had been recorded by 1984. At this point, captive breeding and translocation to other sites was considered and a small number were taken into captivity. However, 1985 was a crisis period as sylvatic plague hit the prairie dog population and ferret numbers again plummeted. Simultaneously the six ferrets taken into captivity were found to have canine distemper contracted in the wild. By the winter of 1985 the known number of black-footed ferrets had been reduced to 10, making it the rarest mammal in the world.

A decision was made in 1986, to capture all remaining animals, making the species extinct in the wild. This was controversial because little success had been achieved in captive breeding to date and the risk of disease was high. Fortunately the disease problem was avoided and the programme has been successful in producing ferrets for reintroduction. The captive population grew from 18 in 1987 to a situation where 2600 kits have now been born in captivity (spread between seven institutions). Techniques such as manipulation of the female reproductive cycle, and sperm cryopreservation have been used.

In 1991 the reintroduction programme began with 49 ferrets, rising to a total of 873 by the end of 1998. Some individuals carried radio collars to monitor movement and early releases were therefore known to be hampered by inappropriate behaviour of the ferrets. Captive breeding had apparently left them unable to catch prey and avoid predation themselves. Subsequent research on aspects of innate and learned behaviour enabled the appropriate captive environment to be created that better prepared the ferrets for the wild. Additionally, keeping ferrets on the release site in prerelease cages appears vital for acclimatisation.

Unfortunately the initial release site in Wyoming had to be abandoned in 1994 after another wave of sylvatic plague hit the area. Subsequently, four new sites have been brought in to the programme. The problems that still remain include the very low genetic variation that now exists, the continuing threat of disease, loss of hunting and predator avoidance skills, and most difficult is the continuing decline of its natural habitat and food source. This case brings in to clear focus the problems of disease in captive populations (and in their prey) and the problem of loss of learned behaviour in captive-bred individuals.

Single species reintroductions as flagships for community conservation

Species reintroductions are often criticised for the level of resourcing required for one species when the outcome is so uncertain. Are there any possible benefits for other species in the process? The example of the large blue butterfly (*Maculinea arion*) below illustrates that it is at the level of the autecological study that some of the complexities of a system can be revealed enabling management for a characteristic community. These would be overlooked if restoration were carried out only at the habitat or landscape scale. This point will be further explored in Chapter 14.

Reintroduction of the large blue butterfly (*Maculinea arion*)

This species suffered from major loss of its dry grassland habitat over the last 100 years, Despite the protection of many remaining sites, *M. arion* continued to decline until its eventual extinction in the UK in 1979. At a very late stage in 1972, when only two populations remained, a study of its ecology and habitat requirements was commissioned. It was already known that this species has a complex life cycle. The larvae spending most of their time as parasites of *Myrmica* ants. They overwinter in the ant nest, pupate and emerge as adults the next summer. The requirement for ants was known at the time of the decline but the perplexing problem was that, despite the presence of *Myrmica* ants on protected sites, *M. arion* continued to disappear (Thomas 1976).

Subsequent research revealed that this species is even more specialised than was first realised. Not only does it have an obligate relationship with *Myrmica* ants, but its survival is dependent on being adopted by one species of ant, *Myrmica sabuleti.* This ant requires closely grazed turf in which to survive, and with the policy of protecting sites rather than actively managing them, many had formed long grass swards and the ant had disappeared. The sites still looked suitable because ant hills of other species were still present (Thomas 1995).

By the time of this discovery it was too late to save the British race of *M. arion*, but other similar European races were identified for a restoration programme. A former site was identified and management begun with the initial objective of increasing the abundance of the host ant. To do this it was necessary to manage carefully the intensity of grazing. A regime of light grazing by ponies in spring and summer and heavier grazing by cattle during the winter was successful in producing a mosaic of short grazed turf and patches of thyme (*Thymus praecox*) on which the female butterflies could lay eggs. The density of the host ant has gradually increased under this management. In 1983 a population of *M. arion* was released for a trial restoration experiment. The initial population was less than 20 individuals but numbers increased over the next 6 years reaching about 200 in 1988. Other sites are now being managed appropriately for future re-establishments and the outlook for this species in Britain is optimistic (Thomas 1989).

The unexpected result of this work was that the intensive management programme produced conditions under which a whole range of species of plants and invertebrates that had recently declined, colonised the site or reappeared from dormant seed. Thus the whole community and not just one species is now of conservation value and much knowledge has been gained of appropriate management for community conservation.

Direct species translocation

It is becoming increasingly common for individuals to be moved from one site to another for conservation purposes. This may be either to found a new population where a population of conspecifics has gone extinct in the past or to add individuals to an existing population. The former is termed reintroduction and the latter reinforcement. But commonly, wild individuals are captured in one location (the donor site or population) and translocated directly to the target site.

Direct translocation has been used on a wide range of plants and animals and was carried out to maintain populations as a source of food long before conservation was a familiar term. The number of translocations carried out under the banner of conservation has increased rapidly and this has led to criticism of the technique because of the lack of evaluation of its efficacy and because of its potential disadvantages. The nature of translocation ranges from highly organised and researched national or international programmes to *ad hoc* releases of rescued animals by well-intentioned animal lovers.

In a fragmented landscape where many populations and habitats are isolated from others, translocations can play an effective role in conservation strategies; they can increase the number of existing populations or increase the size, genetic diversity and demographic balance of a small population consequently increasing its chances of survival. Translocation clearly has a role in the recovery of species that have substantially declined and is the most likely method by which many sedentary species can recover all or part of their former range. However, against this is the potential for reinforcement translocations to spread disease from one population to another or to introduce deleterious or maladaptive genes to a population. Additionally, translocation of predators or competitors may have negative impacts on other species resulting in an overall loss of diversity. Last, but not least of these considerations, is the effort and resources required in this type of action, which need to be justified by evidence of the likely benefits.

Despite the large number of translocations that have taken place, there is surprisingly little evidence of the efficacy of such actions. This is partly because many translocations have not been strictly for conservation, nor official, nor legal, let alone scientific in their approach. Successful translocations inevitably get recorded and gain attention, whereas failures may never be recorded at all. This makes appraisal of the method very difficult. One key problem is a definition of success. Is translocation successful if the individuals survive the first week or a year, or do they need to reproduce for one or several generations? Whatever the answer it is clear that a general framework is required to ensure that (as with reintroductions above) any translocation is justified, has a realistic chance of success and that it will be properly monitored and evaluated for the benefit of future efforts.

Any framework should evaluate the possible benefits and deleterious impacts of the action, the factors affecting chances of success and

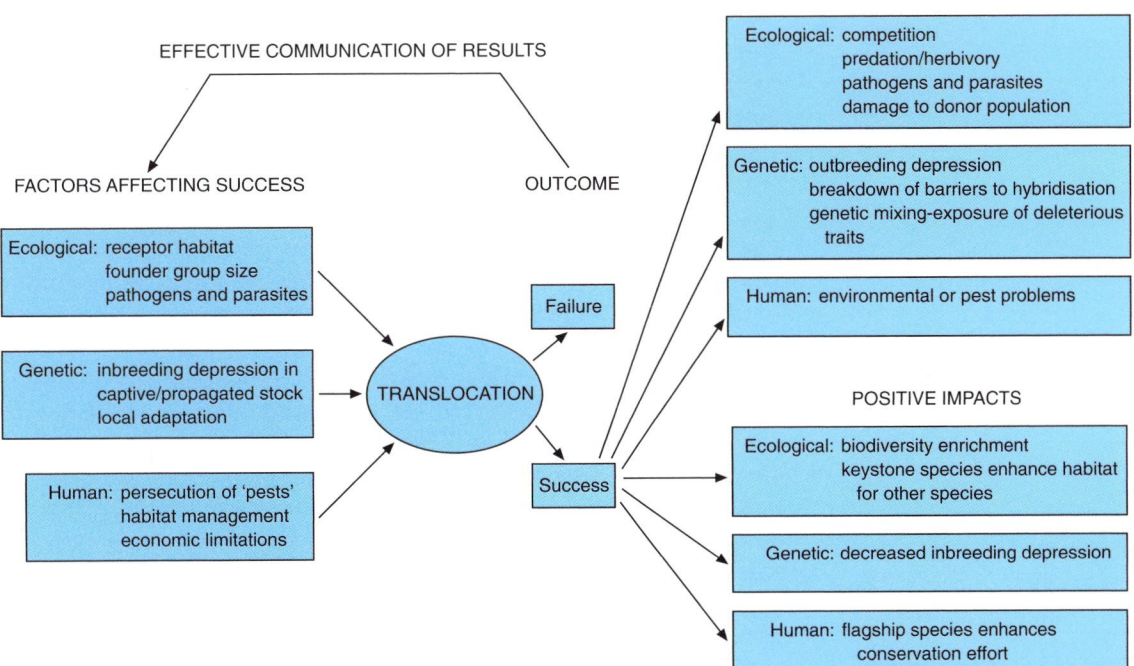

Fig. 11.3 Diagram summarising the factors that should be considered in the evaluation of species translocations. Modified from Hodder & Bullock (1997) with kind permission of Blackwell Science.

the resource implications, including the system of monitoring post-release. Just such a framework has been proposed by Hodder and Bullock (1997) in their appraisal of translocation in the UK (Fig. 11.3)

Translocation examples

An example of apparent translocation success involves the threatened Seychelles warbler (*Acrocephalus sechellensis*). This species was once confined to Cousin Island and reduced to 26 individuals. Careful habitat management increased this number to over 300 birds but the single population remained vulnerable to local catastrophic events. The decision was taken to translocate individuals to two nearby islands to reduce this risk. The translocations took place in 1988 and 1990 and both have resulted in healthy breeding populations (Komdeur 1994). A successful translocation exercise also appears to have been achieved with red howler monkeys (*Alouatta seniculus*) in French Guiana. A howler population was translocated from a site due to be flooded for hydroelectric power generation. The release site was an area where local hunting had reduced the density of the resident howler population. Released troops of monkeys were kept under visual observation and followed by radio tracking of 16 females. Although the troops appeared to undergo initial problems causing them to split up, all the tracked females settled in to normal behavioural patterns (Richard-Hansen *et al.* 2000).

Unfortunately the success stories are at least matched by accounts of failure. Reviewing translocation of amphibians and reptiles, Dodd & Seigel (1991) concluded that most projects have not demonstrated success as conservation techniques and should not be advocated as if they are acceptable management and mitigation practices. A study on the translocation of slow worms (*Anguis fragilis*; a legless lizard) in England released 103 individuals over a period of 3 months in to the receptor site. Subsequent monitoring over 2 years revealed little evidence of breeding and recaptured individuals were in poor condition. The number of recaptures declined over the monitoring period and failure of the release appears likely (Platenberg & Griffiths 1999).

The Zanzibar red colobus monkey (*Procolobus kirkii*)

This monkey is endemic to the island of Zanzibar and a nearby smaller island. Most of its forest habitat has been destroyed making it one of the most endangered primates in Africa. Only 1500–2000 individuals remain in the wild, mainly in Jozani Forest. In the 1970s and 80s some monkeys were translocated to two areas, Masingini and Kichwele, where they probably formerly occurred and others were newly introduced to Ngezi forest on the nearby island of Pemba (Fig. 11.4). The monkeys were caught in nets from areas that were subject to clearcutting. A total of 36 colobus were translocated to Masingini over a 4-year period, 13 were translocated to Kichwele in one release, and approximately 14 were introduced on Pemba. The results of these events were assessed by survey of the areas from 1991 to 1996 (Struhsaker & Siex 1998). Only one of the three sites, Masingini, still contained colobus. Here 56–64 individuals were counted, about the same number that were translocated in the first place. The key point here is that we have little idea of why one translocation has succeeded (at least in the short term) and the others failed. Little or nothing has been learnt from the process. Struhsaker & Siex (1998) make the point that more attention should be given to protecting and studying this species where it currently exists, before carrying out translocations that are as likely to fail as succeed.

In a review of 421 translocations involving birds and mammals, Wolf *et al.* (1996) found significant associations between translocation success and aspects of the release indicating that release into the core of the historical range, good to excellent habitat quality and large numbers released were important factors in success. It seems that translocations remain a useful conservation tool, but only when the situation is right and the knowledge of the species is good. From a conservation perspective it is most important that translocation is not used as a replacement for conservation *in situ*, or an excuse for habitat destruction by claiming it as suitable mitigation.

Population reinforcement

In cases where populations have reached critically low levels from which they are unlikely to recover, a decision may be made to reinforce the population by releasing either captive-bred individuals or individuals directly translocated from another population. The latter is not possible when a single population remains or a group of populations are all endangered. Reinforcement seeks to increase the size of the population

Fig. 11.4 Unguja Island, Zanzibar showing the remaining refuge of wild Zanzibar red colobus monkey (*Procolobus kirkii*) and the reintroduction sites at Kichwele and Masingini. Reproduced from Struhsaker & Siex (1998) with kind permission of Blackwell Science.

so that its viability is significantly increased and recovery becomes possible. There are similar dangers in this type of action to those concerned with reintroduction. There is always a possibility of introducing disease, unsuitable combinations of genes or maladapted individuals such that the overall fitness of the population is reduced, not increased. Care therefore has to be taken in screening the individuals to be released.

The Mauritius pink pigeon (*Columba mayeri*)

An endemic to the island of Mauritius in the Indian Ocean the pink pigeon is one of many threatened oceanic island birds. It has barely managed to survive throughout the last century and in 1980 only 10–20

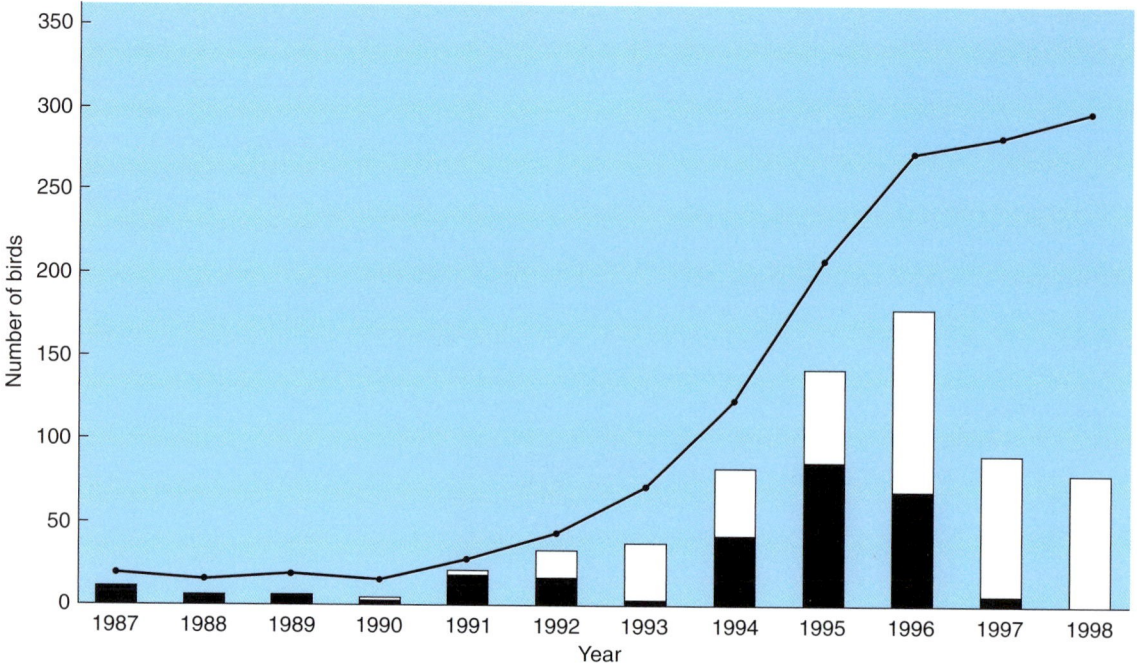

Fig. 11.5 Population increase in the Mauritius pink pigeon (*Columba mayeri*) in the period 1987–1998, including reinforcement from captive breeding. Solid line shows population change; white columns, numbers of wild fledged birds; and black columns, numbers of released birds. Data provided with kind permission of Kirsty Swinnerton.

wild individuals survived. By that time a captive breeding programme had been initiated and the first releases back to the wild began in 1987. The population initially declined from 20 to 16 birds in 1990 with very few wild chicks fledging during this time, but the population recovered and increased at nearly 50% per year up to 1995 (Fig. 11.5). Both the number of captive-released and wild-fledged birds contributed to this increase. More recently the population has been increasing more slowly but without further captive releases, suggesting that it may now be self-sustaining. The strategy employed in this case was to reintroduce the captive-bred individuals to three sites whilst maintaining the wild population in a fourth site. Prior to release, 4–6 birds were held in a release-site aviary to allow familiarisation with their surroundings and with established birds. Supplementary feeding was employed to help birds through the release process and to keep them close to the release site where predator control methods reduced populations of introduced mongooses (*Herpestes auropunctatus*) and cats (*Felis catus*). Prior to release, captive birds were screened for a range of diseases and parasitic infections. Introduced pigeons and doves were possible reservoirs of infection and were controlled at feeding sites to reduce probability of disease spreading to the new populations. Swinnerton *et al.* (2000) identified key elements of the programme that contributed most to the recovery as:

1. the 'soft' release method (i.e. release-site cages allowing acclimatization);
2. post-release support of birds in terms of feeding and protection
3. sufficient numbers of birds for release to establish a functional group.

It is hoped that the separate populations will form one metapopulation on Mauritius and further improve chances of long-term survival.

Overview

A literature review of animal relocations by Fischer & Lindenmayer (2000), including reintroductions and translocations (see below), found data on 180 published examples since 1979. Of the reintroductions conducted solely for conservation purposes, approximately 23% (20/87) were judged successful and 25% were failures, whilst the outcome of the remainder was unknown. The data are likely to be biased toward successes as these are more likely to be published. In general the reintroduction was more likely to succeed if:

1. the source population was wild rather than captive;
2. a large number ($n > 100$) of individuals was released, although the data show this to be somewhat equivocal (Fig. 11.6);
3. the cause of the original decline was removed.

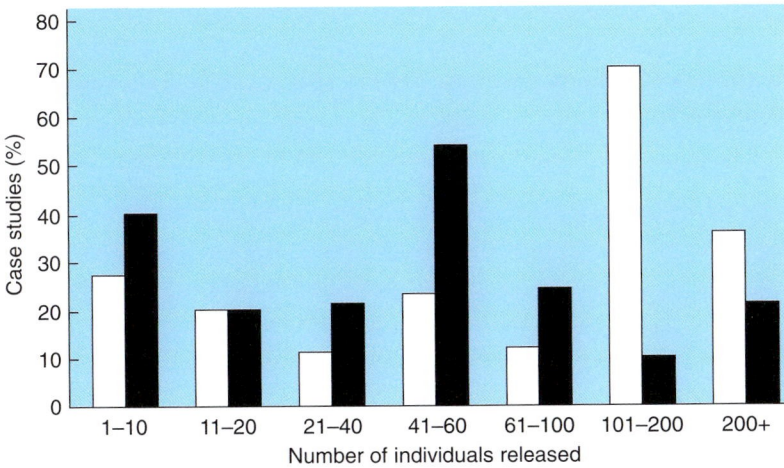

Fig. 11.6 Success of reintroduction attempts in relation to the number of individuals released. White columns, definite successes; black columns, definite failures. Data from Fischer & Lindenmayer (2000).

The authors concluded from the cases studied that the conservation value of animal relocations could, in general, be increased through the following measures:

1. more rigorous evaluation of appropriateness of the intended programme;
2. the establishment of widely accepted criteria for judging success of a programme;
3. better monitoring of relocated populations;
4. better financial accountability;
5. greater effort to publish the results, even ones that are unsuccessful.

Even when reintroductions are carefully considered from a biological point of view, these factors may not be those that decide the issue of whether to go ahead with a programme as illustrated in Box 11.2.

Box 11.2 | Discussion point: should wolves be reintroduced in the UK?

Wolves were eradicated from the UK nearly 400 years ago. The threat they posed to livestock and humans resulted in their persecution and eventual extinction. Today the wolf is seen as an animal of wilderness, and intolerant of human disturbance. Recent evidence from radio-tracking suggests that this perception may be wrong. So long as wolves are not directly persecuted, they are well able to live in and around heavily populated areas, including cities.

The biological feasibility of reintroducing wolves to an area such as the UK focuses around a number of key issues:

Is there sufficient habitat to support a viable population?

Evidence from Isle Royale in Lake Superior where a wolf population has survived in isolation since 1949 suggest that this sort of area (538 km²) could be considered viable, particularly if gene flow was possible from surrounding areas. If this is so then an area such as the Lake District National Park in England might support about four wolf packs. The Scottish Highlands could potentially support many more than this.

Is there a sufficient reservoir of prey species to sustain viable populations?

Wolves prey on medium- to large-sized mammals. The main potential prey in the UK would be deer of which the main species are red, roe and fallow. Recent surveys have shown that one or more of these species are abundant in potential reintroduction areas. The damage caused by these species necessitate annual culls in many areas, particularly in forestry plantations and the level of culling is more than adequate to maintain a wolf population based on known prey requirements of wolves elsewhere.

Is the landscape sufficiently interconnected to allow gene flow between wolf packs?

The long-term survival of wolves is probably dependent on migration between packs preventing inbreeding depression and maintaining viable population sizes. Study of wolves in Europe and America has shown that they have a high capacity to disperse and individuals can travel through less favourable areas, probably even urban areas. They are also recolonising areas of continental Europe as legal protection and public awareness reduces the level of persecution.

In purely biological terms then, the probability of wolves re-establishing in the UK would seem to be high. The barriers seem to be political and sociological. There are also very big sociological issues surrounding public acceptance of an animal perceived by many to be dangerous to humans as well as to their livestock. In the USA, Mech (1995) advocates a system of zonation including areas where wolves are protected and prey on wild ungulates and areas where wolves can be legally controlled because they present a danger to livestock. If such a scheme was socially acceptable and could be effectively policed then it does provide a framework within which the reintroduction in the UK could be planned.

Summary

1. Species are increasingly being taken into captivity to conserve them as they and their habitats become critically endangered.

2. Traditional and modern techniques are being employed to maintain both plant and animal species in *ex situ* facilities.

3. Although captive-breeding technology is becoming ever more successful, resource limitations preclude the vast majority of species from such protection.

4. *Ex situ* conservation is only appropriate in the context of eventual reintroduction and re-establishment of wild populations. Many reintroduction programmes are under way but their success is not yet evaluated and future programmes need to be carefully planned to ensure wise use of scarce resources.

5. Species translocations are increasingly being used to found new populations or to reinforce existing ones. The effectiveness of these strategies has not been fully assessed and there are potential drawbacks to moving individuals around.

Discussion points

- In what circumstances should *ex situ* conservation be employed?
- Are reintroduction programmes a waste of precious resources?
- What are the common problems causing failure of reintroduction programmes?
- What criteria should be used to evaluate success in reintroduction programmes?

Further reading

Bowles M.L. & Whelan C.J. (1994). *Restoration of endangered species: conceptual issues, planning and implementation.* Cambridge: Cambridge University Press

Falk D.A., Millar C.I. & Olwell M. (1996). *Restoring diversity: strategies for reintroduction of endangered plants.* Fort Myers, FL.: Island Press.

Olney, P.J.S., Mace, G.M. & Feistner, A.T.C. (1994). *Creative conservation: interactive management of wild and captive animals.* London: Chapman & Hall.

Web sites
Royal Botanic Gardens Kew: www.rbgkew.org.uk/
IUCN/SSC Captive Breeding Specialist Group: www.cbsg.org/
IUCN/SSC reintroduction Specialist Group:
www.iucn.org/themes/ssc/programs/ rsg.htm

Chapter 12

Landscape-scale conservation

Previous chapters have addressed the traditional view of conservation biology as a subject, looking at the management of protected areas and the small populations they contain. Traditionally conservation action has been orientated towards single species and protected areas. The threat to individual species has formed the focus for action to protect their populations and habitats. However, there is increasing evidence that we should change the emphasis of action to the landscape. The scientific study of landscape-scale processes has been underdeveloped in the field of conservation until recently, but here the subjects of population ecology and landscape ecology meet face to face.

By reading this chapter students will gain an understanding of the importance of landscape-scale processes to the maintenance of biodiversity; how landscape ecology can inform conservation strategies and the ways in which species movement within the landscape may improve probability of survival and persistence.

'Patchiness' in the landscape

Look at any landscape and you can see that it consists of a mosaic of patches reflecting heterogeneity at a range of scales, from patches of moss on the surface of a stone to ecosystems on a continental scale. Biodiversity can also be measured on many different scales (see Chapter 1) and changes in biodiversity over space reflect to some extent the degree of patchiness and patch dynamics. We saw in Chapter 7 that there has been a paradigm shift in ecology and conservation from treating areas and their communities as stable homogeneous units to considering them as dynamic and patchy. Under the latter paradigm, species persistence in the environment is related to size and isolation of patches, influencing the balance between population extinction and foundation through colonisation of empty patches (Wiens 1997a). At the same time the problems identified with small isolated nature reserves and the small populations they contain have brought into focus the need to maximise conservation value of areas outside reserves and to make the whole landscape less hostile to wildlife. Previous chapters have highlighted problems of isolation for communities and single species as predicted by the island biogeography and metapopulation theories.

Ecosystems ecology has taught us that it is the complex relationships between species that maintain the natural processes and the diversity of life. If we simplify these systems through destruction and disturbance we tend to lose species and the complex interactions break down, further threatening the diversity that remains. Christensen (1997) has emphasised the roles of heterogeneity, complexity and diversity in maintaining ecosystem function and the fact that human-driven as well as natural changes in ecosystems are inevitable and need to be incorporated into management plans. All ecosystems are now influenced by human activity and the challenge is therefore to find sustainable ways of managing ecosystems and the landscape.

The transition which is necessary from the traditional management of isolated (and in some parts of the world, quite small) protected areas to management of dynamic patchy landscapes is a big one. This entails moving from the management of the status quo in defined units (though this should not be neglected where it is necessary for short-term persistence of species and habitats) to management for change in larger complex units with potentially conflicting economic and social objectives (such as in urban or agricultural areas). Whilst there is good evidence that this fundamental change should take place, it is equally clear that we do not know enough about the ecology of most systems to define our management goals.

Landscape ecology and conservation

The relevance of landscape ecology (see Box 12.1) to metapopulation dynamics is clear in the significance to both the scale and spatial arrangement of habitat patches to species persistence. Combining the two disciplines helps us to understand how species can be lost from the landscape, or indeed lost from individual patches, even though that patch has not been altered in any way (see Chapter 4). How then does this approach help us in conservation planning?

Box 12.1 | Elements of landscape ecology

When we think of a landscape, we think of a number of separate elements (trees, fields, rivers, buildings, roads, etc.) that combine to form a whole. This is essentially how it is viewed in conservation and ecology. A landscape is a heterogeneous area composed of a mosaic of patches with interacting elements. Some patches may be discrete with clear boundaries, whilst others grade into each other. Thus landscape ecology includes the study of the dynamics of these systems and the movement and persistence of species within them. This is relevant both to natural systems and those heavily influenced by human activity.

Patches in the landscape will vary in quality, for any given species. Each patch will also vary in quality over time. Movement between patches will be critical for the survival of many species, particularly as patches fluctuate in quality. Movement will be influenced by the permeability of patches (how easily individuals of a given species move through the patch to reach other patches), for example, the patch boundaries may be more or less permeable to movement. A river at the boundary of a forest may be an effective barrier to movement. The spatial interaction between suitable and unsuitable patches may be crucial for species persistence in the landscape, particularly if probability of successful movement through unsuitable patches is low.

Some examples of the landscape approach are given in this chapter reflecting the increasing influence of landscape ecology on conservation biology.

Lessons from landscape ecology

The theory of island biogeography encouraged conservationists to question the viability of isolated reserves in a sea of hostile habitat. However, the more realistic view of terrestrial ecosystems offered by landscape ecology, where the land outside the reserve varies in its suitability to any given species, has provided a better framework for conservation planning. At the same time it has further undermined the concept of achieving conservation through the management of protected areas in isolation from their surroundings.

Wiens (1997b) emphasised the difference between classical metapopulation theory where patches are discrete and surrounded by a featureless homogeneous matrix, and landscape ecology, where patches are surrounded by a heterogeneous landscape which varies in its permeability (Fig. 12.1). The landscape approach suggests that migration rates may not simply be a matter of inter-patch distances, but may also depend on migration routes through the matrix and the nature of the boundary between the patch and its surroundings. Wiens recognises four components of landscape ecology in this context:

1. patch quality: the value of the patch as habitat to the species of concern;
2. boundary effects: the extent to which the boundary between the patch and its surroundings influences movement of individuals and within- and between-patch dynamics;
3. patch context: the spatial location of a patch in relation to its surroundings and other similar patches;
4. connectivity: a measure of the ease of movement of individuals between habitat patches within the landscape.

A study by Crist et al. (1992) showed that movement of ground beetles of the genus Eleodes in short-grass prairie varies both with vegetation structure and between species. Three species were released in small plots of 25 m^2 that varied in vegetation structure from bare ground to cactus and scrub. The displacement of individuals from their point of origin varied across the species but was greatest on bare ground and grass cover and least in cactus and scrub vegetation. The distribution and abundance of the beetles at this scale will clearly depend on the percentage cover of different vegetation types and their spatial distribution.

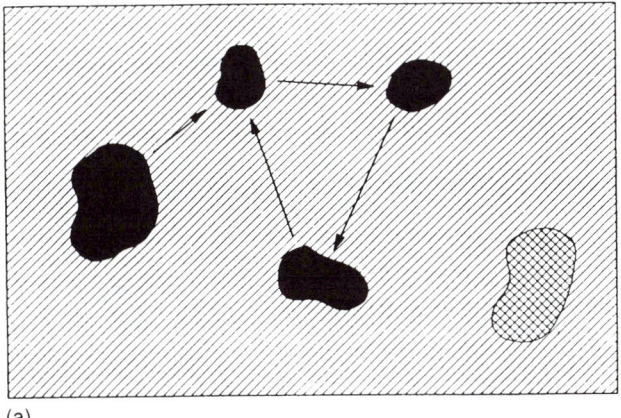

(a)

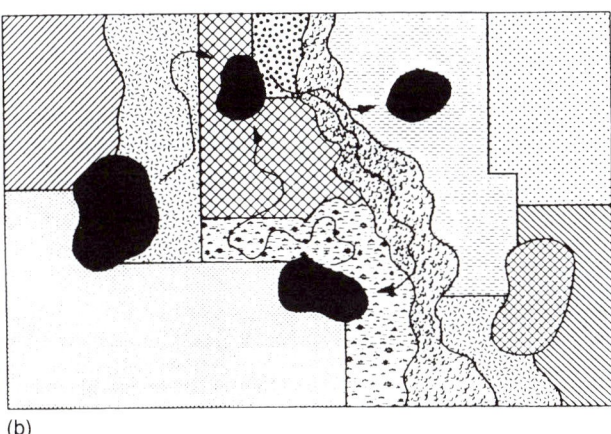

(b)

Lessons from metapopulation biology

The development of metapopulation theory (see Chapter 4) together with empirical field studies have produced a number of pointers towards management of species that persist as metapopulations. Hanski (1997) suggests the following:

1. Many metapopulations may be out of equilibrium, due to destruction of patches and it will only be a matter of time before isolated populations go extinct. One management action must therefore be to reverse the habitat decline by restoration and/or enlargement of suitable patches.

2. A substantial number of fragments is required, certainly more than 10 and probably more than 15 if synchrony in local dynamics is strong, thus making it likely that many populations go extinct at the same time.

3. The spacing of patches must be appropriate for the species' dispersal capacity. The probability of colonisation must be sufficient to counteract extinction. Species movement through the landscape may have to be enhanced (see below).

4. Substantial variance in habitat quality may be beneficial to counteract spatially correlated weather effects. For example, dry sites may enable survival in wet years and wet sites in dry years.

Just as in landscape ecology, these observations point to the importance of understanding heterogeneity at larger spatial scales.

Enhancing species movement in the landscape

Both island biogeography and metapopulation dynamics are determined by the relative rates of colonisation and extinction. These in turn depend on:

1. the spatial distribution of patches;
2. the suitability of the patches as habitat for reproduction;
3. the permeability of the space between patches and therefore how easily individuals can move between patches and what barriers inhibit movement;
4. the mobility of the species in question.

All of these factors can change with land use change. As habitats are destroyed the number of patches declines and the average distance between them increases. The suitability of patches may have declined through inappropriate management and the space in between become more hostile to movement. The mobility of the species may decline over a number of generations, as a result of selection for sedentary behaviour within isolated populations because genes for movement are lost from the population and not replaced by colonisers.

Loss of total area of habitat through fragmentation is thought to be a key driver of species decline, but there is also evidence that the configuration of the remaining patches may be equally significant. A study by Villard *et al.* (1999) on the relative influence of woodland area and configuration on occupancy by a sample of 15 bird species found that variables linked to landscape configuration such as number of woodland fragments, median fragment area and mean nearest neighbour distance were equally as important as total woodland area. Configuration indices predicted occupancy for six of the 15 species in both years of the study suggesting that both woodland cover and its configuration are important in species persistence and responses to both variables are species specific.

What kinds of action can we take, based on this knowledge? The most obvious actions are to protect a network of patches where movement between them is possible and to enhance movement among more distant patches by increasing permeability. Clearly though, any strategy requires a good knowledge of the dispersal capacity of the individual species. Herein lies the biggest problem with applying this approach. Empirical information is available on only a very few species and takes considerable resources to measure.

Integrating reserves into the wider landscape

The paradigm shift in conservation biology from viewing ecosystems as self-regulating systems to dynamic non-equilibrial systems (Chapter 7) has changed the emphasis of reserve design away from the idea of isolated units towards efforts to integrate reserves into the wider landscape.

Realistically, whatever optimal arrangements of habitat might be suggested by metapopulation dynamics, in most cases the course of action will have to be to utilise current reserves as foci or mainland and try and integrate smaller habitat fragments into a network to facilitate movement between patches. Here we briefly consider aspects of reserve boundaries and their relationship with the surrounding land area.

The concept of biosphere reserves

One practical way of scaling up from the reserve to the landscape is to 'soften' the boundaries between land units by using a hierarchy of management. The idea of a biosphere reserve is that it should be designed on a zonal basis that provides a transition from pristine natural environment to highly developed land as follows (Fig. 12.2):

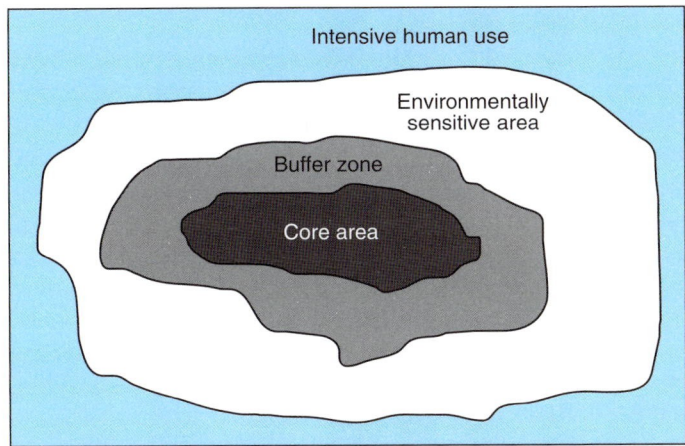

Fig. 12.2 The biosphere reserve concept. The core area is protected by successive zones of increasing human activity toward the outside that buffer the reserve from the most damaging impacts of other land uses.

Area a: undisturbed core area where the habitat is kept as natural as possible with minimal management and disturbance;

Area b: buffer zone in which some human activity may take place but all management should be sustainable;

Area c: further area of environmentally sensitive economic activity where land use can be for material benefit, such as agricultural production, provided its impact on the inner zones is assessed;

Area d: land primarily for human use.

This kind of organised development will rarely be completely possible in practice but the principle of reducing the 'hard edges' between reserve and the surrounding landscape is an important one. The dispersal of many species may be inhibited by 'hard edges' that tend to make dispersing individuals turn back due to the abrupt change in microclimate. This may be an advantage in a very isolated reserve where dispersers are likely to perish, but in an integrated landscape such barriers may prevent sufficient movement between patches.

Wildlife corridors

The most common way in which enhancing permeability has been attempted is by the creation of wildlife corridors. These are zones of relatively high permeability (to the target species) linking primary habitat patches. Corridors can exist at all scales such as the vast areas that form the savanna corridors of the Serengeti in East Africa, or simply a 100-m hedgerow linking two patches of woodland, or they may be even smaller as we shall see below.

Corridors have been supported as a conservation tool because in theory they have a number of advantages.

1. They increase the probability of colonisation by reducing isolation of habitat patches. Therefore more species may be able to persist in a given habitat fragment in line with island biogeography theory, or a group of fragments may be better able to support a given species in line with metapopulation theory.

2. Gene flow between habitat patches will be enhanced, reducing the probability of inbreeding depression and loss of genetic variability through genetic drift (see Chapter 4).

3. Individuals driven out of fragments through territorial behaviour will have a greater probability of finding alternative habitat, thus decreasing mortality, particularly among juveniles.

However, a review of corridors and their use to wildlife (Simberloff et al. 1992) found no good scientific evidence in support of these theoretical assertions. Additionally, they drew attention to the possibility that creation of corridors could have a number of potential drawbacks.

1. They may create gene flow where none has occurred naturally in the recent past. Thus destroying the distinctiveness of populations.

2. Corridors may facilitate movement of, or act as reservoirs for, undesirable species such as introduced species or pathogens that may expose small populations to predation or disease.

3. Corridors may act as sinks for species through increased mortality from predation or simple failure to reach another reserve containing suitable habitat.

Natural corridors, such as riparian forest habitats, are of value in themselves and they are of conservation priority in their own right, but despite their widespread acceptance as a useful conservation management tool, artificially created wildlife corridors require more study before their usefulness can be established.

A recent set of experiments performed at the micro scale has tested the effectiveness of corridors for maintaining species richness in remaining fragments of habitat. Gilbert et al. (1998) used the invertebrate fauna inhabiting layers of moss covering stones to test the hypothesis that corridors could increase movement between patches and therefore persistence of populations. A group of moss-covered stones were selected and on each stone, one half was fragmented into a preset pattern by strategic removal of moss and the other half left as a control. Three experimental patterns were used as shown in Fig. 12.3; the first achieved an isolated pattern of four patches, the second contained corridors connecting the patches and the third contained the same corridor pattern, except the corridors were interrupted, thus controlling for the increased area provided by corridors without the potential connectivity. Their results show that fragmentation into small patches causes

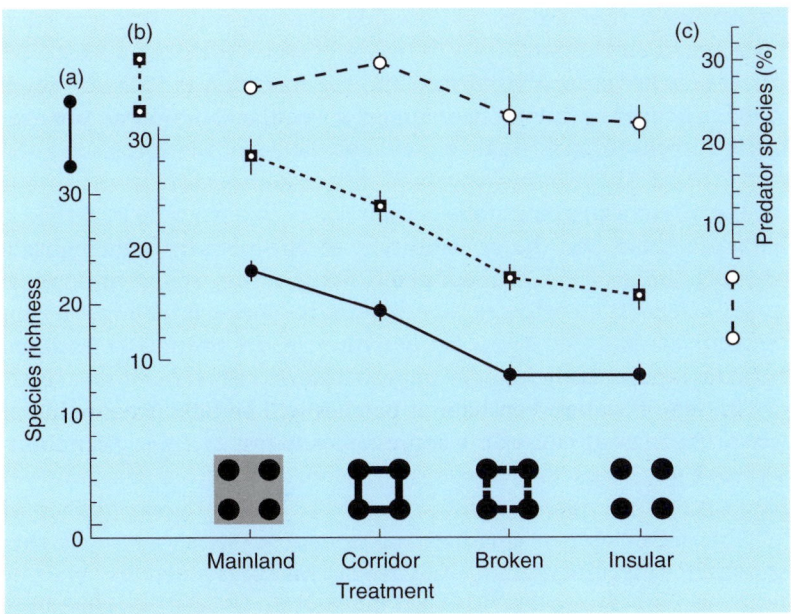

Fig. 12.3 The effect of decreasing connectivity on the diversity of the invertebrate fauna on moss patches. The data show a significant decrease in diversity from mainland and corridor connections to broken corridors and insular patches. Reproduced from Gilbert *et al.* (1998) with kind permission of The Royal Society.

loss in species richness compared with the control, but that this loss is reduced when corridors are added. This was not the case when the corridors were interrupted by a barrier. Whether such corridors would be equally as effective if the whole experiment were to be scaled up to larger organisms at larger scales is unknown, but it is good evidence that corridors can work in some situations.

From a metapopulation theory perspective, an equally useful concept for more mobile species may be stepping stone habitats. These are patches that can in theory be used transitionally by individuals and aid wider dispersal and facilitate movement between habitat patches, rather like using stepping stones to cross a river (Fig. 12.4). The positive or negative effects of stepping stones may depend on how they are used

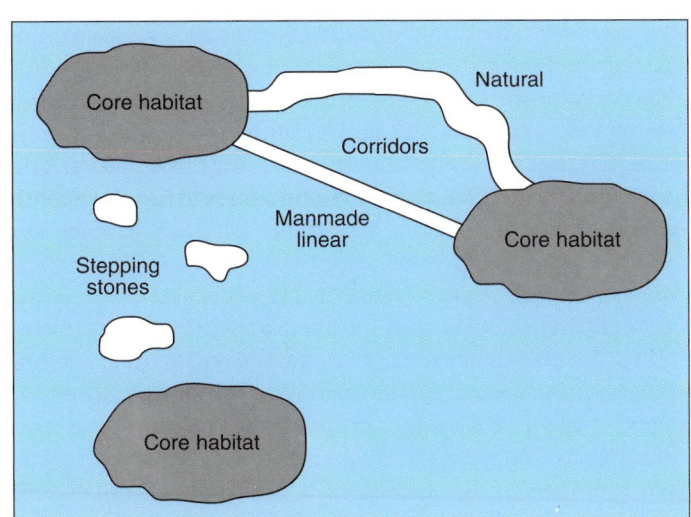

Fig. 12.4 Types of connections between core habitats that may (or may not) aid species dispersal.

by species. If they are used as feeding stops en route between main breeding areas they are likely to have a positive influence on survival. However, if breeding is attempted in these areas they are likely to act as sinks and could have a negative impact in reducing movement between source breeding areas. Again a good knowledge of the species in question is required before any system of stepping stones is planned.

Provision of stepping stone habitat has been advocated by Strong & Bancroft (1994) for the conservation of the white-crowned pigeon (*Columba leucocephala*). This species is listed as threatened in Florida, where they nest on offshore islands (keys) in Florida Bay and forage for fruit in seasonal deciduous forest, either in the Everglades National Park on the mainland or on the mainline Florida Keys. In the latter case, dispersing immature birds are not able to reach northern Key Largo, where the main expanse of forest remains, within the first 72 hours. A series of stepping stone forests is therefore required in southern Key Largo to enable immature birds to reach the main foraging areas.

A special case where corridors and/or stepping stones are vital is that of migratory species. Many species migrate on a seasonal basis, typically from overwintering to breeding grounds and back or following patterns of rainfall. Birds on long migrations often stop to feed and replenish vital energy reserves for the continuing flight. Many feeding grounds are well known for groups such as wading birds and waterfowl. These should be viewed as vital stepping stones, as failure to feed could cause catastrophic mortality on migration. On the ground, migrating mammals require corridors through which to move between main feeding and breeding grounds. Such corridors have been planned for herds of game animals as they follow the rains in search of fresh grass on the East African plains (Mwalyosi 1991). This is vital for their survival as the herds cover long distances and are constantly on the move. The normal route of one such group takes them out of the Tarangire National Park across land which is now being developed for crops and domestic grazing and into the Lake Manyara National Park (Fig. 12.5). To avoid conflict between farmers and conservation interests a corridor has been proposed that will reduce damage to crops and allow safe passage for the animals that have frequently been shot by the farmers. Three possible corridor routes were considered and evaluated based on their capacity to sustain grazing animals as they pass through and the socioeconomic circumstances including the human population and their current activities in the area. The chosen corridor is approximately 60 km long and 1 km wide.

Opportunities from changes in agricultural practice

Economic changes in agriculture in Europe and North America have brought opportunities for conservation activity within the agriculture-dominated landscape of some regions. Within the European Union, a scheme exists to 'set-aside' a proportion of land on each farm to reduce overproduction of arable crops. In the UK 307 000–728 000 hectares have been put in to set-aside each year. These fragments of land have great potential to act as refuges for wildlife within the wider landscape. Unfortunately there is no clear guidance on management of

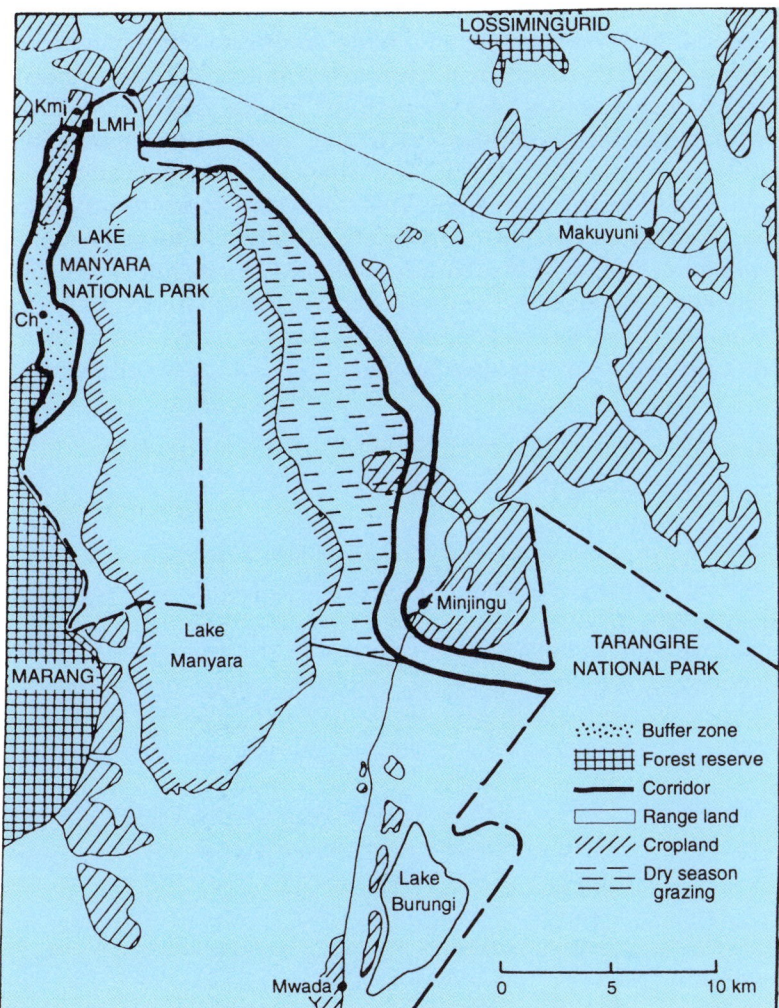

Fig. 12.5 The position of a proposed corridor to allow movement of migrating mammals between grassland refuges in the Tanzanian National Park System. Reproduced from Mwalyosi (1991) with kind permission of Elsevier Science.

set-aside land and little is managed with conservation as an objective. Tattershall *et al.* (2000) illustrated the conservation potential of this land in studying the relationship of field vole (*Microtus agrestis*) populations with management. They found that sowing a grass seed mix followed by cutting once a year and leaving this management in place for more than 2 years was likely to benefit this species, but also recognised that other species of conservation concern may benefit from different management practices. The transient use of these set-aside patches of agricultural land, combined with the complexity of large numbers of management units under different ownership, makes this a particular challenge if it is to benefit conservation in a concerted way.

Conservation in the urban landscape

Just as semi-natural landscapes in the countryside can be viewed as a matrix of patches, so also can the highly developed environment of the urban landscape. The increasing amount of urban development has given rise to a whole branch of ecology devoted to this environment. Many species have found urban areas to their liking and have colonised the new niches as they have been created resulting in global distributions for some such as the brown rat (*Rattus norvegicus*). It is also true that the design of many urban areas leaves room for some green areas, such as inner city parks and gardens. This offers the opportunity for other species not strictly tolerant of urban areas to persist inside city boundaries. In the development of urban areas, planning for maintenance of biodiversity is increasingly a landscape-scale issue and there is a growing realisation that under appropriate management, urban areas can maintain a rich flora and fauna (see Box 12.2).

Box 12.2 | Post-industrial brownfield sites: a neglected habitat in the urban landscape

Many sites within urban areas have a history of development for industrial or housing needs but have subsequently been abandoned and the buildings demolished. These areas are commonly referred to by planners as brownfield sites, to distinguish them from greenfield sites that have never been built on. At the same time as there is increasing pressure on brownfield sites for development, there is an increasing appreciation of their value as sites for urban wildlife (Eyre & Luff 1995). There are a number of examples where brownfield sites have been identified specifically for their high diversity of invertebrates and plants (Lott & Daws 1995). Within the urban mosaic, brownfield sites may be some of the few remaining open areas and are particularly valuable for their early successional status, as vegetation begins to recolonise. Indeed, urban areas may now provide better opportunities for some species assemblages than heavily utilised rural areas.

Many invertebrates associated with early successional habitats are nationally or locally rare in rural as well as urban areas (Eversham *et al.* 1996). Gibson (1998) estimates that 12–15% of Britain's scarce and rare invertebrate species are found in artificial urban habitats. However, the nature of brownfield sites varies greatly according to their past use. Not all sites will be of high conservation value and an evidence-based system is required to evaluate each site to enable sensible planning.

Brownfield sites are transient in nature (as they are commonly targeted for redevelopment) and there is a constant turnover of such sites providing early successional habitats on a temporary basis. This mirrors the transient nature of highly disturbed habitats in more 'natural' environments. Given that these areas can be of significant wildlife value, and it is inevitable that their value will change over time, the challenge is to try and manage the dynamics of the system to retain the overall wildlife value of the urban matrix, rather than considering single sites. Variables describing the spatial and temporal status of sites need to be considered in order to place individual sites in the context of the habitat matrix.

Many brownfield sites are viewed as having potential for development for housing or industrial use, but are also viewed for their potential restoration to green space, amenity areas, or possibly agricultural use. Rarely are they viewed as areas that have inherent value as they are, and in terms of appropriate management to maintain them. Ironically, common (and often expensive) wildlife restoration goals, such as tree planting, may be directly damaging to the wildlife value of the site. It is in this situation that many of the theories describing the spatial distribution of communities and populations can be used to construct a strategy for the management of wildlife. Island biogeography, metapopulation theory, GAP analysis and the theory of wildlife corridors can all be used to help identify suitable distribution of sites within an urban matrix on an ongoing basis, taking into account the dynamics of sites.

Size and isolation of the sites are of prime importance and this needs to be related to the mobility of the species and the permeability of the urban matrix. The latter may be improved by the presence of appropriate corridors. Recommendations for conservation of strategic sites could be made as could appropriate management at sites and along corridors. As landscape-scale conservation develops there is a good prospect of enabling viable populations of species not previously considered urban dwellers to survive in even the largest cities.

The increasing scale of urban development and therefore the increasing number of people seeking high-quality green space within urban areas has focused attention on the ability of the urban landscape to retain elements of semi-natural habitats and their associated species. The occurrence of green space within urban areas can sometimes be attributable to historic accident, but is increasingly a result of planning.

Natural greenspace can be regarded as areas, accessible to humans, within the urban landscape that have been naturally colonised by plants and animals. This definition includes:

1. Encapsulated countryside; semi-natural areas which are now surrounded by urban development, but that have themselves never been built on. These are typically areas of woodland or wetlands and open water.

2. Brownfield sites; sites that have been developed in the past, but have since been abandoned and naturally recolonised by plants and animals (see Box 12.2).

3. Green corridors; land running alongside linear features such as waterways, roads and railway lines which are mixtures of originally planted species and subsequent colonisers.

4. Edges and patches of unmanaged land surrounding more intensively managed areas such as areas within sports grounds, churchyards, golf courses, allotments and gardens.

These areas contrast with intensively managed greenspace, such as sports grounds, parks and gardens that are composed of landscaped assemblages of species maintained by regular human intervention.

Patterns of diversity in the urban landscape

In general the species richness in large urban areas declines toward the city centre. For example, the number of bird species in London declines from 77 in the outer suburbs to 50 in the inner and 43 in the city centre. Similar patterns have been found in plants and invertebrates. However, large areas of green space embedded in city centres can counteract this effect and act as reservoirs of wildlife.

In a study of the butterfly diversity in the Palo Alto area of California, Blair & Launer (1997) found that species number and diversity decreased with the degree of development in the immediate area ranging from a recreational park through a residential area to a business district. Interestingly the species number and diversity in the recreational park was greater than in a nearby nature preserve, suggesting, as in many studies, a moderate degree of disturbance increases diversity in many taxonomic groups.

Simple measurement of change in species number and diversity may mask the actual change in species composition. In semi-natural habitats on the outskirts of cities the flora may be predominantly composed of native species characteristic of that habitat. However, within the inner city the flora may be composed primarily of alien species tolerant of human habitation and almost ubiquitous in urban areas on the same continent and even globally.

Conserving ecosystem function

Species and communities rely on ecosystem processes for their persistence, consequently the most effective large-scale conservation measures could be those aimed at the ecosystem. To keep an ecosystem intact is to conserve a whole range of species, their interactions with one another, and the abiotic environment on which they depend, and the natural heterogeneity within them which contributes to diversity.

Meyer (1997) put forward seven principles as a foundation for ecosystem conservation:

1. ecosystems are open, which should lead to an emphasis on conserving the fluxes across ecosystem boundaries and linkages with surrounding ecosystems;
2. ecosystems are temporally variable and continuously changing; the present bears the legacies of past disturbances;
3. ecosystems are spatially heterogeneous on a range of scales, and essential processes depend on that heterogeneity;
4. indirect effects are the rule rather than the exception in most ecosystems and therefore changes in one part of an ecosystem can have unpredictable knock-on effects in others;
5. ecosystem function depends on its biological structure. Component communities in the ecosystem play vital roles in its function. For example, the soil microbial community plays a vital role in decomposition of organic matter. These communities must be conserved to maintain overall ecosystem function;
6. although several species perform the same function in ecosystems, they respond differently to variations in their biotic and abiotic environment, thereby reducing variation in ecosystem function in a changing environment;
7. humans are a part of all ecosystems. No ecosystems remain unaffected by human activity.

How applicable an approach based on the above principles can be may depend on how natural the ecosystem is or can become, and the extent to which we can understand the natural processes that shape it. Ecosystems that are still fundamentally shaped by natural processes, but have been perturbed by human activities may benefit greatly from this holistic approach. Meyer (1997) provides the example of Knowles Creek in Oregon, USA, which suffered from logging and road-building activities in both the uplands and the valley floor from 1950 to 1985. This shifted the sediment load from the uplands into the valley, but with a decreased sediment storage capacity in the latter the sediment was washed out of the drainage basin, degrading aquatic habitats important for key species such as coho salmon (*Oncorhynchus kisutch*). A migration to the ocean of an expected 100 000 coho smolts was reduced to just 1660 in 1982. Recognition of this knock-on effect led to action to protect remaining refuges for the salmon, to replant trees on the valley floor, and to manage the uplands to reduce major debris torrents whilst providing sediment for restoration of salmon spawning habitat.

In contrast to the above, many ecosystems are so fundamentally altered and influenced by human activities that to organise conservation activities on such a large scale would require either:

a scaling down of human activities (not usually politically possible) and large-scale restoration (not usually technically or economically easy);

or

the neglect of some of the natural remnant habitats and their associated species that require short-term intensive action, to enable longer-term, larger-scale action to proceed.

The result of the latter may be that many of the species representative of that ecosystem may be lost before the ecosystem approach shows any benefit. Examples of this are provided by the wetland systems that remain in Western Europe as fragments surrounded by former wetland areas subsequently drained for intensive agricultural production. The fragments require intensive hydrological management on a small scale. A neglect of this management in favour of a larger-scale approach could quickly see the demise of some species. The answer would seem to lie with an integrated approach at different scales which exploits the advantages of each. Species diversity and ecosystem function are interdependent and require an integrated approach. Conservationists managing small areas may need to scale up their activities gradually in a step-wise fashion.

Ecosystem management

The large-scale management of ecosystems requires not only the integration of many elements of conservation biology and ecology noted above, but also elements of other disciplines related to our position as humans in the ecosystem. Humans require ecosystems to provide a range of services, such as provision of freshwater and food. Maltby *et al.* (1999) proposed 10 principles of ecosystem management which illustrate this mix of the scientific and human sociological perspectives.

Guiding principles:
1. management objectives are a matter of social choice;
2. ecosystems must be managed in a human context;

3. ecosystems must be managed within natural limits;
4. management must recognise that change is inevitable;
5. ecosystem management must be undertaken at the appropriate scale, and conservation must use the full range of protected areas.

Operational principles:

6. ecosystem management needs to address global issues and act on them in a local context;
7. ecosystem management must seek to maintain or enhance ecosystem structure and functioning;
8. decision-makers should use appropriate tools derived from science;
9. managers must follow the precautionary principle;
10. a multidisciplinary approach is needed.

Management at the scale of the ecosystem in perhaps most developed in marine ecosystems. The dynamic and open nature of marine systems lends itself to a large-scale view of resource management, and the relative ignorance we have of marine, compared with terrestrial, ecology inhibits more detailed interventionist-style conservation that has characterised early efforts on land. Despite this, we are as yet unable to truly manage any ecosystems. We are confined to management of the impact that humans have on ecosystems (such as fishing quotas and pollution inputs), not of the ecosystems themselves. We flatter ourselves if we think otherwise.

Management at the landscape scale: the UK Natural Areas concept

We have seen previously that there is good evidence that we should scale up activities from the protected area or nature reserve in many of the most fragmented landscapes such as in Europe, but scale up to what?

A significant move away from the concept of protected areas has been taken by the UK government's conservation body for England, English Nature, in their production of a natural areas map of England. This is an attempt to define conservation management units of the countryside, based on features that determine the landscape and its component species. The primary factors used are geology and soil type, but aspects of hydrology and traditional land management practice are also used. Overall, it is important that these areas are easily identifiable and discrete. This overcomes the problem of trying to identify units of biodiversity from the fragments that remain in a highly modified landscape. English Nature have identified 76 terrestrial and 26 coastal marine areas (Fig. 12.6) providing a clear focus for planning at a regional scale.

An example of a natural area is the Cotswold hills where I grew up. This limestone area was originally covered in beech and oak forest, but was subsequently largely cleared and used for sheep grazing, forming species-rich grassland assemblages. More recently, the grasslands have

Fig. 12.6 (Opposite) Map of the UK Natural Areas Scheme. Reproduced with kind permission of English Nature.

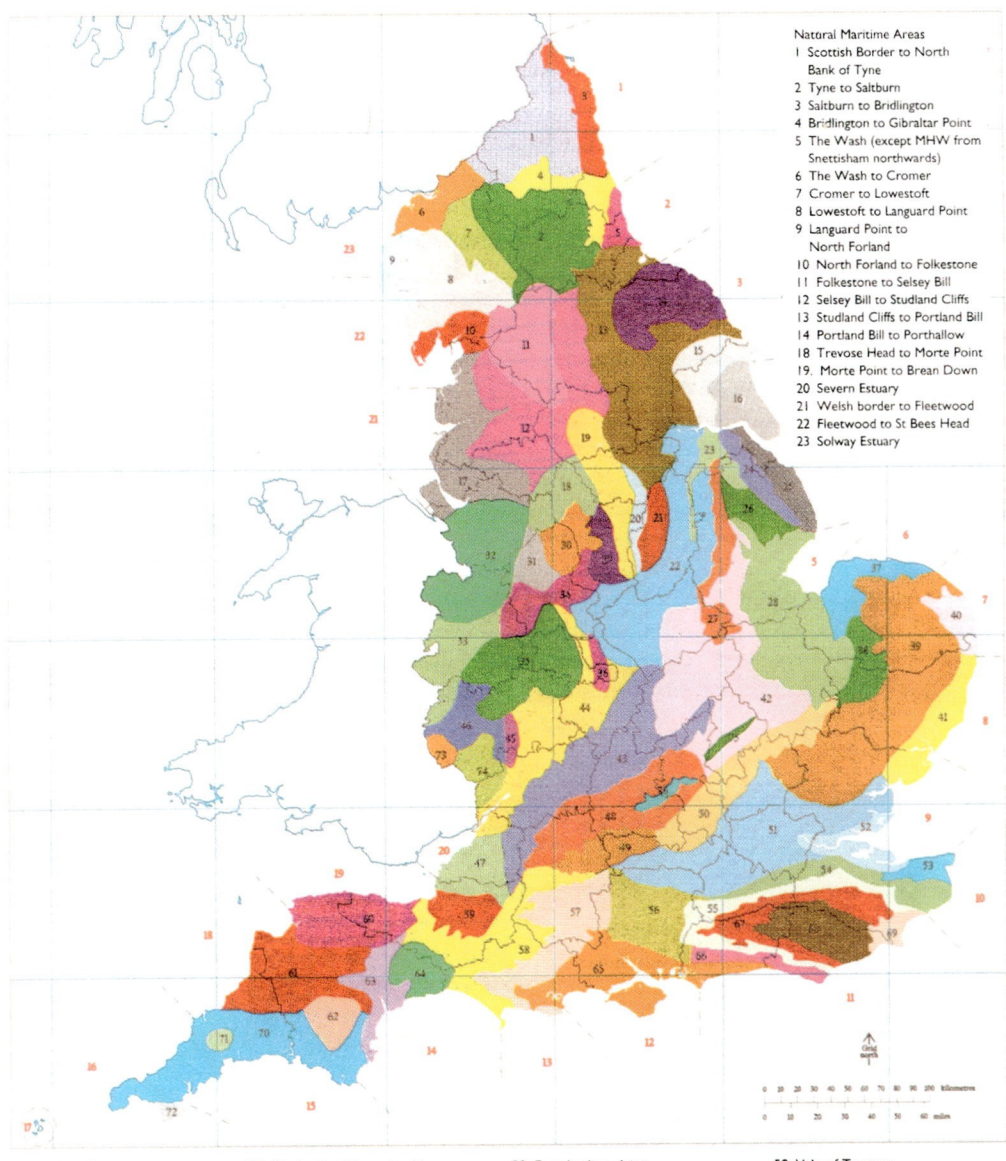

Natural Maritime Areas
1 Scottish Border to North Bank of Tyne
2 Tyne to Saltburn
3 Saltburn to Bridlington
4 Bridlington to Gibraltar Point
5 The Wash (except MHW from Snettisham northwards)
6 The Wash to Cromer
7 Cromer to Lowestoft
8 Lowestoft to Languard Point
9 Languard Point to North Forland
10 North Forland to Folkestone
11 Folkestone to Selsey Bill
12 Selsey Bill to Studland Cliffs
13 Studland Cliffs to Portland Bill
14 Portland Bill to Porthallow
18 Trevose Head to Morte Point
19 Morte Point to Brean Down
20 Severn Estuary
21 Welsh border to Fleetwood
22 Fleetwood to St Bees Head
23 Solway Estuary

1 Border Uplands	20 Derbyshire Magnesian Limestone	39 East Anglian plains	58 Vale of Taunton
2 Northern Pennines	21 Sherwood Forest	40 Broadland	59 Somerset Levels
3 Northumberland Coastal Plain	22 Trent Valley and Levels	41 Sandlings	60 Exmoor and Quantocks
4 Tyne Vale	23 Cover Sands	42 East Midlands Lowlands	61 Culm Measures
5 Durham Magnesian Limestone	24 Lincolnshire Wolds	43 Greater Cotswolds	62 Dartmoor
6 Solway Basin	25 Lincolnshire Coastal Plain	44 Severn Valley	63 Devon Sandstone
7 Eden Vale	26 Lincolnshire Clay Vales	45 Malvern Hills	64 Blackdowns
8 Lake District	27 Lincolnshire Limestone	46 Hereford Plain	65 Hampshire Basin
9 Cumbrian Coastal Plain	28 Fenland	47 Mendips	66 South Downs
10 Morecambe Bay Limestones	29 Lower Derwent Valley	48 Oxford Clay Vales	67 Low Weald
11 Yorkshire Dales	30 The White Peak	49 Wessex Downs	68 High Weald
12 Southern Pennines	31 Staffordshire Northern Upland	50 Chilterns	69 Romney Marsh
13 Vale of York	32 Mosses and Meres	51 London Basin	70 South West Plain
14 North of York Moors	33 Shropshire Uplands	52 Thames Marshes	71 Bodmin
15 Yorkshire Wold	34 Upper Trent Valley	53 North Kent Plain	72 The Lizard
16 Plain of Holderness	35 Birmingham Plateau	54 North Downs	73 Black Mountains
17 Lancashire Plain	36 Wark Sandstone Plateau	55 Greensand	74 Severn/Wye Plateau
18 The Dark Peak	37 North Norfolk	56 Hampshire Chalk	75 Beds Greensand
19 Coal Measures	38 Breckland	57 Salisbury Plain and Dorset Downs	76 Oxford Heights

————— County boundary

been abandoned and the area has been increasingly used for intensive arable production fragmenting both grassland and woodland habitats. Within 'natural areas' the focus is on integration of traditional protected areas with other features of the landscape and the marriage of conservation action with other activities to enhance biodiversity at the landscape scale. Thus, an area with a common history and existing identity such as the Cotswolds is a logical unit to manage from both an ecological and socioeconomic viewpoint.

Summary

1. The landscape can be viewed as a matrix of patches from the micro to macro scale. Species have to persist within this matrix despite the spatial and temporal dynamics.

2. The integration of landscape ecology and population dynamics has given rise to a greater appreciation of the importance of conservation at the landscape scale.

3. Emphasis in conservation has moved from conserving species in isolated reserves to enhancing movement between patches within the landscape matrix through use of wildlife corridors and stepping stone habitats, though the effectiveness of these concepts is yet to be adequately tested.

4. Conservation within the urban areas has progressed rapidly within the framework of a landscape-scale approach. Properly managed urban green space can retain many species not associated with inner city areas.

5. Managing the landscape and its component ecosystems effectively may be partly a question of choosing the appropriate scale, both from an ecological and socioeconomic viewpoint.

Discussion points

- How should we decide on the appropriate scale for conservation activities?
- To what extent can ecosystems be managed?
- How should we balance the need for intensive short-term management of reserves to maintain endangered species with the long-term management of the landscape?

Further reading

Farina, A. (1998). *Principles and methods in landscape ecology.* London: Chapman & Hall.

Green, B. (1996). *Countryside conservation: landscape ecology, planning and management*, 3rd edn. London: E. & F. N. Spon.

Hanski, I.A. & Gilpin, M.E. (eds) (1997). *Metapopulation biology: ecology genetics and evolution*. San Diego: Academic Press.

Pickett, S.T.A., Ostfeld, R.S., Shachak, M. & Likens, G.E. (eds) (1997). *The ecological basis of conservation*. New York: Chapman & Hall.

Web sites

International Association for Landscape Ecology: www.iale.org.uk/

English Nature, Natural Areas Scheme:

www.english-nature.org.uk/science/natural/ na_search.asp

Chapter 13

Conserving the evolutionary process (a longer-term view of conservation)

Conservation action to this day concerns itself with the short-term rescue of species and communities and the medium-term management to maintain them. But there is ample evidence that species and communities are not static but dynamic and evolving. This chapter is concerned with how we might start to think of conservation actions and requirements for the longer term, including management for change rather than stasis.

By reading this chapter students will gain an understanding of; how long- and short-term conservation strategies may differ; how reliant conservation strategies are on the species concept; and methods of formulating conservation strategies that are not habitat- or species-based.

Short-term crisis conservation

We have seen in earlier chapters that the dominant strategy within nature conservation has been to give priority protection to threatened habitats through the nature reserve system. The best and most representative habitat areas are identified and, if possible, protected by procuring ownership or through government legislation. This strategy was undoubtedly right at the time of rapid habitat destruction in the middle of this century, but it has had an undesirable side-effect. It has resulted in the creation of isolated habitat islands between which many species cannot travel due to the wholly unprotected and unsuitable habitat in between. Consequently today species conservation is not only a problem of protecting habitats, but also of how to retain species diversity within small habitat fragments. This is a resource-intensive process.

We have seen in a number of previous chapters how conservation biology has advanced from the idea of preserving species within communities that are at equilibrium to managing systems that are dynamic and non-equilibrial. However, most of our objectives are still set within short time frames of 100 years or often much less. We still treat species and communities as the subjects of conservation despite the fact that we know they are not stable entities. This chapter will examine the idea that conservation policy now needs to start looking to the long term and that it is not strictly species and communities we should be aiming to conserve, but the evolutionary process which has given rise to the rich biodiversity we are so rapidly destroying. This does not mean that species and communities are ignored, but simply that they are not regarded as fixed targets for long-term conservation.

Conservation and the control of nature

The rapidity with which biodiversity has come under threat has necessitated urgent action to save many species and habitats and unfortunately this problem is set to continue for the foreseeable future. By protecting areas and in many cases managing them intensively we have sought to conserve by increasing our control of nature. This is particularly so in semi-natural habitats where complex management plans are constructed to ensure that desired communities of plants and animals are retained from year to year. Any consideration of the historical changes in distribution known for many species, or indeed the projected future changes in climate, suggests that this strategy cannot continue, not least because we won't have the resources for this level of intervention in natural (and human-induced) processes. We will eventually find ourselves trying to hold back the tide of natural change. Is it in any case desirable to continue with our current direction? We may become skilled at maintaining isolated populations and habitats but the process becomes little more than 'zookeeping' if we cannot maintain the natural processes that produced them in the first place. The idea that we are capable of controlling nature has largely been dispelled, but many aspects of our society still reflect this idea. The consequence for conservation is that its priorities are short-term compensation for human activity (e.g. attempting to prevent destruction of habitats and extinction of species) and not long-term management of change to enhance biodiversity.

The realisation, even at a political and economic level, that we are part of nature and that our actions need to be seen in this context, provides an opportunity for conservation to move away from control-oriented objectives and toward facilitation. Species and communities are not fixed in time and space and some of our conservation actions, such as inappropriate reintroductions and expensive intensive management of small isolated reserves, are in danger of working against the conservation of nature. What tools have we got to approach this problem?

The most likely scientific approaches come from the two ends of the scale; genetics and biogeography. If we consider that genes are both the basis of evolution and of biodiversity then we can use genetic diversity to help us to think long term. Biogeography is an important discipline for understanding how natural processes operate in tandem with evolution to change and limit species distributions. These two disciplines or scales of analysis can combine in a form of analysis called **phylogeography**.

The use of phylogeography in conservation

In order to plan conservation strategy for the future in an evolutionary context it is vital first to gain information on what has happened in the past. Advances in molecular genetics have made it possible to trace lineages of species and subspecies and has enabled us to put current situations in the context of past events.

To use an example, a recent succession of ice ages has caused considerable disruption and change in northern temperate communities (in the Southern Hemisphere as well but not so extensively) and this serves as a useful model to look at the problems of longer-term management of biodiversity. A number of studies in both Europe and America have suggested that species have rapidly contracted in range during ice age incursions and have often been fragmented into isolated refugia that provided conditions suitable for survival until subsequent expansion became possible as the climate warmed. The geographical location of refugia in Europe and the patterns of post-glacial recolonisation have been studied through phylogeographic analysis using molecular genetic techniques.

With the Mediterranean Sea as a southern barrier, Europe seems to have had three major refugial areas, The Iberian Peninsula, southern Italy and the Balkans, Greece and Turkey (Fig. 13.1). These areas would

Fig. 13.1 Basic routes of recolonisation from glacial refugia in southern Europe and Asia after the last ice age. Most of the fauna and flora of northern Europe colonised from these areas during the last 10 000 years.

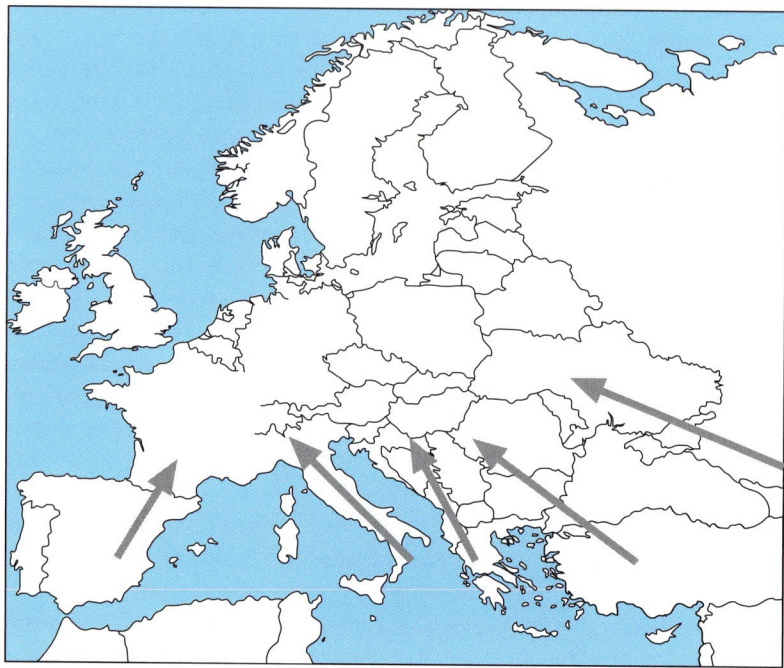

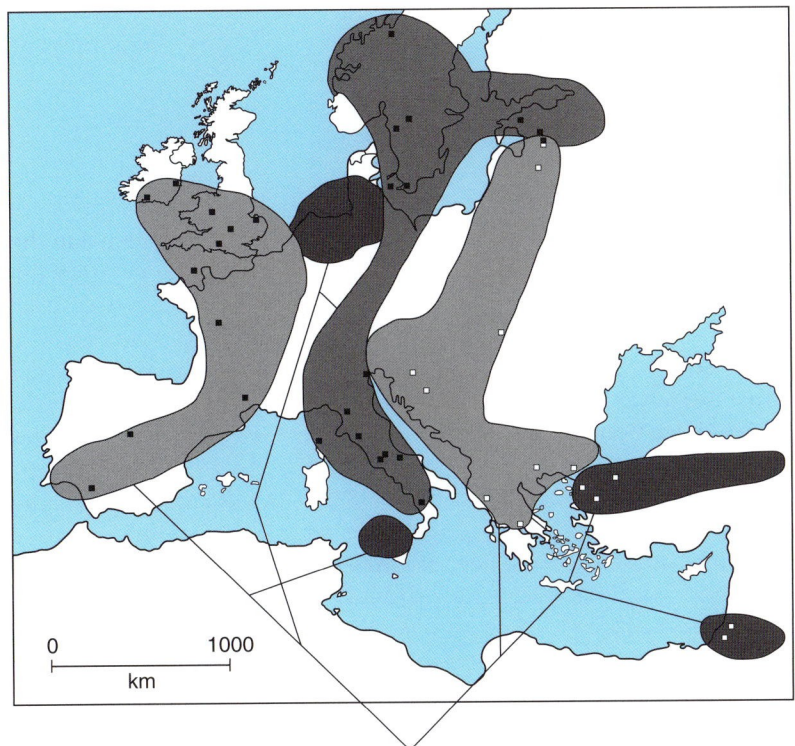

Fig. 13.2 A phylogeography of European hedgehogs derived from mitochondrial DNA haplotypes. Note the divisions that still exist based on the refugial origins and the deep divide between east and west that separates the two recognised species, *Erinaceus concolor* and *E. europeaus*. Reproduced from Hewitt (1999) with kind permission of Academic Press

have remained temperate during the worst of the recent ice age incursions. The repeated contraction of range, isolation and then expansion and contact of populations during interglacial periods has produced a complex mix of closely related species and subspecies. This is further complicated by the mountain ranges that run east–west (e.g. Pyrenees and Alps) and thus inhibit northward expansion.

A phylogeographic study of European hedgehogs (*Erinaceus* spp.) based on mitochondrial DNA analysis revealed one possible result of this cyclic scenario (Fig. 13.2). The current distributions appear to reflect parallel northward expansion from each of the three main refugia. The extent of divergence in their genomes suggests that these clades (separate lines of descent within a phylogeny) have expanded and contracted through many interglacial cycles with some hybridisation (as there is today) but have remained relatively distinct. The two recognised species *E. europeaus* and *E. concolor* appear to have diverged some 6 million years ago whilst the Spanish and Italian clades of *E. europeaus* probably diverged as recently as 3 million years ago (Hewitt 1999).

In other cases populations have expanded from one refugium faster than from others and therefore their genomes currently dominate northern regions, as is the case for the Alder (*Alnus glutinosa*) and Beech (*Fagus sylvatica*) trees and the grasshopper (*Chorthippus parallelus*) (Fig. 13.3). Each of these has emerged from the eastern Balkan refugium fastest, probably because the mountains to the north present less of a

Fig. 13.3 Proposed post-glacial colonisation routes and approximate ice age refuges of a range of plant and animal species in Europe. Reproduced from Hewitt (1999) with kind permission of Academic Press.

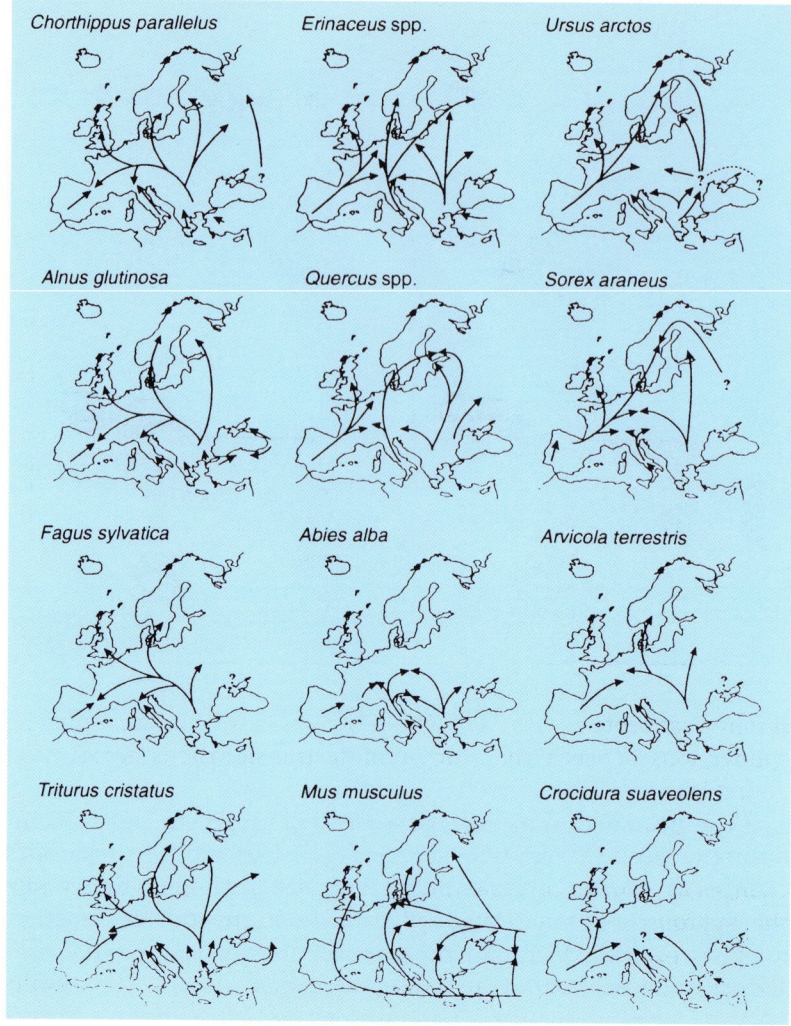

barrier than the Pyrenees or the Alps do to the Iberian and Italian refugia respectively and so the northern populations derive solely from this one origin (Hewitt 1999).

A series of studies on unrelated species by Avise (1996) in south-east USA also serve as a good example of ice age divergence of species. He used a range of DNA techniques to analyse the phylogeography of species in this region. The results show that the intraspecific distribution of genetic diversity suggests significant divisions in many species in a pattern that is concordant across unrelated taxa with similar distributions. In freshwater fish, species were divided into two regions centred on eastern watersheds draining into peninsular Florida and the Atlantic coast, and western watersheds draining in to the Gulf of Mexico (Fig. 13.4). Similarly a number of coastal vertebrates and invertebrates that have been analysed split in to Atlantic and Gulf coast groups. This clearly informs conservation policy suggesting a reserve

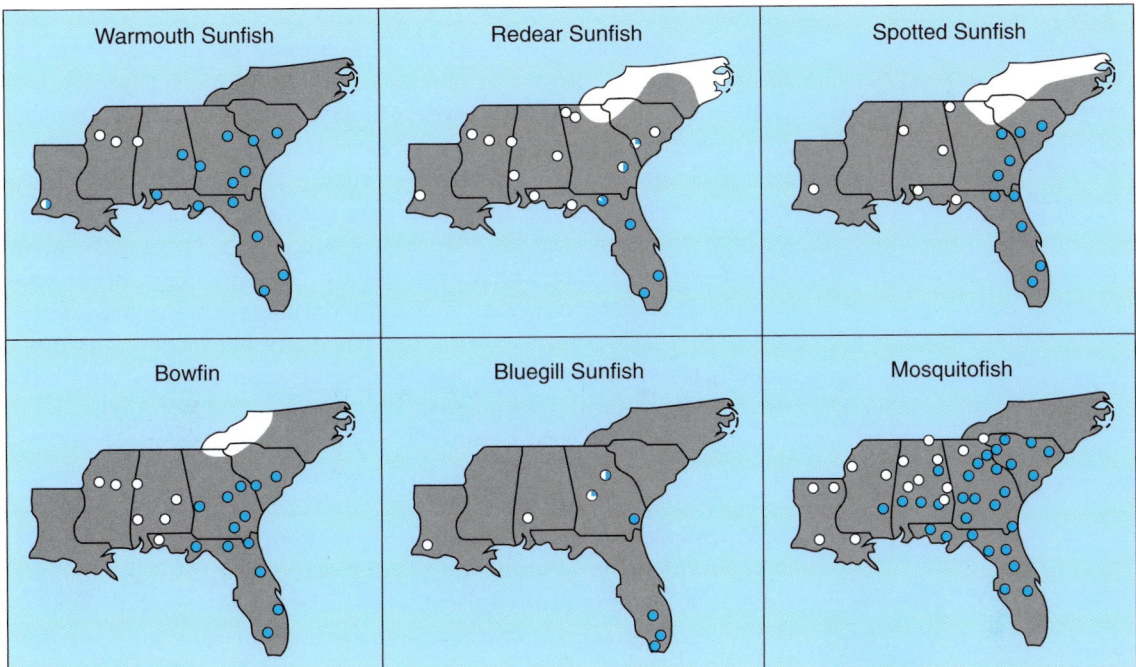

Fig. 13.4 Distribution of major mtDNA clades within six species of fish in the south-east USA. Note they all show a basic east–west divide. Reproduced from Avise (1996) with kind permission of the author.

system that protects diversity in both regions but does not set up false connections between them or promote translocations across their boundaries.

Clearly these studies show that species and their genomes have only been able to survive because of their ability to contract and expand with changes in climate. The new landscape we are creating needs to retain the appropriate connections and barriers to support this ongoing dynamic process as we saw in Chapter 12. The patterns above have formed only over a few tens of thousands of years, a short time in evolutionary terms, but the rapid climate change that is forecast for the future means that we will have to deal with even greater rates of change in species distributions. We must ask ourselves whether, under the current conservation practice, species will be able to contract, expand or shift their ranges as they have done in the past.

Using genetics to plan at evolutionary and biogeographical scales

The nature of genetic data, being somewhat independent from the species concept and traditional taxonomy, has raised some fundamental questions concerning conservation strategy as follows.

What are we trying to conserve?

Taxonomic units, be they species or any other level, are dynamic and evolving. Our ability to look back over evolutionary time enables us to estimate the rates at which speciation has been occurring. Conservation must allow evolution to continue at these natural rates but this has clearly not been the case in the last few hundred years. One view of a natural rate would be where some balance is achieved between the rates of speciation and extinction or even a net increase in species as suggested by the fossil record. Neither exists at the moment because the current levels of habitat fragmentation are far more likely to result in extinction than speciation. We are currently in a period of vastly accelerated extinction rates and the priority must be to reduce this, but what can we do about speciation? We are potentially increasing speciation rates by creating more geographical barriers between populations, making them ever smaller and possibly genetically atypical, but unlike extinction rates we have no way of estimating our impact.

At what level should conservation action be focused?

Conservation still operates largely at the level of the population; but we measure species decline and species extinction, largely because species are convenient recognisable units. All species are divided into populations that are genetically unique semi-independent units, capable of their own evolutionary development. Each population has the potential to evolve into a separate species given time (see Chapter 10). This potential is the basis of the biodiversity we see today but conservation action rarely recognises populations as of value in themselves, unless they are the last few of a species. Populations of common species rarely receive any conservation attention when threatened, simply because there are plenty of other populations left. This ignores their uniqueness and long-term evolutionary potential. Who can say were the next speciation event will come from?

Taxonomic divisions to subspecies level are common and often the focus of conservation effort, but there is no clear definition of a subspecies and this has resulted in problems at a policy level. However, intraspecific phylogenies can reveal many divisions below the species level that are of potential evolutionary significance. To try and cope with this issue Ryder (1986) suggested the concept of the **evolutionary significant unit (ESU)** as a set of populations with a common evolutionary history, distinct from other populations. Despite some doubts over how distinct the lineage has to be, the concept has gained some favour and is now used routinely in conservation genetics, but has rarely been used practically.

The ESU concept has been used in developing a conservation plan for the Atlantic salmon (*Salmo salar*; Dodson *et al.* 1998). This species is not globally endangered but, due to its habit of migrating back to its natal spawning area, the species is divided into a number of locally adapted evolutionary lineages based around river catchments. In this case ESUs were identified using genetic and morphological data from relevant populations to construct a phylogenetic tree (Fig. 13.5). This resulted in four ESUs being identified containing a total of 18 populations. To use this information for practical salmon conservation, Dodson *et al.* combined the biological information with socioeconomic

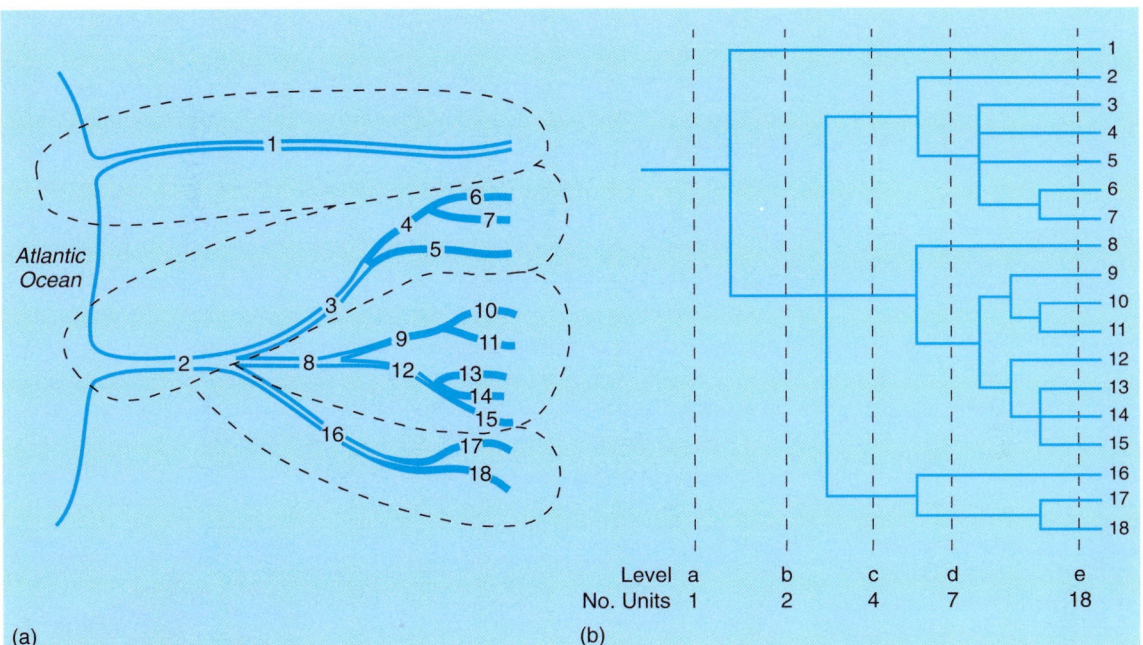

Level a | b | c | d | e
No. Units 1 | 2 | 4 | 7 | 18

(a)   (b)

issues or constraints to produce what they term an **operational conservation unit (OCU)**. In this case OCUs were based on the need to manage commercial and recreational fisheries to conserve and restore populations. The plan could also be used to prevent the introduction of exotic fish from other ESUs, thus preventing genetic contamination and preserving local adaptation.

The use of the ESU has been criticised because its definition overlaps with the species concept and it is a matter of judgement as to which hierarchical level is used to differentiate one ESU from another. For example, in Fig. 13.5 you could call each of the 18 populations an ESU (level e), or reduce these to seven, four, two or one (levels d, c, b, and a respectively). There is no standard level of difference among populations and this could potentially lead to conflicting strategies among different organisations. ESUs also rely on the phylogeny produced and different methods may produce different phylogenies, causing further confusion. However, the concept has been used constructively in cases such as the brown bear (*Ursus arctos*) as explained in Box 13.1.

Fig. 13.5 Four Evolutionary Significant Units (ESU) have been identified among 18 populations of the Atlantic salmon (*Salmo salar*) as shown in the schematic diagram (a). A decision has to be made on the appropriate hierarchical level on which to base the ESU designation. The phylogenetic tree (b) illustrates that anything between 1 and 18 ESUs are possible. Dodson *et al.* chose level d on an operational basis influenced by social, economic and legal considerations. Reproduced from Dodson *et al.* (1998) with kind permission of NRC Canada.

Box 13.1	Using the historical phylogeography of the brown bear (*Ursus arctos*) to formulate a species conservation strategy

The historical distribution of the brown bear covers a vast area of the northern hemisphere, ranging through North America, Asia and across to Europe. Today it has been extirpated from many areas, including large areas of Western Europe and the USA, but is still widespread in other areas such as Alaska and north-west Canada. A number of isolated populations now exist and a long-term conservation strategy is required for the species to avoid further loss of these populations and the genetic diversity they contain.

Historically a large number of subspecies of brown bears has been recognised which potentially makes recovery strategies very complex. An accurate picture of the historical phylogeography is required to assist in decision making on creation of corridors and possible translocations. A study by Waits et al. (1998) using mtDNA sequence analysis has suggested that the remaining populations in North America can be subdivided in to four ESUs covering 1, islands of the south-eastern coast of Alaska; 2, mainland Alaska; 3, eastern Alaska and northern Canada; and 4, southern Canada and US border states. A more complex picture for European populations has been revealed by Taberlet & Bouvet (1994) who found that isolated populations in southern Scandinavia are most closely related to the few remaining populations in the Iberian Peninsula and not to the closest populations in north-eastern Scandinavia and Russia (Fig. 13.6). This suggests that there were probably a number of glacial refugia from which this species recolonised northern Europe after the last ice age.

Fig. 13.6 Distribution of the remaining populations of the brown bear (*Ursus arctos*) in Europe. Letters, denote collection sites. Populations A, Pyrenees; B, Cantabrian mountains; C, Norway and D, Dalarna, Sweden are more closely related than their geographical proximity would suggest. Reproduced from Taberlet & Bouvet (1994) with kind permission of The Royal Society.

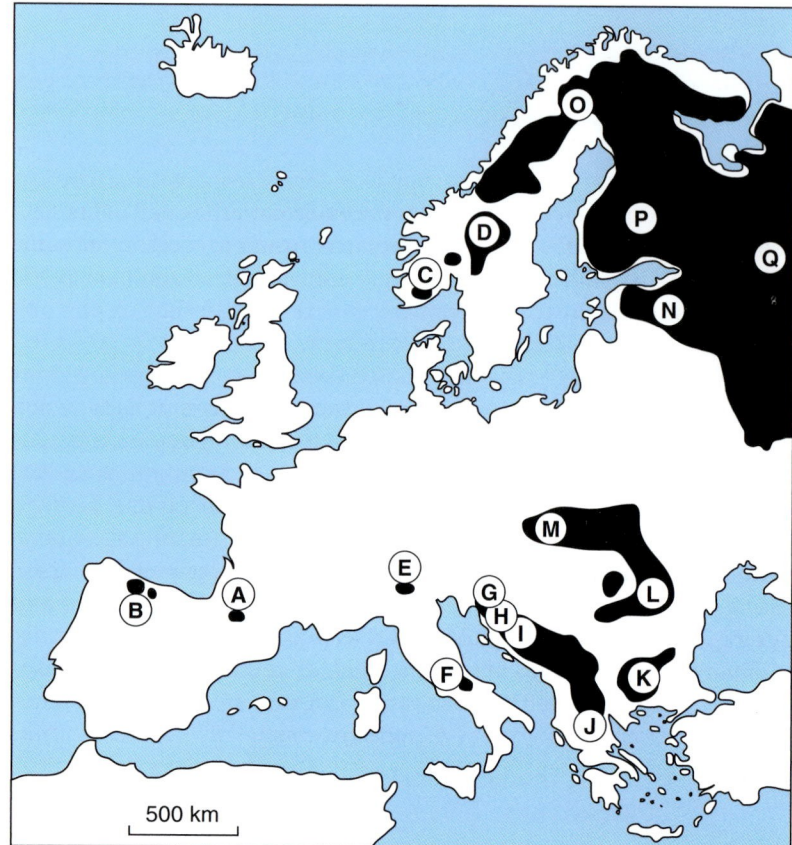

How does this information influence conservation policy?

In the absence of this information, populations in southern Scandinavia may have been thought indistinct from their neighbours. In this situation those isolated populations may not have been regarded as very high priority for conservation when larger groups of interconnected populations were close by. Additionally, if translocation were necessary, there would be no known reason not to transfer individuals or groups between the ranges of the two subgroups. With the genetic information the southern Scandinavian population must be regarded as having higher intrinsic value and no exchange of genetic material should take place between these and other Scandinavian populations other than by natural dispersal processes. The major advantage of this information is that the brown bear populations can be divided into management units that reflect their historical ranges. This can then help define recovery programmes that have the aim of allowing or assisting species to recover their former range.

The concept of management units

Alongside historical patterns of intraspecific diversity, we can recognise groups of populations that are currently independent of others, in that little gene flow occurs between them and has not recently done so. Moritz (1994) advocates identification of such groups, which could be managed independently of others using genetic techniques. He calls such groups **management units** (MU). In this case genetic divergence is not defined by phylogeny, but by significant differences in allele frequency which reflects more contemporary isolation and cessation of gene flow. An understanding of how genetic diversity is structured geographically can help in identifying the appropriate geographical divisions and the scale at which conservation action should be targeted. The division of species into management units (MUs) using genetic data is a potentially important tool. Clearly if genetic analysis can show that groups of populations have been isolated from each other for some time, pre-dating human activity, even though they do not show any deep evolutionary division, it is necessary to manage them separately, especially since, in the absence of migration between them, their demography is likely to differ.

Putting these terms into practice we would probably find that populations of the majority of species in the UK belong to an ESU that covers much of north-west Europe, but they can be regarded as a separate MU from continental Europe because of their current isolation. Many species within the UK do not show any significant difference from their conspecifics on the continent, but they have been isolated from them for approximately 8000 years and are also likely to show independent demography, therefore qualifying as a separate management unit.

Many good examples of species dividing in to management units come from freshwater species separated in isolated river catchments. The alligator snapping turtle (*Macroclemys temminckii*) is found in rivers draining from the southern USA into the Gulf of Mexico (Fig. 13.7). Mitochondrial DNA analysis of samples from 12 rivers revealed clear catchment-level differences suggesting that populations in each river catchment should be regarded as separate management units (Roman *et al.* 1999).

Linking genetic diversity with community diversity

In conservation, genetics is largely used in the context of the above examples to identify intraspecific variation. But can we expend

Fig. 13.7 (a) Distribution and collection sites of the alligator snapping turtle (*Macroclemys temminckii*) in the river catchments of the south-eastern USA and (b) their phylogenetic relationship as shown by mitochondrial DNA analysis. Reproduced from Roman *et al.* (1999) with kind permission of Blackwell Science.

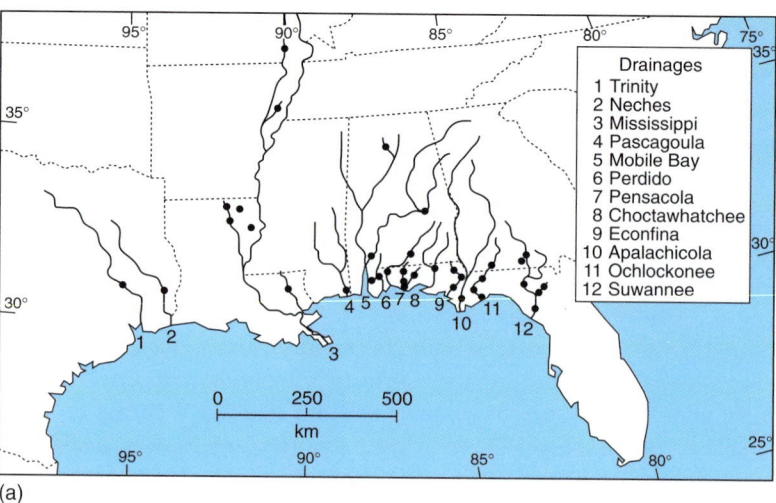

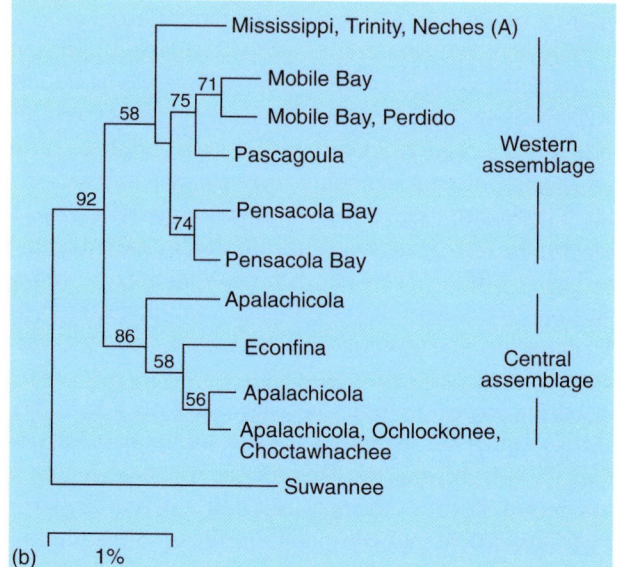

resources looking in detail at each species to define ESUs and MUs? Almost certainly not; if we are to try and maintain evolution at natural rates for all species we must scale up and look for general patterns for ESUs and MUs across species representative of different functions or trophic levels in the community.

It has already been emphasised that any strategy for species conservation must ensure conservation of their habitat. However, in the resource-limited situation in which we find ourselves, conservationists may spend a lot of their time deciding at what scale management activities should be planned. We have seen in Chapter 12 that the problem with applying paradigms such as metapopulation theory to conservation problems is that they tend to be species specific, when we often wish to conserve biodiversity as a whole. How can we get a picture of how existing populations across a whole community relate to each other and therefore on what scale action will be appropriate? One possibility

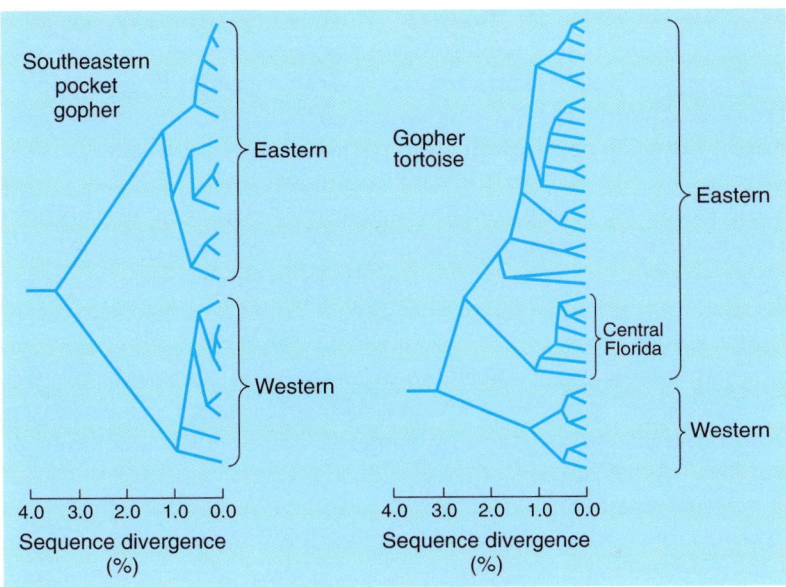

Fig. 13.8 Example of two vertebrates showing distinct eastern and western group among populations in the south-eastern USA. Reproduced from Avise (1996) with kind permission of the author.

is to use genetic analysis to estimate past relationships between populations and provide a measurement of the scale over which they are structured. This at first would also appear to suffer from the same problem of species specificity, but an understanding of the how the genetic diversity is structured geographically across a number of representative species (as surrogates for the community) might help in identifying appropriate scales for action.

An example of this approach is the work of John Avise in south-east USA mentioned above (pp. 273–5). Avise analysed the geographical structuring of populations across a range of vertebrate and invertebrate taxa using mitochondrial DNA sequence analysis. Results suggest that many species from different taxa show the same pattern and scale of regionalisation in south-east USA forming distinct eastern and western assemblages (Fig. 13.8). This data is immediately of use in informing conservation managers that it would be inappropriate to try and link eastern and western populations by creation of corridors that have clearly not been there before. Conservation action should concentrate on linking populations within the assemblages (Avise 1996). Each can be considered a MU as gene flow within them has occurred in the recent past.

Results of studies on genetic relatedness can have a significant impact on the formulation of conservation strategies. They can strengthen arguments for protection, they can be used positively to enable better resource allocation and also help shape our approach to conservation in the future.

The use of systematics in conservation

We saw in Chapter 10 how important it can be for species to gain taxonomic recognition in order to figure in conservation plans or legislation, but populations do not always fit conveniently within species. The science of systematics provides us with many examples of actively speciating groups and of hybrid zones between two closely related species. These are dynamic processes fundamental to biodiversity, yet they take place over such long timescales that they are not easily detected. Soltis & Gitzendanner (1999) have called for systematists to play a larger part in conservation by helping to identify a non-species-based, more evolutionary view of conservation priorities.

This issue is brought more clearly into focus when we consider what we should do to conserve zones of hybridisation between two closely related species. Many such zones have been identified and they are obviously potentially important in evolutionary terms. Some hybrid zones are areas of secondary contact where two species have recently arisen from one through geographical isolation, followed by restoration of contact. The hybrids are often of reduced fitness compared with the parent species and separation is maintained with a narrow hybrid zone. In other cases, one species may be swamping another through superior numbers (see Chapter 4). If this is a natural process it could be argued that we should try to conserve it, even though it could result in the loss of a species. This presents a number of challenges to our current conservation thinking, which advocates action to conserve such species. Clearly our view of what form of conservation (short-term or long-term) is most important dictates our action. Conservation action for the red wolf (*Canis rufus*) (see Box 10.4) may be a relevant example here. If it is a true species there is significant support for its conservation, yet it is in danger of going extinct through the natural process of swamping with coyote (*C. latrans*) genes. It could be argued that this has arisen through human impact on the species's range adding further complication to the problem.

Conserving the evolutionary process

Species ranges will never be natural again in the sense that they are unaffected by human activity, but we must ensure that distributional changes and evolutionary processes can continue at rates that can sustain biodiversity as a whole. If current scenarios of climate change are roughly right, trying to maintain species and communities in isolated reserves will be a futile exercise. Conservation will only be effective if gene flow is re-established and opportunities for colonisation increased, in line with probabilities of extinction. This will require a fundamental change in conservation strategy to scale up our activity both in terms of space (to consider the landscape and ecosystem) and time (to consider more evolutionary time rather than human or political life times).

It is encouraging that a number of policy changes have hinted at moves in this direction with the introduction of landscape-based conservation initiatives mentioned in the previous chapter, but it will be a difficult task to 'reconnect' many reserves in the foreseeable future. But this should not stop us thinking in these positive terms.

Summary

1. Conservation action to date has concentrated on dealing with short-term crisis situations by designating nature reserves and protecting species. The result has been a culture of control of nature rather than a facilitation of its dynamics.

2. The dynamic changes in distribution of species and communities can be tracked through time using phylogeographical analysis employing new techniques in molecular genetics combined with traditional biogeographical studies.

3. In order to recognise the dynamics of nature and formulate appropriate conservation strategies we need some new terminology that does not recognise species as static units in time or space. Evolutionary significant units, management units and operational conservation units have all been used but are not universally accepted.

4. Systematics can help us understand and identify transitional evolutionary events such as hybrid zones, but we need to decide how we should respond to them in terms of conservation action.

5. Conservation priorities should move away from simply species- and habitat-oriented goals toward the idea of conserving the evolutionary process on which all biodiversity depends.

Discussion points

- Are long-term different from short-term conservation objectives?
- Are evolutionary significant units a useful addition to the species concept in conservation?
- Should processes rather than species or habitats be the object of conservation effort?

Further reading

Avise, J.C. (1996). Toward a regional conservation genetics perspective: phylogeography of faunas in the southeastern United States. Pp. 431–470 in *Conservation genetics: case histories from nature*, eds J.C. Avise & J.L. Hamrick. New York: Chapman and Hall.

Hewitt, G.M. (1999). Post-glacial re-colonisation of European biota. *Biological Journal of the Linnean Society* **68**, 87–112.

Moritz, C. (1994). Applications of mitochondrial DNA analysis in conservation: a critical review. *Molecular Ecology* **3**, 401–411.

Myers, N. 1996. The biodiversity crisis and the future of evolution. *The Environmentalist* **16**, 37–47.

Chapter 14

Ecological restoration

Many natural areas have been partly destroyed or degraded through the direct or indirect action of mankind. However, this damage need not be total or permanent. To some extent habitats and ecosystems can be restored on a local basis provided that the materials (e.g. species) and expertise exist. Restoration is a positive process that can be used to great effect in conservation, but can also be misused to seduce us into inappropriate use of resources.

By reading this chapter students will gain an understanding of the aims and scope of ecological restoration, the variety of restoration projects and their challenges, together with the advantages and limitations of the concept.

Introduction

The rise of ecological restoration as a valuable process in conserving biological diversity has largely come about through the need to restore damaged and degraded land arising from agricultural and industrial activity. Early and groundbreaking work in the discipline has been made largely by scientists and land managers engaged in restoring large areas of heavily degraded land to something functional (e.g. Leopold 1949; Bradshaw 1983). As the discipline has matured, more searching questions about goals of restoration have been asked and definitions sought from the community or ecosystem perspective. The end users of this information are most commonly planners and developers, but increasingly ambitious conservation objectives are being set.

When we think of restoration, the repair of a painting may come to mind, and what we may perceive of this is the act of returning the object to its pristine condition. This is essentially what we might aspire to in ecological restoration, even though in practice we will inevitably have to settle for less. A definition used by the Society for Ecological Restoration is *the process of repairing damage caused by humans to the biodiversity and dynamics of indigenous ecosystems.* This reflects the idea that humans are the cause of damage (thus excluding natural catastrophes) and that it is an attempt to return systems back to something that existed prior to the damaging event(s).

It may come as a surprise therefore that there has been a good deal of controversy and debate about definitions in ecological restoration. Bradshaw (1997a) takes on the question 'what do we mean by restoration'? He makes the important distinction between restoration as we would imagine it and as described above, and other processes that are sometimes referred to as restoration, such as rehabilitation and habitat creation. Rehabilitation turns degraded land back into useful land, such as the conversion of open-cast mining sites to playing fields or agricultural land, but does not seek to return the land to its natural ecology. Habitat creation seeks to convert degraded land into useful wildlife habitat, but without any reference to what was formerly present. An example of this is the conversion of gravel pits into a wetland habitat where no wetland had occurred before. Clearly both of these have value and habitat creation can be a strategic conservation action, but neither are ecological restoration in the true sense. A relatively broad view of ecological restoration will be taken in this chapter in order to cover and critically evaluate related practices such as habitat translocation and habitat creation.

The value of ecological restoration lies in its emphasis on positive action to repair damage rather than the negative image of some conservation activities of fighting a desperate battle to save a few remaining fragments. The incentive for ecological restoration can be viewed as falling in to three separate categories; material, existential and heuristic:

1. The material reason is to restore ecosystem processes to benefit ourselves. The underlying assumption is that economies rely on a balance between developed lands and natural areas. It costs money to make polluted water drinkable but natural sources can provide it free of charge. If development impinges on the ability of natural areas to provide basic services, economic well-being declines and quality of life suffers. This imbalance already characterises most national economies and thus there is a case for restoration.

2. Existential reasons stem from the idea that restoration strengthens the relationship of human beings with the rest of nature by providing an opportunity for positive personal participation. When restoration is conducted as a collective effort, the process unites the participants with the restored ecosystem, they feel simultaneously empowered and responsible for their environment, stimulating long-term stewardship and sustainability.

3. Heuristic reasons for restoration arise from the opportunity for the study of ecosystem processes through attempting to reassemble component parts (see Box 14.1). This is essentially a trial and error process that can involve hypothesis construction and testing and is often referred to as **restoration ecology**: the scientific branch of ecological restoration.

Box 14.1 | Butterfly restorations: what have we learnt from invertebrates?

Rare species are increasingly the focus of habitat restoration activity. The single species approach to conservation (Chapters 10 and 11) often gets criticised because it is impossible to deal with every species individually. But political realities dictate that species will often be a focus for activity and resources. There are increasing opportunities for this process arising from biodiversity action plans and the species action plans they contain. So can action for the benefit of a single species be viewed as ecological restoration?

In Chapter 10 we saw evidence that it is at the level of the autecological study that some of the complexities of a system can be revealed. These would be overlooked if restoration were carried out only at the community or ecosystem scale.

The challenge is to ensure that the chosen species are not the only ones to benefit from the activities. No more crucially is this challenge faced than with the invertebrates. Very few invertebrates have been studied in detail (those that have are mostly pest species) and still fewer have been the subject of restoration attempts. As a consequence the examples below are confined to the best-studied taxa, butterflies, in one of the most intensively studied areas, Britain.

To illustrate the progress made, restoration programmes currently under way for two species in the UK are summarised. These examples illustrate two different problems and approaches needed. Some general conclusions about their value are then made.

Heath fritillary (*Mellicta athalia*) and coppiced woodland restoration

This species has experienced a rapid decline in the UK over the last 50 years and has been the subject of detailed ecological study (Warren 1991). In south-east England it relies on woodland habitats, where its larval foodplant is common cow-wheat (*Melampyrum pratense*). Warren was able to show that the adults required hot sunny clearings within the woods to maintain flights, mate and seek out foodplants for oviposition. Traditionally clearings within woodland were maintained on a rotational basis by the practice of coppicing (see Chapter 9). Different areas were cut each year so that areas in each stage of the coppice cycle would always be present. This included newly coppiced areas that provided sheltered, hot, sunny microclimates and suitable habitat for the foodplant. Coppicing became uneconomic by the early twentieth century and coppiced woodland was progressively abandoned and open areas disappeared and so did the species dependent upon them.

The realisation that this was the cause of the decline in the heath fritillary has multiple significance. First it identifies a known management practice which will enable the recovery of the species. But second, it identifies a process for the restoration of a whole community of species typical of southern English semi-natural woodlands. Many woodland-floor species, and particularly the vernal (spring-flowering) flora benefit from rotational coppicing.

A restoration programme initiated in the 1980s has enabled the recovery of the species in one complex of woodlands in Kent and its successful reintroduction in woodlands in Essex (Warren 1991). This is a good example of how an autecological study can lead to the reinstatement of a traditional practice that benefits many species.

Large copper (*Lycaena dispar*) and fenland restoration

The extinction of the large copper butterfly in England resulted from the dramatic 97% reduction in its wetland habitat in East Anglia and abandonment of traditional fen management practices elsewhere. Research has been undertaken in its native habitat in The Netherlands with a view to restoring it in the Broadland area of England (Pullin 1997). Results suggest that the species has a number of key habitat requirements.

Male territories are set up in open fen meadows, cut during late summer, often centred around nectar plants. An extensive network of sites meeting these requirements is needed to complement the dispersive, opportunistic strategy of the butterfly.

Foodplant/egg distribution: eggs are found on the great water dock (*Rumex hydrolapathum*) in a range of sunny, warm situations, especially in habitat edges, which need to be provided in any restoration site. Eggs are not commonly found on plants in open fen meadows where the males form territories.

The ecology and dispersal patterns of this butterfly suggest that the landscape-scale mosaic of habitats is important for its survival and persistence. In the current landscape situation, sufficient foodplants exist in suitable locations, but insufficient habitat is available for male territories and there are too many barriers to movement along some river valleys. This has not always been the case.

Records for some areas of Broadland clearly show that the landscape was much more open in the middle of the last century when the butterfly was present (Fig. 14.3). A fen restoration strategy for Broadland (see page 293) which is currently in its first stages of implementation, advocates the restoration of considerable areas of open fenland and reedland by removal of recently developed scrub and carr woodland (Broads Authority 1993). If this strategy meets its objectives then the future landscape of Broadland may be far more suitable for the restoration of this butterfly. This case illustrates that species often require a mosaic of multiple habitat types and restoration must take account of different scales from microhabitat to landscape.

Implications

These early efforts at the restoration of butterflies and their habitats point to a number of factors that are relevant to future restoration attempts.

1. The links between species and habitat are complex and will rarely be revealed without autecological studies.

This link between species re-establishment and habitat restoration is important. These need to be thoroughly studied in advance of the restoration attempt and then resulting hypotheses can be tested using an experimental approach. These tests should be scientific experiments that enable us to refine our hypotheses and learn by our mistakes. If the habitats are already significantly influenced by human activities the role of management will be vital to the success of the restoration. Not only does the habitat need to be made suitable for the species but the management must be sustainable in the long term.

2. Single species can act as a focus for planning restoration and management activities that also benefit a range of other species.

It is often difficult to plan restoration activity because we are unsure of what we are aiming for. The use of endangered species, which are identified with a particular habitat can act as the necessary focus. The action taken will not suit all species, but carried out in limited areas within a landscape strategy, it need not threaten other species. Using flagship species for restoration programmes is a promising strategy for raising funds and coordinating effort for restoration of the habitat as a whole. Butterflies have taken a leading role in such programmes and are likely to continue to do so in the future, but hopefully other species can do so as well.

3. Rare species test our ability to restore a complex community.

Rare species that are likely to be the subject of restoration attempts may have very complex life cycles and specific habitat requirements on different scales from micro-habitat to landscape. The experience with butterfly re-establishment has been that to restore rare species the habitat has to be restored to its former semi-natural state by appropriate management, and consequently, non-target species, often rare or local themselves, have benefited.

Of course, a single-species approach is far from perfect. It would be an improvement if more than one species that is indicative of a community could be used to integrate knowledge of habitat requirements and produce restoration plans. It is always likely that specific management for some species will be to the detriment of others, but if we retain a historical focus to our restoration activities and think about communities in which species must have occurred then we are likely to retain the widest diversity.

Elements of practical restoration

The size of the restoration task will depend on the scale of damage done and what fundamental elements of the living system remain.

The soil

How easy restoration will be, following damage to a terrestrial ecosystem, depends substantially on what has happened to the soil (Fig. 14.1). Let us consider two extreme cases to illustrate this: first where the damage is simply the removal of all above-ground vegetation, such as following a short period of ploughing and cultivation; and second where the topsoil is also removed leaving only the subsoil or bedrock, such as in open-cast mining activity. In the former all the roots will be intact and many plants will regenerate rapidly; dormant seed will also germinate and ruderals may invade the bare soil and secondary succession will quickly revegetate the area. In the latter case all of the roots and dormant seed will have been removed with the topsoil and its nutrients. Even if the subsoil will support some plant growth, the plants will have to come from surrounding areas and the resulting vegetation will be very different from the original (Bradshaw 1997b).

There are many intermediate scenarios that are commonly met with, including disturbance of the soil over long periods of time, as in

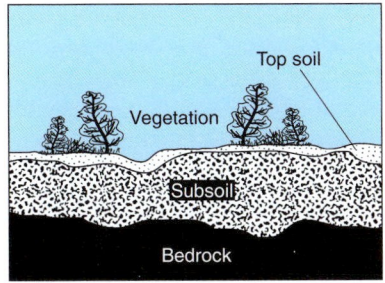

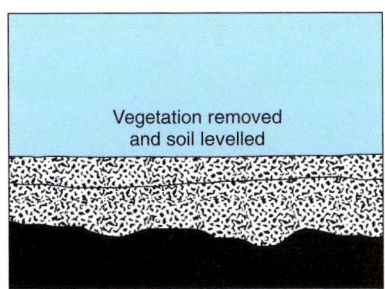

Fig. 14.1 The extent and difficulty of restoration depends on what has been done with the soil on the site. If the soil structure is intact it is easier to restore the vegetation than if the top soil has been removed.

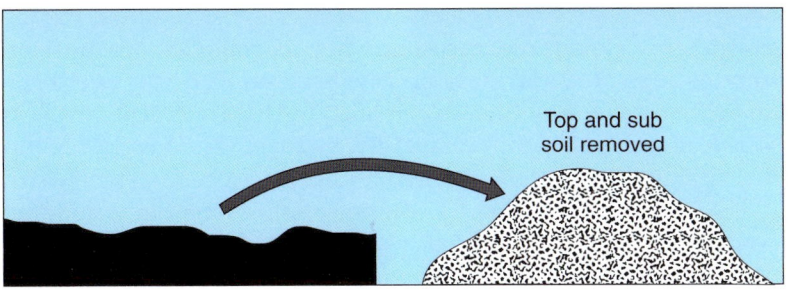

agricultural use, which changes the characteristics of the topsoil. Restoration efforts can involve reintroduction of topsoil if this is feasible. Another common problem is compaction of the soil surface making it difficult for plants to colonise. Some form of mechanical loosening of the soil may considerably improve colonisation rates. Many agricultural soils are rich in nutrients, following years of fertiliser application, in which case stripping off the topsoil to lower the nutrient status may be a preferred option.

Development of vegetation

The development of the vegetation cover cannot be seen as separate from the development of the soil. In the same way that the characteristics of the soil will influence the plants that grow in it, the plants will affect the soil development. As stated above, if the soil is relatively intact and the period of disturbance short, the vegetation will quickly recover and, given time, may be very similar to that which was destroyed. However, in more extreme situations recovery of vegetation of any sort may be very slow. Consequently, in many cases, for reasons of soil conservation or aesthetics, some form of manual restoration is required to speed the process of revegetation and secondary succession.

The most common way of speeding up the process is by bypassing the natural immigration and establishment phases of succession, which may be very slow if the site is isolated from potential colonisers and sufficiently degraded to make establishment difficult and slow. The relative immigration rates of different species are largely determined by the type of propagule used (e.g. spores or seeds), their size and mode of dispersal. Some species that are a natural part of the community and important for natural succession, may take a very long time to colonise, particularly if the source site is some distance away. A good example of this is the legumes, such as clover, which are important for their nitrogen-fixing capability, but which have comparatively large seeds. In such cases establishment can be achieved through collection of seed from a donor site and sowing or drilling the seed mix using established agricultural methods. If seed is taken from donor sites care must be taken to match that site with the receptor site, so that the appropriate species are translocated. Some species in the seed mix may be undesirable, such as alien weeds (Gilbert & Anderson 1998). In some cases the soil may be very poor in nutrients making establishment of plants very slow even though potential colonisers are abundant. Some fertilisation may be necessary to kick-start the succession when the soil is left in a nutrient-poor condition. However, the level of application of fertiliser can be critical to the type of vegetation that results. Too high a level of nutrients made lead to a species-poor competitive sward of vigorous grasses. It is then difficult to reduce the nutrient levels to increase species diversity.

The concept of safe sites for seedling establishment in restoration programmes has been developed by Urbanska (1997). This involves identification of environments which are favourable to seedling germination and establishment. In practice this means identification of microenvironments which enable successful establishment. This may include such aspects as competitor-free space, low grazing pressure and presence of nurse species that aid establishment and survival. Clearly knowledge of these factors will inform the restoration process and help set objectives.

The pollinator community

The reproduction and spread of many plant species will depend on the presence of specific pollinator species, usually insects (but sometimes birds or bats). For example, spring-flowering species may require early flying insects, such as queen bumble bees, for pollination. These have a small foraging range and specific habitat requirements for their nests. If there is no similar vegetation nearby then the pollinators will also be absent. Initial restoration may have to rely on more generalist plant–pollinator interactions. Synchrony of flowering and pollinator activity is also a potential problem and Handel (1997) has advocated creating sequentially flowering plant communities to ensure a pollen source throughout the summer, increasing the probability that some fraction will be visited by local pollinators producing a positive feedback on future pollination success. This may require a compromise between restoration of old and creation of new communities.

Seed dispersal

In many communities the role of seed dispersers will be vital to the achievement of natural patterns of plant distribution. A whole range of animals act as dispersers, many of which will have been lost along with the original plant community. Birds and mammals commonly disperse seed as it passes through their gut to be deposited in a readily available source of nutrients. Mechanisms to bring back essential seed dispersers into the community will have to be identified at an early stage in some restoration programmes. This has been identified as particularly important in tropical forest restoration, as we shall see in the Costa Rica example below (Janzen 1983)

Herbivores

The dynamics of many plant communities are dependent on the selective action of herbivores. Potentially dominant plant species may be kept in check by grazing, and the disturbance caused may provide extra niches for other species. Herbivores (from ants to elephants) cause heterogeneity at many scales that enable greater plant diversity to persist by maintaining a balance between early and late successional species. The successful restoration of vegetation communities may therefore be dependent on the successful reintroduction of the native herbivores.

Case studies in restoration

Prairie restoration in the USA

The vast prairie lands that once covered the mid-western states of the USA were largely destroyed by agricultural development during the first half of the twentieth century. The subsequent abandonment of much of this land for economic reasons has left opportunities for restoration of the prairie ecosystem. In many areas much of the soil remains but the seed bank has been almost completely destroyed through intensive cultivation. This cultivation has been so intensive in some areas that the native seed bank only remains in odd areas that have been safe from the plough, such as graveyards and railway sidings. However, seed has been collected from such areas and sown in restoration plots. Alternatively, transplantation of turf and planting of individual plants can be used. The last two are more costly and small scale, but the establishment success rate is higher.

A major problem in trying to restore the native plant community is the presence of exotic weeds. These can be invasive species that take up dominant positions in early successional communities, preventing the natural vegetation composition developing and therefore must be eradicated. Methods such as selective herbicide application or intensive cultivation have been tried, but the most promising technique in the case of the prairie vegetation is the use of fire. Fire is a natural phenomenon in prairie systems and most native plants are tolerant of it, so this can be used to selectively eliminate exotic weeds. Another major issue in prairie restoration is whether to use only local varieties of plant species, or to increase genetic diversity by bringing in more distant strains. Little is known of the genetic diversity or local adaptation that may have been present in native populations. Use of seed of local provenance is usually advocated in vegetation restoration in order to protect locally adapted traits, but where local populations have lost genetic diversity it may be advantageous to reintroduce diversity from more remote sources.

The ultimate challenge is to recreate the dynamics of prairie systems (Fig. 14.2). Prairies form a dynamic heterogeneous mosaic pattern in

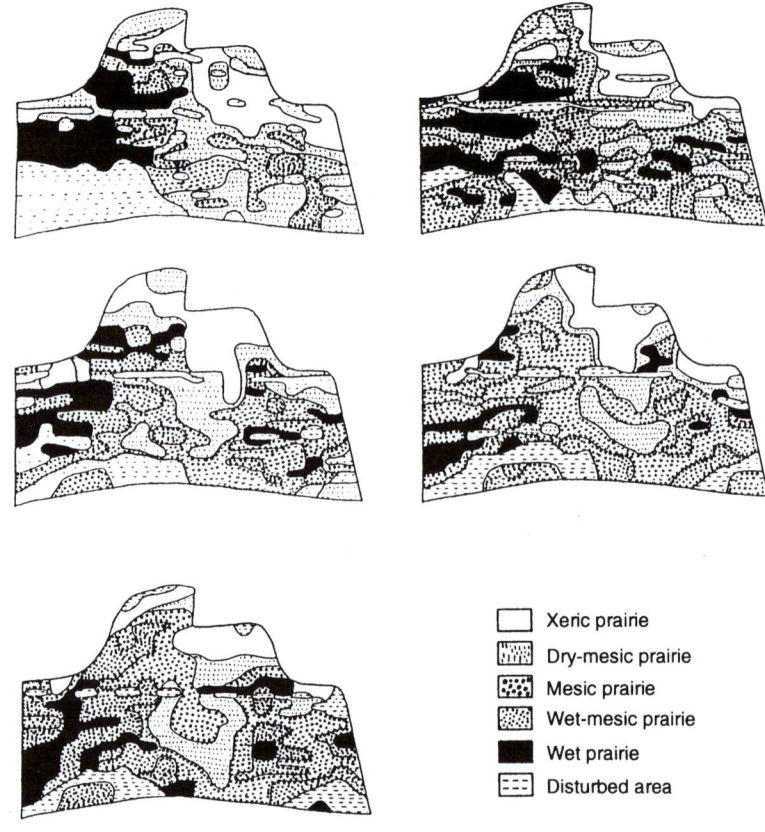

- ☐ Xeric prairie
- ▦ Dry-mesic prairie
- ▦ Mesic prairie
- ▦ Wet-mesic prairie
- ■ Wet prairie
- ⊡ Disturbed area

response to climatic events and local disturbance, particularly fire, mound building ants and grazing and trampling by large herbivores (Cottam 1987). The fire may be recreated artificially with some care but it is probable that disturbance by animals can only be restored through the reintroduction of the animals themselves. American bison (*Bison bison*) have long since disappeared from most of their former range and reintroducing these large herbivores will require substantial areas of prairie to be restored to support viable populations. If successful, how can their numbers be controlled without reintroduction of their natural predators? At this point it becomes evident how difficult it might be to truly restore a natural system.

Tropical dry forest in Costa Rica

The biodiversity of tropical dry forest is often ignored in favour of tropical rainforest, but the former is also highly diverse, although rarer and highly threatened. Large areas of tropical dry forest in Central America have been cleared and the land used for cattle ranching. Only small fragments remain in national parks, such as Santa Rosa in Costa Rica.

An ambitious project to restore large tracts of forest surrounding Santa Rosa has been started by tropical biologist Dan Janzen. His idea was to allow the forest to regenerate naturally from remaining fragments rather than embarking on an expensive programme of planting. The first priority was to remove the large numbers of cattle from the area and create the conditions for regeneration of the native trees. Small fragments of forest remain that may act as nuclei from which surrounding areas could be restored, but regeneration of tree cover is critically dependent on the presence of pollinators and seed dispersers. Research revealed the seed dispersal and seedling establishment can be enhanced by the presence of large herbivores that deposit seed in their dung, that in turn acts as a nutrient source for young trees. Horses were fed with meal containing seeds of important large forest trees, especially the Guanacaste tree (*Enterolobium cyclocarpum*) and were allowed to roam freely around the restoration area (at much lower density than present under the former cattle ranching). Once established, the tree then acts as focus on which birds and arboreal mammals gather. They deposit more seeds around it and the forest slowly regenerates. The other key factor is the suppression of fire that has been used by farmers to maintain quality of grassland for their cattle. This frequently invades the forest edge and suppresses spread of the forest.

Wetland restoration in Broadland, UK

Broadland is the premier UK wetland area and is internationally recognised for its nature conservation value with extensive fens as well as open water. However, long-term changes in the area have necessitated action to restore the broads and surrounding fenland (wetland irrigated both by precipitation and groundwater seepage; see Chapter 9) areas and find a sustainable management strategy to maintain them.

Looking at the Broadland area today, you might think it heavily influenced by human activity, but essentially a natural wetland system. In fact the broads (areas of open water) are themselves the creation of humans. They were formed by peat digging or cutting for fuel, a practice that has been going on for a least 1000 years in this area. The peat itself had accumulated because of the waterlogged conditions in this low-lying basin. As peat cuttings were exhausted and abandoned, they flooded, producing open fen and reed marsh. Peat cutting reached a peak in the Middle Ages and declined in the middle of the nineteenth century as fossil fuels became increasingly available. The wetland margins were traditionally used for harvesting common reed (*Phragmites australis*) for thatch roofing, for grazing of livestock (grazing marsh) and production of marsh hay for fodder. Changes in the profitability of such practices led to progressive abandonment of the fens and marshes from the middle of the nineteenth century. As a result, succession of open fen to fen carr woodland changed the landscape completely from an open windswept wetland, to enclosed, drier woodland. (Fig. 14.3). Of the current 5000 hectares of semi-natural wetland, less than 2000 hectares remains as open fenland, and much of this is in a poor state. Many other areas of former fenland have been drained for intensive agricultural use.

This rapid change in landscape was accompanied by the decline and disappearance of many species reliant on open fen and reed marsh such

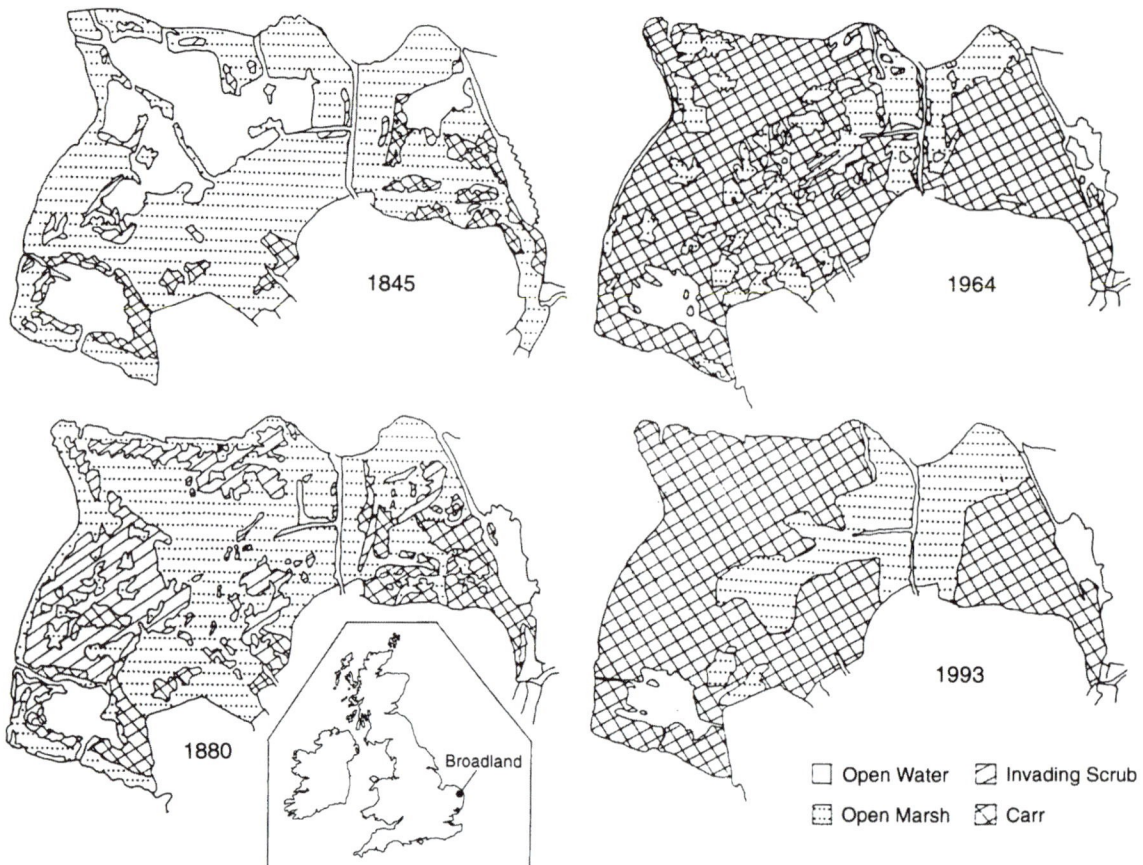

Fig. 14.3 A time series of vegetation maps of Woodbastwick Fen, Broadland, UK, dating from 1845 to 1993 showing changes in cover of different vegetation types associated with succession. Reproduced with kind permission of English Nature.

as the bittern (*Botaurus stellaris*), a bird of the heron family, which had declined from 60 male territories (recorded by the booming call males make in the breeding season) to just two males in 1997; the large copper butterfly (*Lycaena dispar*), which disappeared much earlier around 1860; and the fen orchid (*Liparis loeselii*), which is now recorded at only three Broadland sites. More recently, the intensification of agriculture around the broads in the last 50 years has led to increased levels of nutrient input from surface runoff and the growth of the human population (around this popular tourist area) has resulted in increased sewage input. The resulting progressive eutrophication of the water bodies has caused fundamental changes in the aquatic flora and fauna.

The land is largely privately owned, but many areas are leased as nature reserves and/or designated as Sites of Special Scientific Interest (SSSI). A partnership was formed in 1993 between the Broads Authority (the UK Government body responsible for overall management and protection of the Broadland area), English Nature (the UK Government body with responsibility for nature conservation), local conservation bodies, land owners, and other interested parties in order to formulate a strategy for the restoration and future management of Broadland (Broads Authority 1993).

After a period of consultation a set of general aims and objectives were agreed upon (Broads Authority & English Nature 1997):

1. expand existing open fen and optimise conservation value of all open fen habitats;
2. retain all internationally important woodland;
3. develop a mosaic of habitats and vegetation types;
4. maintain and increase areas of open water;
5. maintain and enhance populations of all nationally rare species;
6. maintain and increase existing biodiversity;
7. develop sustainable management techniques.

Of major interest here are the restoration strategies for open fenland and the open water bodies (the broads themselves). Old maps, such as those in Fig. 14.3, indicate where and how much open fenland formerly existed before abandonment. These maps have been used together with woodland surveys to identify areas for restoration. Once this has been done, there are a number of early stages in the restoration process:

1. clearance of the woodland using heavy machinery. This involves grubbing out of roots and disposing of the timber (Fig. 14.4a);
2. removal of accumulated peat so that the peat surface is below the water table.
3. creation of 'turf ponds' by banking up peat around the scrapes to produce an area of open shallow water (Fig. 14.4b).

These areas then represent the beginning of the successional process and can be managed in various ways to form desired community types. For example, they can be cut annually during the winter, which favours the development of reedland, which is good bittern habitat, or cut annually during the summer, which favours fen meadow vegetation with a rich flora and invertebrate fauna.

The ecology of the open water bodies of Broadland (the broads), as in all water bodies, is heavily dependent on the prevailing chemistry. When first formed, the broads would have been relatively nutrient poor. Agriculture was not well developed or intensive in the surrounding regions and the human population was relatively low, but over time the nutrient inputs in the form of nitrogen and phosphorus have increased and changed their ecology. This is partly a natural successional process, but the changes that have been recorded since 1950 are due to excessive nutrient inputs from agricultural runoff and sewage effluent into the rivers and then into the broads to which they are connected (Fig. 14.5).

The progressive eutrophication of the broads caused a change in ecology from a community dominated by water weeds to a community dominated by phytoplankton, causing turbidity of the water and toxicity to fish and waterbirds. This switch in aquatic flora seems to take place when the mean total phosphorus concentration in the water exceeds 100 μg l^{-1}. The changes in the aquatic ecosystem are complex and progress differently in each water body, but the overall result is always a loss of biodiversity; the water weed harbours large populations of aquatic invertebrates reliant on the plants for food and for shelter from predators such as fish. The monitoring of these changes and the realisation that the

Fig. 14.4 (a) Mechanical removal of recently developed fen carr woodland and scrub to (b) restore open water and early succession vegetation in Broadland, UK

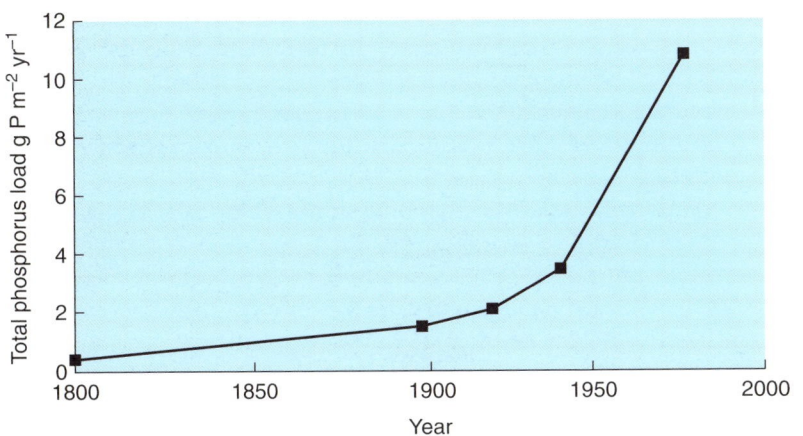

Fig. 14.5 Changes in phosphorus concentration in Barton Broad, UK from 1800 to 1970s. Data from Moss (1980) and George (1992).

whole aquatic ecosystem was becoming degraded led to a strategy for the restoration of the broads. A partnership between conservation bodies and the water authority concentrated on reducing the phosphorus inputs into the system by improved sewage treatment and diversion of sewage outlets. In a short period of time between 1978 and 1985 the phosphorus loads received by the River Ant, for example, were reduced from 40 to 4 kg per day. Mean total phosphorus concentrations in Barton Broad dropped to the target figure of 100 μg l^{-1} in 1980 but rose rapidly during the next summer as a result of phosphorus being released from the sediment surface in the broad. It was clear that rapid restoration required the removal of recent sediment layers to take out the stored phosphorus. This was successfully achieved in the smaller Cockshoot Broad in the Bure valley. Re-establishment of the aquatic plants required restocking of species and their protection in cages from grazing waterbirds. Zooplankton also had to be increased to graze off the high numbers of phytoplankton which were causing turbidity of the water and inhibiting growth of the plants. The zooplankton were kept at low numbers by the fish in the broad and the lack of hiding places among the plants. This cycle had to be broken, by excluding fish by netting them off and electrofishing. The intensive treatment has produced promising results, but constant monitoring will be required to judge long-term effectiveness of this technique (George 1992).

Where should restoration take place?

Many of the conservation methods covered in previous chapters relating to effects of fragmentation, reserve design and landscape-scale conservation can be applied to the question of where to restore habitat within a larger damaged landscape. In many areas where fragmentation has occurred there are reasonable records of what has recently been lost; however, restoration usually has to be strategic and is limited in resources, so one wants to restore an area that will be most effective in enhancing the viability of other fragments. In the case of heathland areas of Dorset, UK, Webb (1997) advocates a landscape-based approach which uses conservation principles to formulate a list of possible actions. The most important actions were thought to be:

1. reconnecting small patches to form larger ones;
2. infilling areas surrounding existing patches to minimise edge effects;
3. creation of corridors or stepping stones where existing patches are isolated.

In addition, more specialised goals may be to restore patches large enough to maintain viable populations of key endangered species such as the Dartford Warbler (*Sylvia undata*), a heathland specialist (see Chapter 9), or to restore whole water catchment areas, which would contain a gradation of vegetation from dry to wet heath.

On the basis of the earlier chapters, these all seem like sensible ideas, but do they work. Here, as in other restoration schemes it is vital that sufficient monitoring is carried out after the restoration is complete to be able to test the hypothesis that the action has been effective (see Chapters 9 & 15).

Agri-environment schemes

Agriculture has rightly been blamed for much of our habitat and species loss in the developed world. The drive for ever greater and more efficient production of food has ignored the impact on our ecosystems. Recently, governments in the European Union have recognised that subsidising farmers to overproduce crops through the Common Agricultural Policy (CAP), has a direct cost in terms of environmental degradation. This has resulted in some reform of the CAP, reducing subsidies and, in many countries, designating Environmentally Sensitive Areas (ESAs) where farmers are encouraged by grant aid to manage their land in an environmentally sensitive way. In many areas this involves taking some land out of intensive crop production and restoring more traditional farming practices that maintain higher levels of diversity and some of the rarest species. At the heart of this scheme is the assumption that land that has been intensively farmed can be restored relatively easily to high biodiversity semi-natural habitats. This will then increase the area and connectivity of these habitats to the benefit of the landscape and wildlife. It is a new approach to conservation, because it attempts to integrate the practice of agriculture with conservation of semi-natural landscapes (c.f. Chapter 12).

In the UK there are currently 43 ESAs, designated between 1986 and 1994, covering 15% of the agricultural land area (Fig. 14.6). Most ESAs concentrate on the restoration of grassland landscapes and over 8000 farmers have signed up to the scheme, covering 33% of the land area of ESAs. Not all of the resulting management agreements involve restoration, but many involve specific agreements to restore grassland where arable crops have recently been grown. This type of ecological restoration scheme appears very positive in theory, but there is limited scien-

Fig. 14.6 Location of UK Environmentally Sensitive Areas.

tific evidence, as yet, supporting the view that restoration of high-value habitats is feasible and is occurring. Gilbert & Anderson (1998) draw a distinction in this context between 'ecological' and 'political' habitat creation/restoration. The former activity attempts to restore a functioning ecosystem and its component biodiversity, the latter is undertaken for show, to create public interest for short-term political gain. As stated earlier only appropriate monitoring will sort the good scheme from the bad.

Habitat creation

The creation of new habitats that may be quite different from the original natural habitat has a questionable role in conservation. Some would argue that this is not conservation at all. Being a human construct, newly created habitat does not have the continuity of form and 'naturalness' that is normally of high value in conservation. However, the new habitat may have an amenity value and provide new space for valued plants and animals. Is there perhaps also a scientific argument for habitat creation? The process certainly suffers from all the drawbacks of habitat restoration and more; there is no evidence that we can create habitat approaching the same diversity as equivalent natural communities, except perhaps in certain circumstances where natural succession quickly takes over, such as in some wetland and aquatic habitats. Habitat creation is also rarely documented to the standards required to test a specific hypothesis that would enable us to judge its relative success. Despite this there may be circumstances in which strategic creation of a habitat may be beneficial to species in the surrounding landscape. A possible example is where communities in small water bodies (ponds and lakes) are threatened due to habitat destruction. These habitats are naturally fragmented and many species inhabiting such places survive as a type of metapopulation or patchy population, where loss of individual ponds will threaten persistence in all the others. Strategic creation of ponds in such landscapes could therefore improve chances of persistence. However, these should be monitored carefully to ensure that they are not acting as sinks (see Chapter 4) at the expense of established ponds.

It is difficult to define the boundaries between creation and restoration and appropriate creation of strategic sites can play a part in restoring a landscape, through planting of new woodland or hedgerow for example. Gilbert & Anderson (1998) put forward a process for designing new habitat that includes consideration of the context in which it is taking place (Fig. 14.7). Within this framework they identify a number of key stages as follows:

1. Objectives: it is crucial to be clear about the desired end point of the work and what you are trying to achieve.

2. Site context and integration: the objectives should be firmly embedded in the context of the surrounding landscape. Are the objectives appropriate for the area and what will the project add to the conservation value of the landscape as a whole.

3. Site survey: the site should be fully surveyed to understand its current ecology. What already exists of value and how is your action going to affect this? For example, planting a new woodland could be reducing the area of valuable grassland. Are their particular features of the site, such as nutrient levels, which may pose significant problems in the achievement of your objectives?

4. Practical work: once these considerations have been fed back into the process of setting objectives and appropriate modifications made to the project the practical process can begin. These will be so specific to the project that no generalisations can be made here.

5. Long-term management: once the initial creation process is complete the maintenance of the site will probably require regular management, such as mowing or coppicing; a plan therefore needs to be drawn up with appropriate consideration of resources and expense.

6. Long-term monitoring and dissemination: a clear plan needs to be put in place to monitor key aspects of the site in such a way that the achievement of the objectives can be tested. This will involve formulating

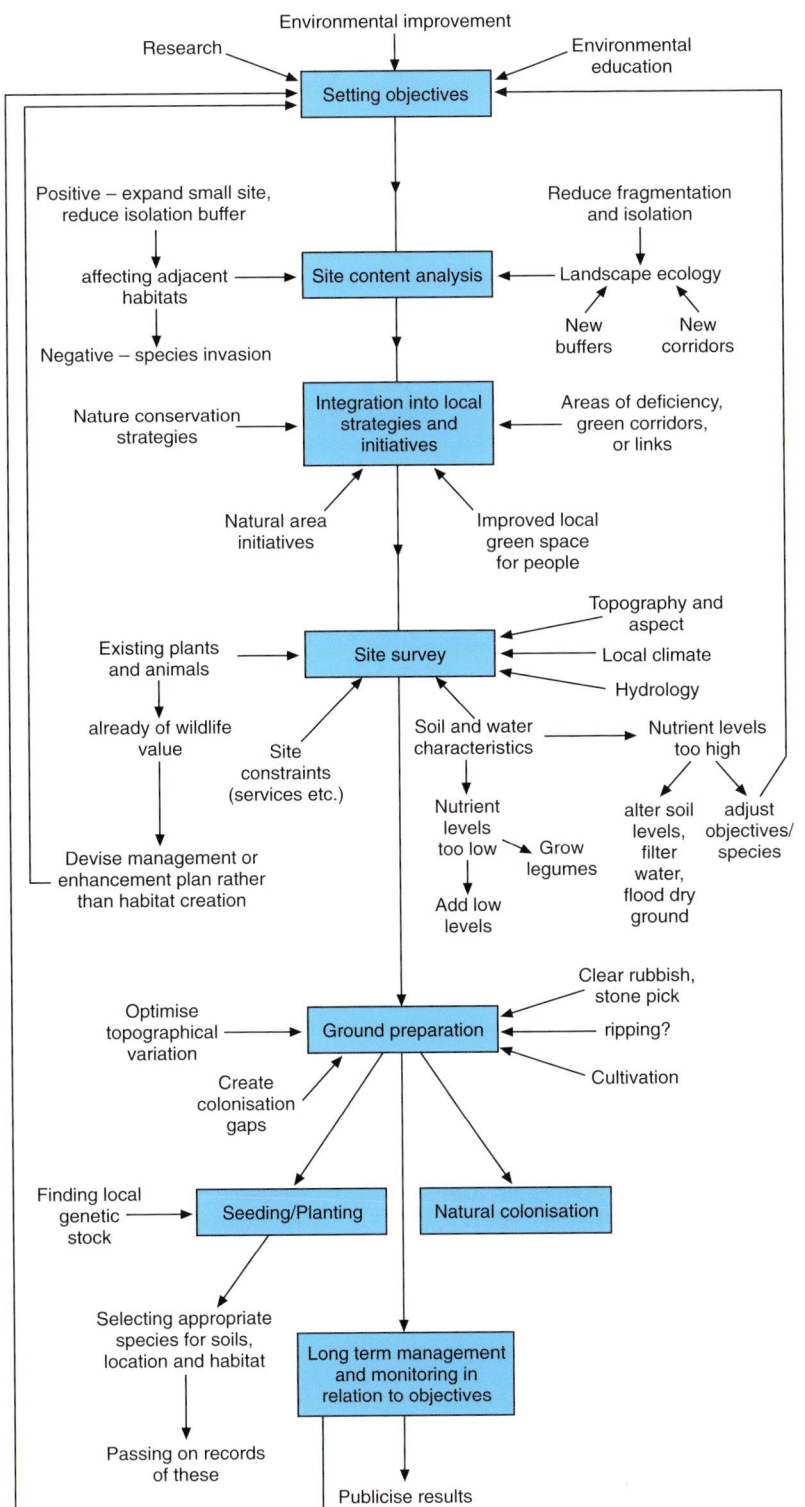

Fig. 14.7 A flow chart of the design process for habitat creation. Reproduced from Gilbert & Anderson (1998) with kind permission of Oxford University Press.

hypotheses and the monitoring programmes to test them. The results should then be made generally available (preferably published) so that the conservation community can learn from the process and improve techniques appropriately.

Few habitat creation efforts have followed the above guidelines and even fewer have achieved their objectives. Weighing up the evidence, habitat creation would seem to be on the periphery of mainstream conservation, it may be useful in certain circumstances if the required objectives are achievable, but should not, as in restoration, be used as an excuse for destruction of natural habitat.

The good and the bad of ecological restoration as conservation practice

Ecological restoration can be carried out at all scales and small-scale projects are now quite common. The process provides opportunities for local involvement (thinking globally, acting locally), doing something positive, learning by the process and the possibility of individuals and communities rediscovering the complexity and value of the natural world. These opportunities are increasing in the developed world through de-intensification of agriculture, abandonment of agricultural land, and the availability of post-industrial sites, often in close proximity to large centres of population. In the developing world restoration of degraded land offers further opportunities for preservation of land-based cultural traditions of indigenous peoples, including environmental knowledge. In essence, getting people involved in the 'health' of their local environment will make them less inclined to degrade it and more inclined to conserve it and use it more sustainably.

The constraints on ecological restoration are: the costs; the limits of what ecological restoration can do (these are very severe limits at the present time); and the danger of overly optimistic mitigation. The last is perhaps the most serious, because compensatory mitigation is frequently offered as part of development plans to limit environmental damage. The development of the practice of ecological restoration brings with it the danger that the opportunity of mitigation will increasingly be used to excuse environmentally damaging development. This problem is compounded because many environmental consultancies that are developing expertise in ecological restoration, can profit from compensatory mitigation, and some may be all too willing to claim that damage can be expertly repaired when they actually have no evidence that this is true.

Habitat translocations

One of the commonest forms of mitigation for damage is habitat translocation. This most commonly involves the removal of turfs of vegetation and top soil from the area to be developed and its translocation to a prepared area (usually near by). This is increasingly frequent in the densely populated regions of Western Europe, where space for residential and commercial development is now at a premium. In a recent survey by Bullock (1998) of 24 UK translocation efforts he found that changes in the community were *always* encountered and many of these were major, resulting from disturbance during translocation, environmental differences between the receptor and the donor sites, poor aftercare and poor management. On current evidence, habitat translocations rarely achieve their conservation goals and are certainly *not* an adequate alternative to *in situ* conservation.

Overview

The concept of restoring damaged items of value is regarded as a positive action and can be applied to components of the natural environment in a similar way to works of art. With a little encouragement and awareness-raising, this can be very much a bottom-up movement, and if properly directed can be used as a significant tool towards the goal of reinstating the vital relationship between society and its environment on which it so fundamentally depends. *But conservation must come first.* The possibility of ecological restoration should *not* be used as an excuse to allow more development that will further damage remaining natural and semi-natural systems.

Summary

1. Ecological restoration offers a positive action to turn back the tide of biodiversity loss and repair some of the damage done.

2. Ecological restoration can take place in many ways, from single species to whole ecosystems, and on many scales from the local to regional.

3. The biggest challenge for restoration is understanding the complexity of systems and how to make them work again, following disruption. Ecological restoration projects are mostly employing the ability of the system to repair itself. Practical attempts at restorations should be adequately monitored to assess reasons for success or failure.

4. Basic conservation principles laid out in earlier chapters can be used to decide where restoration should take place to gain maximum benefit for the whole system.

5. Ecological restoration can be very beneficial to local communities but can also be misused by some interest groups to argue for habitat translocation and creation schemes that have little chance of success and are rarely monitored adequately to expose their inadequacy.

Discussion points

- What is your definition of ecological restoration?
- How do you determine a reference point in time and habitat type to which you might restore an area?

- Why not just leave areas to recover from damage rather than use expensive techniques to restore them?

Further reading

Gilbert, O.L. & Anderson, P. (1998). *Habitat creation and repair.* Oxford: Oxford University Press.

Hey D.L. & Philippi, N.S. (1999). *A case for wetland restoration.* New York: Wiley.

Urbanska, K.M., Webb, N.R. & Edwards, P.J. (eds) (1997). *Restoration ecology and sustainable development.* Cambridge: Cambridge University Press.

Web sites

The Society for Ecological Restoration: www.ser.org and www.sercal.org

World Resources Institute: www.wri.org/biodiv/ecorest.html

Prairie Restoration in the USA:

edweb.fnal.gov/help/prairie/Prairie_Res/index.html

Chapter 15

Putting the science into practice

Throughout this book there has been an emphasis on the development of the science of conservation biology. It is a fast-developing subject that has benefited from the advances in related subjects, ranging from genetics to landscape ecology. The utility of conservation biology is realised through changes in conservation policy. In many cases, practical conservation lags far behind advances in the science, but equally the science may not be addressing the real problems faced by practitioners and policy-makers. This chapter explores this problem and looks for solutions and effective frameworks to enable the latest science to be put into practice and the latest questions to be addressed by scientific research.

By reading this chapter students will gain an understanding of: the problems of getting conservation science into practical action; the importance of evidence-based conservation practice; the type of framework that could facilitate improvements in conservation practice; and the barriers and limitations faced in achieving change toward more effective conservation actions.

Introduction

As the need for conservation action rapidly grows, so the demand for information on which to base that action increases. The scientific information should originate from conservation biologists, but conservation policy-makers and practitioners have to interpret the information and turn it into effective action. There is no established framework for this and it is generally left to the individual to seek out information if they wish (or have the time). Conservation practitioners are commonly faced with situations where action is needed but where information on the system they are dealing with is inadequate (either because little relevant information exists or because it is inaccessible) or conflicting. In such a situation the practitioner must rely on anecdotal information or knowledge of traditional practices, and their actions are therefore **experience-based** (action based on personal experience or disseminated information that 'it has worked before'). This does not necessarily mean that the action is wrong or ineffective, but it does not allow conservation practice to progress through scientific evaluation to produce effective actions. A scientific approach to conservation demands that actions should be **evidence-based** (action taken because scientific experimentation has indicated that it is effective in achieving the desired goals). Unfortunately, making this evidence available to the practitioner has proved a problem. Bridging the gap between scientist and practitioner is one of the biggest challenges we face in conservation.

The contrasting positions of the practitioner and the scientist

The practitioner and the scientist face very different challenges in very different circumstances, despite working towards the same goals. Rogers (1997) takes the constructive view that it is essential that the way scientists operate in ecology and managers operate in conservation gains mutual understanding and respect (Fig 15.1). Scientists operate within a structure of hypothesis generation and testing rewarded through achieving publication of their work, financial support for further research and peer recognition of their contribution to the subject. This has led to a rapid development of ecological theory that has leapt ahead of practical action (which takes much longer to implement and evaluate) and indeed, in many cases, of empirical data (which can require lengthy field experiments!). This is far removed from the pragmatic approach of conservation practitioners who operate in a world of budgets and adaptive action to try and achieve targets set out in action plans for species, habitats or reserves.

There is no dispute that a general gap exists between science and practice in many fields of biology, but it is surprising and worrying that

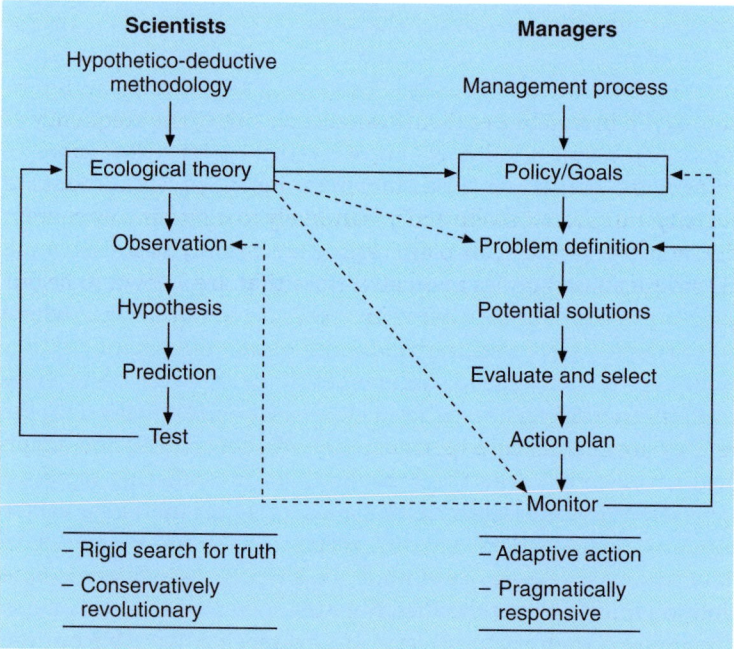

Fig. 15.1 The contrasting processes and goals of scientists and managers. Reproduced from Rogers (1997) with kind permission of Kluwer Academic Publishers.

a similar gap exists between scientists working directly in the applied field of conservation biology and their practitioner colleagues. Conservation needs both sets of people and the challenge is therefore to find a framework to bridge the gap. We can hardly blame practitioners for carrying out actions based on anecdotal evidence if the scientific research has not been done to determine the correct management action or if the research has not been disseminated in an accessible form. Practitioners will use whatever information is available and this is often limited to personal experience, gained either by themselves or their colleagues, and knowledge of the traditional land management practices that influenced the development of the habitat.

An example of the problem is the operation of grazing management regimes for the conservation of calcareous grassland communities in Europe. These grasslands are semi-natural ecosystems resulting from 'traditional' agricultural practices. In the absence of good evidence on the best form of management (e.g. what stock to use, how many head of stock and when to graze), managers rely on their interpretation of the 'traditional' practices for guidance (see Chapter 9). There are probably as many different interpretations as managers. Consequently, there is little or no consensus on effective grazing management for the mainte-nance of calcareous grassland biodiversity. Furthermore, the objectives of the traditional agriculturalist are unlikely to have been the same as those of today's conservation manager: the former was certainly not concerned with maintaining biodiversity.

A second example of traditional management is the technique of coppicing (cutting trees at base to harvest poles for fencing and basket making; the trees then regrow and are harvested on a regular cycle) of woodland blocks, which has been viewed as standard practice for main-taining open areas in woodland for the benefit of ground flora and sun-loving insects such as butterflies. The focus on these attractive but minority elements of overall woodland biodiversity has led to wide-spread use of coppicing despite the fact that mature woodland contains greater species richness, especially of shade- and moisture-loving plants and saproxylic invertebrates (Southwood *et al.* 1979). The frequency of the coppice cycle and the distribution of coppiced patches within wood-land blocks are likely to be key factors in optimising overall woodland biodiversity; but overall biodiversity is unlikely to figure in any current coppice management action plans which are usually based on tradi-tional, product-based cycles and patch sizes that are known to favour key species. Coppicing is even being imposed in some woodlands where it has never previously been practised.

The process of adaptive management has been suggested as a way forward for practitioners, in which their reserves become laboratories where they are constantly experimenting with techniques and adapt-ing their practices based on their results (Walters 1986). This approach has some merit but managers rarely have time to set up the necessary experiments, with appropriate controls and sample sizes that will give them the answers they require. It would be much more efficient to base decisions on information that already exists.

A key issue is that often the scientific evidence is available but the framework does not exist to ensure that it is used in formulating action plans. There is no general mechanism by which managers are challenged to justify their plans by citing scientific evidence, although specific examples exist such as the legal requirement under the US Endangered Species Act (Box 15.1). Prendergast *et al.* (1999) take the example of reserve selection (see Chapter 7) to emphasise the abundant theory that exists, in contrast to the obvious lack of its use in practice. Their proposed solution is an improvement in communication and therefore understanding of the issues. Conservation biologists tend to see species and habitats as the major issue, whereas practitioners face planning regulations and issues of land ownership together with costs of maintenance and labour. Mechanisms must be put in place to bring the two groups closer together and increase the flow of information in both directions. Practitioners need to be able to tell scientists what their most pressing problems are and scientists need to be able to effectively communicate possible solutions.

Box 15.1 | The US Endangered Species Act

The Endangered Species Act (ESA) was passed as law in the United States in 1973. The responsibility for its administration falls to the US Fish and Wildlife Service (FWS). Species listed under the ESA receive protection from persecution, trade and destruction of habitat, and plans are developed for the species' recovery.

Nicholopoulos (1999) identified five factors that were taken into account when considering a species for listing under the Act:

1. the present or threatened destruction, modification, or curtailment of the species' habitat or range;
2. overutilisation for commercial, recreational, scientific or educational purposes;
3. disease or predation;
4. the inadequacy of existing regulatory mechanisms; and
5. other natural or man-made factors affecting the species' continued existence.

Species can be considered for protection under the Act either through identification by the FWS itself or by petition by any interested person or body. If the latter occurs the FWS must reach an initial decision on whether to proceed within 90 days through the petition process shown in Fig. 15.2. The key stages in this process are the evaluation of the data provided by the petitioner, the acquisition of additional data available to assess the species' status and the threat to its survival, and the peer review process which enables independent experts to comment on the accuracy and reliability of the scientific information. This therefore serves as an example of a mechanism by which scientific data can be used directly to inform conservation action through a formal process.

Evidence-based conservation: lessons from medicine and public health

As mentioned in Chapter 7, conservation is a crisis discipline, and in this sense it has often been compared with medicine in that decisions have to be taken quickly with incomplete knowledge of the present situation

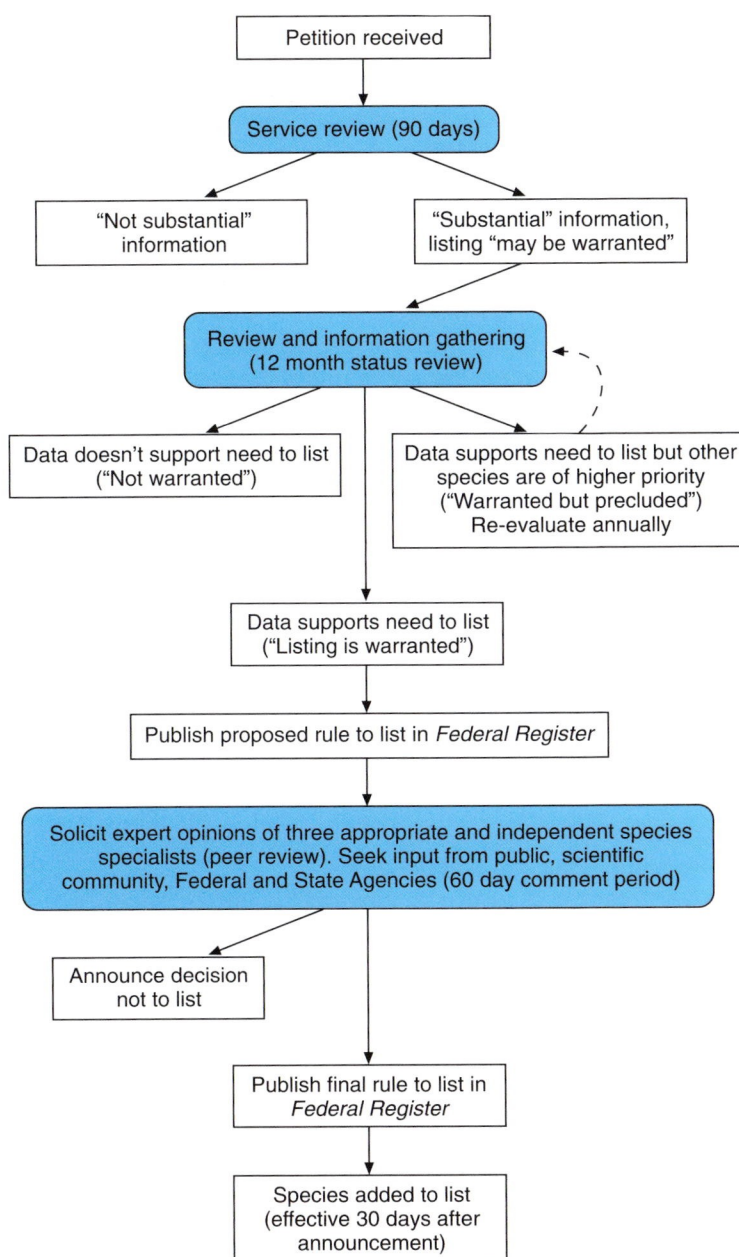

Fig. 15.2 A flow chart illustrating the petition process for listing species under the US Endangered Species Act. Reproduced from Nicholopoulos (1999) with kind permission of the US Fish and Wildlife Service.

or of the possible consequences of our actions. Both disciplines also contain key moral and ethical elements that often present us with dilemmas. For centuries medicine has progressed by trial and error because of the necessity of action without sufficient knowledge of the system (the human body and its diseases). The extent of medical research today is vast compared with conservation biology, and the practice of medicine is far better developed and resourced. Yet the relationship between scientist and practitioner is almost exactly the same (Pullin & Knight 2001). The medical practitioner wishes to base the management of human health on the best available evidence. To this end medicine has been through an **effectiveness revolution** essentially about 'cost effectiveness' and 'evidence-based action'. Translated, this means 'what works and what doesn't', and at what cost. An early pioneer was Cochrane (1972), who advocated use of the 'randomised controlled trial' (patients are randomly assigned to either treatment or control groups) to assess the effectiveness of medical treatments and procedures. The public were appalled to learn how few commonly used procedures had been rigorously evaluated in this way. Equally shocking was the notion that where such research had been carried out, it was being largely ignored by practitioners. A whole sub-branch of the revolution developed, aimed at 'getting research into practice', and the policy decisions were made to reduce the number of less effective procedures carried out.

The concept of basing decisions on 'evidence of effectiveness' has now been extended to the wider health field covering the promotion of health and prevention of disease and into determining management policy. Essentially, the process is about ensuring that decision-making, be it at the level of choice of treatment for a particular medical condition or at the level of national policy-making, is based on good quality research evidence of the effectiveness of the planned intervention. There are three key stages in the process:

- Ensuring that good quality research, relevant to the important public health needs, is funded and conducted.
- Critical assessment of research against rigorous criteria to ensure that policy and practice are informed by good quality research.
- The establishment of mechanisms whereby such research evidence is translated into policy and practice.

A major development in evaluating existing scientific evidence on a given subject has been that of **'systematic reviews'** that help to translate the results of research into practice. A systematic review is itself a form of research. It takes the findings of primary research and evaluates them as a combined data set. Obviously some research is better than others and a 'hierarchy of evidence' has been developed to help judge the quality of the research design (Table 15.1). This method rates as most important those findings of the most rigorous studies and enables the rejection of studies that are considered unreliable or flawed, based on their design. Systematic reviews are at their most straightforward when all the research studies on a particular topic have used good quality RCT methodology. In these cases, the results of all the separate trails are combined and re-analysed in a 'meta-analysis' (data sets are combined and subjected to statistical analysis to test a hypothesis). This is undertaken using the original raw data when available. As a minimum, however, the systematic review would summarise and tabulate the main design features of comparable studies such as target population and sample size and also the results, noting where there is consistency or dissonance in the findings. The field has now advanced so much that there are 'rules' for conducting systematic reviews and special training courses are organised to teach the methodology. There are also entire institutions dedicated to undertaking systematic reviews. The effectiveness revolution has spawned an impressive industry.

Table 15.1	Hierarchy of quality of evidence based on the type of research undertaken

Category	Quality of evidence
I	Strong evidence obtained from at least one properly designed, randomised controlled trial of appropriate size
II-1	Evidence from well-designed controlled trials without randomisation
II-2	Evidence from well-designed co-host or case-controlled analytic studies, preferably from more than one centre or research group
II-3	Evidence obtained from multiple time series or from dramatic results in uncontrolled experiments
III	Opinions of respected authorities based on clinical evidence, descriptive studies or reports of expert committees
IV	Evidence inadequate owing to problems of methodology, e.g. sample size, length or comprehensiveness of follow-up or conflicts of evidence

Source: Stevens & Milne (1997).

Relevance of the effectiveness revolution to Conservation

Pullin & Knight (2001) argue that, just as in medicine and public health, conservation action should not remain largely experience based. We can no longer accept management practices that remain untested by proper scientific methods, and which are justified purely on personal experience or anecdotal evidence. We would not allow a doctor to embark on a new line of treatment for their patients based solely on the fact that it worked on the last patient they tried it on! For the same reasons, we should no longer give unqualified support to conservation practices that are untested by proper scientific methods, and justified purely on personal experience or anecdotal evidence. Experience clearly has its place in conservation and is a valued commodity, but there is a difference between using one's experience to increase the effectiveness of a specific action, and promoting wider use of that action based on personal experience alone. The requirement for urgent action may necessitate the continuation of some experience-based practices, and achieving the highest level of evidence (Table 15.1) may be difficult when dealing with rare species or ecosystems, but the identification of such situations should help focus appropriate research to evaluate effectiveness. The argument that conservation activities are an experiment in themselves does not hold if the experiment is poorly designed. The issue is how to enable practitioners to enter an era of evidence-based conservation action.

Good examples of reviews already exist in the literature, but they are few in number, especially those that contain some elements of a systematic review (e.g. Griffith *et al.* 1989; Dodd & Seigel 1991; Hobbs & Huenneke 1992; Bender *et al.* 1998; Menges 2000; Buckland *et al.* 2000).

Hartley & Hunter (1998) combined 13 separate studies to analyse the effect of forest cover and edge effects on bird nest predation rates. Each of the 13 studies had used some form of artificial nest and although many aspects of the studies such as period of exposure varied, they were sufficiently similar to combine. The results of these studies suggested that daily nest predation rates decreased as forest cover increased over spatial scales from 5 to 25 km. However, edge effects became significant only in highly fragmented landscapes. More systematic reviews need to be undertaken and conservation journals should encourage their publication. Furthermore, production of these reviews should be seen as good practice in government-based conservation bodies, particularly those in a position to fund conservation projects.

The way forward

Analysis of the key changes within the medical effectiveness revolution provides an instructive framework with which to move conservation into an era of evidence-based action. The basic steps for each conservation organisation are:

- Formulate policy that action should be evidence-based.
- Promote methods of systematic review with provision of funding.
- Identify priority areas for systematic review.
- Identify gaps in knowledge and prioritise these for research funding.
- Develop mechanisms to promote and maintain the concept of evidence-based practice among practitioners.

Can the above framework be operated within current conservation infrastructures? Conservation managers are not subject to the same sorts of regulation as medics or other public health practitioners, but most governments do have statutory conservation bodies that can set standards that others should follow. Conservation bodies involved in the management of land or species for conservation should examine their management actions and consider:

1. On what quality of evidence is this action based (see Table 15.1)?
2. What action is required to improve the quality of that evidence and thus the justification for the management?

Some organisations may be pleased with the answers they can provide to these questions whilst others may find them useful in improving their standards.

So how might we enable practitioners to move away from experience-based toward evidence-based actions? A direct way to get the message across is to encourage organisations that fund conservation action (governmental and non-governmental) to discriminate between experience- and evidence-based practice when deciding on allocation of grants. Many organisations act simultaneously as conservation manager through their ownership of nature reserves, as policy-maker through their role as advisor to government, and as grant provider for both research and management. They are thus in a unique position to do the following: (1) formulate policy on evidence-based action; (2) identify priority areas for systematic review and provide appropriate funding; (3) commission the appropriate research where evidence is found to be lacking by the systematic review process; and (4) set

Table 15.2 Summary of the typical content of a reserve management plan

Sections of management plan	Content of section
Description of site	Location, size, site history, geology, topography, climate, soils, hydrology, general ecological classification, position within the surrounding landscape, current use
Conservation evaluation	Historic and current conservation status, features of value on the site (species diversity, naturalness, representative communities), threats to site, potential value, specific species of note
Management aims and objectives	Hydrology, plant communities, specific species, education and research
Limitations and constraints	Limitations of site, natural processes, outside influences, disturbance, pollution, problem species, legal constraints, resources, safety
Management prescription	Specific projects, rationale, objectives (including definitions of success), work schedule, research plans and methodology
Monitoring of actions	Project monitoring and evaluation, time scale and project reporting
Appendices	Maps, data sheets, protocols

minimum standards of conservation practice for grants given and promote this among practitioners.

Formulation of action plans: an opportunity to bridge the gap

A fundamental part of conservation planning is the production of an action plan. These are most commonly produced for species, habitats or reserves and set out the course of action over a specified period and the monitoring necessary to evaluate progress in achieving objectives. It is the construction and approval process of action plans that offers the best opportunity for getting evidence-based action into conservation practice and also for identifying areas where scientific research is required. Let us first look at the typical form of an action plan and then explore ways of incorporating evidence.

The most common form of action plan is probably the reserve management plan. The typical content of such a plan is summarised in Table 15.2. This format has generally been followed by reserve managers and conservation organisations that own or manage reserves. As a framework it is very useful and encourages reserve managers to think ahead and formulate objectives rather than just dealing with the day-to-day

Table 15.3	Summary of the content of UK Species Action Plans
Action Plan sections	Content of section
Part 1. Overview	Statement of conservation status and priority for action, legal status, summary of actions to be undertaken and timetable
Part 2. Biological assessment	Summary of knowledge of species ecology, distribution, population trends, threats and limiting factors and conservation action taken to date
Part 3. Actions and work programme	Proposed actions in the following areas: policy and legislation, advisory, site safeguard, international, land acquisition and reserve management, future research and monitoring, species management and protection, communication and publicity

challenges, but it does not encourage the use of scientific evidence to formulate actions.

The format for UK species action plans has been set out in the UK Biodiversity Action Plan: a document produced in response to the Rio Summit meeting (see Chapter 7). The basic plan is set out as in Table 15.3. Species and Habitat Action Plan formats (see examples in Boxes 15.2 and 15.3 respectively) encourage the gathering together of the literature on the species ecology and conservation but they do not explicitly require the compilers to justify their proposed actions by citing evidence for their effectiveness. Consequently, many current actions carried out by conservation organisations, government organisations and private companies are undertaken without any clear scientific rationale. Despite this their benefit is rarely questioned and almost never evaluated. This is partly because the scientific information is lacking or inaccessible, but partly because the link between science and practice is not formalised.

Box 15.2 | Example species action plans

Example 1. Corncrake (*Crex crex*)

1. Current status

1.1. over the last 100 years the corncrake has shown a sustained decline in numbers in the UK and a contraction in range. By the early 1970s there were only 3250 calling males, falling to 478 in 1993. Over 90% of calling males are located in the Hebrides, with the remainder in Orkney (all these islands off the Scottish coast). There are very few in England and Wales and, in recent years, few calling males in Northern Ireland.

1.2. The corncrake is a globally threatened species. It is listed on Appendix II of the Bern Convention and Annex I of the European Community Birds Directive. In the UK it is protected under Schedule I of the Wildlife and Countryside Act 1981 and the Wildlife (Northern Ireland) Order 1985.

2. Current factors causing loss or decline

2.1. Loss of traditional grassland habitat mosaics, especially tall vegetation throughout the breeding season.

2.3. Changes in grass management and cutting techniques (e.g. earlier cutting).

2.4. Predation and disturbance may be contributing to the decline in some localities.

3. Current action

3.1. Approximately 10% of the British corncrake population is protected on nature reserves.

3.2. Corncrake grant schemes, under the Joint Corncrake Initiative, provide incentives for corncrake-friendly grass cutting and management to protect corncrakes, but it is hoped to supersede this approach by improved Environmentally Sensitive Area (ESA) prescriptions with advice to land managers.

4. Action Plan objectives and targets

4.1. The reasons for decline of this species have been elucidated by an excellent programme of research and the means of reversing the decline are now known. This species responds rapidly to favourable management of meadows and an increase in numbers and range is perfectly feasible.

4.2. Halt the decline in UK corncrake population and range.

4.3. Maintain the numbers of corncrakes in the UK at or above the 1993 level.

4.4. Maintain the range of corncrakes in the UK at or above the 1993 level (82 occupied 10 km squares).

4.5. By 1998, increase the range of the corncrake in Britain to at least the same number of 10 km squares occupied in 1988 (90 squares).

4.6. In the longer term re-establish corncrakes in parts of their former range in the UK.

5. Proposed action with lead agencies

5.1. Policy and legislation

5.1.1. Support and promote the uptake of corncrake grant schemes in Scotland and Northern Ireland.

5.1.2. Support and promote the uptake of ESA agreements and review the effectiveness of existing ESAs in Scotland. Seek to improve where necessary.

5.1.3. If existing ESAs are effective as conservation measures, consider designating remaining core corncrake areas in the Western Isles, Inner Hebrides and Orkney as ESAs, to encourage continued hay production and sympathetic management.

5.2. Site safeguard and management

5.2.1. Seek to secure favourable management on all suitable land within designated sites, and in all non-designated areas supporting populations of corncrake.

5.2.2. Consider designating sites of particular importance as Sites of Special Scientific Interest (SSSI).

5.3. Species management and protection

5.3.1. Seek to reduce damage to nests and mortality of adults and young from mowing operations by wardening and promoting corncrake-friendly techniques.

5.3.2. Ensure crofters and farmers are advised of risks to species from predation by domestic cats, and support local mink and ferret control, preventing their spread to new areas.

5.4. Advisory

5.4.1. Provide advice to agricultural advisors and to all those managing corncrake areas, on corncrake-friendly cutting methods and other beneficial management practices.

5.4.2. Provide advice on corncrake-friendly management techniques to agricultural colleges to aid their inclusion in land management courses.

5.5. Future research and monitoring

5.5.1. Conduct a full survey of the breeding population of corncrake in Britain and Northern Ireland every three years.

5.5.2. Study economic, technical and agronomic aspects of modifying grassland management in key corncrake areas to benefit the species.

5.5.3. Investigate the responses of corncrakes to approaching mowing machinery, and conduct 'after mowing' surveys to assess the density of nests and broods, and the mortality rate. Seek to identify the least damaging time for mowing.

5.5.4. Investigate levels of mortality due to cat, mink and feral ferret predation and assess the possibility of reducing mortality.

5.5.5. Encourage annual monitoring of breeding numbers and periodic surveys of habitat at key sites.

5.5.6. Review the factors affecting corncrake migration and wintering grounds.

5.5.7. Pass information gathered during survey and monitoring of this species to the Biological Records Centre so that it can be incorporated in national databases.

5.5.8. Provide information annually to BirdLife International on the UK status of the species to contribute to maintenance of an up-to-date global Red List.

5.6. Communication and publicity

5.6.1. Consider projects to develop controlled 'green tourism' based on the species.

5.6.2. Consider publishing a code of practice for birdwatching to reduce the pressure on this species in sensitive areas.

Example 2: Starfruit (*Damasonium alisma*)

1. Current status

1.1. Starfruit occurs in muddy or gravel margins of shallow ponds with seasonally fluctuating water levels on commons or village greens. It was formerly recorded in several English counties northward to Shropshire and Yorkshire but, by 1990, the species was restricted to three native sites: one in Surrey and two in Buckinghamshire. Populations of starfruit are subject to wide fluctuations: one site in Buckinghamshire produced 300 plants in 1992, following pond clearance, but a total of only 15 plants occurred in 1994 at two native sites, probably as a result of high winter rainfall.

1.2. The UK represents the northern edge of the species' range, with a scattered distribution across Europe, from Spain to Asia Minor and North Africa. It is listed as endangered on the GB Red List and is protected under Schedule 8 of the Wildlife and Countryside Act 1981.

2. Current factors causing loss or decline

2.1. Neglect and mismanagement of ponds on grazed commons or greens, including overshading by trees and shrubs, with associated collection of leaf litter and the excessive growth of submerged and marginal plants.

2.2. Loss of habitat through development, drainage and infilling of pools and wet hollows.

2.3. Introduction of water level controls reducing seasonal fluctuations.

2.4. Introduction of invasive, non-native species of water plants.

3. Current action

3.1. Recovery work has been undertaken on this species since 1990 to relocate former sites and establish whether any remain suitable for regeneration of the seed bank.

3.2. Reintroduction has been attempted at several sites including a pond specially created for starfruit in 1994. Long-term monitoring at these sites will determine whether reintroduction has been successful.

3.3. Work at the Royal Botanic Gardens, Kew has included both seed storage and germination techniques.

4. *Action Plan objectives and targets*

4.1. Safeguard populations at all known sites, including considering SSSI notification.

4.2. Establish suitable conditions and restore to a minimum of ten former sites by 2004.

4.3. Organise long-term management of the restored ponds to ensure the plant's future survival.

5. *Proposed actions with lead agencies*

5.1. Policy and legislation

5.1.1. No action proposed.

5.2. Site safeguard and management

5.2.1. Promote measures to maintain water quality at all extant sites

5.2.2. Control marginal and submerged vegetation in the area around any starfruit populations and ensure that bare substrate is provided for germination.

5.2.3. Prepare and promote an appropriate water level management plan for sites containing this species.

5.2.4. Restore appropriate management at former sites with a view to regeneration from seed bank or reintroduction.

5.2.5. Consider the need to notify sites as SSSIs.

5.3. Species management and protection

5.3.1. Collect and deposit seeds from all sites in the National Seed Bank.

5.3.2. Continue programme of restoration and, following analysis of previous attempts, aim to restore ten populations to suitable sites by 2004. Where reintroduction is attempted, ensure the use of seed of local provenance only.

5.4. Advisory

5.4.1. Ensure landowners, managers and local authorities are aware of the presence, legal status and importance of conserving this species and appropriate methods of habitat management.

5.5. Future research and monitoring

5.5.1. Survey former sites with a view to regeneration of the seed bank or identification of suitable sites for reintroduction.

5.5.2. Monitor population size, water quality and water levels at all sites regularly.

5.5.3. Work closely with other European countries to establish the status, ecology and conservation requirements of this species and use information and expertise towards its conservation in the UK.

5.5.4. Pass information gathered during survey and monitoring of this species to Biological Records Centre for incorporation in national databases.

5.5.5. Provide information annually to the World Conservation Monitoring Centre on the UK status of the species to contribute to the maintenance of an up-to-date global Red Data list.

5.6. Communication and publicity

5.6.1. Ensure local communities are made aware of the presence and importance of this species and the reasons for carrying out management.

Box 15.3 | Habitat action plan for Fens

1. Current status

The UK is thought to host a large proportion of fen surviving in the European Union. As in other parts of Europe fen vegetation has declined dramatically in the past century.

Fen habitats support a diversity of plant and animal communities. Some can contain up to 550 species of higher plants, a third of our native plant species; up to and occasionally more than half the UK's species of dragonflies, several thousands of other insect species, as well as being an important habitat for a range of aquatic beetles.

In intensively farmed areas fens occur less frequently, are smaller in size and more isolated than in other parts of the UK. There are, however, exceptions to this. The UK's largest area of base-poor fen, the Insh marshes in the floodplain of the River Spey in Scotland, covers an area of 300 ha, the calcareous rich fen and swamp of Broadland covers an area of 3000 ha and the Lough Erne system in Fermanagh has extensive areas of fen and swamp. In some lowland areas such as the scottish borders and southern Northern Ireland there are concentrations of small fens of particular importance.

2. Current factors affecting the habitat

Fens are dynamic semi-natural systems and in general management is needed to maintain open-fen communities and their associated species richness. Without appropriate management (e.g. mowing, grazing, burning, peat-cutting, scrub clearance), natural succession will lead to scrub and woodland forming. Current factors affecting this habitat type are:

- Past loss of area by drainage and conversion to intensive agriculture.
- Excessive water abstraction from aquifers has dried up or reduced spring-line flows, and generally lowered water tables. Abstraction also has affected the natural balance between the differing water qualities of groundwater and surface water.
- Small total area of habitat and critically small population sizes of several key species dependent on the habitat.
- Lack of or inappropriate management of existing fens leading to drying, scrub encroachment and succession to woodland.
- Valley fens are particularly susceptible to agricultural runoff and afforestation within the catchment.
- Enrichment or hypertrophication resulting in changing plant communities.

3. Current action

3.1 Legal status

The majority of fens are notified as SSSIs and many are notified as Wetlands of International Importance under the Ramsar Convention and as Special Protection Areas under the European Community (EC) Birds Directive. Several of the larger fens are managed as NNRs or other nature reserves. Several types of fens are listed in the EC Habitats Directive including transition mire, poor and rich fen and alkaline fen, and a number have been proposed as Special Areas for Conservation (SACs).

3.2 Management research and guidance

The Countryside Council for Wales (CCW) has an active programme of positive management focused on NNRs and undertakes active management to restore favourable conditions to key fen sites.

The Broads Authority conducts a fen management programme within their executive area in association with English Nature, who negotiate management agreements with owners/occupiers for reedbed management. The Broads ESA and Suffolk rivers ESA both play an important role in protecting the fens.

The statutory conservation agencies have negotiated several management agreements on SSSIs to help secure sympathetic fen management and have worked with key partners to create an extensive fen on former peat workings in the Somerset levels. Statutory conservation agency staff provide advice to a range of fen owners on appropriate management, rehabilitation extension and creation. Voluntary and statutory agency staff monitor the population size and productivity of key fen species.

The Environment Agency has been encouraged to incorporate fen protection, management or creation in its catchment and shoreline management plans. Many fens are subject to water level management plans prepared by flood defence operating authorities.

4. Action Plan objectives and proposed targets

Identify priority fen sites in critical need of rehabilitation and initiate action by 2005. All rich fen and other sites with rare communities should be considered.

Ensure appropriate water quality and water quantity for the continued existence of all SSSI fens by 2005.

5. Action required

5.1. Policy and legislation

Review water quality and set standards for fens by 1998 through the appropriate government agencies and departments. Aim to meet these targets by year 2010.

Review water resource uses by 1998 and aim to meet these targets where they affect fens by year 2010.

Consider modifying or expanding existing habitat and countryside schemes such as ESAs and Nitrate Sensitive Areas to encourage the protection of fens from agricultural contaminants.

Prepare and implement water level management plans.

5.2. Site safeguard and management

Continue to notify important sites as SSSIs by 1998.

Progress with the existing programme for designation as Ramsar, SPA and SACs by the year 2004.

Ensure that development schemes do not affect the integrity or the conservation interest of fens.

Agree a list of fens requiring remedial treatment by 1998.

Ensure that favourable management is in place for priority fen sites by 2005, by NNR establishment and SSSI management agreement or equivalent.

5.3. Advisory

Agree conservation strategies with relevant statutory and non-statutory agencies.

Initiate or participate in training courses appropriate to the management of fens.

5.4. International

Promote the interchange of management techniques, conservation strategies and cooperation on research affecting fens.

5.5. Future research and monitoring

Undertake necessary research to inform and monitor attempts to restore and re-create rich fen and related habitats.

Promote research into the ecology of fen species, particularly in relation to water quality, water quantity and management requirements.

5.6. Communication and publicity

No action proposed.

Costings

The successful implementation of the action plan will have resource implications for both the private and public sectors. The data below provide a preliminary estimate of the likely resource costs to the public sector in the years 1997, 2000 and 2010.

The data are based on targets whereby 1200 hectares of fens will be appropriately maintained and improved through to 2010. Costs: 1997 (£40000): 2000 (£70000): 2010 (£70000).

Models for combining science and practice

If the current protocols for the production of action plans are not encouraging the use of scientific information in conservation practice, then what changes need to be made?

One way of addressing this problem was presented by Meffe *et al.* (1998), who called for the establishment of an independent scientific review process to be established as part of the planning review in US resource management. They state the goals of independent scientific review are to help ensure that:

1. the best available scientific knowledge is brought into the decision- or policy-making process;
2. the influences of bias and special interests are minimised;
3. science is separated clearly from non-scientific issues;
4. decisions or policies are achieved in an open and transparent manner;
5. all relevant information is considered and evaluated;
6. all conclusions drawn are consistent with the available scientific information;
7. the risks associated with different interpretations of data or alternative management decisions are articulated.

This is certainly a useful model but one that will be far more familiar to the scientist than the practitioner.

A further mechanism is for the scientific community to provide a **decision support system** (DSS) to practitioners to provide information that will help them make decisions both in formulating action plans and also in the management process during the operation of the plan. The DSS acts as an interface between the scientist and the practitioner. The scientist feeds information to the DSS as it becomes available and the practitioner uses the DSS as a tool kit in making decisions and solving problems in everyday management.

This type of approach is currently being used in the Kruger National Park in South Africa in their Kruger Rivers Programme. Here the challenge is to be able to predict and monitor effects of changes in river

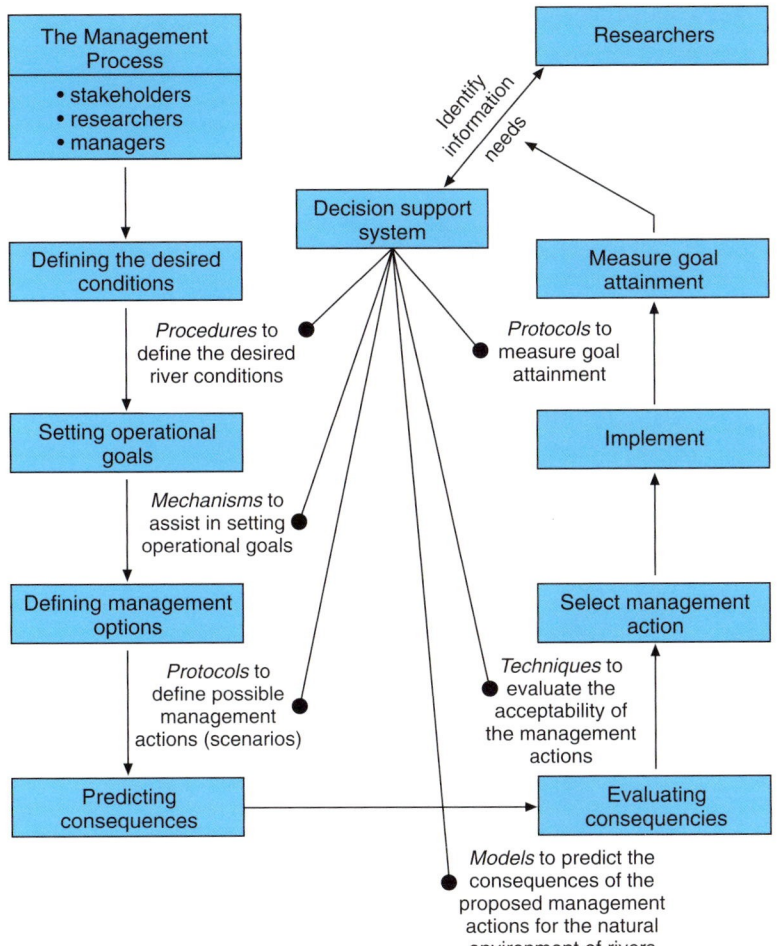

The Management Process
- stakeholders
- researchers
- managers

Defining the desired conditions

Procedures to define the desired river conditions

Setting operational goals

Mechanisms to assist in setting operational goals

Defining management options

Protocols to define possible management actions (scenarios)

Predicting consequences

Decision support system

Identify information needs

Researchers

Measure goal attainment

Protocols to measure goal attainment

Implement

Select management action

Techniques to evaluate the acceptability of the management actions

Evaluating consequences

Models to predict the consequences of the proposed management actions for the natural environment of rivers

Fig. 15.3 A Decision Support System for conservation management in the Kruger National Park, South Africa. Reproduced from Rogers (1997) with kind permission of Kluwer Academic.

hydrology on the biodiversity in different sections of the river catchment. A DSS has been constructed that feeds ecological information into the process of management at all key stages of decision-making (Fig. 15.3). The model uses the DSS to help in the key areas of setting objectives for management, predicting the outcomes of management actions and in monitoring the response of the system to management actions and natural events (Rogers 1997). This approach has considerable strengths but it does assume that partnerships between scientists and practitioners have already been formed around a common challenge. How do we get to this stage?

A more process-based model that involves modification of action plans to encourage evidence-based practice may be seen by practitioners as a more adaptable process that can form the basis for many types of action (species or habitat based) that may look very different in their final form. Most conservation practitioners now formulate action plans of one kind or another as part of a conservation planning and resource allocation process, either within conservation organisations or in

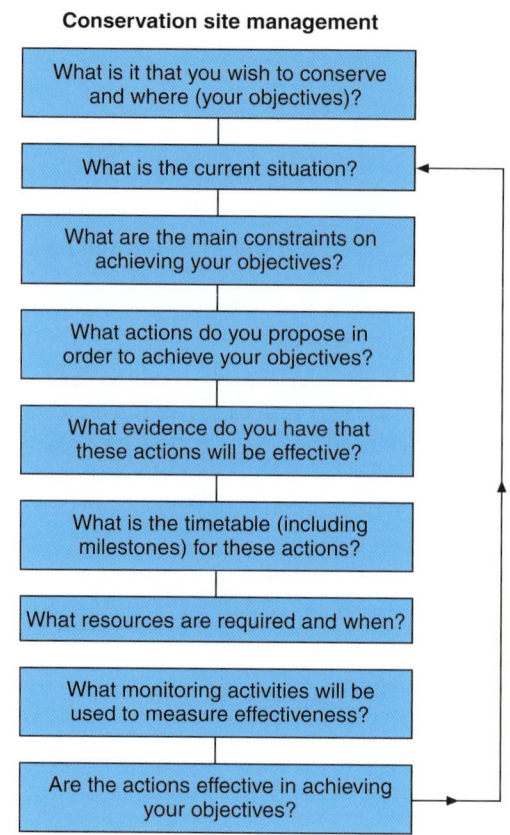

competing for resources (funds) from other institutions. It is at the formulation stage that the action should be justified through citing of evidence or the lack of relevant information identified and plans for research produced. The flow of resources for the plan should be consequent on these qualities and at the same time needs for research and decision support systems identified and the research commissioned. A flow diagram for the production of a generalised action plan that encourages evidence-based practice is shown in Fig. 15.4. A key addition is the section or stage where evidence has to be cited in support of the action(s) proposed. The quality of this evidence should also be assessed according to the guidelines in Table 15.1. As a result of this assessment, the compilers must decide if there is sufficient evidence simply to undertake this action or, if there is insufficient evidence of effectiveness, how the action will be pursued so as to test its effectiveness (usually in the form of a research programme or experiment). Crucially the latter does not mean that the actions are delayed as long as they are judged to be the best option, only that they should be undertaken in a provisional and precautionary way until their effectiveness has been demonstrated. Proper monitoring and evaluation of the actions can then lead to the progression to the next stage of actions through a periodic review process.

Taking action

I hope that throughout this book you have been given the impression that significant advances are being made in the science of conservation biology. But equally, I hope that it is clear that much remains to be done and there is considerable need and urgency for this work. Future generations will judge us by the actions we take and at some point we all have to put our knowledge to good use.

As the finale to this book I think it a useful exercise for the reader to combine all the knowledge gained from previous chapters and try to apply this in a practical context. This is, after all, what conservation biology is all about. Box 15.4 supplies background information on a UK nature reserve in sufficient detail for you to be able to construct a management action plan using the model provided in Fig. 15.4. You will need to seek evidence from other sources on the effectiveness of conservation actions to inform your decision-making, just as you would in the real situation. The problems are typical of small isolated reserves and the challenges are considerable. Over to you.

Box 15.4 | Case study in reserve management

Write a management plan for Woodwalton Fen National Nature Reserve based on the plan and information given. Use your knowledge of conservation biology and the appropriate general points made earlier in the book to put forward your own proposals for management. Think critically about the current management and suggest how it might be improved and provide justification for any changes you would make. Remember to base your decisions on evidence and make it clear where research is required to provide evidence.

You should address major problems that the reserve management team faces such as:

1. reserve size and isolation
2. succession of vegetation
3. hydrology
4. pollution, including eutrophication
5. management of small populations

You should also assume that resources are limited and that grand schemes are unlikely in the short term.

Woodwalton National Nature Reserve, Cambridgeshire, UK

The following case study considers a nature reserve that has many features that present challenges for management which are typical of the UK and continental European situation.

Background

The fenlands of eastern England formerly covered an area totalling some 1500 km² stretching from Lincoln in the north to Cambridge in the south. This area was progressively drained for agriculture from the sixteenth century until, by the late nineteenth century, only small fragments remained, representing just 3% of the original area (Fig. 4.1, p. 77). One of these remaining fragments of relict peatland is Woodwalton Fen National Nature Reserve. This might itself have been lost if an area of it had not been purchased in 1910 by N.C. Rothschild as an area for sport shooting of wildfowl and other game birds. In 1919 it was presented to the Society for the Promotion of Nature Reserves along with some surrounding land. It was leased to the Nature Conservancy Council and declared a National Nature Reserve in 1954. Today it covers an area of 210 hectares.

Its history is complex because it did not escape drainage and reclamation completely. It is possible, from stratigraphical studies of the peat, to show that the fen was once covered by a greater depth of peat allowing the development of acid mire vegetation under the influence of acid rain water. It is now criss-crossed by a drainage system which was cut in the mid-nineteenth century and used as access for peat-cutters who probably removed most of the surface peat suitable for fuel. The maximum depth of the peat is now 3.5 m. Following the removal of much of the surface peat over the northern two-thirds of the reserve, peat influenced by base-rich groundwater from surrounding calcareous ridges was exposed. Fen vegetation has therefore developed over an artificial surface. Some areas appear to have been farmed, involving grazing and hay cutting. These activities probably continued until its purchase in 1910. Acid peat still remains in the farmed area at the southern end of the reserve.

The surrounding land has been ploughed and used for intensive agriculture, particularly in the last 50 years. The exposed peat has oxidised and decomposed, causing it to shrink and the soil surface to fall below the level of the fen. Wind erosion has also played its part in this process. The fen surface is now several metres above the surrounding land. Maintaining a high water table has therefore become a totally artificial process. Water comes in from the surrounding upland hills to the Great Raveley drain which flows along its east side. This can then be pumped on to the reserve and kept there by a series of sluices. It is not an entirely controlled system as the water in the drain is controlled by the water authority and in times of high water levels the reserve receives flood water. This is common and probably beneficial for periods during the winter, but can cause problems if extended over long or unseasonal periods.

Pollution problems include the increasing eutrophic status of the water entering the fen system from surrounding agricultural land, causing the spread of nutrient loving competitive weeds such as stinging nettle, *Urtica dioica*. Additionally, crop spraying of the surrounding land is often done by aircraft and the potential for spray drift of herbicides and pesticides is considerable.

The ecology of the fen

Fenland is relatively nutrient-rich and vegetational succession can take place rapidly making this a very dynamic system. There are two recognised seres (pathways of vegetation succession) on the fen: the *Molinia–Betula* sere on acid peat and the *Calamagrostis, Phragmites–Salix* sere on basic peat. There are currently several types of early successional plant communities present which are described as open fen and swamp. Where acid peat remains the vegetation typically includes purple moorgrass, *Molinia caerulea*, with ling heather, *Calluna vulgaris*, bog myrtle, *Myrica gale*, tormentil, *Potentilla erecta*, and saw sedge, *Cladium mariscus*. The base-rich areas are dominated by purple small-reed (a grass), *Calamagrostis epigejos*, but often forms a herb-rich mixed fen community containing nationally rare fen plants such as fen wood-rush, *Luzula pallescens*, and fen violet, *Viola persicifolia*. Appropriate management (see below) can lead to the formation of reed beds dominated by common reed, *Phragmites australis*.

The network of drainage ditches holds many uncommon water plants including bladderwort, *Utricularia vulgaris* and water violet, *Hottonia palustris*. The late successional vegetation (fen carr and woodland) may not be of equal plant conservation interest to the above, but includes extensive stands of birch, *Betula* spp. and willows, *Salix* spp. and is important for both invertebrates and birds, including the nightingale, *Luscinia megarhynchos* and long-eared owl, *Asio otus*.

The UK invertebrate site register lists 181 species of Coleoptera, 72 species of Lepidoptera and 63 species of Diptera recorded on the reserve as being of national importance, making it one of the UK's most important invertebrate sites.

Current management

Since its establishment as a reserve, a variety of management practices have been used at Woodwalton, including reed cutting and grazing to maintain some open areas and delay the successional process. Despite this, occasional neglect of some areas has allowed succession to birch woodland on more acid peat and sallow scrub in more calcareous areas so that large areas of the reserve are still covered by lower value late successional communities.

In order to maintain the diversity of vegetation on the reserve, the philosophy has been to divide the fen in to a patchwork of management areas. The drains which cross the reserve define compartments that have become individual management areas (Fig. 15.5). Each one can have different management aims and objectives. Most management objectives have involved maintaining or restoring early successional vegetation communities of both seral types. This has often involved the use of heavy machinery to remove bushes and scrub. However, some compartments have been managed for specific species or species groups and others have been used to create open-water features to further increase the diversity of habitat types. Current management objectives for vegetation in each compartment are shown in Fig. 15.5. Typical management practices include:

1. Maintenance of high summer water table – favours formation of reed beds. Occasional winter mowing is necessary to maintain its early successional status.

2. Summer cutting for mixed fen – cutting and removal of vegetation during the summer on base-rich peat favours formation of mixed fen meadow community. Some grazing during the autumn has been imposed which can help maintain floristic diversity. These areas are frequently flooded during the winter.

3. Grazing to maintain neutral/acidic grassland – cattle grazing is imposed during the winter and spring, followed by summer mowing in some years.

4. Management of woodland/carr – coppice management and ride management maintain diversity of microhabitats within the woodland blocks and provide habitat for song birds such as the nightingale.

In addition, the water table is managed by a series of sluices that enable limited variation of water table between compartments

Conservation objectives on the reserve

Woodwalton is one of the few remnants of a range of fenland habitats and these need to be maintained by careful management. In addition, a range of plant and animal species, rare or endangered in the UK, occur on the reserve and need particular management plans.

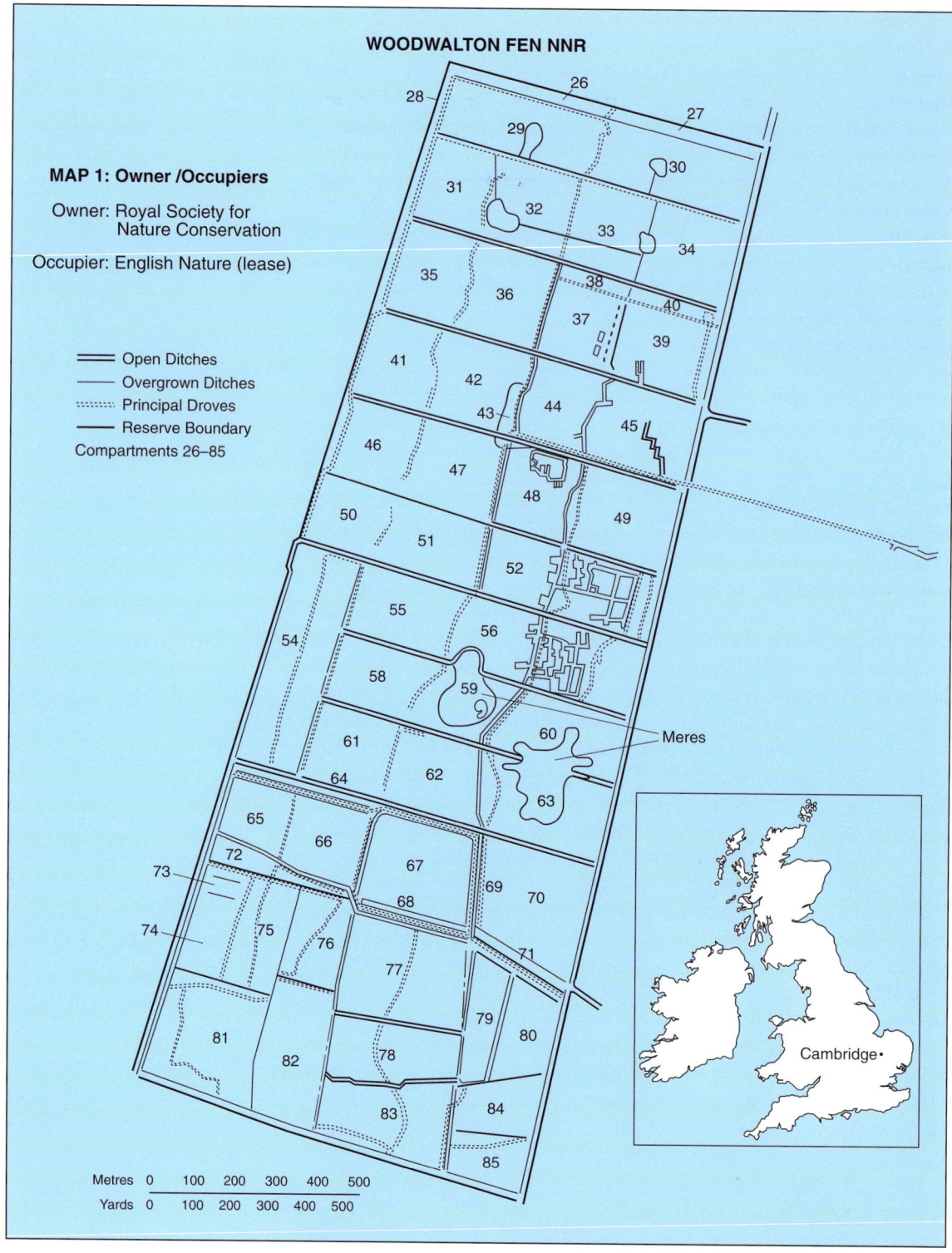

WOODWALTON FEN NNR

MAP 1: Owner /Occupiers

Owner: Royal Society for
Nature Conservation

Occupier: English Nature (lease)

═══ Open Ditches
─── Overgrown Ditches
········ Principal Droves
━━━ Reserve Boundary
Compartments 26–85

Meres

Cambridge•

Metres 0 100 200 300 400 500
Yards 0 100 200 300 400 500

Fig. 15.5 Map of Woodwalton Fen National Nature Reserve, UK showing the pattern of compartments, which are managed individually for different conservation goals.

Fenland is a habitat which can undergo rapid succession to woodland and management is required to maintain representative patches of each stage of succession. The early successional stages need intensive management, through cutting or grazing to avoid scrub encroachment. However, each of these management practices produces its own community. Indeed, the timing and intensity of each of these practices produce unique communities.

One rare species that is the subject of management at Woodwalton is the fen violet, *Viola persicifolia*. This plant was unknown on the fen until scrub clearance in the 1960s resulted in an abundance of flowering plants. It seems that disturbance of the peat surface results in germination of dormant seed. Since that time, a range of research and management trials have taken place to try and maintain populations, but periodic disturbance seems to be the only long term solution (Pullin & Woodell 1987). You might consider adding specific plans for this species.

Summary

1. There is a significant gap between the scientist and practitioner in conservation that is inhibiting progress in the discipline.

2. In the past most conservation practices have been experience-based rather than evidence-based.

3. Advances in medical and public health practice provide a model of how to move from experience-based to evidence-based actions.

4. Current action plan formats used by conservation practitioners do not generally encourage the application of evidence in justification of actions. Modifications to these formats can encourage evidence-based decision-making and identification of priority areas for research.

5. Conservation organisations will have to be the major drivers of this change by acting as users and commissioners of research, evaluators of action plans and grant awarding bodies.

Discussion points

• What is the difference between experienced-based and evidence-based action?
• What are the advantages and disadvantages of using traditional land management practices to guide conservation management?
• Who should be formulating conservation policy?
• Do we need to be so prescriptive as using evidence-based action in our approach to managing nature?

Further reading

Meffe, G.K., Boersma, P.D., Murphy, D.D., Noon, B.R., Pulliam, H.R., Soul(, M.E. & Waller, D.M. 1998. Independent scientific review in natural resource management. *Conservation Biology* **12**, 268-270.

Pullin, A.S. & Knight, T.M. (2001). Effectiveness in conservation practice: pointers from medicine and public health. *Conservation Biology*. **15**, 50–54.

Stevens, A. & Milne, R. (1997). The effectiveness revolution and public health. In *Progress in public health*, ed. G. Scally, pp. 197–225: London. Royal Society of Medicine Press.

Walters, C.J. (1986). *Adaptive Management of Renewable Resources*. New York: Macmillan.

Web sites

Australian Government Environmental Site:
www.environment.gov.au/corporate/ about.html
Cochrane web site: www.cochrane.de/
US Fish & Wildlife Service Endangered Species Program:
endangered.fws.gov/
UK Government, Department of Environment, Food and Rural Affairs:
www.defra.gov.uk/
UK National Biodiversity Network: www.nbn.org.uk/

References

Andrewartha, H.G. & Birch, L.C. (1954). *The distribution and abundance of animals.* Chicago: University of Chicago Press.

Ault, J.S., Bohnsack, J.A. & Meester, G.A. (1998). A retrospective (1979–1996) multispecies assessment of coral reef fish stocks in the Florida Keys. *Fisheries Bulletin*, **96**, 395–414.

Avise, J.C. (1996). Toward a regional conservation genetics perspective: phylogeography of faunas in the southeastern United States. Pp. 431–470 in *Conservation genetics: case histories from nature*, eds J.C. Avise & J.L. Hamrick. New York: Chapman and Hall.

Bender, D.J., Contreras, T.A. and Fahrig, L. (1998). Habitat loss and population decline: a meta-analysis of the patch size effect. *Ecology*, **79**, 517–533.

Berger, J. (1990). Persistence of different-sized populations: an empirical assessment of rapid extinctions in bighorn sheep. *Conservation Biology*, **4**, 91–98.

Berger, J. (1999). Intervention and persistence in small populations of bighorn sheep. *Conservation Biology*, **13**, 432–435.

Bibby, C.J. (1979). Foods of the Dartford warbler *Sylvia undata* on southern English heathland (Aves: Sylviidae). *Journal of Zoology*, **188**, 557–576.

Billington, H.L. (1991). Effect of population size on genetic variation in a dioecious conifer. *Conservation Biology*, **5**, 115–119.

Blair, R.B. & Launer, A.E. (1997). Butterfly diversity and human land use: species assemblages along an urban gradient. *Biological Conservation*, **80**, 113–125.

Bowman, D.M.J.S. (1998). Tansley Review No. 101. The impact of aboriginal landscape burning on the Australian biota. *New Phytologist*, **140**, 385–410.

Bradshaw, A.D. (1983). The reconstruction of ecosystems. *Journal of Applied Ecology*, **20**, 1–17.

Bradshaw, A.D. (1997a). What do we mean by restoration? Pp. 8–14 in *Restoration ecology and sustainable development,* eds K.M. Urbanska, N.R. Webb & P.J. Edwards. Cambridge: Cambridge University Press.

Bradshaw, A.D. (1997b). The importance of soil ecology in restoration science. Pp. 33–64 in *Restoration ecology and sustainable development,* eds K.M. Urbanska, N.R. Webb & P.J. Edwards. Cambridge: Cambridge University Press.

Broads Authority (1993). *No easy answers. Draft Broads plan.* Norwich: Broads Authority.

Broads Authority and English Nature (1997). *Fen management strategy.* Norwich: Broads Authority.

Brown, J.H. (1981). Two decades of homage to Santa Rosalia: toward a general theory of diversity. *American Zoologist*, **21**, 877–888.

Brunet, J. (1993). Environmental and historical factors limiting the distribution of rare forest grasses in south Sweden. *Forest Ecology and Management*, **61**, 263–275.

Buckland, S.T., Goudie, I.B.J. & Borchers, D.L. (2000). Wildlife population assessment: past developments and future directions. *Biometrics*, **56**, 1–12.

Bullock J.M. (1998). Community translocation in Britain: setting objectives and measuring consequences. *Biological Conservation*, **84**, 199–214.

Bullock, J.M. & Pakeman, R.J. (1997). Grazing of lowland heath in England: management methods and their effects on heathland vegetation. *Biological Conservation*, **79**, 1–13.

Burley, F.W. (1988). Monitoring biological diversity for setting priorities in conservation. Pp. 227–230 in *Biodiversity*, ed. E.O. Wilson. Washington, DC: National Academy Press.

Carson, R. (1962). *Silent spring*. Boston: Houghton-Mifflin.

Channell, R. & Lomolino, M.V. (2000). Dynamic biogeography and conservation of endangered species. *Nature*, **403**, 84–86.

Chiras, D.D. (1994). *Environmental science: action for a sustainable future*, 4th edn. Redwood City, CA: Benjamin/Cummings.

Choquenot, D. & Bowman, D.M.J.S. (1998). Marsupial megafauna, Aborigines and the overkill hypothesis: application of predator–prey models to the question of Pleistocene extinction in Australia. *Global Ecology and Biogeography Letters*, **7**, 167–180.

Christensen, N.L. Jr. (1997). Managing for heterogeneity and complexity on dynamic landscapes. Pp 167–186 in *The ecological basis of conservation*, eds S.T.A. Pickett, R.S. Ostfeld, M. Shachak & G.E. Likens. New York: Chapman & Hall.

Cislaghi, C. & Nimis, P.L. (1997). Lichens, air pollution and lung cancer. *Nature*, **387**, 463–464.

Clarke, K.R. & Warwick, R.M. (1998). A taxonomic distinctness index and its statistical properties. *Journal of Applied Ecology*, **35**, 523–531.

Cochrane A. (1972). *Effectiveness and efficiency. Random reflections on the health service*. London: Nuffield Provincial Hospitals Trust.

Coffey, M. (1978). The dust storms. *Natural History*, **87**, 72–83.

Cohen, J.E. (1995). How many people can the Earth support? New York: Norton.

Cohen, J.E. (1997). Conservation and human population growth: what are the linkages? Pp. 29–42 in *The Ecological basis of conservation*, eds S.T.A. Pickett, R.S. Ostfeld, M. Shachak & G.E. Likens. New York: Chapman & Hall.

Cook, R.E. (1969). Variation in species density of North American birds. *Systematic Zoology*, **18**, 63–84.

Connell, J.H. (1978). Diversity in tropical rain forests and coral reefs. *Science*, **199**, 1302–1310.

Costanza, R., dArge, R., deGroot, R., Farber, S., Grasso, M., Hannon, B., Limburg, K., Naeem, S., Oneill, R.V., Paruelo, J., Raskin, R.G., Sutton, P. & vandenBelt, M. (1997). The value of the world's ecosystem services and natural capital. *Nature*, **387**, 253–260.

Cottam, G. (1987). Community dynamics on an artificial prairie. Pp. 257–270 in *Restoration Ecology*, eds W.R. Jordan III, M.E. Gilpin & J.D. Aber. Cambridge: Cambridge University Press.

Courchamp, F., Clutton-Brock, T. & Grenfell, B. (1999). Inverse density dependence and the Allee effect. *Trends in Ecology and Evolution*, **14**, 405–410.

Cowley, M.J.R., Thomas, C.D., Thomas, J.A. & Warren, M.S. (1999). Flight areas of British butterflies: assessing species status and decline. *Proceedings of the Royal Society of London (B)*, **266**, 1587–1592.

Crist, T. O., Guertin, D.S., Wiens J.A. & Milne, B.T. (1992). Animal movement in heterogeneous landscapes: an experiment with *Eleodes* beetles in shortgrass prairie. *Functional Ecology*, **6**, 536–544.

Darby, H.C. (1976). Domesday England. Pp. 39–74 in *A new historical geography of England before 1600*, ed. H.C. Darby. Cambridge: Cambridge University Press.

Den Boer, P.J. (1998). The role of density-independent processes in the stabilization of insect populations. Pp. 53–80 in *Insect populations: in theory and practice*, eds J.P. Dempster & I.F.G. McLean. Dordrecht: Kluwer Academic Publishers.

Dodd, C.K. & Seigel, R.A. (1991). Relocation, repatriation, and translocation of amphibians and reptiles: are they conservation strategies that work? *Herpetologica*, **47**, 336–350.

Dodson, J.J., Gibson, R.J., Cunjak, R.A., Friedland, K.D., de Leaniz, C.G., Gross, M.R., Newbury, R., Nielsen, J.L., Power, M.E., Roy, S. (1998). Elements in the development of conservation plans for Atlantic salmon (*Salmo salar*). *Canadian Journal of Fisheries and Aquatic Sciences*, **55**(Suppl 1), 312–323.

Duffey, E., Morris, M.G., Sheail, J., Ward, L.K., Wells, D.A. & Wells, T.C.E. (1974). *Grassland ecology and wildlife management*. London: Chapman & Hall.

Ehrlich, P.R. (1984). The structure and dynamics of butterfly populations. Pp. 25–40 in *The biology of butterflies*, eds R. I. Vane-Wright & P.R. Ackery. Princeton., NJ: Princeton University Press.

Ehrlich, P.R. (1995). The scale of the human enterprise and biodiversity loss. Pp. 214–226 in *Extinction rates*, eds J.H. Lawton & R.M. May. Oxford: Oxford University Press.

Ehrlich, P.R., Ehrlich, A.H. & Holdren, J.P. (1977). *Ecoscience: population, resources, environment*. San Francisco: W. H. Freeman.

Eldridge, M.D.B., King, J.M., Loupis, A.K., Spencer, P.B.S., Taylor, A.C., Pope, L.C. & Hall, G.P. (1999). Unprecedented low levels of genetic variation and inbreeding depression in an island population of the black-footed rock-wallaby. *Conservation Biology*, **13**, 531–541.

English Nature (1994). *Priorities for habitat conservation in England*. Research report no. 97. Peterborough: English Nature.

Englund, R.A. (1999). The impacts of introduced poeciliid fish and Odonata on the endemic *Megalagrion* (Odonata) damselflies of Oahu Island, Hawaii. *Journal of Insect Conservation*, **3**, 225–243.

Erwin, D.H., Valentine, J.W. & Sepkoski, J.J. (1987). A comparative study of diversification events: the early Paleazoic versus the Mesozoic. *Evolution*, **41**, 1177–1186.

Erwin, T.L. (1982). Tropical forests: their richness in Coleoptera and other arthropod species. *Coleopterists Bulletin*, **36**, 74–75.

Evans, P.G.H. (1987). *The natural history of whales and dolphins*. London: Academic Press.

Eversham, B.C., Roy, D.B. & Telfer, M.G. (1996). Urban, industrial and other manmade sites as analogs of natural habitats for Carabidae. *Annales Zoologici Fennici*, **33**, 149–156.

Eyre, M.D. & Luff, M.L. (1995). Coleoptera on post-industrial land: a conservation problem. *Land Reclamation and Decontamination*, **132**.

Ferry, B.W., Baddeley, M.S. & Hawksworth, D.L., eds (1973). *Air pollution and lichens*. London: Athlone Press.

Fischer, J. & Lindenmayer, D.B. (2000). An assessment of the published results of animal relocations. *Biological Conservation*, **96**, 1–11.

Fischer, M. & Matthies, D. (1998). RAPD variation in relation to population size and plant fitness in the rare *Gentianella germanica* (Gentianaceae). *American Journal of Botany*, **85**, 811–819.

Flenley, J.R., King, A.S.M., Jackson, J., Chew, C., Teller, J.T. & Prentice, M.E. (1991). The late quaternary vegetational and climatic history of Easter Island. *Journal of Quaternary Science*, **6**, 85–115.

Frankel, O.H., Brown, A.D.H. & Burdon, J.J. (1995). *The conservation of plant biodiversity*. Cambridge: Cambridge University Press.

Franklin, I.R. (1980). Evolutionary change in small populations. Pp. 135–149 in *Conservation biology: an evolutionary-ecological perspective*, eds. M.E. Soulé & B.A.Wilcox. Sunderland, MA: Sinauer Associates.

Fuller, R.J. & Henderson, A.C.B. (1992). Distribution of breeding songbirds in Bradfield Woods, Suffolk, in relation to vegetation and coppice management. *Bird Study*, **39**, 73–88.

Gaston, K.J. & Spicer, J.I. (1998). *Biodiversity: an introduction*. Oxford: Blackwell Science.

George, M. (1992). *The land use, ecology and conservation of Broadland*. Chichester: Packard Publishing.

Gibson, C.W.D. (1998). *Brownfield red data: the values artificial habitats have for uncommon invertebrates*. Report no. 273. Peterborough: English Nature.

Gilbert, F., Gonzalez, A. & Evans Freke, I. (1998). Corridors maintain species richness in the fragmented landscapes of a microecosystem. *Proceedings of the Royal Society of London (B)*, **265**, 577–582.

Gilbert, O.L. & Anderson, P. (1998). *Habitat creation and repair*. Oxford. Oxford University Press.

Godwin, H. (1981). *The archives of the peat bogs*. Cambridge: Cambridge University Press.

Goldschmidt, T., Witte, F. & Wanink, J. (1993). Cascading effects of the introduced Nile perch on the detritivorous/phytoplanktivorous species in the sublittoral areas of Lake Victoria. *Conservation Biology*, **7**, 686–700.

Goltsman, M., Kruchenkova, E.P. & Macdonald, D.W. (1996). The Madnyi Arctic foxes: treating a population imperilled by disease. *Oryx*, **30**, 251–258.

Gould, S.J. (1989). *Wonderful life: the Burgess Shale and the nature of history*. New York: Norton.

Griffith B., J.M. Scott, J.W. Carpenter and C. Reed. (1989). Translocation as a species conservation tool: status and strategy. *Science*, **245**, 477–480.

Groombridge, B., ed. (1992). *Global biodiversity*. London: Chapman & Hall.

Groombridge, B., ed. (2000). *Global biodiversity: earth's living resources in the 21st century*. Cambridge: World Conservation Monitoring Centre.

Handel, S.N. (1997). The role of plant-animal mutualisms in the design and restoration of natural communities. Pp. 111–132 in *Restoration ecology and sustainable development,* eds K.M. Urbanska, N.R. Webb, & P.J. Edwards. Cambridge: Cambridge University Press.

Hanski, I. (1997). Metapopulation dynamics: from concepts and observations to predictive models. Pp. 69–91 in *Metapopulation biology: ecology genetics and evolution*, eds. I.A. Hanski & M.E. Gilpin. San Diego: Academic Press.

Hanski, I., Kuussaari, M. & Nieminen, M. (1994). Metapopulation structure and migration in the butterfly *Melitaea cinxia*. *Ecology*, **75**, 747–762.

Hanski, I., Pakkala, T., Kuussaari, M. & Lei, G. (1995). Metapopulation persistence of an endangered butterfly in a fragmented landscape. *Oikos*, **72**, 21–28.

Harding, M. (1994). Restoring Redgrave and Lopham Fen. *Enact*, **2**, 12–15.

Harrison, S. (1989). Long-distance dispersal and colonization in the bay checkerspot butterfly. *Ecology*, **70**, 1236–1243.

Harrison, S., Murphy, D.D. & Ehrlich, P.R. (1988). Distribution of the bay checkerspot butterfly, *Euphydryas editha bayensis*: evidence for a metapopulation model. *American Naturalist*, **132**, 360–382.

Hartley, M.J. & Hunter, M.L. (1998). A meta-analysis of forest cover, edge effects, and artificial nest predation rates. *Conservation Biology*, **12**, 465–469.

Hewitt, G.M. (1999). Post-glacial re-colonisation of European biota. *Biological Journal of the Linnean Society*, **68**, 87–112.

Heywood, V.H. (1995). *Global biodiversity assessment*. Cambridge: Cambridge University Press.

Hillel, D. (1991). *Out of the earth: civilisation and the life of the soil*. Berkeley, CA: University of California Press.

Hobbs R.J.,& Huenneke, L.F. (1992). Disturbance, diversity, and invasion: implications for conservation. *Conservation Biology*, **6**, 324–337.

Hodder, K.H. & Bullock, J.M. (1997). Translocation of native species in the UK: implications for biodiversity. *Journal of Applied Ecology*, **34**, 547–565.

Holdridge, L.R. (1967). *Life zone ecology*. San José: Tropical Science Center.

Holmquist, J.G., Schmidt-Gengenbach, J.M. & Yoshioka, B.B. (1998). High dams and marine–freshwater linkages: effects on native and introduced fauna in the Caribbean. *Conservation Biology*, **12**, 621–630.

Holt, W.V. (1994). Reproductive technologies. Pp. 144–166 in *Creative conservation*, eds P.J.S. Olney, G.M. Mace & A.T.C. Feistner. London: Chapman & Hall.

Hooker, S.K., Whitehead, H. & Gowans, S. (1999). Marine protected area design and the spatial and temporal distribution of cetaceans in a submarine canyon. *Conservation Biology*, **13**, 592–602.

Hoole, J.C., Joyce, D.A. & Pullin, A.S. (1999). Estimates of gene flow between populations of the swallowtail butterfly, *Papilio machaon* in Broadland, U.K. and implications for conservation. *Biological Conservation*, **89**, 293–299.

Howarth, F.G. (1990). Hawaiian terrestrial arthropods: an overview. *Bishop Museum Occasional Papers*, **30**, 1–26.

Huntley, BJ. (1988). Conserving and monitoring biotic diversity: some African examples. Pp. 248–260 in *Biodiversity*, ed. E.O. Wilson. Washington, DC: National Academy Press.

Ingrouille, M. (1995). *Historical ecology of the British flora*. London: Chapman and Hall.

IUCN (1994a). *Guidelines for protected areas management categories*. Cambridge, UK and Gland, Switzerland: IUCN.

IUCN (1998). *Guidelines for re-introductions*. IUCN/SSC Re-introduction Specialist Group. Gland, Switzerland & Cambridge, UK: IUCN.

IUCN (2001). *International Union for the Conservation of Nature red list categories* version 3.1. Gland, Switzerland: IUCN.

Jaarsveld, A. S. van, Freitag, S., Chown, S.L., Muller, C., Koch, S., Hull, H., Bellamy, C., Kruger, M., Endrody-Younga, S., Mansell, M.W. & Scholtz, C.H. (1998). Biodiversity assessment and conservation strategies. *Science*, **279**, 2106–2108.

Janzen, D. H. (1983). Dispersal of seeds by vertebrate guts. Pp. 232–262 in *Coevolution*, eds D.J. Futuyma & M. Slatkin. Sunderland, MA: Sinauer Associates.

Johnson, L.E. & Padilla, D.K. (1996). Geographic spread of exotic species: ecological lessons and opportunities from the invasion of the zebra mussel *Dreissena polymorpha*. *Biological Conservation*, **78**, 23–33.

Joy, J. & Pullin, A.S. (1999). Field studies on flooding and survival of overwintering large heath butterfly, *Coenonympha tullia* larvae on Fenn's and Whixall Mosses in Shropshire and Wrexham, UK. *Ecological Entomology*, **24**, 426–431.

Kemf, E. & Jackson, P. (1994). *Rhinos in the wild*. WWF Species Status Report.

Kerr, J.T. (1997). Species richness, endemism, and the choice of areas for conservation. *Conservation Biology*, **11**, 1094–1100.

Kirby, P. (1992). Habitat management for invertebrates: a practical handbook. Sandy: RSPB.

Kinnaird, M.F. & O'Brien, T.G. (1998). Ecological effects of wildfire on lowland rainforest in Sumatra. *Conservation Biology*, **12**, 954–956.

Kock, K-H. (1992). *Antarctic fish and fisheries*. Cambridge: Cambridge University Press.

Komdeur, J. (1994). Conserving the Seychelles warbler *Acrocephalus-sechellensis* by translocation from Cousin island to the islands of Aride and Cousine. *Biological Conservation*, **67**, 143–152.

Kotze, D.J. & Samways, M.J. (1999). Support for the multi-taxa approach in bio-diversity assessment, as shown by epigaeic invertebrates in an Afromontane forest archipelago. *Journal of Insect Conservation*, **3**, 125–143.

Krebs, C.J. (1994). *Ecology*, 4th edn. New York: Harper Collins.

Kremen, C., Colwell, R.K., Erwin, T.L., Murphy, D.D., Noss, R.F. & Sanjayan, M.A. (1993). Terrestrial arthropod assemblages: their use in conservation planning. *Conservation Biology*, **7**, 796–808.

Lacy, R.C. (1987). Loss of genetic diversity from managed populations: interacting effects of drift, mutation, immigration, selection, and population subdivision. *Conservation Biology*, **1**, 143–158.

Lamberson, R.H., McKelvey, R., Noon, B.R. & Voss, C. (1992). A dynamic analysis of northern spotted owl viability in a fragmented forest landscape. *Conservation Biology*, **6**, 505–512.

Laurance, W.F., Ferreira, L.V., Rankin-De Merona, J.M., Laurance, S.G., Hutchings, R.W. & Lovejoy, T.E. (1998). Effects of forest fragmentation on recruitment patterns in amazonian tree communities. *Conservation Biology*, **12**, 460–464.

Lawton, J.H., Bignell, D.E., Bolton, B., Bloemers, G.F., Eggleton, P., Hammond, P.M., Hodda, M., Holt, R.D., Larsen, T.B., Mawdsley, N.A., Stork, N.E., Srivastava, D.S. & Watt, A.D. (1998). Biodiversity inventories, indicator taxa and effects of habitat modification in tropical forest. *Nature*, **391**, 72–75.

Leopold, A. (1949). *A Sand County almanac and sketches here and there*. New York: Oxford University Press.

Levins, R. (1969). Some demographic and genetic consequences of environmental heterogeneity for biological control. *Bulletin of the Entomological Society of America*, **15**, 237–240.

Lips, K.R. (1998). Decline of a tropical montane amphibian fauna. *Conservation Biology*, **12**, 106–117.

Lott, D. & Daws, J. (1995). The conservation value of urban demolition sites in Leicester for beetles. *Land Reclamation and Decontamination*, 79–81.

Lovelock, J.E. (1979). Gaia. Oxford: Oxford University Press.

Lubchenco. J. (1998). Entering the century of the environment: a new social contract for science. *Science*, **279**, 491–497.

MacArthur, R.H. & Wilson, E.O. (1967). *The theory of island biogeography*. Princeton, NJ: Princeton University Press.

Mace, G. M. & Lande, R. (1991). Assessing extinction threats: toward a reevaluation of IUCN threatened species categories. *Conservation Biology*, **5**, 148–157.

Mace, R.D. & Waller, J.S. (1998). Demography and population trend of grizzly bears in the Swan Mountains, Montana. *Conservation Biology*, **12**, 1005–1016.

Magin, C.D., Johnson, T.H., Groombridge, B., Jenkins, M. & Smith, H. (1994) Species extinctions, endangerment and captive breeding. Pp. 3–31 in *Creative conservation*, eds P.J.S. Olney, G.M. Mace & A.T.C. Feistner. London: Chapman & Hall.

Maltby, E., Holdgate, M., Acreman, M. & Weir, A. (1999). *Ecosystem management: questions for science and society*. Virginia Water: Royal Holloway Institute for Environmental Research.

Marsh, G.P. (1864). *Man and nature; or, physical geography as modified by human action*. Reprinted in 1965, ed. D. Lowenthal. Cambridge, MA: Harvard University Press.

Martikainen, P., Kaila, L. & Haila, Y. (1998). Threatened beetles in white-backed woodpecker habitats. *Conservation Biology*, **12**, 293–301.

Martin, P.S. (1973). The discovery of America. *Science*, **179**, 969–974.

May, R.M., Lawton, J.H. & Stork, N.E. (1995). Assessing extinction rates. Pp. 1–24 in *Extinction rates,* eds. J.H. Lawton & R.M. May. Oxford: Oxford University Press.

Mech, L.D. (1995). The challenge and opportunity of recovering wolf populations. *Conservation Biology*, **9**, 270–278.

Meffe, G.K., Boersma, P.D., Murphy, D.D., Noon, B.R., Pulliam, H.R., Soulé, M.E. & Waller, D.M. (1998). Independent scientific review in natural resource management. *Conservation Biology*, **12**, 268–270.

Menges E.S. (2000). Population viability analyses in plants: challenges and opportunities. *Trends in Ecology and Evolution*, **15**, 51–56.

Meyer, J.L. (1997). Conserving ecosystem function. Pp. 136–145 in *The ecological basis of conservation*, eds S.T.A. Pickett, R.S. Ostfeld, M. Shachak & G.E. Likens. New York: Chapman & Hall.

Miller, G.H., Magee, J.W., Johnson, B.J., Fogel, M.L., Spooner, N.A., McCulloch, M.T. & Ayliffe, L.K. (1999). Pleistocene extinction of *Genyornis newtoni*: human impact on Australian megafauna. *Science*, **283**, 205–208.

Mittermeier, R.A., Myers, N., Thomsen, J.G., da Fonseca, G.A.B. & Olivieri, S. (1998). Biodiversity hotspots and major tropical wilderness areas: approaches to setting conservation priorities. *Conservation Biology*, **12**, 516–520.

Moritz, C. (1994). Applications of mitochondrial DNA analysis in conservation: a critical review. *Molecular Ecology*, **3**, 401–411.

Morris, M.G. (2000). The effects of structure and its dynamics on the ecology and conservation of arthropods in British grasslands. *Biological Conservation*, **95**, 129–142.

Moss, B. (1980). Further studies on the palaeolimnology and changes in the phosphorus budget of Barton Broad, Norfolk. *Freshwater Biology*, **10**, 261–279.

Mwalyosi, R.B. (1991). Ecological evaluation for wildlife corridors and buffer zones for Lake Manyara National Park, Tanzania and its immediate environment. *Biological Conservation*, **57**, 171–186.

Nalepa, T.F. & Schloesser, D.W., eds (1993). *Zebra mussels: biology, impacts, and control.* Boca Raton, FL: Lewis Publishers.

Newhouse, J.R. (1990). Chestnut blight. *Scientific American*, **263** (July), 74–79.

Newmark, W.D. (1987). The land-bridge island perspective on mammalian extinctions in western North American parks. *Nature*, **325**, 430–432.

Newton, I. (1979). *Population ecology of raptors*. Berkhamsted: T. & A. D. Poyser.

Newton, I. (1986). *The Sparrowhawk*. Waterhouses: T. & A. D. Poyser.

Newton, I. (1998). Pollutants and pesticides. Pp. 66–89 in *Conservation science and action*, ed. W.J. Sutherland. Oxford: Blackwell Science.

Nicholopoulos, J. (1999). The endangered species listing program. *Endangered Species Bulletin*, **24**, 6–9.

Nicholson, A.J. & Bailey, V.A. (1935). The balance of animal populations. *Proceedings of the Zoological Society of London*, **3**, 551–598.

Nott, M.P. & Pimm, S.L. (1997). The evaluation of biodiversity as a target for conservation. Pp. 125–135 in *The ecological basis of conservation*, eds S.T.A. Pickett, R.S. Ostfeld, M. Shachak & G.E. Likens. New York: Chapman & Hall.

Nowak, R.M. (1992). The red wolf is not a hybrid. *Conservation Biology*, **6**, 593–595.

Okubo, A., Maini, P.K., Williamson, M.H. & Murray, J.D. (1989). On the spatial spread of the grey squirrel in Britain. *Proceedings Of The Royal Society Of London Series B*, **238**, 113–125.

Oliver, I. & Beattie, A.J. (1993). A possible method for the rapid assessment of biodiversity. *Conservation Biology*, **7**, 562–568.

Olney, P.J.S. & Ellis, P., eds (1991). *1990 International Zoo Yearbook*. London. Zoological Society of London.

Olsen, D.M. & Dinerstein, E. (1998). The global 200: a representation approach to conserving the Earth's most biologically valuable ecoregions. *Conservation Biology*, **12**, 502–515.

Ostrowski, S., Bedin, E., Lenain, D.M. & Abuzinada, A.H. (1998). Ten years of Arabian oryx conservation breeding in Saudi Arabia: achievements and regional perspectives. *Oryx*, **32**, 209–222.

Pearson, D.L. (1994). Selecting indicator taxa for the quantitative assessment of biodiversity. *Philosophical Transactions of the Royal Society, London Series B*, **345**, 75–79.

Pickett, S.T.A. & Thompson, J.N. (1978). Patch dynamics and the design of nature reserves. *Biological Conservation*, **13**, 27–37.

Pickett, S.T.A., Parker, V.T. & Fiedler, P.L. (1992). The new paradigm in ecology: implications for conservation biology above the species level. In Pp. 65–88 *Conservation biology: the theory and practice of nature conservation preservation and management*, eds P.L. Fiedler & S.K. Jain. New York: Chapman & Hall.

Pimentel, D. (1976). Land degradation: effects on food and energy resources. *Science*, **194**, 149–155.

Pimm, S.L., Moulton, M.P. & Lenora, J.J. (1995). Bird extinctions in the central Pacific. Pp. 75–87 in *Extinction rates,* eds J.H. Lawton & R.M. May. Oxford: Oxford University Press.

Platenberg, R.J. & Griffiths, R.A. (1999). Translocation of slow-worms (*Anguis fragilis*) as a mitigation strategy: a case study from south-east England. *Biological Conservation*, **90**, 125–132.

Plowden, C. & Bowles, D. (1997). The illegal market in tiger parts in northern Sumatra, Indonesia. *Oryx*, **31**, 59–66.

Polasky, S., Csuti, B., Vossler, C.A. & Meyers, S.M. (2001). A comparison of taxonomic distinctness versus richness as criteria for setting conservation priorities for North American birds. *Biological Conservation*, **97**, 99–105.

Potts, G.R. (1986). The partridge: pesticides, predation and conservation. London: Collins.

Prendergast, J.R., Quinn, R.M., Lawton, J.H., Eversham, B.C. & Gibbons, D.W. (1993). Rare species, the coincidence of diversity hotspots and conservation strategies. *Nature*, **365**, 335–337.

Prendergast, J.R., Quinn, R.M., Lawton, J.H. (1999). The gaps between theory and practice in selecting nature reserves. *Conservation Biology*, **13**, 484–492.

Pullin, A.S. (1997). Habitat requirements of *Lycaena dispar batavus* and implications for re-establishment in England. *Journal of Insect Conservation*, **1**, 177–185.

Pullin, A.S. & Knight, T.M. (2001). Effectiveness in conservation practice: pointers from medicine and public health. *Conservation Biology*, **15**, 50–54.

Pullin, A.S. & Woodell, S.R.J. (1987). Response of the fen violet, *Viola persicifolia* Schreber, to different management regimes at Woodwalton Fen National Nature Reserve, Cambridgeshire, England. *Biological Conservation*, **41**, 203–217.

Pykala, J. (2000). Mitigating human effects on European biodiversity through traditional animal husbandry. *Conservation Biology*, **14**, 705–712.

Rabinowitz, D. (1981). Seven forms of rarity. Pp. 205–217 in *The biological aspects of rare plant conservation*, ed H. Synge. New York: Wiley.

Rackham, O. (1986). *The history of the countryside*. London: J.M. Dent & Sons.

Reynolds, J.C. (1985). Details of the geographic replacement of the red squirrel (*Sciurus vulgaris*) by the grey squirrel (*Sciurus carolinensis*) in eastern England. *Journal of Animal Ecology*, **54**, 149–162.

Richard-Hansen, C., Vie, J.C. & de Thoisy, B. (2000). Translocation of red howler monkeys (*Alouatta seniculus*) in French Guiana. *Biological Conservation*, **93**, 247–253.

Rieseberg, L.H. & Swenson, S.M. (1996). Conservation genetics of endangered island plants. Pp. 305–334 in *Conservation genetics: case histories from nature*, eds J.C. Avise & J.L. Hamrick. New York: Chapman & Hall.

Rogers, K.H. (1997). Operationalizing ecology under a new paradigm: an African perspective. Pp. 60–77 in *The ecological basis of conservation*, eds S.T.A. Pickett, R.S. Ostfeld, M. Shachak & G.E. Likens. New York: Chapman & Hall.

Roman, J., Santhuff, S.D., Moler, P.E. & Bowen, B.W. (1999). Population structure and cryptic evolutionary units in the alligator snapping turtle. *Conservation Biology*, **13**, 135–142.

Rosenweig, M.L. (1995). *Species diversity in space and time*. Cambridge: Cambridge University Press.

Roy, M.S., Geffen, E., Smith, D. & Wayne, R.K. (1996). Molecular genetics of pre-1940 red wolves. *Conservation Biology*, **10**, 1413–1424.

Ryder, O.A. (1986). Species conservation and systematics: the dilemma of sub-species. *Trends in Ecology and Evolution*, **1**, 9–10.

Saccheri, I.J., Kuussaari, M., Kankare, M., Vikman, P., Fortelius, W. & Hanski, I. (1998). Inbreeding and extinction in a butterfly metapopulation. *Nature*, **392**, 491–494.

Sedlakova, I. & Chytry, M. (1999). Regeneration patterns in a central European dry heathland: effects of burning, sod-cutting and cutting. *Plant Ecology*, **143**, 77–87.

Shaffer, M.L. (1981). Minimum population sizes for species conservation. *BioScience*, **31**, 131–134.

Sherwin, W.B., Timms, P., Wilcken, J. & Houlden, B. (2000). Analysis and conservation implications of Koala genetics. *Conservation Biology*, **14**, 639–649.

Shigesada, N. & Kawasaki, K. (1997). *Biological invasions: theory and practice*. Oxford: Oxford University Press.

Simberloff, D., Farr, J.A., Cox, J. & Mehlman, D.W. (1992). Movement corridors: conservation bargains or poor investments. *Conservation Biology*, **6**, 493–504.

Simpson, G.G. (1964). Species density of North American recent mammals. *Systematic Zoology*, **13**, 57–73.

Soltis, P.S. & Gitzendanner, M.A. (1999). Molecular systematics and the conservation of rare species. *Conservation Biology*, **13**, 471–483.

Somerville, M. (1858). *Physical geography*, 4th edn. London: Murray.

Soule, M.E. (1985). What is conservation biology. *Bioscience*, **35**, 727–734.

Southwood, T.R.E., Brown V.K. & Reader P.M. 1979. The relationships of plant and insect diversities in succession. *Biological Journal of the Linnean Society*, **12**: 327–348.

Spencer, J.E. & Thomas, W.L. (1978). *Introducing cultural geography*, 2nd edn. New York: Wiley .

Stevens A., & Milne R. 1997. The effectiveness revolution and public health. Pp. 197–225 in *Progress in public health*, Ed. G. Scally. London: Royal Society of Medicine Press.

Stork, N.E. & Samways, M.J. (1995). Inventory and monitoring of biodiversity. Pp. 453–544 in *Global biodiversity assessment*, ed. V.H. Heywood. Cambridge: Cambridge University Press.

Strong, A.M. & Bancroft, G.T. (1994). Postfledgling dispersal of white-crowned pigeons: implications for conservation of deciduous seasonal forests in the Florida Keys. *Conservation Biology*, **8**, 770–779.

Struhsaker, T.T. & Siex, K.S. (1998). Translocation and introduction of the Zanzibar red colobus monkey: success and failure with an endangered island endemic. *Oryx*, **32**, 277–284.

Stuart, A.J. (1991). Mammalian extinctions in the Late Pleistocene of northern Eurasia and North America. *Biological Reviews*, **66**, 453–562.

Stuttard, P. & Williamson, K. (1971). Habitat requirements of the Nightingale. *Bird Study*, **18**, 9–14.

Swinnerton, K., Jones, C., Lam, R., Paul, S., Chapman, R., Murray, K. & Freeman, K. (2000). Conservation of the pink pigeon in Mauritius. *Re-introduction News*, **19**, 10–12.

Taberlet, P. & Bouvet, J. (1994). Mitochondrial DNA polymorphism, phylogeography, and conservation genetics of the brown bear *Ursus arctos* in Europe. *Proceedings of the Royal Society London Series B*, **255**, 195–200.

Tattershall, F.H., Avundo, A.E., Manley, W.J., Hart, B.J. & Macdonald, D.W. (2000). Managing set-aside for field voles (*Microtus agrestis*). *Biological Conservation*, **96**, 123–128.

Thomas, J.A. (1976). *The biology and conservation of the large blue butterfly* Maculinea arion L. Monks Wood: Institute of Terrestrial Ecology.

Thomas, J.A. (1989). The return of the large blue. *British Wildlife*, **1**, 2–13.

Thomas, J.A. (1991). Rare species conservation: case studies of European butterflies. Pp. 149–197 in *The scientific management of temperate communities for conservation*, eds I.F. Spellerberg, F.B. Goldsmith & M.G. Morris. Oxford: Blackwell Scientific Publications.

Thomas, J.A. (1995). The ecology and conservation of *Maculinea arion* and other species of large blue butterfly. Pp 180–197. in *Ecology and conservation of butterflies*, ed A.S. Pullin. London: Chapman & Hall.

Thomas, W.L. (1956). *Man's role in the changing face of the earth*. Chicago: University of Chicago Press.

Thorsen, M., Shorten, R., Lucking, R. & Lucking, V. (2000). Norway rats (*Rattus norvegicus*) on Frégate Island, Seychelles: the invasion; subsequent eradication attempts and implications for the island's fauna. *Biological Conservation*, **96**, 133–138.

Trine, C.L. (1998). Wood thrush population sinks and implications for the scale of regional conservation strategies. *Conservation Biology*, **12**, 576–585.

Turner, J.R.G., Lennon, J.J. & Lawrenson, J.A. (1988). British bird species distributions and the energy theory. *Nature*, **335**, 539–541.

Tyler, G.A., Smith, K.W. & Burges, D.J. (1998). Reedbed management and breeding bitterns, *Botaurus stellaris* in the UK. *Biological Conservation*, **86**, 257–266.

US National Research Council. (2000). Genetically modified pest-protected plants: science and regulation. Washington, DC: National Academy Press.

Urbanska, K.M. (1997). Safe sites: interface of plant population ecology and restoration ecology. Pp. 81–110 in *Restoration ecology and sustainable development*, eds K.M. Urbanska, N.R. Webb, & P.J. Edwards. Cambridge: Cambridge University Press.

Veríssimo, A., Júnior, C.S., Stone, S. & Uhl, C. (1998). Zoning of timber extraction in the Brazilian Amazon. *Conservation Biology*, **12**, 128–136.

Villard, M-A., Trzcinski, M.K. & Merriam, G. (1999). Fragmentation effects on forest birds: relative influence of woodland cover and configuration on land-scape occupancy. *Conservation Biology*, **13**, 774–783.

Vincent, A.C.J. (1997). Trade in pegasid fishes (sea moths), primarily for tradi-tional Chinese medicine. *Oryx*, **31**, 199–208.

Vitousek, P.M. (1988). Diversity and biological invasions of oceanic islands. Pp. 181–189 in *Biodiversity*, ed. E.O. Wilson. Washington, DC: National Academy Press.

Vucetich, J.A. & Waite, T.A. (1998). Number of censuses required for demo-graphic estimation of effective population size. *Conservation Biology*, **12**, 1023–1030.

Waits, L.P., Talbot, S.L., Ward, R.H. & Shields, G.F. (1998). Mitochondrial DNA phylogeography of the North American brown bear and implications for con-servation. *Conservation Biology*, **12**, 408–417.

Walk, J.W. & Warner, R.E. (2000). Grassland management for the conservation of songbirds in the Midwestern USA. *Biological Conservation*, **94**, 165–172.

Walker, D., Orti, G. & Avise, J.C. (1998). Phylogenetic distinctiveness of a threat-ened aquatic turtle (*Sternotherus depressus*). *Conservation Biology*, **12**, 639–645.

Walters, C.J. (1986). *Adaptive management of renewable resources*. New York: Macmillan.

Warren, M.S. (1991). The successful conservation of an endangered species, the heath fritillary butterfly, *Mellicta athalia*, in Britain. *Biological Conservation*, **55**, 37–56.

Warwick, R.M. & Clarke, K.R. (1998). Taxonomic distinctness and environmen-tal assessment. *Journal of Applied Ecology*, **35**, 532–543.

Wayne, R.K. & Jenks, S.M. (1991). Mitochondrial DNA analysis implying exten-sive hybridization of the endangered red wolf, *Canis rufus. Nature*, **351**, 565–568.

Webb, M.R. & Pullin, A.S. (1997). The orange argus: a history of the large copper butterfly in Britain. *British Wildlife*, **9**, 29–37.

Webb, N.R. (1986). *Heathlands*. London: Collins.

Webb, N.R. (1997). The development of criteria for ecological restoration. Pp. 133–158 in *Restoration ecology and sustainable development,* eds K.M. Urbanska, N.R. Webb, & P.J. Edwards. Cambridge: Cambridge University Press.

Wehausen, J.D. (1999). Rapid extinction of mountain sheep populations revis-ited. *Conservation Biology*, **13**, 378–384.

Wiens, J.A. (1997*a*). Metapopulation dynamics and landscape ecology. Pp. 43–62 in *Metapopulation biology*, eds I.A. Hanski & M.A. Gilpin. San Diego, CA: Academic Press.

Wiens, J.A. (1997*b*). The emerging role of patchiness in conservation biology. Pp. 93–107 in *The ecological basis of conservation*, eds S.T.A. Pickett, R.S. Ostfeld, M. Shachak & G.E. Likens. New York: Chapman & Hall.

Williams, P., Gibbons, D., Margules, C., Rebelo, A., Humphries, C. & Pressey, R. (1996). A comparison of richness hotspots, and complementary areas for con-serving diversity of British birds. *Conservation Biology*, **10**, 155–174.

Williams-Linera, G., Domínguez-Gastelú, V. & García-Zurita, M.E. (1998). Microenvironment and floristics of different edges in a fragmented tropical rainforest. *Conservation Biology*, **12**, 1091–1102.

Wilson, E. O. (1994). *The diversity of life*. Harmondsworth: Penguin Books.

Wilson, E.O. & Peters, F.M., eds (1988). *Biodiversity*. Washington, DC: National Academy Press.

Wisenfeld, J. (1995). Experience at Hatfield Forest, Essex, with restoration of old pollards and establishment of new ones. *Biological Journal of the Linnean Society*, **56** (suppl.), 181–183.

Witte, F., Goldschimdt, T., Goudswaard, P.C., Ligtvoet, W., van Oijen, M.J.P. & Wanink, J.H. (1992*a*). Species extinction and concomitant ecological changes in Lake Victoria. *Netherlands Journal of Zoology*, **42**, 214–232.

Witte, F., Goldschimdt, T., Wanink, J.H., van Oijen, M., Goudswaard, K., Witte-Maas, E. & Bouton, N. (1992*b*). The destruction of an endemic species flock:quantitative data on the decline of the haplochromine cichlids of Lake Victoria. *Environmental Biology of Fishes*, **34**, 1–28.

Wolf, C.M., Griffith, B., Reed, C. & Temple, S.A. (1996). Avian and mammalian translocations: update and reanalysis of 1987 survey data. *Conservation Biology*, **10**, 1142–1154.

Wright, S. (1931). Evolution in mendelian populations. *Genetics*, **16**, 97–159.

Wynne, G., Avery, M., Campbell, L., Gubbay, S., Hawkswell, S., Juniper, T., King, M., Newbery, P., Smart, J., Steel, C., Stones, T., Stubbs, A., Taylor, J., Tydeman, C. & Wynde, R. (1995). *Biodiversity challenge*, 2nd edn. Sandy: Royal Society for the Protection of Birds.

Zohary, M, & Hoff, H. (1993). *Domestication of plants and animals in the old world: the origin and spread of cultivated plants in West Asia, Europe and the Nile Valley*, 2nd edn. Oxford: Clarendon Press.

Index